CREATIVE
HOMEOWNER®

ULTIMATE GUIDE
WIRING
9TH UPDATED EDITION

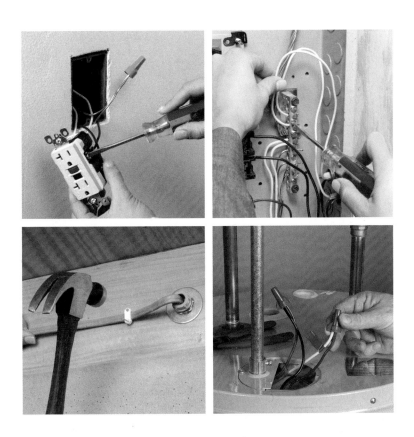

Technical Editor for Updated Edition: Charles T. Byers

Assistant Professor, Residential Remodeling Technology, AAS, AST,

Thaddeus Stevens College of Technology

CREATIVE HOMEOWNER®

ULTIMATE GUIDE: WIRING

MANAGING EDITOR	Fran J. Donegan
CONTRIBUTING WRITERS	John Caloggero, Rex Cauldwell, Steve Willson
PHOTO COORDINATOR	Mary Dolan
PROOFREADER	Sara M. Markowitz
DIGITAL IMAGING SPECIALIST	Frank Dyer
INDEXER	Schroeder Indexing Services
TECHNICAL ADVISORS	John Caloggero; Perter Eng; Charles L. Rogers, Certified Instructor, National Center for Construction and Research; Joseph A. Ross, Ross Electrical Assessments; David Shapiro
COVER DESIGN	David Geer
ILLUSTRATIONS	Clarke Barre, Robert Strauch, Charles Van Vooren, Ian Warpole
FRONT COVER PHOTOGRAPHY	Freeze Frame Studio
BACK COVER PHOTOGRAPHY	John Parsekian/CH

UPDATED EDITION

MANAGING EDITOR:	Gretchen Bacon
EDITOR:	Jeremy Hauck
TECHNICAL EDITOR:	Charles T. Byers, Assistant Professor, Residential Remodeling Technology, AAS, AST, Thaddeus Stevens College of Technology
DESIGNER:	Wendy Reynolds

Printed in China
First Printing

Ultimate Guide: Wiring, 9th Updated Edition
ISBN 978-1-58011-575-9

Library of Congress Control Number: 2022938737

We are always looking for talented authors. To submit an idea, please send a brief inquiry to acquisitions@foxchapelpublishing.com.

Creative Homeowner®, *www.creativehomeowner.com*, is distributed exclusively in North America by Fox Chapel Publishing Company, Inc., 800-457-9112, 903 Square Street, Mount Joy, PA 17552, and in the United Kingdom by Grantham Book Service, Trent Road, Grantham, Lincolnshire, NG31 7XQ.

Safety

Although the methods in this book have been reviewed for safety, it is not possible to overstate the importance of using the safest methods you can. What follows are reminders—some do's and don'ts of work safety—to use along with your common sense.

▌Always use caution, care, and good judgment when following the procedures described in this book.

▌Always be sure that the electrical setup is safe; be sure that no circuit is overloaded, and that all power tools and electrical outlets are properly grounded. Do not use power tools in wet locations.

▌Never modify a plug by bending or removing prongs. When prongs are bent, loose or missing, replace the entire device.

▌Don't use 3-prong-to-2-prong cord adapters to overcome ground connections.

▌Be sure all receptacles and electrical conductors are properly grounded.

▌If a plug prong breaks off in a receptacle, do not attempt to remove it. Turn off the circuit, and call a licensed electrician.

▌Be sure receptacles are mounted securely in their boxes and do not move when the plug is inserted. A loose receptacle can cause a short circuit.

▌Do not use loose receptacles or other faulty electrical equipment until it is repaired or replaced and inspected by a licensed electrician.

▌Replace all damaged electrical enclosures such as receptacle, switch, and junction boxes.

▌Use extension cords only when necessary, on a short-term basis; never use extension cords in place of permanent wiring.

▌Be sure all extension cords are properly sized and rated for the use intended.

▌Keep electrical cords away from areas where they may be stepped on, pinched between door jambs, or otherwise damaged.

▌Don't use appliance or extension cords that show signs of wear, such as frayed or dried sheathing or exposed wires.

▌Visually inspect all electrical equipment and appliances before use.

▌Never staple, nail, or otherwise attach an extension cord to any surface.

▌Always turn off tools and appliances before unplugging them.

▌Never unplug a tool or appliance by yanking on the cord; always remove the cord by the plug.

▌Always keep the area in front of your main panel clear and dry. Work on a rubber mat or dry board and maintain an unobstructed area of at least 3 feet in front of the panel. The panel must be easily accessed.

▌Keep dust, lint, and other combustible materials away from electrical panels, receptacles, and appliances.

▌Keep electrical panel doors closed and latched when not in use.

▌Keep all electrical equipment away from any source of water unless it is rated for use in wet areas, such as a wet-dry shop vacuum.

▌Use ground-fault circuit interrupters (GFCIs) wherever possible. GFCIs are required in all wet, damp, or moist areas.

▌Limit use of receptacles to one appliance. If more than one appliance will be on a circuit, use an approved plug strip with a built-in circuit breaker.

▌Use proper lighting in areas where the risk of an electrical hazard is present and keep emergency backup lighting readily available.

▌Keep all energized parts of electrical circuits and equipment enclosed in approved cabinets and enclosures.

▌Use only tools that have double insulated casings.

▌Always be aware of the potential hazards when doing electrical work of any kind.

▌Be sure to use appropriate protective equipment when doing electrical work (safety glasses, insulated gloves, rubber mats, etc.).

Contents

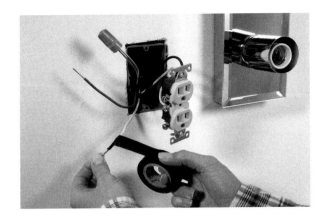

Introduction

ULTIMATE GUIDE: WIRING provides you with the information and confidence you need to make electrical repairs and improvements to your home safely and effectively. Written in easy-to-understand language that is accompanied by informative illustrations and photographs, **Ultimate Guide: Wiring** gives a clear understanding of how electricity works, how it is delivered to your house, how it is distributed throughout your home. Step-by-step sequences guide you through the most common electrical projects, including installing switches and outlets, repairing and adding light-

ing fixtures, and hooking up major appliances. You'll also find information on low-voltage wiring systems, outdoor lighting and wiring, home networks, Wi-Fi applications, lightning protection, surge protection, and standby generators. The information that accompanies each project includes the tools and materials you will need to perform the work at hand. This latest edition includes changes to the most recent version of the National Electrical Code. But before beginning any electrical project, check with your local building department for requirements in your area.

Ultimate Guide: Wiring will teach you to approach your home wiring projects with the confidence that comes from knowledge. You will see that there is really nothing mystical about installing a dimmer switch or changing a receptacle. As with changing a lightbulb, the work can be simple once you know how to do it, and to do it safely.

As a teaching tool, **Ultimate Guide: Wiring** provides clear instruction, ease of use, and an entertaining presentation. Some of the book's features include:

▌ **Updated notes on material availability and pricing,** because these considerations have become a major issue in the industry since the spring of 2020 and will continue for the foreseeable future, as demand for limited supplies has caused prices to elevate dramatically. For example, the stocked quantities of breakers that protect AFCI and GFCI are in the single digits at home centers, and the same applies for generic single and double pole breakers. Rising copper futures and a limited supply of the PVC conductor insulation and the cables' outer sheathing has likewise led to a shortage of Romex wire. It pays huge dividends to check pricing and availability from several sources before beginning any electrical project. Careful planning and execution of every aspect of your work is essential in today's market.

▌ **Step-by-step photographs** illustrate how to wire electrical boxes, switches, receptacles, and even specific appliances. Great effort has been made to include photos that will help you to understand how circuits work, show you real components and wiring, and take you step-by-step through projects. Projects include difficulty ratings (opposite), tools, and materials.

▌ **Informative art,** including cutaway drawings, clarify concepts not easily demonstrated in photographs.

▌ **Charts and tables** provide information such as the correct size and type of wire for a particular project.

▌ **Detailed how-to wiring diagrams** reinforce the step-by-step procedures and often add variations and alternative approaches.

▌ **Smart Tips** provide tidbits of interesting and insightful information about various subjects, often related to your project.

▌ **Sidebars** accompanying the how-to steps frequently discuss related topics that don't require a tremendous amount of detail.

Of course, mastering this book will not qualify you to become a licensed electrician, but it will provide you with enough knowledge of electrical work to realize when someone else is doing it wrong. Inevitably, either for reasons of safety or simply because it is required by your local or state electrical code, you may need the services of a licensed electrician, especially for work on your service entrance or within your main electrical panel. In those cases, you should know not only what an electrician must do, but also how he or she must do it. **Ultimate Guide: Wiring** will help you to do just that.

Ultimate Guide: Wiring conforms to the current National Electrical Code® (NEC). However, electrical codes are not design manuals. Codes are written to establish minimal standards. It is always better to exceed code requirements. Also, be aware of local code restrictions that may be more stringent than the NEC. If you are ever uncertain about an electrical requirement, don't take unnecessary risks! When in doubt, call a licensed electrician.

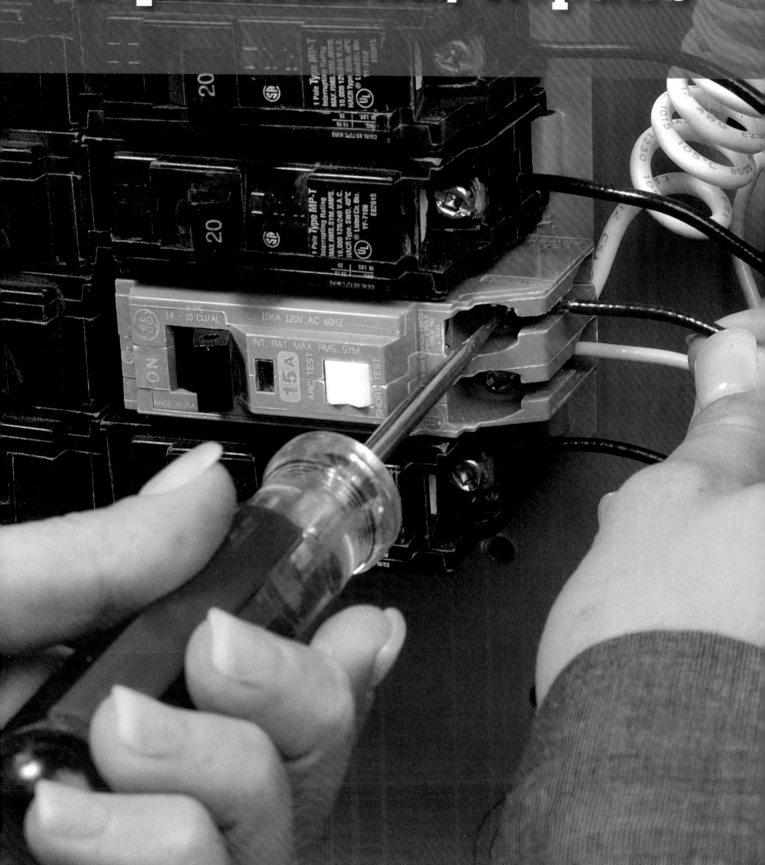

wiring methods

BECOMING ACQUAINTED with basic wiring methods will enable you to tackle a variety of electrical projects. In many cases, these include running cable through walls or between floors, connecting receptacles and switches to the system, and installing new circuits—the subjects covered in this chapter. For the basics, including an explanation of the workings of the home electrical system and the tools and equipment used in residential wiring, review the material in Part II, which begins on page 254.

FUSE AND CIRCUIT BREAKER CAPACITIES

Fuse or Circuit Breaker		Wire Gauge Capacity	Load Capacity
15-Amp Fuse	15-Amp Circuit Breaker	14/2G	15 Amps
20-Amp Fuse	20-Amp Circuit Breaker	12/2G	20 Amps
30-Amp Fuse	30-Amp Circuit Breaker	10/2G	30 Amps

BASIC CIRCUITRY

Charting Circuits

Whether working with fuses or circuit breakers, you must know which switches, receptacles, fixtures, or equipment are on the circuits they control. You must also know how they work. There are many types of fuses and circuit breakers, each with its own function. The purpose of fuses and circuit breakers is to protect the wiring—not the appliance.

Keep this in mind as you chart circuits, verifying that no fuse or circuit breaker has more amperage than the wire it is protecting. The maximum allowable current a wire can carry, measured in amps, is called its *ampacity*.

While you are inspecting your fuse box or breaker panel, look for any obvious problems. For example, if you unscrew a fuse from a fuse box, examine both the fuse and its screw shell. (To be safe, first pull the main fuse.) Check the fuse or the screw shell for any damage from arcing or burning.

Once you are certain that there is no damage to your fuse box or breaker panel, you may begin to chart your circuits. A plug-in radio will come in handy, as will an assistant, if you can find one. If necessary, you can do the work alone—it will just take a bit longer.

Wiring Methods

CHARTING CIRCUITS

Identifying which circuits service all the receptacles, switches, lights, and appliances in your house takes some time. And it works best if you do it with a helper, so you'll have to draft someone for the afternoon and expel everyone else so things are quiet. The time and effort you spend on this job, however, are well worth it. By knowing which breaker controls which device, you can quickly turn off power to anything you are working on and avoid the risk of serious shock.

TOOLS & MATERIALS

▌ Felt tip marker
▌ Stick-on labels
▌ Graph paper

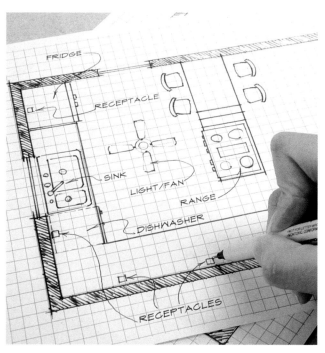

1 Before you label anything in your service panel box, make a scaled drawing of every room in your house. Draw the location of all the receptacles, light fixtures, switches, and appliances, and note where all the cabinets and furniture are positioned.

3 If you are working by yourself, adjust the radio to a high volume so that when you turn on the power you can hear from the service panel area if the radio comes on.

4 As you go from outlet to outlet, note on your room drawings which ones occupy which circuits. You'll need help to check if lights and ceiling fans turn on when you switch the breakers.

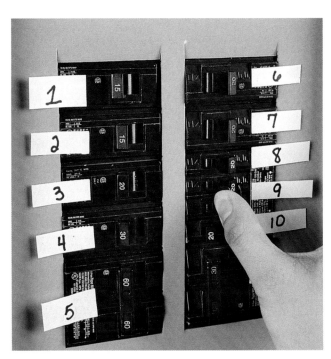

2 Once all the circuits are identified, go to the service panel and mark which breakers go to which circuits using stick-on labels. Then test each circuit by turning off the power, plugging in a radio (that's turned on) to any given outlet, and then turning the power on at the panel to see if the radio plays.

5 You will also need help from someone to check any appliance circuits. To do this with a range, for example, first turn off the breaker; then have a helper turn on the range. Next, turn on the breaker and see if the range comes on.

CHECKING FOR DAMAGE

You can easily diagnose a blown fuse element by looking through the fuse glass. A burned element suggests an overload; a broken element and darkened glass suggests a short circuit.

When a plug fuse is blown, the fuse shell may also be damaged. Check it for signs of burning and arcing.

A damaged plug fuse will clearly show marks caused by burning and arcing.

Burn flashes in a circuit breaker panel are a telltale sign of serious damage.

Wiring Methods

DESIGNING A KITCHEN WIRING PLAN

A WIRING PLAN must accommodate lighting fixtures, outlets for small appliances, and other devices that are often moved from one area to another, and outlets for large permanent appliances, such as dishwashers, washing machines, and electric ranges.

Creating the Plan

A kitchen probably requires the most complicated plan. For clarity and ease of viewing, we've provided two wiring diagrams: one for small-appliance outlets and the other for general lighting outlets. The National Electrical Code defines a general-purpose branch circuit as a circuit that supplies two or more receptacles or outlets for lighting and appliances. An appliance branch circuit is a circuit that supplies energy to one

or more outlets to which appliances are to be connected and that has no permanently connected lighting fixtures that are not a part of an appliance.

As a minimum, Section 210.52(B) of the NEC requires that the dining room, pantry, and kitchen, including countertop receptacles, be supplied by no less than two 20-ampere branch circuits. Remember, the NEC provides the minimum requirements. It is recommended that more than two circuits be provided for these areas. However, these circuits are allowed to also supply the other receptacles in the dining room, pantry, and kitchen.

Gas ranges, such as the one shown here, require a 15-amp circuit to control clocks, burner ignition devices, and lights. For electric ranges, use a 50-amp range receptacle placed on a dedicated circuit.

SMALL APPLIANCE BRANCH CIRCUITS

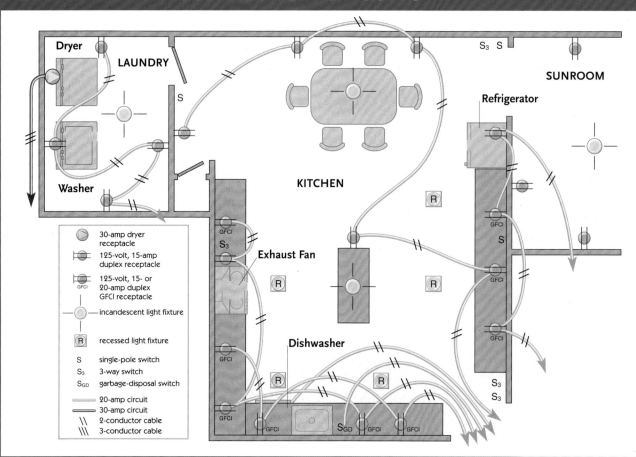

Countertop Receptacles. Place receptacles so that kitchen appliances supplied with 2-foot power cords, such as toasters, coffee makers, and electric griddles, can reach a receptacle without the use of an extension cord. For example, there must be a receptacle within 2 feet of the end of the counter. There must be a receptacle within 2 feet from each end of the sink. The maximum distance between receptacles is 4 feet. Therefore, if an appliance is placed between the receptacles, the 2-foot cord can reach either receptacle. The spacing around an inside corner is measured on the top of the counter along the wall line.

GFCI Protection. To protect users of kitchen appliances in the vicinity of water, Section 410(A)(6) requires all kitchen countertop receptacles to be provided with ground-fault circuit-interrupter (GFCI) protection, regardless of how far they are located from the sink. Provide GFCI protection by one of two methods. Either install a GFCI receptacle as the first one in the circuit and connect regular receptacles to the load side of the GFCI, which will protect those receptacles downstream, or install a GFCI circuit breaker to protect the entire circuit.

Lighting. You will notice in the wiring diagram that there are no lighting outlets on the 20-ampere small appliance branch circuits. Lighting should be provided by 15-ampere circuits. Arrange the lighting circuits in such a manner that should one circuit fail, the space will still be at least partially illuminated by lights on another circuit.

Plan on installing three-way switches in such a manner that lights can be turned on in the adjoining room before turning off the lights in the room that you are leaving. Should table or floor lamps be desired in the kitchen or dining area, install switch-controlled receptacle outlets that are supplied by a 15-ampere circuit.

GENERAL PURPOSE LIGHTING OUTLETS

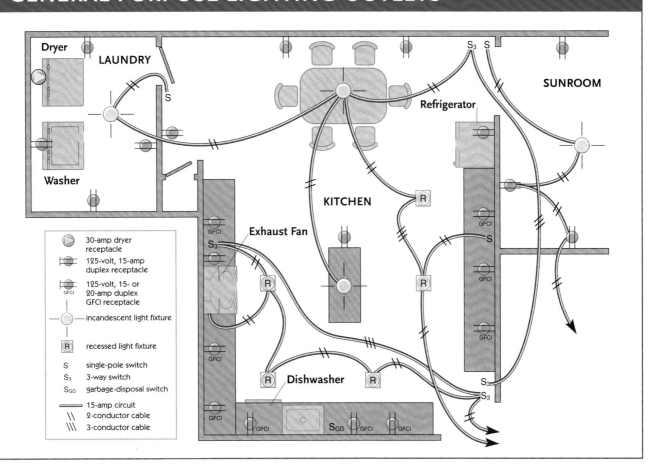

Wiring Methods

MAXIMUM WIRES IN A BOX

Box Type and Size	Maximum Number of Wires Permitted						
Electrical boxes must be of sufficient size to safely contain all enclosed wires. (Table 314.16(a), NEC)	18 GA	16 GA	14 GA	12 GA	10 GA	8 GA	6 GA
4" x 1¼" Round or Octagonal	8	7	6	5	5	4	2
4" x 1½" Round or Octagonal	10	8	7	6	6	5	3
4" x 2⅛" Round or Octagonal	14	12	10	9	8	7	4
4" x 1¼" Square	12	10	9	8	7	6	3
4" x 1½" Square	14	12	10	9	8	7	4
4" x 2⅛" Square	20	17	15	13	12	10	6
3" x 2" x 2" Device Box	6	5	5	4	4	3	2
3" x 2" x 2½" Device Box	8	7	6	5	5	4	2
3" x 2" x 2¾" Device Box	9	8	7	6	5	4	2
3" x 2" x 3½" Device Box	12	10	9	8	7	6	3
4" x 2⅛" x 1½" Device Box	6	5	5	4	4	3	2
4" x 2⅛" x 1⅞" Device Box	8	7	6	5	5	4	2
4" x 2⅛" x 2⅛" Device Box	9	8	7	6	5	4	2
3¾" x 2" x 2½" Device Box	9	8	7	6	5	4	2
3¾" x 2" x 3½" Device Box	14	12	10	9	8	7	4

CALCULATING AMPACITY

AN OVERLOADED CIRCUIT is a real danger in any electrical system and can easily lead to a blown fuse or tripped circuit breaker. Worse, it poses a potential fire hazard and can be a threat to both your life and property. The NEC requires that the demand on a given circuit be kept below its safe capacity (Section 220.14).

To calculate the total amperage of the circuit, add up those loads of which you know the amperage. For those loads that are listed in wattage instead of amperage, divide the wattage by the circuit voltage to get the amperage (amps = watts/volts), and add the values to the other am-

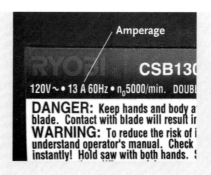

This product label provides information about the amperage used by the device.

perage loads. Total amperage load for the circuit should not exceed the breaker or fuse rating. The safe capacity of a circuit equals only 80 percent of the maximum amp rating. For a typical 20-amp circuit, the circuit should carry just 16 amps. If you can't find the amperage or wattage of the appliance, use "Appliance Wattage," page 263.

BASIC WIRING

Height and Clearance Requirements

New-construction wiring proceeds from a power or light-ing plan. Use these floor plans to lay out what is known as rough-in work. This includes installing the outlet boxes, running the wiring through the rough framing, stripping the wires inside the electrical boxes, and connecting the grounding wires. Because the electrical inspector will re-view the construction site and approve or reject the rough-

in wiring, it is necessary to follow NEC requirements when installing wiring and electrical fixtures.

Clearance requirements are especially important to re-duce the potential for fire hazards. For example, recessed fixtures not approved for contact with insulation must be spaced at least ½ inch from combustible materials [NEC Section 410.116(A)(1)]. When locating receptacles and switches, adhere to specific height requirements both for reasons of safety and accessibility. Switches, for instance, are not permitted to be any higher than 6 feet 7 inches above the floor or working level (Section 404.8).

INSTALLING ELECTRICAL BOXES

BOTH FOR EASE OF USE and aesthetics, receptacle and switch boxes should be kept at a uniform height above the finished floor or work surface. A general rule of thumb is to center receptacle boxes 12 inches above the floor—18 inches for handicapped accessibility. Cen-ter receptacle boxes over countertops 4 feet above the finished floor, as well as receptacle boxes in bathrooms and garages. Laundry receptacles are placed at a height of 3½ feet. Switch boxes, on the other hand, are nor-mally centered 4 feet above the finished floor—the max-imum for handicapped accessibility.

A common type of electrical box used in residential work today is a nonmetallic (plastic or fiberglass) box that may include integral nails for fastening it to stud fram-ing. Nonmetallic boxes such as this are inexpensive and easy to install. You place the box against a stud, bring the face of the box flush to where the drywall will be after it is installed, and then nail the box in place. Be sure to pur-chase boxes that have enough depth—at least 1¼ to 1½ inches. This will give you approximately 23 cubic inches of interior box volume in which to tuck your wires. Using cable staples, secure the nonmetallic cable no more than 12 inches from the single-device electrical box. Make sure that at least ¼ inch of fully insulated cable will be secured inside of the box after the wires are stripped. Many switch boxes have gauge marks on their sides that allow you to position the box on a framing stud without having to measure depth. Recess boxes no more than ¼ inch from the finished wall surface. Mount boxes flush with the sur-

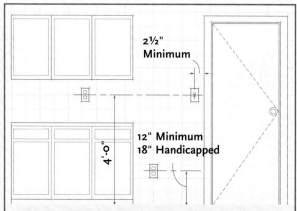

Receptacles should be centered 12 in. above the finished floor—18 in. for handicapped acces-sibility. Receptacles over countertops should be centered 4 ft. above the finished floor. Switches are generally centered at this same height, which is the maximum for handicapped accessibility.

face of combustible materials, such as wood.

Another type of electrical box is the handy box: a sin-gle-switch/receptacle box that is often screwed directly to a framing member, using a portable electric drill with a screwdriver bit. They sometimes come with a side-mount-ing flange to aid in installation. One danger, however, is that most handy boxes do not have adequate depth and can, therefore, only accommodate one cable safely. Mis-use of this type of box is a code violation and should be avoided.

On masonry surfaces, attach boxes using masonry anchors and screws. Simply drill anchor holes in the ma-sonry; then insert the anchors, and mount the box.

Wiring Methods

STRIPPING WIRES AND CABLES

There are many different ways to strip electrical cable, but probably the easiest is to use a combination of a cable ripper to peel off the plastic sheathing, followed by a multipurpose tool or wire strippers to remove the insulation on the wires. Most boxes require that about 8 inches of cable wire extend into the box. So strip off 8 inches of sheathing first; then take off about ⅝ inch of insulation from the end of each wire. Slide this cable into the box, and attach the outlet device.

TOOLS & MATERIALS

- Multipurpose tool
- Cable ripper
- Cable

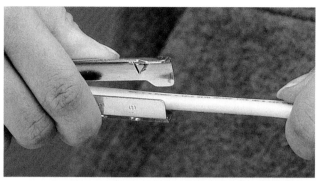

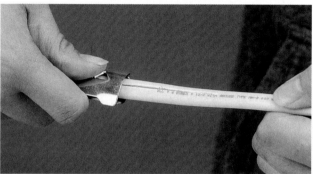

1 To remove the plastic sheathing from an electrical cable, use a cable ripper. Slide this simple tool over the end of the cable; then squeeze the halves together to pierce the sheathing (top). To cut the sheathing, pull the ripper to the end of the cable (above).

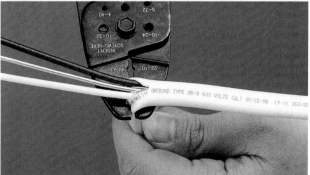

2 Once the sheathing is cut to the end of the cable, pull back the sheathing to where the cable was first pierced (top), and cut off the sheathing using a multipurpose tool or a utility knife at this point (bottom).

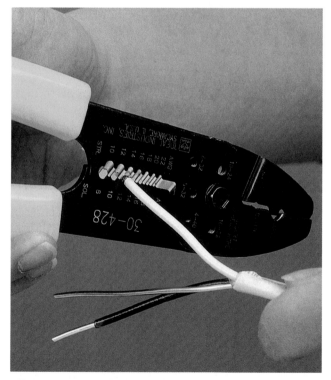

3 Use a multipurpose tool to strip the insulation from the ends of the wire. Take off about ⅝ in. of insulation, using the appropriate slot on the tool that matches the gauge of the wire.

Preparing for Inspection

Once new framing walls are ready to be wired and electrical boxes have all been put in place, carefully begin pulling the cable through the framing. When you insert a cable end into an electrical box, leave a minimum of 6 inches of extra cable, cutting away the excess. Using a cable staple, secure the cable at a maximum of 12 inches above the single-device box. After you have run all cables through the framing and into the electrical boxes, rip back and remove the sheathing from the cable ends in each box; then strip the individual wires. Before a rough-in inspection can be done, you must also splice together the grounding wires using either green wire connectors or wire crimping ferrules. Then place the wires securely in their boxes.

After a rough-in inspection is performed, install the receptacles and switches. Wait until the drywall is in place before doing this work. When the walls are completed and all of the boxes wired, you can install cover plates and turn on the power. Check each receptacle, using a plug-in receptacle analyzer, to verify that all of the wiring has been properly done. Install the light fixtures; then confirm that they are all working. Once you have completed all of this, your work will be ready for final inspection. The inspector will reexamine your work, performing many of the same circuit tests as you.

GRANDFATHERING EXISTING ELECTRICAL WORK

QUESTIONS SOMETIMES ARISE as to whether it's necessary to update a certain electrical issue, or what wiring conditions will or won't be flagged in a home inspection report. When you are unsure what is permitted and what is not, your local building department is a great source of knowledge, especially if your work to be completed will require a permit, which means an inspection. But before the permit comes the plan review where you can find out if your ideas are correct, or if you need someone with a specific license to do the work.

Most home improvement jobs can be accomplished by the do-it-yourselfer homeowner, with exceptions for plumbing, gas piping, and heating. In these areas, municipalities have found it best to have licensed contractors perform the work to ensure uniformity and public safety. That is, after all, the goal of the permit process—uniformity and public safety no matter who performs the work. Plans, permits, and inspections go a long way to keeping everyone safe and healthy in your community. And keep in mind that the goal of the National Electrical Code (NEC)

This is just one example of grandfathered outdoor receptacle covers still in use today.

is to ensure a safe, reliable electrical system inside your home—for your own protection.

Grandfathering as used in the building industry refers to cases where an outdated building method is permitted to remain in place as long as that area of a home or building does not require repair, renovation, or demolition. If the area is going to be repaired, renovated, or demolished, then it—along with any new parts or construction—must meet current building codes for that community.

There are many 100-amp services provided to homes across America that still have fuses to control a dryer circuit, or have receptacles with only two prongs without the third ground prong. Are they as safe as the state-of-the-art circuit breakers for a dryer, or a grounded receptacle connected to a GFCI breaker? Of course not. But are they legal? Under grandfather clauses, yes, they are.

The real estate industry across America has become very competitive, and the best-kept homes, sometimes regardless of location, can at times bring very high sale prices and sell in the blink of an eye. This is where the home inspection industry comes into play. Inspectors look at the current conditions in a home, and find potential issues due to the home's age, and list their concerns for the perspective buyer. It is then up to the seller and the buyer to negotiate what gets fixed and who pays for it. But in the pandemic-era market, the demand for housing is so high that some homes are being bought without any home inspections. Still, if you as a buyer have the opportunity to require a home inspection, it's always in your best interest to do so.

Wiring Methods

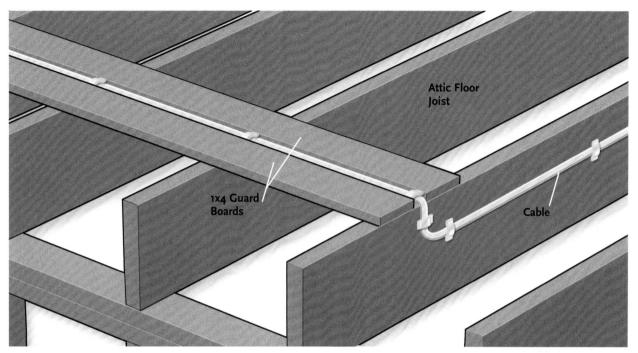

Attic Runs. To run cable perpendicular to framing joists in an unfinished attic, construct a channel space along an edge wall, using two 1x4 furring strips as guard boards, as shown. You can also drill holes through the middle of the joists and run the cable through these holes. This option is a poor choice if insulation is in the way.

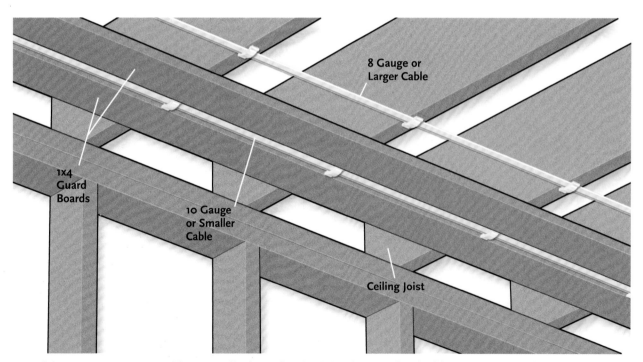

Crawl Space Runs. To run cable perpendicular to framing joists in an unfinished basement or crawl space, construct a runway using a 1x4 furring strip along the bottom edge of the framing or bore holes in the joists. You can staple cable containing three 8-gauge conductors or larger directly to the underside of the joists.

smart tip

SPLICING GROUNDING WIRES

IN EXISTING WIRING YOU'RE LIKELY TO COME ACROSS THE PIGTAIL METHOD OF SPLICING GROUNDING WIRES (IN THE PHOTO AT RIGHT), SO THAT'S THE METHOD DEMONSTRATED THROUGHOUT THIS BOOK. HOWEVER, GROUNDING WIRE CONNECTORS ARE MANUFACTURED WITH A HOLE AT THE TOP SO THAT WIRES CAN BE SPLICED AS SHOWN AT FAR RIGHT. THIS IS THE METHOD ACTUALLY PREFERRED BY ELECTRICIANS THESE DAYS.

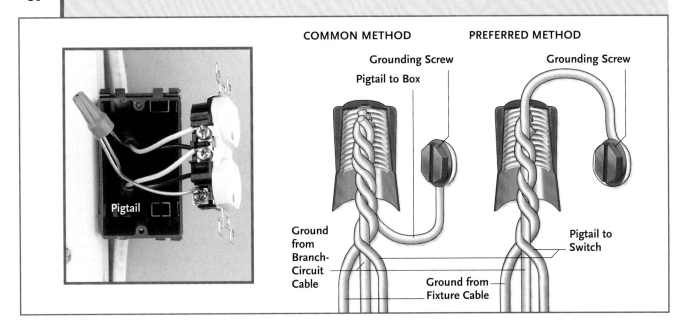

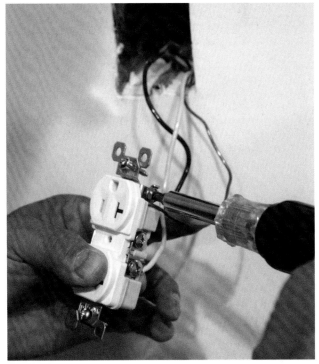

When multiple ground wires are present in a junction box, a copper crimp sleeve is used to trim all ground wires except the one(s) necessary to connect to the device ground screw.

Wiring Methods

INSTALLING A JUNCTION BOX

No wire splices outside an electrical box are permitted by the NEC. But this doesn't mean that they don't occur, particularly in old houses that have suffered at the hands of sloppy or un-informed electricians. If you have any of these splices in your house, you must take apart the existing splice; install a junction box; make the new splices using wire connectors; and cover the box with a protective metal cover plate.

For descriptions of the parts and tools used in this project, **see pages 278** and **279**. For an in-depth tutorial on splicing wires together, **see page 291**.

TOOLS & MATERIALS

▪ Insulated screwdrivers ▪ Multipurpose tool ▪ Hammer ▪ Neon circuit tester ▪ Wire connectors ▪ Screws/nails ▪ Grounding pigtail and screw ▪ Junction box ▪ Cable clamps ▪ Cable

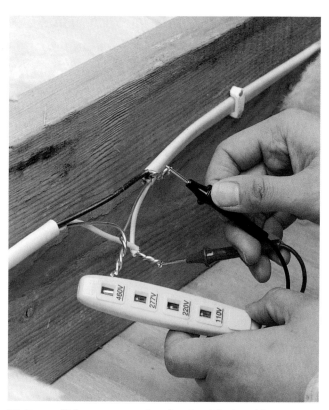

1 Turn off the power to the circuit with the splice in the cable. Remove any wire connectors or electrical tape from the wires. Then check for any power with a neon circuit tester. If you find power, immediately locate the proper circuit breaker and turn it off.

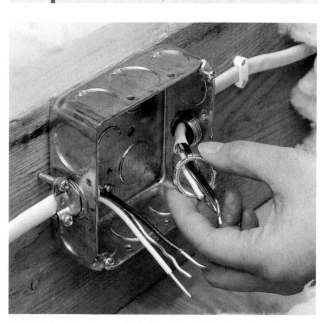

3 Put cable connectors into both knockout openings; then slide the cables through the connectors; and tighten the cable clamps onto the cable. Finish up by turning the locknuts onto the connectors from inside the box. Secure these nuts using slip joint pliers.

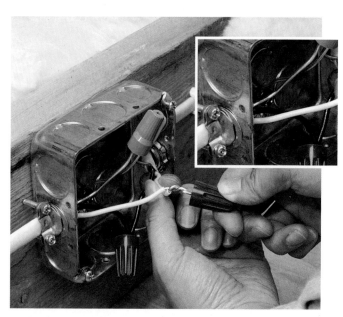

4 Connect a length of grounding wire to the green grounding screw inside the box (inset). Then splice all the like-colored wires in the box using the proper wire connectors for the wire gauge in the cable. Red-colored connectors usually work for both two 14-gauge wires and two 12-gauge wires. Green connectors are used for ground wires.

2 For the wires to have access to the junction box, remove a couple of knockout plates using a screwdriver and a hammer. Then separate the splices, and install the box so it falls midway between the ends of both cables. Screw or nail the box in place (inset).

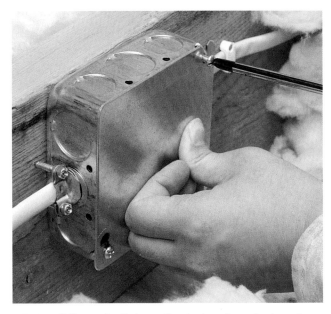

5 Carefully push all the spliced wires into the junction box, and install the box cover plate. Turn on the circuit power at the breaker panel, and check to see if all the receptacles, switches, and lights on the circuit are working properly.

SURFACE WIRING

CONDITIONS EXIST where concealed wiring isn't possible—for example, a basement having exposed concrete or masonry walls. In this case, surface wiring is the only option. Surface-mounted conduit, or raceway, provides a rigid flat metal or plastic pipe to convey wire across instead of inside a wall or ceiling. Special receptacle and fixture boxes are used in conjunction with raceway to offer a safe way to install surface wiring. A plastic raceway requires a separate grounding wire; a metal raceway connected to a properly grounded electrical box is self-grounding. (See "Raceways," page 311.)

Raceway Receptacle Box

Raceway Channel

Elbow Connector

Raceway channels protect exposed wire along a wall or ceiling surface.

21

Wiring Methods

RUNNING CABLE THROUGH FRAMING

INSTALLING WIRING through new construction is relatively easy. The most common electrical installations are those in which outlet boxes are mounted alongside a stud or joist, although this is not always possible. Once electrical boxes are in place, run the cable through the framing members. Do this by drilling ¾-inch holes directly through the center of the studs or joists. Center the holes at least 1⅝ inches in from the edge of the framing member. If you must drill closer, then attach a wire shield to the outer edge of the framing to prevent nails or screws from penetrating the hole and causing damage to the cable during the course of future work.

If you cannot drill holes through framing because the framing cavity contains ductwork or plumbing, you may have to resort to surface wiring to do the job properly. (See "Surface Wiring," page 21.)

Avoiding Damage. Be careful not to jerk the wire cable violently as you pull it through the drilled holes in the framing. The friction from pulling cable through rough-cut wood can cause the cable sheathing to tear, exposing the wires to serious damage. You should also avoid making sharp bends or kinks in the cable, as these too can damage the wiring. In addition, be careful when running cable along the bottom of a wall—there are likely to be toenailed fasteners near the bottom of each wall stud.

Getting around windows and doors can also be a problem. If there are cripple studs above the header, then you can

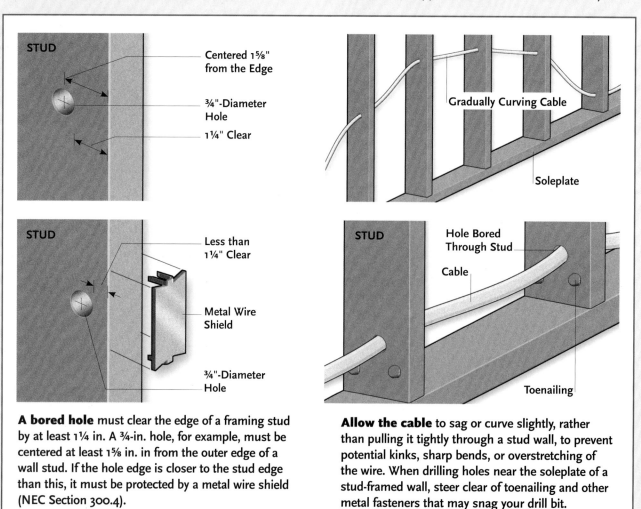

A bored hole must clear the edge of a framing stud by at least 1¼ in. A ¾-in. hole, for example, must be centered at least 1⅝ in. in from the outer edge of a wall stud. If the hole edge is closer to the stud edge than this, it must be protected by a metal wire shield (NEC Section 300.4).

Allow the cable to sag or curve slightly, rather than pulling it tightly through a stud wall, to prevent potential kinks, sharp bends, or overstretching of the wire. When drilling holes near the soleplate of a stud-framed wall, steer clear of toenailing and other metal fasteners that may snag your drill bit.

drill holes through them for cable. However, you can't drill through the length of a solid-wood header. If possible, you can go over or under such obstacles. As a last resort, use a router to cut a channel deeply enough across the surface of the header to accommodate a cable; protect the cable by installing metal plates over it.

Holes and Notches. If you bore holes through ceiling and floor joists, the holes must be located so that they will not undermine the structural integrity of the framing. (See illustration below.) This is also a concern if you notch the wood along the top or bottom edge to run cable perpendicular to the joists. In this instance, you must install metal wire shields to protect the cable from damage. Even cable that runs parallel with framing should not be left vulnerable or hanging loosely in a wall or floor space. Use cable staples to secure it in place along the center of the stud, joist, or rafter.

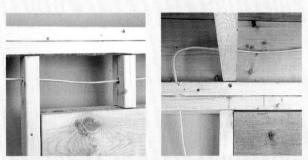

Cripple studs, left, over a header offer a simple and convenient path for wiring around a door or window opening. The best way to go around a solid header, right, is to run your wiring through the ceiling joists above or the floor joists below the rough opening.

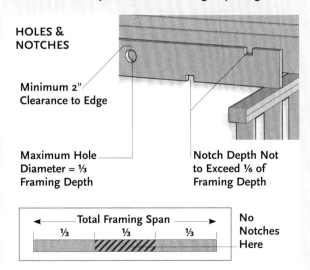

HOLES & NOTCHES

Minimum 2" Clearance to Edge

Maximum Hole Diameter = ⅓ Framing Depth

Notch Depth Not to Exceed ⅙ of Framing Depth

Total Framing Span

⅓   ⅓   ⅓

No Notches Here

smart tip

ROUTING A SOLID HEADER

USE A ROUTER TO CUT A CABLE CHANNEL ACROSS A SOLID HEADER ONLY IF YOU HAVE NO OTHER ALTERNATIVE. ATTACH A SERIES OF METAL PLATES (SHOWN AS CUTAWAY, BOTTOM) OVER THE ROUTED CABLE CHANNEL TO PROTECT THE CABLE FROM POTENTIAL NAIL DAMAGE.

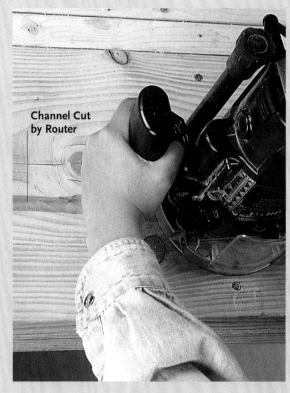

Channel Cut by Router

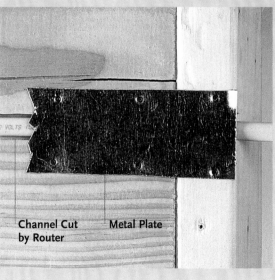

Channel Cut by Router   Metal Plate

Wiring Methods

Opening and Closing Walls

Running cables through existing walls and joist spaces is a lot more complicated than running cables in new construction. Because you cannot see into finished framing cavities, fishing cables through walls and ceilings requires great patience and more than a little skill.

If you have access to walls from a basement or attic, you can get power into walls by fishing the cable vertically instead of horizontally through the structural framing. In many cases, running cable the long way around to complete a circuit may be the easiest route, even if you have to spend more money for cable. The cost of the cable is likely to be much less than that of ripping into walls and ceilings. If you must run cable across existing framing, for example, you may have to cut into drywall in order to position the cable properly. It is a good idea to take time initially to explore alternative routes the cable might follow. Try to determine the best route; then make a rough sketch or map of the cable route. This will undoubtedly save you time and money later.

Before running cable, first decide where to locate your new switch, outlet, or junction box; then determine which walls or ceilings, if any, need to be opened to efficiently route the cable to this point. You can cut openings in drywall using a utility knife, mini-hacksaw, or keyhole or saber saw. After you make your cut, either remove the scrap or knock it back between the framing members.

In an unfinished basement, you may encounter hollow concrete-block walls or poured steel-reinforced solid concrete walls. Although it is possible to cut into a hollow concrete block wall, it isn't practical. For block and concrete walls, it is best to install metal surface raceways or electrical conduit, and surface-mount your electrical boxes and wiring. Use a masonry bit on your power drill to make pilot holes for masonry anchors; then anchor the boxes and conduit clamps directly to the wall.

Flat square electrical boxes are specially made to fit in shallow furred-out wall cavities. A–shallow boxes; B–box extension; C–box cover

project

Fishing cable through closed walls can be difficult. Here are some tips to make it easier: always use a cut-in box for the outlet; use a guide wire to establish one reference point for two different floors; be willing to waste some wire by running the cable into the basement and then to its destination, instead of taking the shorter, but usually much harder, route through the wall.

TOOLS & MATERIALS

- Keyhole or saber saw
- Cordless drill
- ⅛-inch bit
- ¾-inch spade bit
- Fish tape
- Guide wire

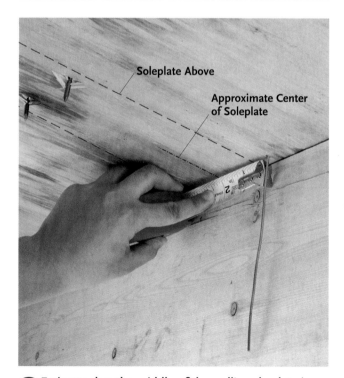

Soleplate Above

Approximate Center of Soleplate

3 Estimate that the middle of the wall's sole plate is about 2 in. away from the guide wire. Mark this centerline along the bottom surface of the floor plywood.

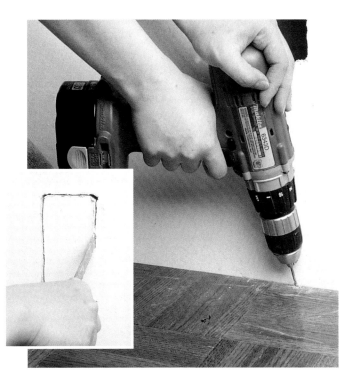

1 Trace the outline of a cut-in box on the wall, and cut along this line using a drywall or keyhole saw (inset). Then drill a small hole through the floor directly below this box opening in the wall.

2 Use a piece of scrap wire as a guide to locate the hole under the floor. Just slide the wire into the hole; go downstairs and find the wire. Because the hole was drilled right next to the wall, the wall framing should begin about ½ in. away from the guide wire.

4 Using a drill with a ¾-in. spade bit, bore a hole up through the plywood and wall plate. Unwind some cable from the roll, and push the free end up through this hole. Be sure to push up enough cable to reach the box hole. Tape the cable in place so it doesn't fall out of the hole.

5 If you can fit your hand into the box hole, reach in and grab the cable. If not, get some help from someone with smaller hands. Once you pull the cable out, install it in a cut-in box; then push the box into the wall, and secure it in place.

Wiring Methods

RUNNING CABLE BEHIND A BASEBOARD

project

One of the best places to run new cable in a finished room is to remove the baseboard and install the cable in the stud space behind. The job isn't very hard, and you can make it even easier by being careful when you remove the baseboard. By reusing the old baseboard, you can save some money, but more importantly, you can save a lot of time and effort.

TOOLS & MATERIALS

▌Pencil ▌Utility knife ▌Metal paint scraper ▌Wood chisel ▌Straightedge ▌Backsaw ▌Hammer ▌Finishing nails ▌Drywall nails ▌Nail set ▌Fish tape ▌Wire shields ▌Measuring tape ▌Wood shim ▌Cable ▌Paintbrush and paint

1 Installing cable behind a baseboard is one of the best ways to route cable through existing walls. The first step is to mark the wall along the top of the baseboard (top). Then cut along the joint between the baseboard and the wall to break the seal made by caulk and paint (bottom).

4 Use a utility knife or a keyhole saw to cut through the drywall along the cut line. Once the piece is free, pull it away from the wall. If the drywall was screwed in place, remove the screws so the piece of drywall comes out cleanly and can be reused.

5 The cable can run either in notches cut in the edge of the studs, as shown here, or in holes drilled through the middle of the studs. If you notch the studs, install a metal shield on each stud to protect the cable.

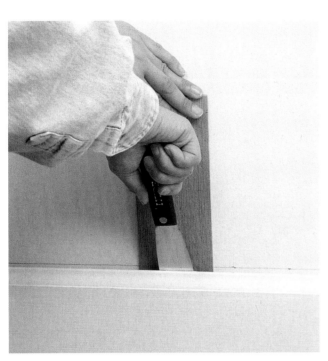

2 Carefully pry off the baseboard using a putty knife and a shimming shingle. Work the knife blade between the two, and pry them apart enough to slide the shingle behind the knife. The shingle protects the wall surface from damage.

3 Measure down from the wall reference line ½ in., and mark the wall every couple of feet. Using a long straightedge and pencil, draw a cut line through these marks.

6 Once the cable is entirely installed, cover up the opening with the piece of drywall you removed, if it's still useable, or with a new piece. Drive the nails or screws in the studs and bottom plate to avoid hitting the metal shields.

7 Reinstall the old baseboard, or cut and install a new baseboard that matches the other trim in the room. Then caulk the joint between the baseboard and the wall, and paint the joint and the baseboard.

Wiring Methods

WIRING AROUND AN EXISTING DOORWAY

IF AN EXISTING DOORWAY IS IN THE PATH OF YOUR CABLE, YOU WILL HAVE TO RUN THE CABLE UP AND AROUND THE DOOR FRAME. IN THIS SITUATION, RATHER THAN CUTTING OUT SECTIONS OF THE DRYWALL, YOU MAY BE ABLE TO TAKE ADVANTAGE OF THE SHIM SPACE. REMOVE THE MOLDING FROM AROUND THE DOOR, GENTLY PRYING IT AWAY FROM THE WALL. USE A RIGID PAINT SCRAPER WITH A SCRAP PIECE OF WOOD UNDER IT TO PROTECT THE WALL. IF YOU CANNOT REMOVE THE TRIM WITHOUT CAUSING IT DAMAGE, YOU MAY HAVE TO REPLACE THE MOLDING. IF THE MOLDING IS IRREPLACEABLE, YOU MAY WISH TO RECONSIDER USING THIS METHOD TO ROUTE THE CABLE AROUND YOUR DOOR. ONCE THE SHIM SPACE IS EXPOSED, NOTCH OUT THE SHIM SPACERS JUST ENOUGH TO ACCOMMODATE THE CABLE. STRING THE CABLE AROUND THE SHIM SPACE; THEN COVER THE NOTCHED AREAS, USING METAL WIRE SHIELDS.

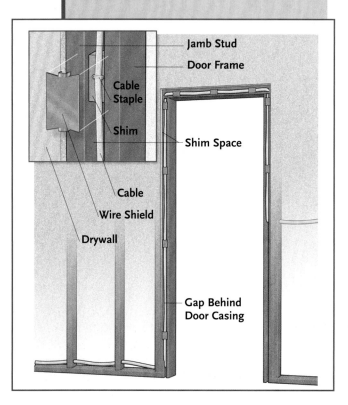

- Jamb Stud
- Door Frame
- Cable Staple
- Shim
- Shim Space
- Cable
- Wire Shield
- Drywall
- Gap Behind Door Casing

FISHING CABLE ACROSS A CEILING

Running cable through an existing but inaccessible ceiling may require that you cut both a ceiling and a wall opening in order to fish the cable from a vertical wall cavity to a horizontal ceiling cavity. Once the ceiling is opened, use a fish tape to get the cable across to the new electrical box.

TOOLS & MATERIALS

- ❚ Stepladder
- ❚ Utility knife
- ❚ Keyhole or saber saw
- ❚ Wood chisel
- ❚ Pencil and straightedge
- ❚ Plumb bob
- ❚ Hammer
- ❚ Cordless drill
- ❚ ¾-inch spade bit
- ❚ Electrical tape
- ❚ Nonmetallic fish tape
- ❚ Wire shields
- ❚ Safety glasses
- ❚ Dust mask

1 Determine where you want your ceiling outlet; then trace around the fixture box. Using a drywall or keyhole saw, cut along the line and remove the drywall. Then trace around the fixture box or use the manufacturer's paper template supplied with many old work/remodel plastic electrical boxes.

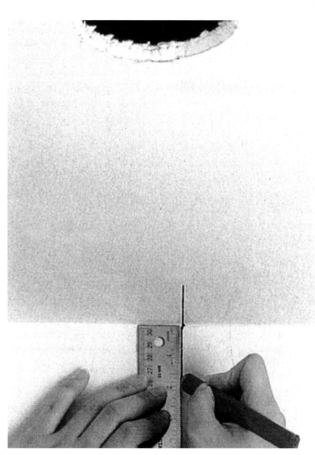

2 Measure from the end wall of the room to the ceiling hole. Then go to the side room wall and transfer this measurement to the corner between the wall and ceiling.

3 Cut a 2-in.-wide by 6-in.-long opening in the ceiling and the wall. Use a utility knife to cut the wall opening because the top plates are behind it. Use a keyhole saw for the ceiling.

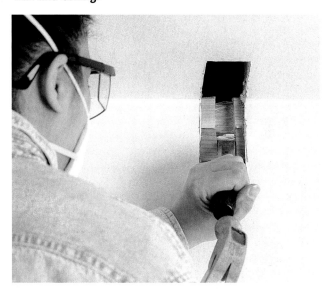

4 Using a sharp chisel and a hammer, cut a ¾-in.-wide by 1-in.-deep notch in the wall plates. This notch will act as a raceway for the electrical cable that will service the ceiling fixture. If you run into a nail, stop chiseling and cut it out with a hacksaw to prevent more damage to the chisel blade.

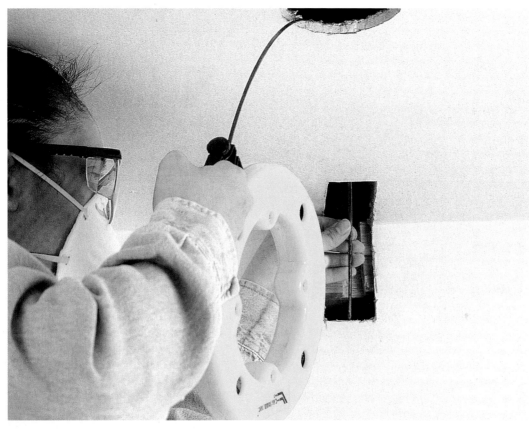

5 Use a fish tape to pull cable into the box. Start by feeding the tape into the ceiling hole, directing it through the access hole in the ceiling and down to the box hole near the floor.

6 Tape the end of some electrical cable to the end of the fish tape, and pull the cable up through the box hole at the floor.

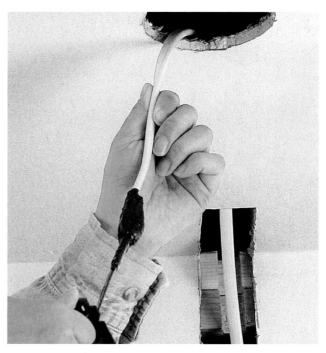

7 Gently pull the cable through the access hole and the outlet hole in the ceiling. Cover the cable at the top plates notch with a metal shield.

If removing your existing baseboard is not a reasonable option (see page 26), you will simply have to cut out a limited section of visible drywall in order to gain access to the stud framing. The resulting wall damage can probably be minimized if you use a specialized flex-drill—one that is long and flexible—to bore through several adjacent framing studs, rather than having to notch them all at the wall surface. Nevertheless, some patching and repair work, as well as refinishing, will still be necessary. (The long section of drywall in this photo has been removed for clarity.)

FISHING WIRE THROUGH A WALL

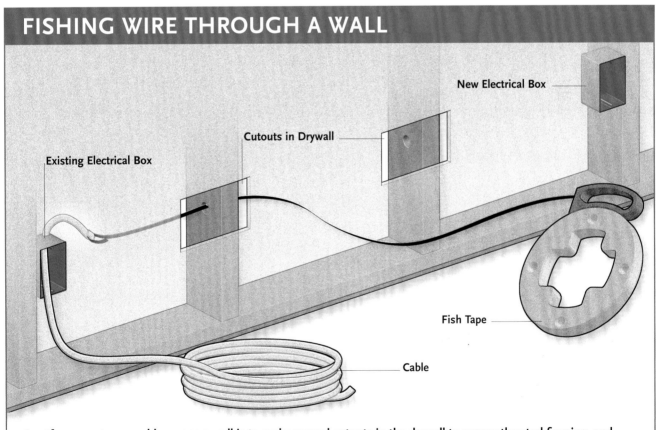

New Electrical Box

Cutouts in Drywall

Existing Electrical Box

Fish Tape

Cable

Another way to run cable across a wall is to make several cutouts in the drywall to expose the stud framing, and bore holes through the studs. Fish the cable gradually from the existing box to the new location.

RECEPTACLES

Duplex Receptacles

Although there are two basic types of receptacles—single and duplex—only duplex receptacles are commonly found in modern homes. A duplex receptacle accommodates two plugs at the same time. Originally, receptacles were neither grounded nor polarized; later, they became polarized but not grounded. Today, receptacles include a screw terminal for a grounding connection. These receptacles have a total of five terminal screws: two brass screw terminals on the right side for black/red hot-wire connections; two silver screw terminals on the left side for white neutral-wire connections; and one green screw terminal on the left side for a bare copper or green grounding-wire connection. The NEC now requires that in new construction all 125-volt, 15- and 20-amp receptacles installed in living areas must be listed as tamper-proof. (See "Tamper-Proof Receptacles," page 307.) Check with your building department for requirements in your area.

RECEPTACLE HISTORY

NONGROUNDED NON-POLARIZED RECEPTACLE

A

Hot or Neutral

NONGROUNDED POLARIZED RECEPTACLE

B

Neutral

NM Cable

Hot

GROUNDED RECEPTACLE

C

Neutral

Ground

NM Cable

Hot

Early receptacles had two nonpolarized connections (A). For this type of receptacle, the colored wires could go to either screw terminal. Later, manufacturers made polarized receptacles (B). These require that a specific color wire be connected to a specific screw terminal, but they are not grounded. Today, receptacles also include a green grounding screw terminal (C).

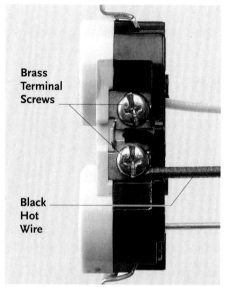

Brass Terminal Screws

Black Hot Wire

Receptacle, right side. The hot black or red wires are connected to the brass terminal screws on a receptacle.

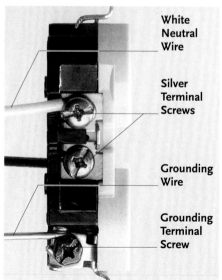

White Neutral Wire

Silver Terminal Screws

Grounding Wire

Grounding Terminal Screw

Receptacle, left side. The silver terminal screws on a receptacle receive the white neutral wires, while the green terminal screw receives the grounding wire.

INSTALLING USB/120-VOLT DUAL-PURPOSE RESIDENTIAL RECEPTACLES

THESE RECEPTACLES ARE AVAILABLE in both 20-amp and 15-amp 120-volt receptacles in the Decora style cover plate that will provide the required 3.6-amp USB charging current for your electronic devices. The advantage is the adapter plug to convert your USB cable to the 3-prong outlet is no longer necessary in the event it gets lost or broken. To meet the latest NEC requirements, these dual-purpose receptacles are being produced in the tamper-proof style to prevent accidental electrical shock to children.

Be sure to match the amperage of the receptacle to the amperage of the branch circuit breaker or fuse. To begin, disconnect the power to the receptacle by locating the relevant fuse or breaker in the panel box. Test the receptacle by plugging in a device to be sure the power is disconnected. With the grounding lugs facing the same way, up or down, detach one wire at a time, and connect each wire to the matching screw terminal on the dual-purpose receptacle.

New dual-use receptacles support back wiring as shown in the figures above. Back wiring results in the fastest, highest quality connection, but the device will also support side wiring under the connection screws. Follow the strip wire gauge on the back for proper length to assure the best connection.

Fasten the device screws to the junction box and install the Decora cover plate with the two supplied cover plate screws. Complete the installation by restoring power to the branch circuit and test the receptacle with an electrical device.

Wiring Methods

WIRING AN END-OF-RUN RECEPTACLE

An end-of-run receptacle is one of the easiest devices to install. Because only one cable comes into the box, there's only one black (hot) wire, one white (neutral) wire, and one bare ground wire. Just hook the black to a brass terminal, the white to a silver terminal, and the ground wire to the receptacle's grounding screw.

TOOLS & MATERIALS

▪ Insulated screwdriver ▪ Diagonal cutting pliers ▪ Long-nose pliers
▪ Wire stripper ▪ Multipurpose tool
▪ Cable ripper ▪ Duplex receptacle
▪ Receptacle box ▪ 12/2G NM cable
▪ Green wire connector ▪ Grounding pigtail and screw (for metal boxes)
▪ Cable clamps (for metal boxes)

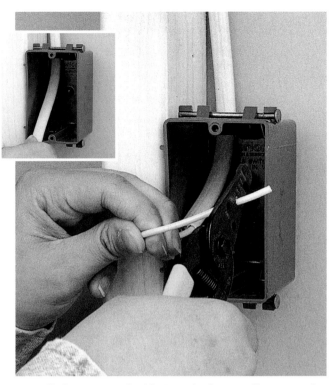

1 Pull about 8 in. of cable into the box to allow enough wire to easily attach the receptacle (inset). Strip off most of the cable sheathing; then strip the insulation from the ends of both wires.

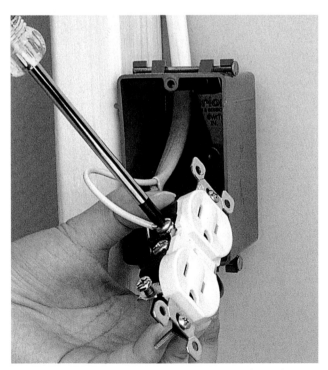

2 Using long-nose pliers, form a small hook on the ends of the cable wires. Then loop the hook around its terminal screw and tighten it in place. The white wire goes on a silver screw. The black wire is attached to a brass- or gold-colored screw.

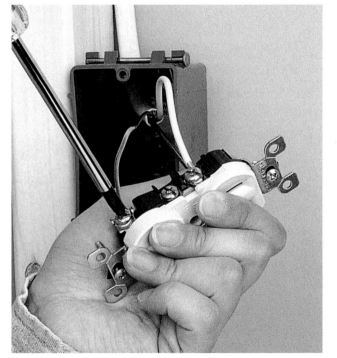

3 Attach the grounding wire to the receptacle's grounding screw. Once all the wires are attached, push the receptacle into the box, and attach the receptacle to the box using screws. Add a receptacle cover and the job is done.

WIRING A MIDDLE-OF-RUN RECEPTACLE

project

The conventional way to wire a middle-of-run receptacle is to connect all of the wires to the receptacle, letting it act as the splice between the connecting black or white wires. Wiring a receptacle this way is easy but connects all of the devices on the circuit in series—if you temporarily remove one receptacle, the current to the rest of the line will be cut. As an alternative,

TOOLS & MATERIALS

▌ Insulated screwdriver ▌ Diagonal cutting pliers ▌ Long-nose pliers ▌ Wire stripper
▌ Multipurpose tool ▌ Cable ripper
▌ Duplex receptacle ▌ Receptacle box
▌ 12/2G NM cable ▌ Green wire connector
▌ Grounding pigtail and screw (for metal boxes) ▌ Cable clamps (for metal boxes)

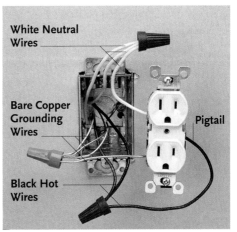

White Neutral Wires

Bare Copper Grounding Wires

Black Hot Wires

Pigtail

This type of connection, using a metal box, allows the receptacles on a circuit to be wired independently.

wire the receptacles on the circuit independently. Splice each pair of hot and neutral wires using wire connectors; then connect a pigtail from each splice to the appropriate receptacle terminal. Only current drawn by the appliance plugged into it will flow through the receptacle. If you remove the receptacle from the circuit, the rest of the circuit will continue to work. This type of connection is necessary where three or more cables must be spliced together because more than one wire is not permitted under a single screw terminal.

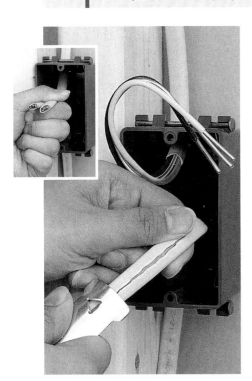

1 Pull the cable through the box cable clamps until 8 in. of both cables are in the box (inset). Strip away the cable sheathing; then the insulation from the ends of the wire.

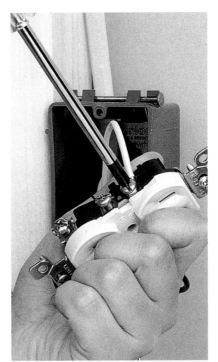

2 Make small hooks on the ends of all the wires using long-nose pliers. Then attach the wires to the receptacle by tightening a terminal screw against each wire.

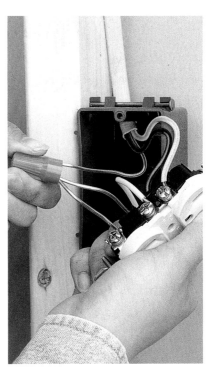

3 Join both grounding wires with a grounding pigtail inside a wire connector. Attach the other end of the pigtail to the grounding screw on the receptacle.

Wiring Methods

Sequential 120-Volt Duplex Receptacles

Start- or middle-of-run receptacles are connected to all wires from both directions. End-of-run receptacles are the last on the circuit and have only two terminations and a ground connection.

Multiple 120-Volt Duplex Receptacle Circuit

On multiple 120-volt receptacle circuits, three-wire cable is used to connect all but the last receptacle. The white neutral wire is shared by both circuits.

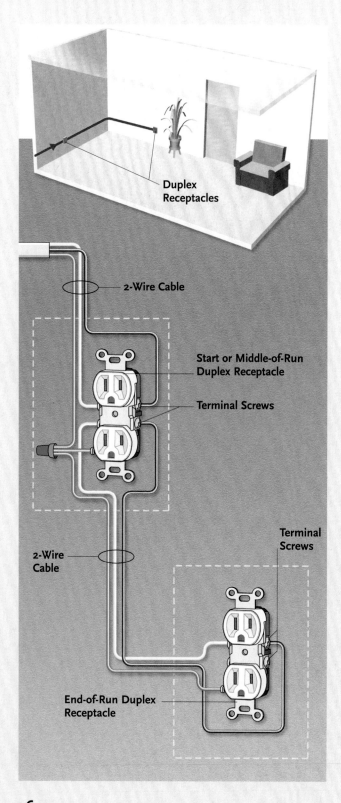

Duplex Receptacles

2-Wire Cable

Start or Middle-of-Run Duplex Receptacle

Terminal Screws

2-Wire Cable

Terminal Screws

End-of-Run Duplex Receptacle

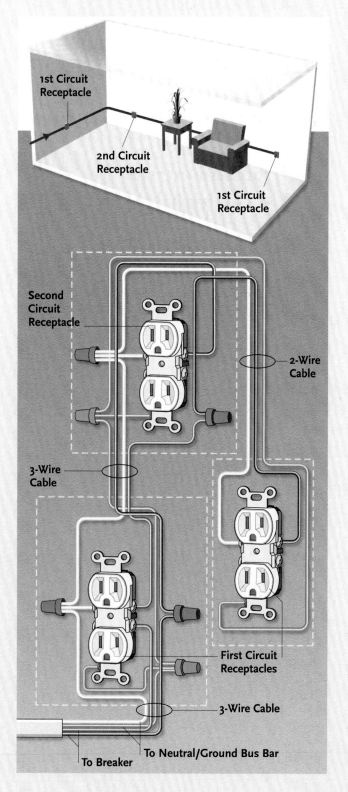

1st Circuit Receptacle

2nd Circuit Receptacle

1st Circuit Receptacle

Second Circuit Receptacle

2-Wire Cable

3-Wire Cable

First Circuit Receptacles

3-Wire Cable

To Breaker

To Neutral/Ground Bus Bar

WIRING A SPLIT-CIRCUIT RECEPTACLE

The metal tabs connecting the screw terminals on each side of a receptacle can be removed. By breaking the connection between the brass screw terminals you can wire the top outlet of the receptacle independently from the bottom. The silver tabs are normally left intact. This permits two appliances in a single receptacle to be powered by different circuits.

TOOLS & MATERIALS

▪ Insulated screwdriver ▪ Diagonal cutting pliers ▪ Long-nose pliers ▪ Wire stripper ▪ Multipurpose tool ▪ Cable ripper ▪ Duplex receptacle ▪ Receptacle box ▪ 12/3G NM cable ▪ Green wire connector ▪ Grounding pigtail and screw (for metal boxes) ▪ Cable clamps (for metal boxes)

smart tip

AVOID PUSH-IN TERMINALS

SOME RECEPTACLES HAVE WIRE HOLES INSTEAD OF SCREW TERMINALS. ON THIS TYPE OF RECEPTACLE, THE END OF EACH STRIPPED WIRE (14-GAUGE COPPER ONLY) IS PUSHED INTO THE APPROPRIATE HOLE TO COMPLETE THE CONNECTION. ALTHOUGH SIMPLE TO USE, THESE KINDS OF CONNECTIONS CAN BE PROBLEMATIC AND ARE NOT RECOMMENDED.

Push-In Terminals

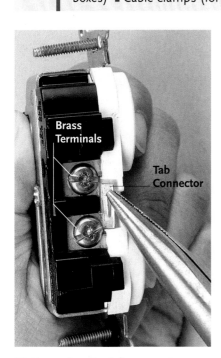

Brass Terminals

Tab Connector

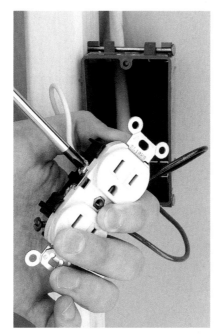

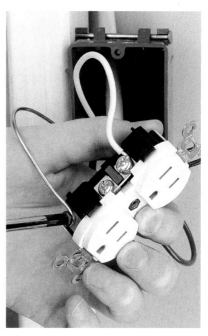

1 Removing the tab connector between the brass terminal screws by breaking it away with long-nose pliers. This allows you to wire outlets on a duplex receptacle independently.

2 Once the tab has been removed, attach the two hot wires to the brass terminal screws. Don't remove the tab that joins the silver screws. Just attach the white (neutral) wire to either silver screw.

3 Attach the grounding wire to the grounding screw on the receptacle. Then push the receptacle into the box; attach it with screws; and install a cover plate.

Wiring Methods

WIRING A SWITCH/RECEPTACLE

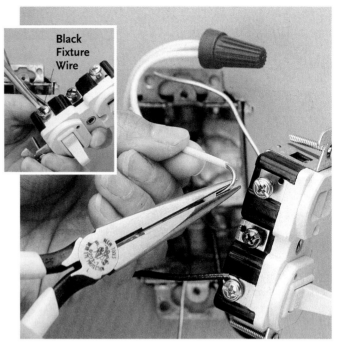

project

Combine a grounded receptacle with a single-pole switch to make up for a lack of receptacles in a room. You can wire a switch/receptacle combination in one of two ways—either the switch controls the receptacle or, more commonly, the receptacle remains constantly active while the switch powers a separate fixture. This type of circuit must occur in the middle of a run.

TOOLS & MATERIALS

▪ Insulated screwdriver ▪ Diagonal cutting pliers ▪ Long-nose pliers ▪ Wire stripper ▪ Cable ripper ▪ Electrical box ▪ Switch/receptacle ▪ 12/2G NM cable ▪ Green and red wire connectors ▪ Grounding pigtail and screw (for metal boxes) ▪ Cable clamps (for metal boxes)

1 Connect the ground wire to the metal box grounding screw. Connect the black fixture wire to the brass screw on the side of the switch unit (inset). Then attach the black power wire to the terminal screw on the other side of the switch. Join the white neutral wires with a pigtail, and attach the other end of the pigtail to the silver receptacle screw.

2 Join the ground wires and two pigtail grounds with a wire connector. One pigtail is attached to the grounding screw in the metal box. The other is attached to the grounding screw on the side of the switch/receptacle.

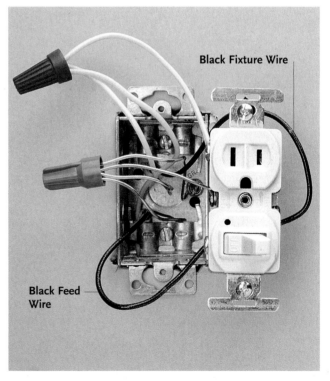

3 If you want to control the receptacle with the switch, instead of controlling another device, such as a light fixture, then just switch the locations of the black wires as shown above.

Single-Pole Switch with Light Fixture and Duplex Receptacle

Wire a middle-of-run light fixture through a single-pole switch using two-wire cable to power the switch and three-wire cable from the switch to the fixture. Continue the circuit to an end-of-run receptacle using two-wire cable.

Split Receptacle Controlled by End-of-Run Switch

In this configuration, one-half of a split receptacle (tab removed) is powered by a switch located at the end of the circuit run. The other half of the receptacle is constantly powered. Mark the white neutral wire with black tape to indicate that it is hot.

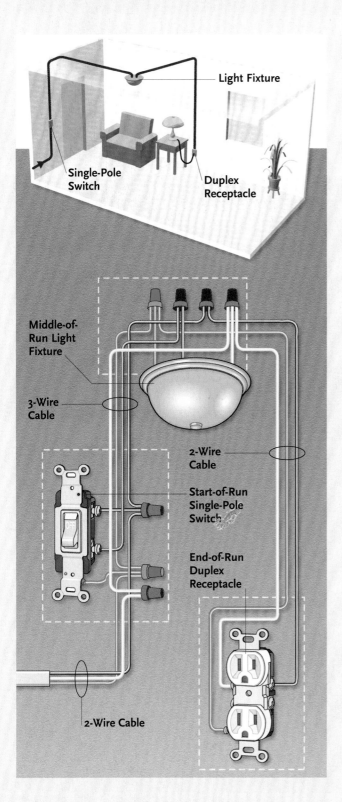

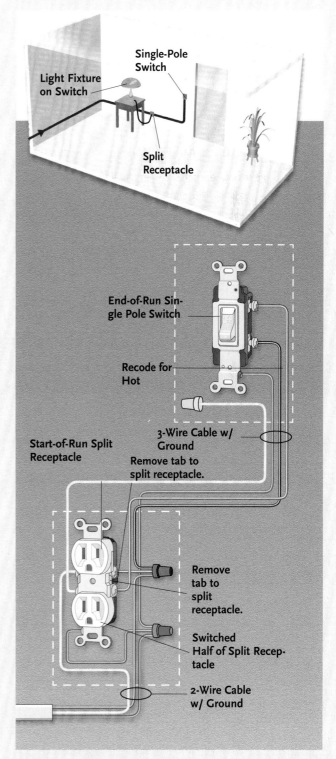

Wiring Methods

Duplex Receptacle with Split Receptacle Controlled by Start-of-Run Switch

To install a split receptacle controlled by a switch, remove the tab on the receptacle. Using two-wire cable, connect the switch to the power source. One hot wire from the switch connects to each half of the receptacle.

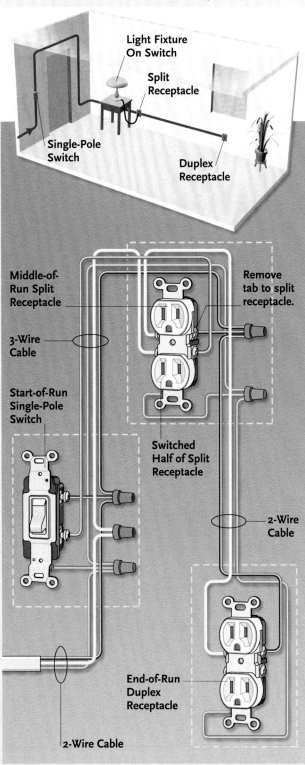

Light Fixture On Switch

Split Receptacle

Single-Pole Switch

Duplex Receptacle

Middle-of-Run Split Receptacle

3-Wire Cable

Start-of-Run Single-Pole Switch

Remove tab to split receptacle.

Switched Half of Split Receptacle

2-Wire Cable

End-of-Run Duplex Receptacle

2-Wire Cable

Duplex Receptacle with Split Receptacle Controlled by End-of-Run Switch

In this combination, the split receptacle is located at the start of the cable run. One-half of the receptacle is controlled by the switch. The other half of the receptacle is always hot and feeds the remainder of the circuit.

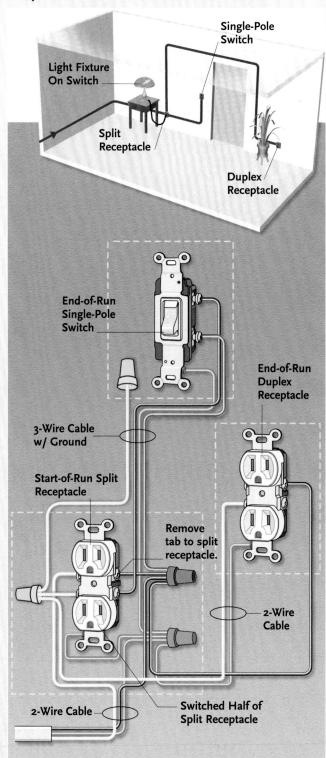

Single-Pole Switch

Light Fixture On Switch

Split Receptacle

Duplex Receptacle

End-of-Run Single-Pole Switch

End-of-Run Duplex Receptacle

3-Wire Cable w/ Ground

Start-of-Run Split Receptacle

Remove tab to split receptacle.

2-Wire Cable

2-Wire Cable

Switched Half of Split Receptacle

smart tip

INTERPRETING A RECEPTACLE

THE LABELS OR MARKINGS THAT APPEAR ON A RECEPTACLE CONVEY IMPORTANT INFORMATION ABOUT SAFETY AND USAGE. A UL LABEL, FOR INSTANCE, MEANS THAT THE DEVICE HAS BEEN CERTIFIED FOR SAFETY BY THE AMERICAN UNDERWRITERS LABORATORIES, WHILE A CSA LABEL INDICATES APPROVAL BY THE CANADIAN EQUIVALENT—THE CANADIAN STANDARDS ASSOCIATION. ALSO SHOWN ARE AMPERAGE AND VOLTAGE RATINGS, WHICH STATE THE MAXIMUM PERMITTED FOR THE DEVICE. YOU SHOULD BE ESPECIALLY ALERT TO THE ACCEPTABLE WIRE USAGE DESIGNATION, WHICH INDICATES WHAT KIND OF WIRE IS SAFE TO CONNECT TO THE RECEPTACLE. A CU LABEL MEANS THAT ONLY COPPER WIRE CAN BE USED; CO/ALR INDICATES THAT ALUMINUM WIRES ARE ACCEPTABLE; AND CU/AL SPECIFIES COPPER OR COPPER-CLAD ALUMINUM WIRES ONLY.

THE SCREW TERMINAL COLORS ON A RECEPTACLE ALSO DENOTE SPECIFIC INFORMATION.

USE THE BRASS SCREW TERMINALS FOR BLACK/RED HOT WIRES, THE SILVER SCREW TERMINALS FOR WHITE NEUTRAL WIRES, AND THE GREEN TERMINAL SCREW FOR THE GROUNDING CONNECTION.

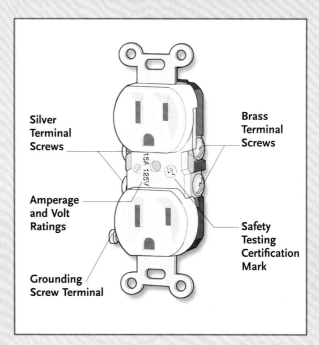

Silver Terminal Screws

Brass Terminal Screws

Amperage and Volt Ratings

Safety Testing Certification Mark

Grounding Screw Terminal

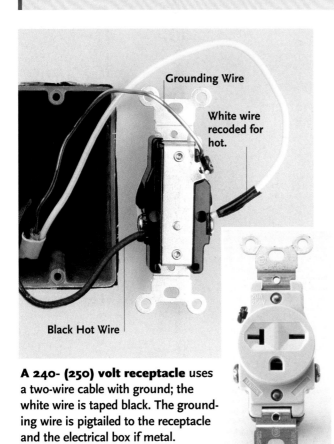

Grounding Wire

White wire recoded for hot.

Black Hot Wire

A 240- (250) volt receptacle uses a two-wire cable with ground; the white wire is taped black. The grounding wire is pigtailed to the receptacle and the electrical box if metal.

High-Voltage Receptacles

Large appliances in a home often draw significantly more current than smaller appliances. For this reason, contemporary homes usually have two types of receptacles—one type provides low-voltage power (120 volts), and the other provides high-voltage power (240 volts). Appliances that are rated for 240 volts—such as cooking ranges, clothes dryers, and air conditioners—are required to be connected to a single circuit. Most high-voltage appliances are connected to either a flush- or surface-mounted receptacle box. A nonmetallic sheathed cable containing two hot wires, each carrying 120 volts, and a grounding wire typically form an end-of-run connection within the receptacle box, which must be located within the length of the appliance cord. Because no neutral wire is needed, the white wire is coded, using black tape, to indicate that it is hot. However, a high-voltage circuit that also requires 120-volt current to operate clocks, timers, and lights does need to have a white neutral wire connected to the receptacle—so that the appliance can split the entering current between 120 volts and 240 volts. These circuits use three-wire cable.

Wiring Methods

All receptacles for high-voltage appliances have specific slot configurations that can only mate with the corresponding type of plug. (See the table, "High-Voltage Receptacle Patterns," below.) Note that such plugs are labeled with X and Y to designate connections for the current-carrying wires, W for the white grounding wire connection, and the G for the receptacle grounding wire connection.

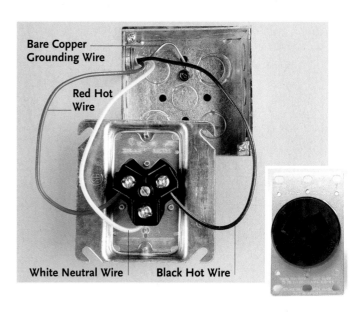

Bare Copper Grounding Wire

Red Hot Wire

White Neutral Wire

Black Hot Wire

Older three-slot 120/240-volt receptacles use a three-wire cable with ground; the black and red wires are connected to brass setscrew terminals, and the white wire goes to neutral. Newer four-slot receptacles include a ground connection (opposite, right).

HIGH-VOLTAGE RECEPTACLE PATTERNS

Slot Configuration	NEMA No.	Amps	Volts	Phase	Poles	Wires	With Grounding	Without Grounding
	5-30R	30A	125V		2	3	x	
	6-30R	30A	250V		2	3	x	
	7-30R	30A	277V		2	3	x	
	10-30R	30A	125/250V		3	3		x
	14-30R	30A	125/250V		3	4	x	
	15-30R	30A	250V	3	3	4	x	
	18-30R	30A	120/208V	3	4	4		x
	5-50R	50A	125V		2	3	x	
	6-50R	50A	250V		2	3	x	
	7-50R	50A	277V		2	3	x	
	10-50R	50A	125/250V		3	3		x
	14-50R	50A	125/250V		3	4	x	
	18-50R	50A	120/208V	3	4	4		x
	14-60R	60A	125/250V		3	4	x	

The National Electrical Manufacturer's Association (NEMA) assigns a number to each receptacle slot pattern. All NEMA receptacle numbers end with the letter R. The corresponding plug number ends with the letter P. These numbers are universal and identify compatible receptacles and plugs, regardless of manufacturer.

240-Volt Appliance Receptacle

Wire a 240-volt appliance receptacle using a two-wire cable with a ground. Connect the white wire to one brass terminal and the black wire to the other. Tape the white wire black to indicate that it is hot. Pigtail the grounding wire to both the receptacle and box grounding screws.

120/240-Volt Appliance Receptacle

Red and black wires in a three-wire cable provide 240-volt power to this type of appliance receptacle. Either wire, combined with the white wire, provides 120-volt power. Connect the grounding wire to the receptacle and the receptacle box.

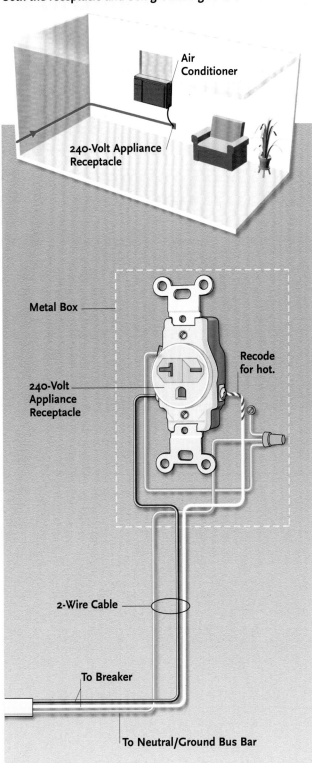

Air Conditioner

240-Volt Appliance Receptacle

Metal Box

240-Volt Appliance Receptacle

Recode for hot.

2-Wire Cable

To Breaker

To Neutral/Ground Bus Bar

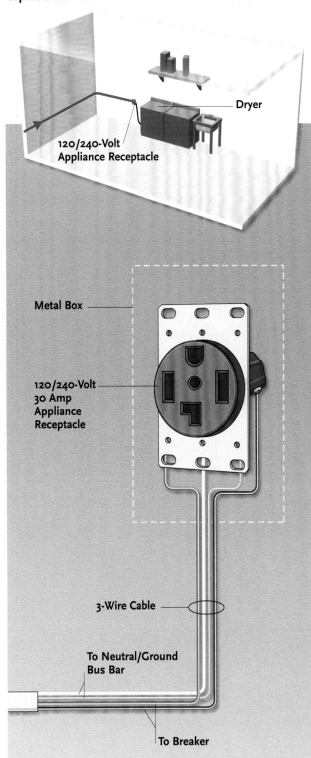

Dryer

120/240-Volt Appliance Receptacle

Metal Box

120/240-Volt 30 Amp Appliance Receptacle

3-Wire Cable

To Neutral/Ground Bus Bar

To Breaker

Wiring Methods

GFCI RECEPTACLES

A GROUND-FAULT CIRCUIT INTERRUPTER (GFCI) is an electrical device that prevents electrocution caused by an accident or equipment malfunction. In a general-purpose, 120-volt household circuit, current moves along two insulated wires—one white and one black. Power is brought to the device or appliance by the black wire and returns from it by the white wire. As long as these two current flows remain equal, then the circuit operates normally and safely. However, if a portion of the return current is missing, or "faulted," a GFCI will immediately open the circuit in $\frac{1}{25}$ th to $\frac{1}{30}$ th of a second—25 to 30 times faster than a heartbeat. In this fraction of a second, you may receive a jolt of a shock, rather than the dangerous or potentially lethal shock that would otherwise occur in a circuit without the protection of a ground-fault circuit interrupter.

A GFCI receptacle, however, is not foolproof. For a ground-fault circuit interrupter to succeed, a ground-fault must first occur. This happens when current flows out of the normal circuit to a ground pathway, causing the imbalance between the black and white wires mentioned earlier. In this instance, if you place your body between the black and white wires, and you are not grounded, the GFCI will not function properly because it has no way of distinguishing your body from any other current-drawing device. The number of electrons entering the circuit is equal to the number of electrons returning from the circuit, except that they are passing first through the resistance within your body—causing your heart to go into fibrillation, beating erratically. If your heartbeat is not quickly restored to normal, then you will die. Even if the circuit is connected to a breaker panel, the breaker will

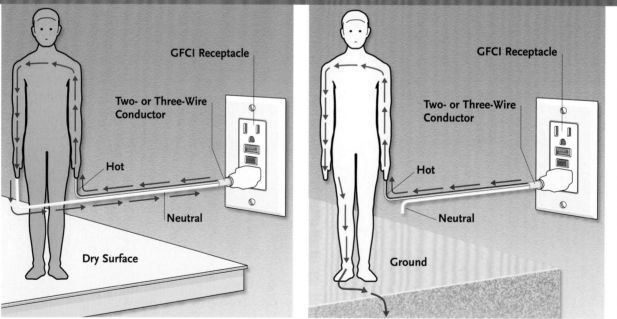

If an electrical current flows through your body from a hot wire to a neutral wire, this completes an electrical circuit—just as though you were an appliance or fixture. In this case, a ground-fault circuit interrupter cannot save you from being electrocuted because it cannot distinguish you from your microwave. If you hold only one wire, however, the resulting imbalance in current entering and leaving the circuit will trip the GFCI and protect you from serious shock or electrocution.

not trip unless the internal current exceeds 15 or 20 amps—2,500 times more than is necessary to cause electrocution. A breaker or fuse is only designed to protect your household wiring against excessive current—it is not designed to protect you.

Required GFCI Locations. Even though GFCI circuits are not foolproof, they are nevertheless required in certain locations within a dwelling unit, specified by the NEC (Section 210.8). These locations include, but are not strictly limited to, bathrooms, garages, outbuildings, outdoors, crawl spaces, unfinished basements, kitchens, and wet-bar sinks. A good general rule to follow is that if you are working in a damp or wet environment, then the receptacle you use should be GFCI-protected. This includes dedicated-appliance receptacles.

A GFCI receptacle resembles a conventional receptacle, except that it has built-in RESET and TEST buttons. A GFCI can also be directly installed at the panel box as a circuit breaker. This type of ground-fault circuit interrupter has a test button only; when tripped, the switch flips only halfway off to break the circuit. To reset the circuit, the breaker must be switched completely off and then flipped back on again. A GFCI receptacle is less expensive than a breaker-type GFCI and has the advantage of letting you reset a circuit at the point of use.

Reset Button

Test Button

A GFCI receptacle has both TEST and RESET buttons. When a ground fault occurs or a test is made, the RESET button will pop out. Once a fault is eliminated or the test completed, press the button back in to reset the circuit.

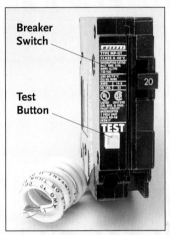

Breaker Switch

Test Button

A GFCI circuit breaker has a TEST button, but no RESET button. To reset a GFCI breaker, first push the switch to the OFF position; then flip it back to the ON position.

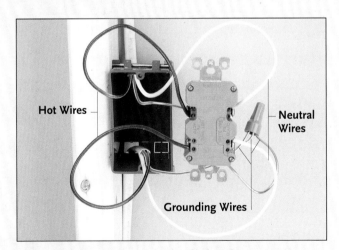

Hot Wires

Neutral Wires

Grounding Wires

If you want several receptacles farther down circuit, or downstream, from the GFCI receptacle to also have GFCI protection, then use the method of wiring for multiple locations. One set of hot and neutral wires is connected to the LINE terminals and the other set to the LOAD terminal screws.

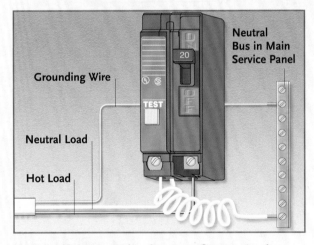

Grounding Wire

Neutral Load

Hot Load

Neutral Bus in Main Service Panel

To install the circuit breaker type of GFCI, simply insert the device into the panel box in the same way as a conventional circuit breaker; then connect the black and white load wires from the circuit you wish to protect. Connect the white corkscrew wire attached to the GFCI circuit breaker to the white neutral bus in the panel.

Wiring Methods

GFCI PROTECTION IN ELECTRICAL CIRCUITS—A BRIEF HISTORY

1968 Ground Fault Circuit Interrupter (GFCI) protection introduced and required by the NEC code for underground swimming pool lighting fixtures.

1971 The mandate to protect home occupants in other wet areas such as kitchens and outdoor spaces begins.

1975 Bathrooms required to have protection against ground faults.

1987 Any receptacle within six feet of a kitchen sink must be GFCI.

1990 Receptacles in unfinished basements. Eventually applies to finished basements too.

1996 All kitchen counter receptacles.

2014 Receptacles near any sink, including laundry and utility.

THE PROTECTION PROVIDED by GFCI receptacles and GFCI breakers relies on a complex circuitry that detects circuit imbalance between the black (line, or hot) wire and the white (neutral) wire when current is flowing through the circuit. A properly balanced electrical circuit carries the same 120 volts on both the black and white wires of a circuit simultaneously. Any imbalance will trip the GFCI receptacle in the room or the GFCI breaker in the main service panel.

The ground (bare copper) wire also plays an important role in this circuit, as the white (neutral) wire is also grounded at the main service panel through the bus bar. This connection creates the direct path to ground for un-

wanted electrical currents, maintaining a safe electrical environment in the home.

Whether to use a GFCI breaker vs. a GFCI receptacle is a decision made by the electrician and the homeowner when the electrical plan is being designed. Initially it was beneficial to use a GFCI receptacle at the beginning of any required circuits and have the correct number of standard receptacles beyond the GFCI receptacle to meet code. The advantage of this circuit design is that when the GFCI receptacle trips and stops the flow of electrical current to all of the devices, resetting the circuit after the ground fault issue is corrected only requires pushing in the reset button on the GFCI receptacle.

With today's higher demand on electrical receptacles and more locations where GFCI technology is required, the use of the GFCI breaker over the GFCI receptacle is becoming more popular. In addition, the cost of GFCI receptacles continue to increase—especially with the self-testing devices being introduced into the market. The disadvantage of this circuit design is that it requires the homeowner to open the main service panel door and correctly identify the GFCI breaker that has tripped and reset the breaker after the ground fault issue is corrected, rather than simply pressing the reset button on a receptacle.

GFCI Receptacles and GFCI breakers are designed to work with specific amperages of 15 amps connected to 14-gauge wires and 20 amps connected to 12-gauge wires. Be sure the receptacle or breaker being replaced matches the correct installation.

Both GFCI breakers and GFCI receptacles have a test button and it is highly recommended that the test feature be performed each month to ensure the proper operation of the GFCI device. The newer self-testing GFCI receptacles are capable of automatically performing this procedure every three seconds.

Care has to be taken so a freezer or refrigerator/freezer appliance is not connected to a GFCI circuit, because when the GFCI circuit is tripped due to a ground fault the current to these devices will also be interrupted and may not be detected for some time, which would allow food to spoil or defrost.

Holiday outdoor lighting and extension cords plugged into outdoor receptacles can also create ground fault issues that could cause GFCI receptacles in the home to trip, due to moisture from rain, snow, and ice. Care has to be taken to assure that outdoor electrical connections are not exposed to the elements. Many outdoor receptacles are connected to a first-floor bathroom or powder room GFCI electrical circuit.

Wiring Methods

INSTALLING A GFCI RECEPTACLE

project

Installing a GFCI receptacle isn't much harder than installing a standard receptacle. The only difference is that the GFCI has two sets of terminal screws, each with a different purpose. One is marked LINE and is used for the incoming power line. The other set is marked LOAD and is used for the out-going wires that connect to downstream receptacles in the circuit.

TOOLS & MATERIALS

▌Insulated screwdriver ▌Diagonal cutting pliers ▌Long-nose pliers ▌Wire stripper ▌Neon circuit tester ▌Cable ripper ▌GFCI receptacle ▌Receptacle box ▌12/2G NM cable ▌Wire connectors ▌Copper grounding wire ▌Grounding pigtail and screw (for metal boxes) ▌Cable clamps (for metal boxes)

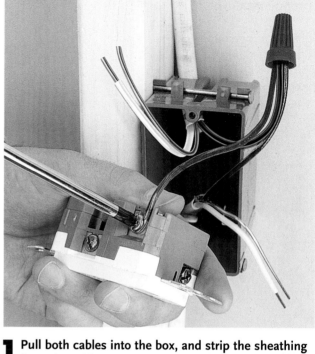

1 Pull both cables into the box, and strip the sheathing from the cable and the insulation from the ends of all the wires. Join the black cable wires with a black pigtail with a wire connector. Then attach the black pigtail to the HOT LINE terminal screw on the side of the GFCI receptacle.

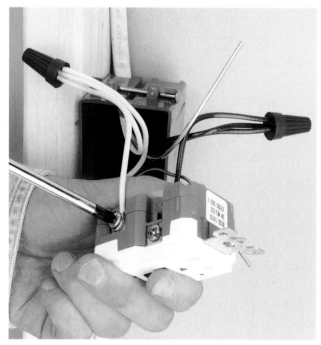

2 Join the white neutral wires from both cables with a white pigtail using a wire connector. Then securely attach the pigtail to the WHITE LINE screw on the side of the receptacle.

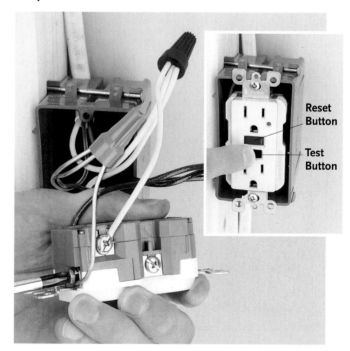

Reset Button

Test Button

3 Finish up the wire connections by joining the ground wires from the cables and a grounding pigtail with a wire connector. Then attach the pigtail to the receptacle's grounding screw. Install the receptacle, and test the RESET button by pushing in the TEST button. The RESET button should pop out.

Single-Location GFCI Receptacle Circuit

All kitchen countertop and bathroom receptacles—and receptacles within 6 ft. of a wet-bar sink—must be GFCI protected. To protect a single location using a GFCI receptacle, connect the feed cable to the line terminals. Receptacles downstream will remain unprotected.

Multiple GFCI Receptacle Circuit

In some locations the electrical code may require more than one protected receptacle where multiple receptacles must be GFCI protected, such as over kitchen counters. They should be wired for single-location protection. This will require both two- and three-wire cables.

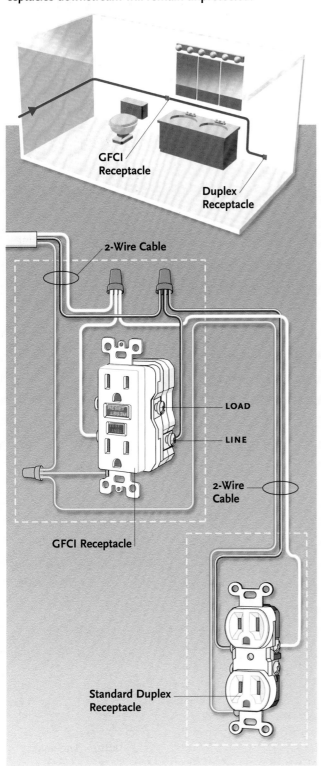

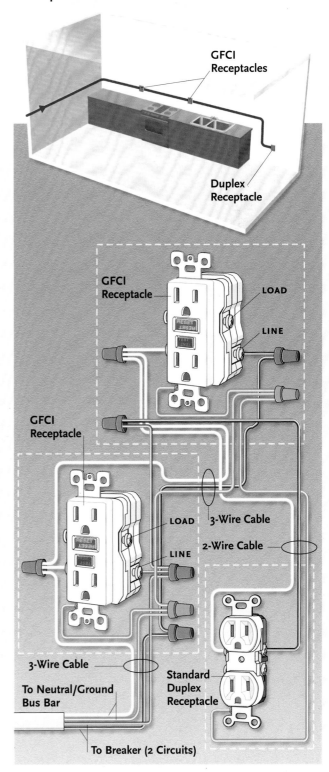

Wiring Methods

SWITCHES

Single-Pole Switches

A switch controls the flow of power in a circuit. Single-pole switches have two screw terminals; it can control a circuit from one location only. Power is connected to one side of the switch at all times. When the switch is on, electricity flows from the wire attached to the powered screw terminal, through the switch, and into the fixture or appliance wiring connected to the other terminal.

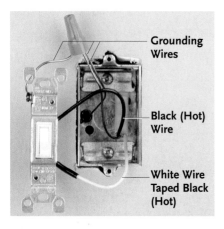

Grounding Wires

Black (Hot) Wire

White Wire Taped Black (Hot)

At the end of a circuit, both the black and white wires connecting to a switch are hot. To indicate this, wrap the white wire with black tape.

project

Wiring a middle-of-run, single-pole switch is one of the easiest wiring projects. Only two cables come into the box. The white wires are joined with one wire connector, the ground wires are joined with a pigtail under another connector. The other end of the pigtail is attached to the ground screw on the switch. And the black wires (one from each cable) are attached to the two screw terminals on the switch.

TOOLS & MATERIALS

▪ Insulated screwdriver ▪ Long-nose pliers ▪ Multipurpose tool ▪ Cable ripper ▪ Switch box and switch ▪ 12/2G NM cable ▪ Wire connectors ▪ Grounding pigtail and screw (for metal boxes) ▪ Cable clamps (for metal boxes)

SINGLE-POLE SWITCH ANATOMY

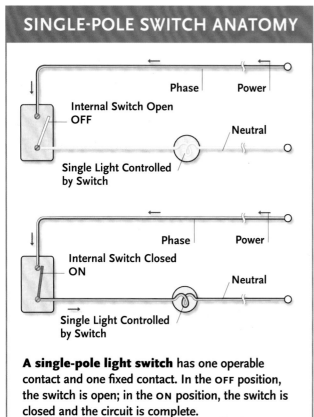

Phase   Power

Internal Switch Open
OFF

Neutral

Single Light Controlled by Switch

Phase   Power

Internal Switch Closed
ON

Neutral

Single Light Controlled by Switch

A single-pole light switch has one operable contact and one fixed contact. In the OFF position, the switch is open; in the ON position, the switch is closed and the circuit is complete.

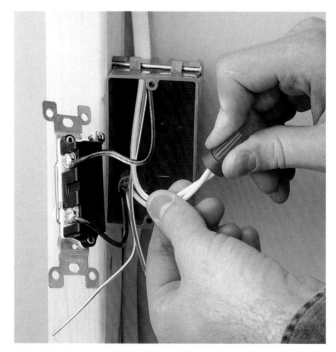

2 Join the two white wires with a wire connector. Then join the two ground wires and a separate grounding pigtail together in another wire connector. If it's a metal box, join two pigtails to the grounding wires. One is attached to the metal box and the other to the grounding screw on the switch.

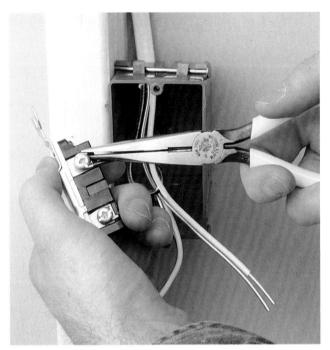

1 In a middle-of-run switch circuit the box contains two cables. Strip the sheathing from the cables and the insulation from the ends of the wires. Using long-nose pliers, form a hook at the end of both black wires, and attach these hooks to the screw terminals on the side of the switch.

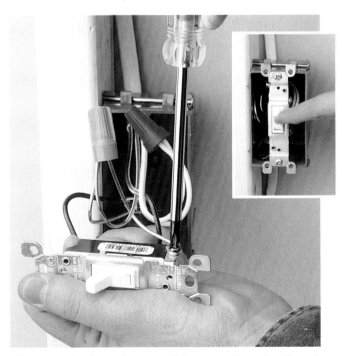

3 Form a hook on the end of the grounding pigtail, and attach it to the switch's grounding screw. Then carefully push the switch and the wiring back into the box, and attach the switch to the box with screws. Test the circuit to make sure it works properly.

Single-Pole Switch to Light Fixture

In a standard lighting circuit, the power is supplied by a two-wire cable with a grounding wire. In this configuration, the light fixture is located at the end of the cable run.

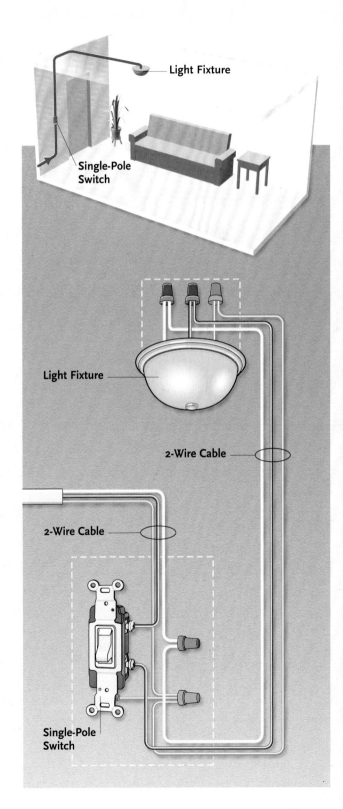

Light Fixture

Single-Pole Switch

Light Fixture

2-Wire Cable

2-Wire Cable

Single-Pole Switch

Wiring Methods

Light Fixture to an End-of-Run Single-Pole Switch

Use two-wire cable to wire a light fixture where the switch comes at the end of the cable run. This configuration is known as a switch loop. Mark the white neutral wire with black tape to indicate that it is hot.

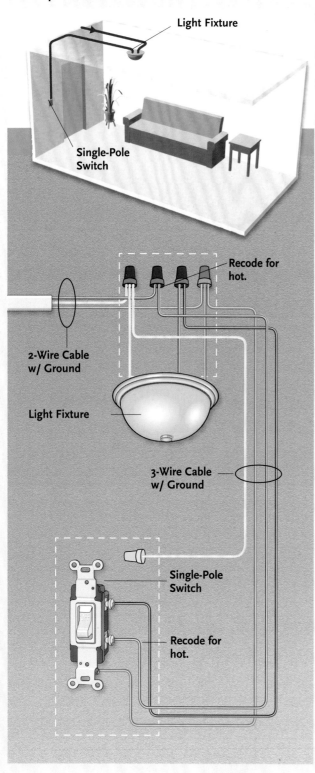

Light Fixture

Single-Pole Switch

Recode for hot.

2-Wire Cable w/ Ground

Light Fixture

3-Wire Cable w/ Ground

Single-Pole Switch

Recode for hot.

Double-Ganged Switches to End-of-Run Light Fixtures

In this setup, power is fed first through the switches and then to the light fixtures. Only two-wire cable is needed for the wiring connections. The switches occupy one double-ganged electrical box.

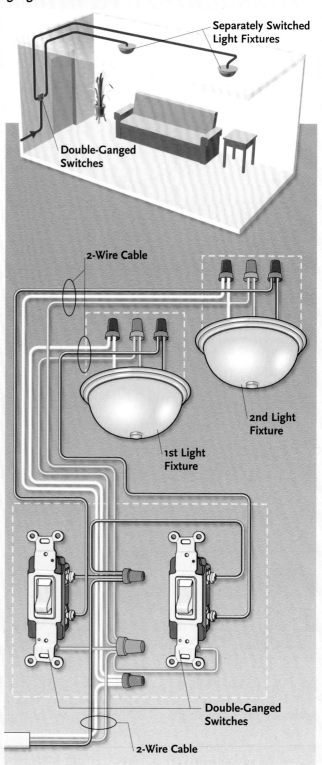

Separately Switched Light Fixtures

Double-Ganged Switches

2-Wire Cable

2nd Light Fixture

1st Light Fixture

Double-Ganged Switches

2-Wire Cable

Three-Way Switches

Like a single-pole switch, a three-way switch controls the flow of power in an electrical circuit, but from two different locations instead of just one. This type of switch is useful, for example, when you want to be able to turn on a stairway light from either the top or bottom of the stairway, or a detached garage light from either the house or the garage. Such switching requires special three-conductor or three-way switch cable with ground. This type of cable is usually round, rather than flat like conventional nonmetallic (NM) cable, and it contains an additional, insulated conductor—a red wire.

Three-way switches also differ from single-pole switches in that they have three screw terminals instead of two: a COM terminal (dark screw), and two traveler screws to connect wires that run between switches. The switch also has a grounding screw. The switch does not have either an ON or an OFF marked position because the COM terminal alternates the connection between two different switch locations, allowing either position to potentially close the circuit.

You must consider three different cables when wiring a three-way switch: the feeder cable, the fixture cable, and the three-wire cable. The typical wiring method is to run the two-wire hot feeder cable into the first switch box, and then the three-way switch cable between the first and the

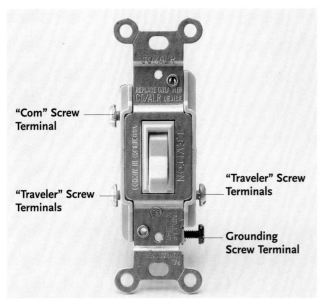

A three-way switch has three terminal screws and no ON/OFF positions. The dark colored screw terminal screw is the COM, or common, terminal. The two light screw terminals are switch leads, known as "travelers."

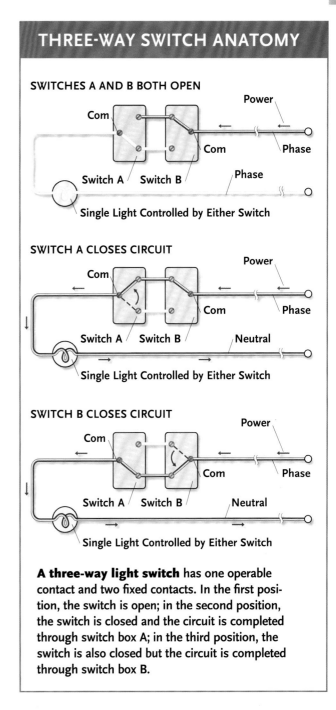

THREE-WAY SWITCH ANATOMY

A three-way light switch has one operable contact and two fixed contacts. In the first position, the switch is open; in the second position, the switch is closed and the circuit is completed through switch box A; in the third position, the switch is also closed but the circuit is completed through switch box B.

second switch box. You can then run a second two-wire fixture cable between the second switch box and the fixture box. An alternative method is to run the hot feeder into one switch box; then run the three-way switch cable from the first switch box to the light fixture and then to the second switch box. Either method initially requires that you run the hot feeder to a switch box. It's also possible to run power first to the light fixture, but this method is not preferred because it's more difficult to troubleshoot if there's a problem in the circuit.

Wiring Methods

project

The hardest thing about wiring a three-way switch is to keep track of the common wires and the traveler wires. The common wire is the black wire from the cable that supplies power to the circuit. It is screwed to the common terminal. The traveler wires are the black and red wires from the three-wire cable that joins the two switches. These wires are screwed to the traveler terminals.

TOOLS & MATERIALS

- Insulated screwdriver ■ Diagonal cutting pliers ■ Long-nose pliers ■ Wire stripper
- Multipurpose tool ■ Cable ripper
- Switch boxes ■ Three-way switches
- Two-wire cable ■ Wire connectors
- Three-way switch cable ■ Copper wire
- Cable clamps

FIRST SWITCH

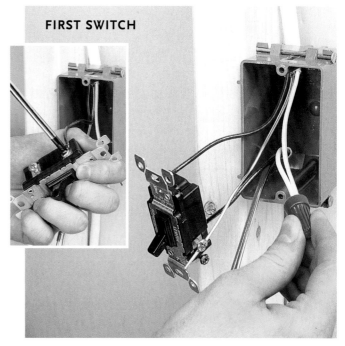

1 First, bring a two-wire power cable and a three-wire cable that goes between the switches into the box. Strip the sheathing and wire insulation from both cables and all wires. Then attach the black wire from the power cable to the common screw terminal (inset). Join the white wires with a wire connector.

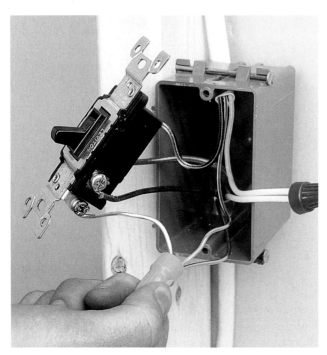

4 Join the ground wires from the two cables to a grounding pigtail wire using a wire connector. Attach the other end of the grounding pigtail to the green grounding screw on the switch. Push the switch and all the wires into the box, and attach the switch to the box using screws.

SECOND SWITCH

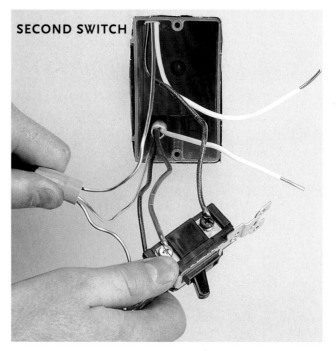

5 Strip the sheathing from the cables and the insulation from the wires, and attach the black common wire to the common terminal. Attach the black wire of the two-wire cable to the black common screw. Then attach the black and red wires, from the three-wire cable, to the traveler terminals. Join the ground wires to the grounding screw using a pigtail and a wire connector.

2 Connect the black wire from the three-wire cable to one of the traveler terminals on the first switch. When you install the second three-way switch, attach the other end of this black wire to the same traveler terminal on the second switch.

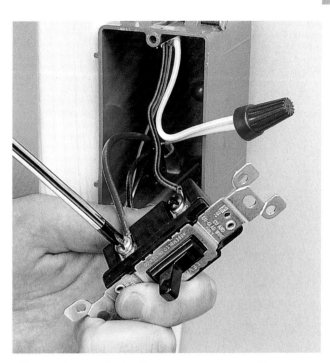

3 Attach the red wire from the three-wire cable to the remaining traveler terminal. As with the black traveler, the other end of this red wire should be attached to the same traveler terminal on the second three-way switch.

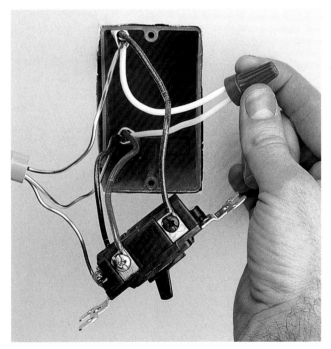

6 Join the white neutral wires from both cables using a wire connector. Push the switch and all the wires into the box, and attach the switch to the box using screws.

7 Complete the circuit by attaching the cable wires to fixture wires using wire connectors, white-to-white, black-to-black, and ground-to-ground. Attach the light fixture to the ceiling box. Then turn on the circuit power, and test the switches.

Wiring Methods

Three-Way Switches with Fixture at End-of-Run

In this switch circuit, power goes from the first switch box through the second, and then to the light fixture. A three-wire cable with ground is run between the switches and a two-wire cable runs between the second switch and the fixture.

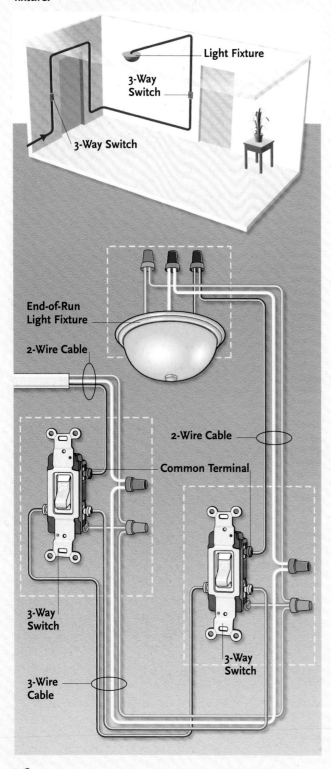

Light Fixture

3-Way Switch

3-Way Switch

End-of-Run Light Fixture

2-Wire Cable

2-Wire Cable

Common Terminal

3-Way Switch

3-Way Switch

3-Wire Cable

Three-Way Switches with Fixture at Start-of-Run

In this setup, power enters the light fixture on a two-wire grounded cable. It proceeds to the three-way switches and then returns to the fixture. Two-wire cable connects the fixture to the first switch and three-wire cable runs between the switches.

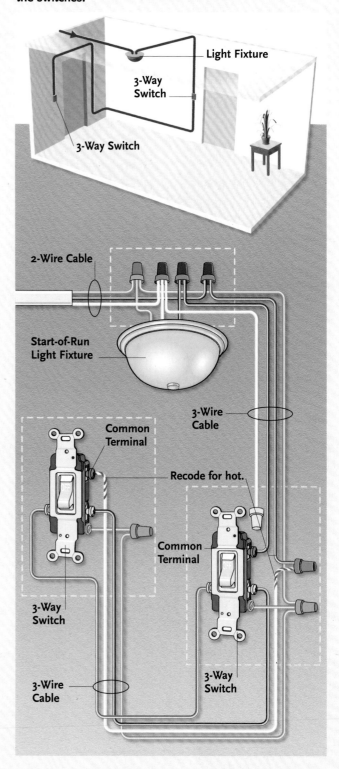

Light Fixture

3-Way Switch

3-Way Switch

2-Wire Cable

Start-of-Run Light Fixture

3-Wire Cable

Common Terminal

Recode for hot.

Common Terminal

3-Way Switch

3-Way Switch

3-Wire Cable

Three-Way Switches with Fixture at Middle-of-Run

Here, the light fixture is positioned between the two three-way switches. Power comes to the first switch on a two-wire grounded cable. It passes through the light fixture, proceeds to the second switch, and then returns to the fixture on three-wire cable.

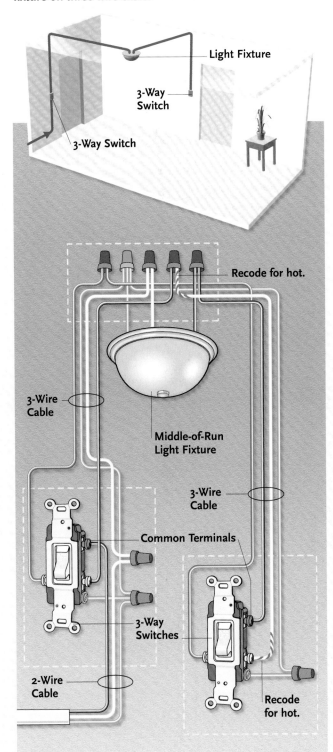

Light Fixture

3-Way Switch

3-Way Switch

Recode for hot.

3-Wire Cable

Middle-of-Run Light Fixture

3-Wire Cable

Common Terminals

3-Way Switches

2-Wire Cable

Recode for hot.

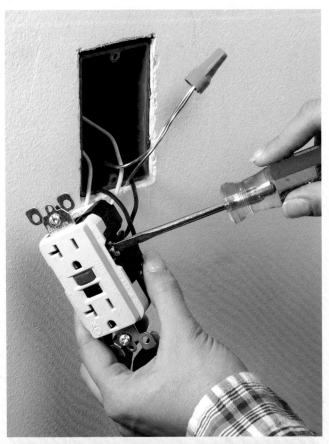

Wiring Methods

Four-Way Switches

A four-way switch can be connected between two three-way switches to allow you to control a light from three different locations. A four-way switch is installed in line or "series" with the travelers between the two three-way switches. A three-wire cable should be run from the first three-way switch to the four-way switch and from the second three-way switch to the four-way switch. The red and black wires from the first switch connect to the brass-color screws, and the black and red wires from the second switch connect to the dark- or copper-color screws. The white neutral conductor is carried all the way through all switches. Pigtail the grounding wires to the green grounding screw inside the metal switch box. Check the wiring diagram of the switch before connecting wires.

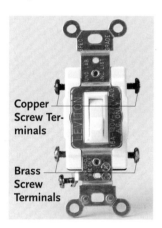

Copper Screw Terminals

Brass Screw Terminals

A four-way switch has four terminal screws. It looks similar to a double-pole switch, but does not have any dedicated ON or OFF position. A four-way switch controls an outlet or fixture from three separate locations, in tandem with two three-way switches; it must always be located between the other two switches on the circuit.

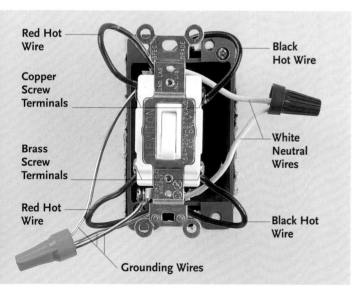

Red Hot Wire

Black Hot Wire

Copper Screw Terminals

Brass Screw Terminals

White Neutral Wires

Red Hot Wire

Black Hot Wire

Grounding Wires

The internal levers in a four-way switch either connect the screw terminals in a straight vertical configuration or in a diagonal X pattern. In combination with the two three-way switches, this permits the circuit to be completed or broken by any one of the three switches.

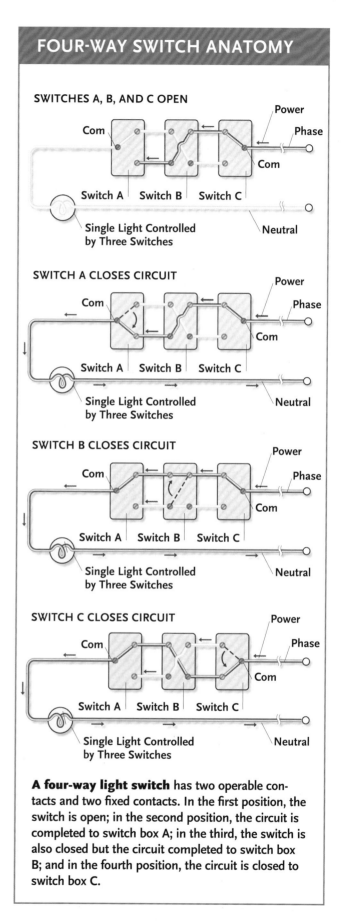

FOUR-WAY SWITCH ANATOMY

SWITCHES A, B, AND C OPEN

Com · Power · Phase · Com · Switch A · Switch B · Switch C · Single Light Controlled by Three Switches · Neutral

SWITCH A CLOSES CIRCUIT

Com · Power · Phase · Com · Switch A · Switch B · Switch C · Single Light Controlled by Three Switches · Neutral

SWITCH B CLOSES CIRCUIT

Com · Power · Phase · Com · Switch A · Switch B · Switch C · Single Light Controlled by Three Switches · Neutral

SWITCH C CLOSES CIRCUIT

Com · Power · Phase · Com · Switch A · Switch B · Switch C · Single Light Controlled by Three Switches · Neutral

A four-way light switch has two operable contacts and two fixed contacts. In the first position, the switch is open; in the second position, the circuit is completed to switch box A; in the third, the switch is also closed but the circuit completed to switch box B; and in the fourth position, the circuit is closed to switch box C.

Four-Way Switch

A four-way switch must be combined with two three-way switches to control a light fixture from three or more locations. Two-wire cable feeds power through the fixture to the first three-way switch. The four-way switch is connected to the other switch using three-wire cable.

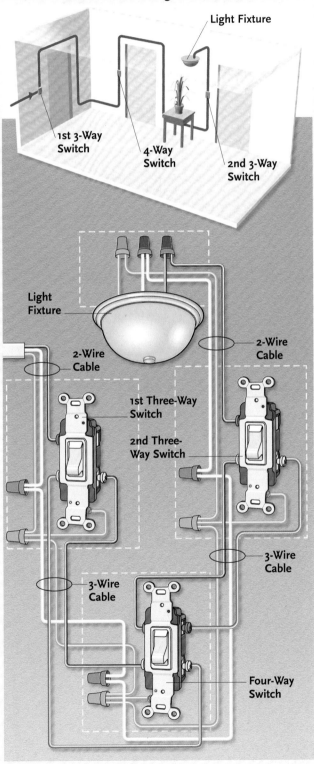

Dimmer Switches

A dimmer switch allows you to regulate luminosity, or brightness, of light emanating from a light fixture—either to set a mood or conserve energy. Dimmer switches can be single-pole or three-way switches. In a three-way configuration, only the dimmer switch regulates brightness, while the paired toggle switch merely turns the fixture on or off. Though not commonly used, dimmer switches are also available for fluorescent lighting.

Dimmer switches are controlled by a solid-state device within the switch that alternately turns the current on and off as many as 120 times per second. By restricting the flow of current, the switch dims the light. The longer the current is off, the dimmer the light. Standard dimmer switches are rated for 600 watts.

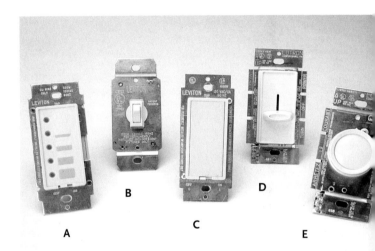

A–automatic switch; B–toggle switch; C–push-button switch; D–slider switch; rotating dial switch

In an end-of-run switch, the travelers are a red wire and a white wire taped black, or a black wire and a white wire taped black.

A middle-of-run dimmer switch has traveler wires that are either both black or one red and the other black.

59

Wiring Methods

WIRING A SINGLE-POLE DIMMER SWITCH

Dimmer switches don't cost much (you can find them for about $10–$15) and they're easy to install if you are just replacing an existing single-pole switch. But they can have an impact that far outweighs their cost. To change the entire mood of a room by simply turning a small dial is one of the biggest home improvement bargains out there.

TOOLS & MATERIALS

- Insulated screwdriver
- Long-nose pliers
- Wire stripper
- Multipurpose tool
- Neon circuit tester
- Wire connectors
- Dimmer switch

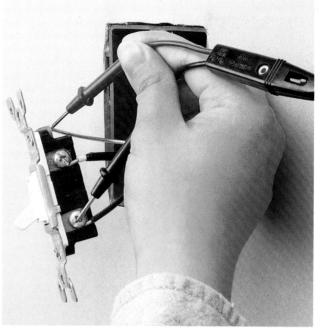

1 To replace a standard switch with a dimmer switch, first turn off the power to the circuit. Then remove the switch cover plate and the screws that hold the switch to the box. Pull out the switch, and check for current using a neon tester. If you find current, you turned off the wrong circuit.

2 Remove all the wires from the old switch, and set it aside (top). Then cut off the screw hooks on the ends of the wire, and straighten the wire ends using pliers. Strip off enough insulation on each wire so that about ½ in. of bare wire is exposed.

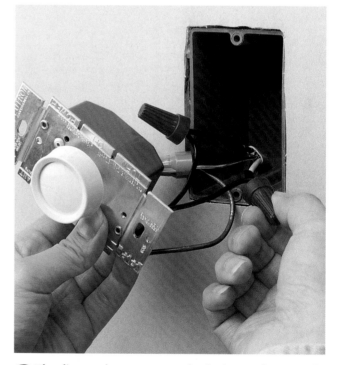

3 The dimmer has two power lead wires and a grounding wire attached to the back. Join these leads to the circuit cable wires with wire connectors. Either lead wire can be connected to either circuit wire.

smart tip

TESTING A SWITCH

WHEN YOU FLIP ON A SWITCH AND THE SWITCH CIRCUIT DOESN'T WORK, THE PROBLEM MAY NOT BE WITH THE SWITCH. IT COULD BE A BLOWN FUSE, A TRIPPED CIRCUIT BREAKER, OR A FAULTY FIXTURE. FIRST CHECK THE SERVICE PANEL; THEN TEST THE SWITCH. BEGIN BY REMOVING THE FUSE OR SETTING THE BREAKER ON THE SWITCH CIRCUIT TO THE *OFF* POSITION; THEN REMOVE THE SWITCH COVERPLATE. APPLY THE PROBES ON A MULTI-TESTER TO THE BLACK AND WHITE WIRE TERMINAL SCREWS TO VERIFY THAT THE POWER IS TURNED OFF; THEN TURN ON THE SWITCH. NEXT, TOUCH THE PROBE AND CLIP OF A BATTERY-OPERATED CONTINUITY TESTER TO THE WIRE TERMINALS. IF THE SWITCH IS GOOD, THEN THE TESTER WILL EITHER LIGHT UP OR BUZZ. FINALLY, TURN OFF THE SWITCH. IF IT IS GOOD, THEN THE TESTER SHOULD NO LONGER LIGHT UP OR BUZZ. REPLACE THE SWITCH IF IT FAILS ANY OF THESE TESTS. IF THE SWITCH IS GOOD, THE FAULT MUST BE IN THE FIXTURE.

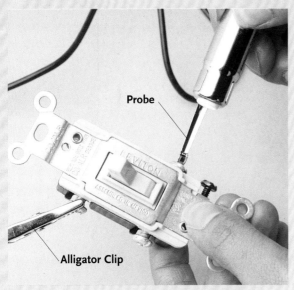

Probe

Alligator Clip

Use a continuity tester to test the integrity of an unwired or disconnected switch. Attach the alligator clip to one terminal screw, and touch the probe to the other. If the switch is good, the probe will light when you turn the switch on, but will not light when you turn it off.

PLUGS, CORDS, AND SOCKETS

Standard Plugs

Plugs come in a variety of different styles and shapes, including flat- or round-corded, grounded, polarized, and quick-connect. Round-corded plugs are typically used on larger appliances that require three-pronged, grounded plugs; smaller appliances commonly use flat-corded plugs. A polarized plug has one wide and one narrow prong and can only be inserted into a receptacle so that the neutral and hot cord wires properly align with the neutral and hot receptacle wires.

Some homeowners may still be using fixtures that have older-style, permanently attached cords and plugs. Because such cords and plugs no longer meet NEC standards, it is simply cheaper and safer for you to replace them, rather than attempting to repair them. When you do replace a plug or cord, be sure that the new device meets current code requirements (NEC Article 406). If your existing cord is in good condition, but the plug needs to be replaced, cut the cord just behind the plug, and strip the insulation off the end of the cut wires. Then properly reconnect them to the new plug.

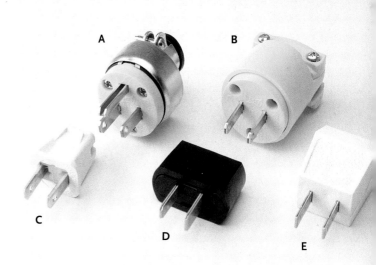

A   B

C

D

E

Plugs come in various configurations for different purposes; be sure that the replacement plugs you buy are appropriate for the appliances, receptacles, or wires to which they will be connected. A–grounded round-cord plug; B–round-cord plug; C–quick-connect plug; D–polarized plug; E–flat-cord plug

Wiring Methods

project

Most extension cords these days have integral, molded plugs on both ends. So if one of these plugs is damaged, you have to cut it off and replace it with a separate plug. These are common hardware store and home-center items. To make sure you get the right plug, cut off a 6-inch length of the cord and take it with you to the store. This will allow you to compare the size and type of your cord with the plugs that are available.

TOOLS & MATERIALS

- Insulated screwdriver
- Long-nose pliers
- Diagonal cutting pliers
- Wire stripper or multipurpose tool
- Replacement plug

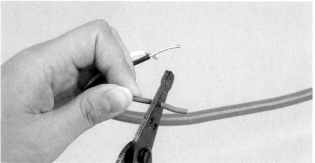

1 Damaged extension cord plugs, such as this one with the missing ground prong, should be replaced. If the cord has a separate plug, just remove the old plug. If the cord has an integral cord, cut off the plug (top). Then strip the cable sheathing and the wire insulation using a multipurpose tool.

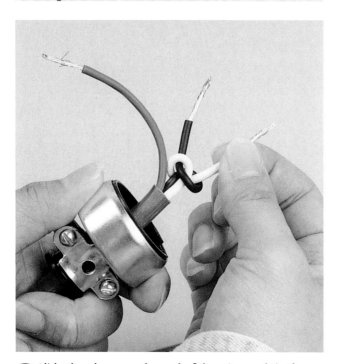

2 Slide the plug over the end of the wire, and tie the white and black wires together as shown. This knot, called an Underwriter's Knot, is designed to reduce the chance that pulling on the cord will pull the wires off their plug terminals.

3 Attach the white wire to the silver screw, the black wire to the brass screw, and the ground wire to the grounding screw (top). Pull the prongs back into the plug body; then attach the plug cover over the prongs. Finish up by tightening the cable clamp screws so the plug is securely attached to the cable.

INSTALLING A QUICK-CONNECT PLUG

project

The most common extension cord for home use is the flat cable type that matches the cable found on just about every floor and table lamp that's sold these days. Because there are so many of these cords in use, fixing them has become easy because manufacturers have created so many clever solutions. Probably the best is the simple quick-connect plug. All that's required is to cut off the old plug and slide the cut wire into the new plug and you're done.

TOOLS & MATERIALS

▪ Diagonal cutting pliers
▪ Quick-connect plug

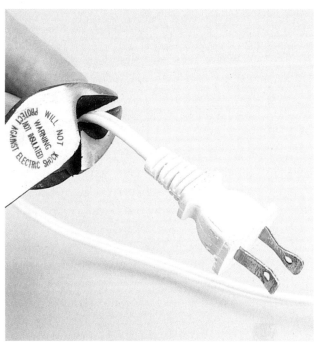

1 Flat cords with integral plugs like this can't be repaired when the plug fails. The only option is to cut off the plug and install a new separate plug. If you chose a quick-connect plug, you don't even need to strip the insulation from the wire.

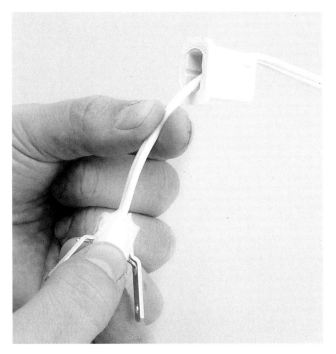

2 The quick-connect plug comes in two pieces: the plug housing and the prong assembly that goes into the housing. The housing goes on the cable first. Then insert the cable into the prong assembly following the directions on the product packaging.

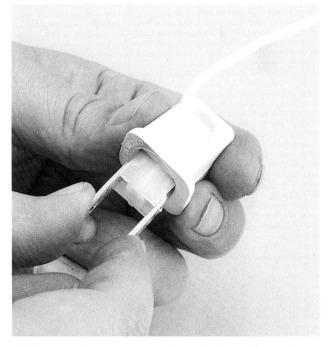

3 Squeeze the prongs together with the cable inside. Barbs on the sides of the prongs will pierce the wire insulation and make contact with the wires. Then pull the housing over the prong assembly until the two snap together.

Wiring Methods

project

Whenever you replace a plug, you should also check the cord. If it's worn or damaged, then replace it too. Although a cord with an integral plug is preferable, you can purchase a cord by the foot and attach a plug to it so that you get the length of cord you want. In either case, select a cord that is appropriate for the appliance and that matches the original type of cord—do not use a light-duty cord in place of a heavy duty one. Also, if the appliance is metal, the cord should contain a green grounding wire.

TOOLS & MATERIALS

▌Insulated screwdriver
▌Utility knife
▌Wire stripper
▌Lamp cord

1 Whenever you replace a damaged plug, take the time to examine the whole cord for other damage. If you find any cracked, frayed, or dried sections where the wires are exposed, replace the entire cord (top). To remove the cord, untie the knot at the top, and pull it out through the bottom of the lamp.

2 Feed the new cable into the bottom of the lamp and up through the socket base. Strip about ½ in. of insulation from the end of both wires.

3 Pull the two wires apart so there's enough free wire to tie an Underwriters' Knot. Once the knot is tied, push the wire down into the socket so just the ends stick up.

4 Attach the copper wire to the brass terminal screw and the silver wire to the silver terminal screw. Then reassemble the socket; install a bulb; and plug it into a receptacle.

Light Sockets and Switches

Occasionally, you may have a problem with a faulty light socket or switch. To test a socket, first unplug the lamp. Next, remove the socket from the lamp; then separate it from its outer shell and insulating sleeve. Clip a continuity tester to the socket shell; then touch the probe to the neutral (silver) terminal screw. If the tester lights, the continuity of the circuit is unbroken. To test the switch, clip the tester to the brass terminal screw; then touch the probe

TESTING SOCKETS AND SWITCHES

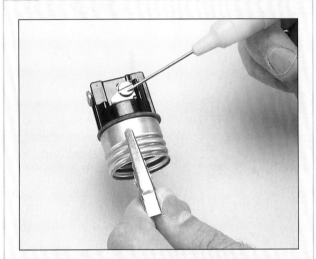

To test a socket, clip a continuity tester to the socket; then touch the probe to the silver (neutral) terminal screw.

To test the switch clamp the tester to the brass (hot) terminal screw, and touch the probe to the brass tab in the socket. The tester will light if connections are not broken.

SOCKET AND SWITCH ANATOMY

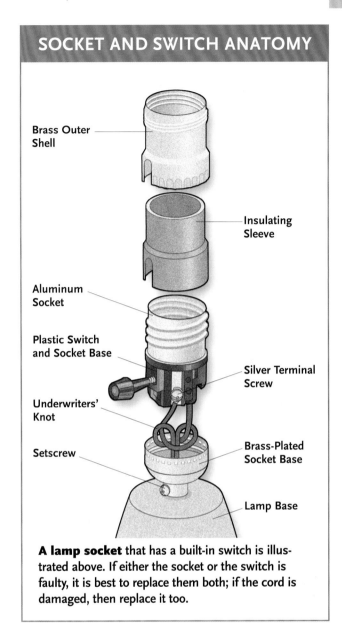

Brass Outer Shell

Insulating Sleeve

Aluminum Socket

Plastic Switch and Socket Base

Underwriters' Knot

Silver Terminal Screw

Setscrew

Brass-Plated Socket Base

Lamp Base

A lamp socket that has a built-in switch is illustrated above. If either the socket or the switch is faulty, it is best to replace them both; if the cord is damaged, then replace it too.

to the brass tab inside the socket shell. If the tester does not light in either switch position, the switch needs to be replaced.

If a lamp has no metal parts that must be grounded, then a zip cord with only two wires may be used to wire its socket and switch. This type of cord has one ribbed side and one smooth side; the ribbed side contains the neutral wire and connects to the silver terminal screw. The smooth side contains the hot wire and connects to the brass screw terminal. This difference aids in maintaining the correct polarity of all the wiring and fixture components—neutral to neutral, hot to hot. A reversal of polarity can result in a shock hazard, even when the lamp is switched off.

REPLACING A LIGHT SOCKET AND SWITCH

1 Squeeze the brass sleeve above the base cap, and slip off both the sleeve and the inside insulator (often cardboard).

2 Loosen the terminal screws, disconnect the wires, and remove the old switch.

3 Connect the hot wires to the new socket. The wires should fit snugly under the terminal screws; if not, then re-twist them.

4 Place the insulator and brass shell over the socket. Tighten the set-screw holding the cord in the socket, if there is one, and replace the harp.

Multi-Socket Switches

Lamps that have two sockets are generally controlled by a single ON/OFF switch. In contrast, a three-socket lamp may have a single switch or multiple switches.

In a two-socket lamp, the sockets are commonly soldered together, in which case the wiring is run internally. Because the switch operates both bulbs simultaneously, if one socket doesn't light, then you will first need to undo the wire connectors splicing together the switch and the power wires before you will be able to connect a new switch. If the two sockets are independently wired, then each can be replaced separately. Because both bulbs are still operated simultaneously, by one switch, the socket wiring is more complicated. In this instance, each power wire must be spliced to both sockets. Aside from the additional jumper wires, the switch can be replaced using the same method as before.

Lamps that have three sockets may have either a sep-

arate switch for each bulb or one four-way switch. In the case of separate switches, each socket will have jumper wires that are spliced together with the power wires. You can simply disconnect the jumper wires from the socket screw terminals and replace the faulty socket and switch. If a three-socket lamp has only one switch, then that switch will have three positions. The first position will operate the first socket only; the second position will operate both the second and third sockets; and the third position will operate all three sockets. A black wire attaches the switch to the line cord. A wire-connector splice connects the switch to a black jumper wire from the first socket, while a second splice connects the switch to black jumper wires from both the second and third sockets. Each socket may be individually replaced by disconnecting the wires from the terminal screws. To replace the switch, disconnect the wire-connector splices between the lamp cord and the socket.

REPAIRING MULTI-SOCKET SWITCHES

SOLDERED DOUBLE SOCKET

Soldered Double Socket

Load Power

Single Switch

To replace a soldered double socket, simply remove the wires from the socket terminal screws. To replace the switch, disconnect the wire-connector splice between the switch and the socket.

SEPARATE SOCKETS

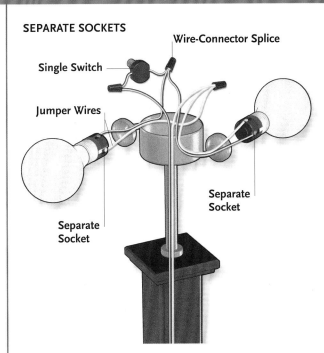

Wire-Connector Splice

Single Switch

Jumper Wires

Separate Socket

Separate Socket

If the sockets are separated, then you can replace them independently. Replace the switch by disconnecting the wire-connector splice between the switch and the black jumper wires.

MULTIPLE SOCKETS WITH SEPARATE SWITCHES

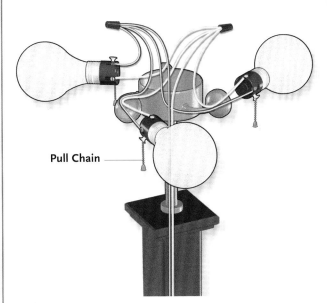

Pull Chain

When every socket has its own switch—for example, pull-chain switches for each lightbulb—each one can be easily disconnected at its own socket terminal screws for repair or replacement.

MULTIPLE SOCKETS ON A FOUR-WAY SWITCH

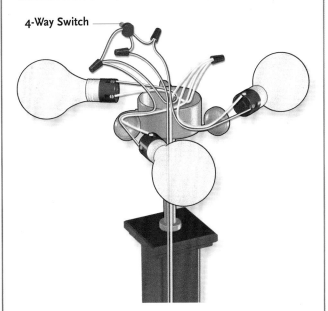

4-Way Switch

Multiple sockets on a four-way switch can also be disconnected at their terminal screws. Replace the four-way switch by undoing the wire-connector splices between it and the three black jumper wires.

Wiring Methods

NEW CIRCUITS AND SERVICE PANELS

ADDING A NEW CIRCUIT

project

Remodeling plans often call for adding new electrical circuits to meet increased demands. In addition, appliances such as dishwashers and waste-disposal units often require a separate circuit to power the appliance. You will need to run wiring from the appliance to the main panel.

Working on a service panel is dangerous, so take all safety measures. If your installation is special in any way or if you are not confident of completing the hookup correctly, have a licensed electrician do the work at the panel after you have done the room wiring. Many local building codes require that a licensed electrician make the final hookups at the panel anyway.

Start by turning off the power at the top of the service panel. Then bring your new circuit cable into the box by removing one of the knockout plates at the side or bottom of the box. Install a cable connector, and secure the connector to the panel with a locking nut. Feed the cable through the connector and tighten the two cable clamp screws snug. Strip the Romex PVC jacketing from the cable inside the box (see page 16 step 1). Route the white wire and bare ground to the neutral/grounding bus bar, and the black wire to the breaker position. Strip ⅜ in. from the ends of the black-and-white wires. Place the wires under the corresponding screw location on the breaker and neutral/grounding bus and tighten the screws firmly.

If you need to add a breaker for a 240-volt circuit, get a special breaker that occupies two slots in the panel box. The cable will have two hot wires—one black and one red. Insert one of the hot wires into each of two holes in the double breaker.

TOOLS & MATERIALS

- Insulated screwdrivers ▪ Cable stripper
- Utility knife ▪ Multipurpose tool ▪ Flashlight
- Cable ▪ Cable clamps ▪ Circuit breaker

1 Open the door to the panel box, and turn off the main breaker switch, usually at the top of the box. Remove the panel cover by backing out the screws at the corners. Note the circuit identification list (inset). This list should reference every circuit that is wired into the panel.

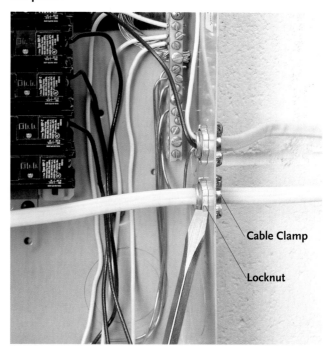

Cable Clamp

Locknut

4 Once the cable clamps are tight, return to the locknut and tighten it securely. Do this by holding the blade of a flat-blade screwdriver against one of the locknut ridges and driving it in a clockwise direction using a hammer.

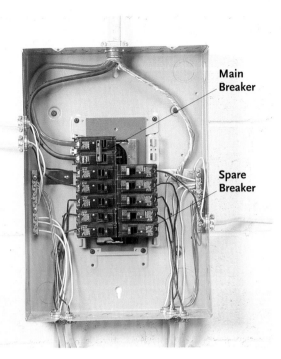

1

2 When you add a new circuit, you have to add a new circuit breaker to protect it. Check your panel box to see if you have room for another breaker, or if you have a breaker installed that's not being used (see above). You can tell it's not being used because no black wire is attached to it.

3 To attach a cable to the panel box, first remove a knockout plate from the side of the box. Then install a cable connector in this hole by threading a locknut on the inside end of the connector. Slide the cable through the connecter, and tighten the cable-clamp screws.

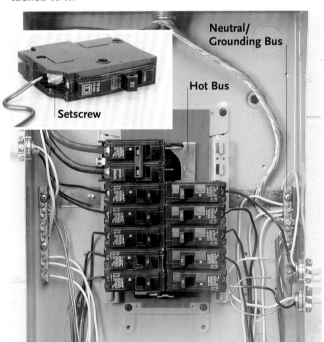

5 In most service panels, there are two bus bars for attaching the neutral and ground wires. Both bars can take both colored wires but only one wire should be put into each hole. The black circuit wire goes under the setscrew on the breaker (inset).

6 If you added a new breaker to the panel, then remove the knockout for this breaker space on the panel cover. If you are using a spare breaker, the knockout is already gone and you can just put the cover back on. Record the new circuit on the panel door, and turn on the main breaker.

Wiring Methods

INSTALLING AN ARC-FAULT CIRCUIT INTERRUPTER IN AN EXISTING CIRCUIT

project

The National Electric Code requires the use of arc-fault circuit-interrupter (AFCI) breakers to be installed on all new 125 volt, 15- and 20-amp single-pole breakers for main service as well as auxiliary service panels. This requirement includes GFCI locations as well. The purpose is to provide the maximum amount of protection of the electrical circuit. The requirement applies to all new construction, but switching existing circuits will supply this protection to existing buildings as well.

TOOLS & MATERIALS

▌Insulated screwdrivers ▌Voltage tester
▌Wire stripper ▌Long-nose pliers
▌Flashlight ▌AFCI breaker

What Is an Arc Fault? When a live wire makes a solid contact with a grounded object or a neutral wire, the current drawn causes a short and trips a standard circuit breaker. But if the contact is intermittent because of loose or corroded connections or damaged insulation, an arc of current develops. The arc causes heat in the range of thousands of degrees F, which left to continue might ignite combustible material in the vicinity and cause a fire.

AFCIs prevent fires by shutting down the circuit once it detects an arcing situation. The AFCI recognizes normal arcing and sparking created by normal use of electrical equipment and devices, such as when you unplug an appliance that is still on. But when the AFCI detects abnormal sparking or arcing, it is programmed to shut down the power to the circuit.

AFCI Breakers. AFCI circuit breakers have a test button and look similar to ground-fault circuit-interrupter (GFCI) circuit breakers. The breaker is wired to the hot and the neutral of the branch circuit, with a pigtail from the breaker to connect to the neutral bus, similar to the wiring of a GFCI breaker. Some designs combine GFCI and AFCI protection. AFCI/GFCI breakers meet code requirements for both applications with one combination breaker.

AFCIs do not protect against all faults in older wiring where there is no ground. However, they will provide protection against some arcing in these homes. In all homes they would add to the level of protection against fires caused by arcs, and in modern wired homes, they would add a significant level of protection. The AFCI circuit breaker provides protection for the branch circuit wiring and limited protection for power cords and extension cords. Single-pole, 15- and 20-ampere AFCI circuit breakers are currently available. Before installing any electrical devices or equipment, always read the accompanying installation instructions and follow the sequence for installation and testing.

With the adaptation of plug-on neutral breakers, caution must be exercised to choose the correct AFCI or AFCI/GFCI breaker. A wire-on breaker utilizes the existing neutral/grounding bus bar with an additional wire attached to the breaker, while a plug-on breaker does not. The current style of plug-on breakers can only be used with new panels designed to accept them.

Identifying the Breakers. Each breaker manufacturer has established their own dimensions for breaker styles. For example, a **CH** breaker will not fit in a panel designed for **BR** breakers. These designations have their own mounting dimensions between the hot bus and the breaker clip mounting bar and are not interchangeable. To be sure you select the correct breaker type, take the breaker you are replacing to the home improvement center or hardware store to match it correctly.

Identify the Circuits. Open the panel board door and read the circuit chart that identifies which circuit breaker(s) supply circuits in the living area. Turn the circuit breaker to the off position. Plug a lamp in the receptacles, or use a voltage tester to ensure that the correct circuit breaker is identified on the panel board chart. Turn off all other branch circuit breakers. Turn off the main circuit breaker last, it is normally located at the upper section of the panel board. Loosen or remove the panel board trim screws. Different manufacturers use different methods of securing the trim.

1 Using the circuit chart on the service panel door, identify the circuit where you want to install the AFCI breaker. Then turn off the main breaker, and remove the panel cover. Remove the black wire from the circuit breaker in question, and pull out the breaker.

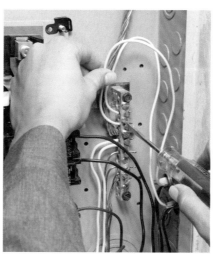

2 Find the white wire that goes with this circuit, and remove it from the neutral/ground bus bar. Bend this wire out of the box so you can see it clearly.

3 The AFCI breaker fits in the same space as the breaker that was removed. Engage the breaker in the panel clip, and push it into the hot bus bar. Make sure this breaker sits flush with the other breakers.

4 Connect the white neutral wire that was removed from the neutral/ground bus bar to the new breaker in the slot labeled LOAD NEUTRAL. Then connect the black hot wire that was attached to the removed breaker to the new breaker in the second slot.

5 Connect the end of the white pigtail to a terminal on the neutral/ground bus. Install the cover. To test, turn on the main breaker and each of the circuit breakers except for the AFCI. With everything off on the circuit, switch the handle on, and push the test button. The breaker should trip. If it doesn't, call an electrician.

Wiring Methods

ARC FAULT CIRCUIT INTERRUPTER (AFCI) BREAKERS

ARC FAULT CIRCUIT INTERRUPTER (AFCI) breakers have been available since the 2002 National Electric Code (NEC) adopted their use in dwelling bedrooms, requiring 120 volt 15 and 20 ampere outlets—including lighting fixtures—to provide protection for all of the branch circuits. This included any and all new installations.

Additionally, the 2008 NEC expanded the mandate so that AFCI-protected branch circuits had to be used in new installations in family rooms, dens, recreational rooms, parlors, libraries, dining rooms, sun rooms, closets, hallways, etc. Virtually all single-pole breakers are now required to be AFCI for any and all new installations.

AFCI breakers are designed to apply intelligent algorithms to differentiate normal, acceptable arcing, such as from mechanical switches being turned on and off, from unwanted and unsafe arcing. Conventional circuit breakers cannot achieve this, as they are only designed to detect sustained current overloads and short-circuit occurrences. Only an AFCI breaker can detect the presence of an arc that can be attributed to erratic current flow, which will cause the control circuitry inside an AFCI breaker to trip. When this occurs, it will de-energize the circuit and therefore eliminate further arcing conditions that can cause a fire.

The adaptation of AFCI technology stems from attempts to use modern appliances in homes with old wiring systems. It was very common to not have the necessary number of outlets needed for the increased electronic equipment usage, so residents would use multi-socket power strips to plug in all of their devices, overloading circuits and blowing fuses or tripping breakers.

New wiring can be damaged by wire staples, the sharp tips of framing nails, drywall screws, structural wood joint connectors, and even metal junction boxes. Such damage can create unsafe electrical conditions that the AFCI breaker will detect and shut down, alerting residents to a potential hazard. AFCI breakers provide that extra layer of protection.

Some standard breaker panel boxes can be retrofitted to accept AFCI breakers. However, do NOT do this yourself—the job requires a professional electrician, and inspector to verify the work, since it involves rewiring a portion of the neutral wire requirements.

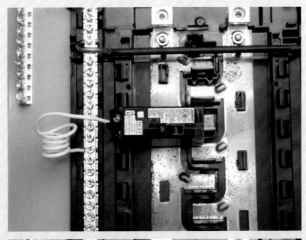

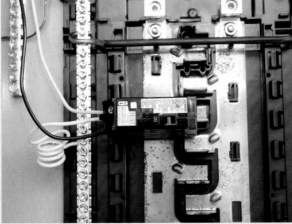

DUAL-FUNCTION AFCI/GFCI BREAKERS

WITH NEW ELECTRICAL WIRING codes required by the NEC for laundry and kitchen locations, the use of combination AFCI/GFCI breakers that contain self-testing technology has become widespread. These dual-function breakers combine the class A 5mA GCFI sensitivity to detect ground fault conditions in addition to the AFCI circuitry to detect unwanted arcing. The breaker will trip and shut off the flow of electricity to the entire circuit when protection has been compromised in either way.

The dual function breaker has many advantages, including a) it's more cost efficient than buying separate GFCI and AFCI breakers to meet code requirements, and b) it saves space by combining two state-of-the-art safety technologies in one device. Both screw lugs are provided at the same angle to allow for easier wire installation.

In addition, the dual function breaker provides both automatic and continuous self-testing that will ensure the breaker is performing properly. If the self test determines the breaker has been compromised, it will automatically trip the breaker and stop the flow of electrical current, thus alerting you to a problem in the wiring.

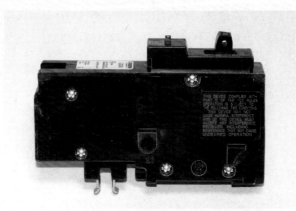

Standard 15-amp breaker installed above 20-amp AFCI/GFCI breaker in panel box.

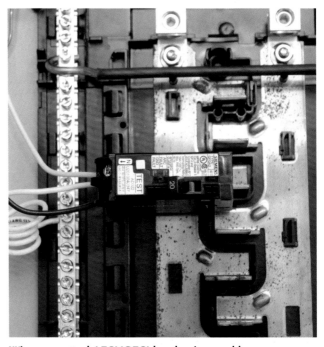

Wire on neutral AFCI/GFCI breaker in panel box.

Wiring Methods

INSTALLING AN AUXILIARY SERVICE PANEL

project

Service panels with no room for new circuits are commonplace these days. One way to correct this is to have an electrician upgrade your service panel, bringing a higher amp service into your house. If you plan a major remodeling that adds a lot of new appliances to the load, you may have to do this. But if you plan on adding just a few more circuits, installing a main lug subpanel is easier.

TOOLS & MATERIALS

▌Insulated screwdrivers ▌Multipurpose tool ▌Pliers ▌Cable ripper ▌Drill/driver and bits ▌60-amp subpanel with grounding bus ▌60-amp, 240-volt circuit breaker ▌6-gauge service cable ▌Conduit and fittings ▌Protective conduit bushings ▌20-amp, 120-volt breakers

1 Begin by preparing the subpanel for installation. On this job we used a 60-amp panel that had room for four 120-volt breakers. These panels have a neutral bus, or terminal, bar installed by the manufacturer, but not always a grounding bus bar. If your model doesn't, buy a separate bus, and screw it to the back of the panel box.

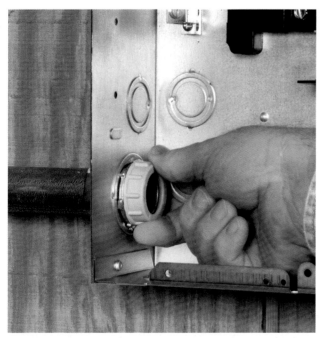

4 Install locknuts and protective plastic bushings on both ends of the conduit. These bushings cover the threads on the conduit, or the adapter that attaches the conduit to the box, and prevents these sometimes-sharp threads from abrading the wires that go between panels.

5 This subpanel is served by 6-gauge wires, one black hot, one red hot, one white neutral, and one green grounding wire. Start attaching these wires by feeding a ground wire through the conduit and attaching the end to the grounding bus bar inside the subpanel.

2 Install a length of conduit in the side of the sub-panel to connect it to the main service panel and to provide a protected route for the wires that join the two. Turn off the power at the main panel, and remove the cover.

3 Remove a convenient knockout in the side of the main service panel to receive the conduit from the subpanel. Push the end of this conduit into the hole, and mount the subpanel on the wall. Make sure the box is level and that it sits flat against the wall.

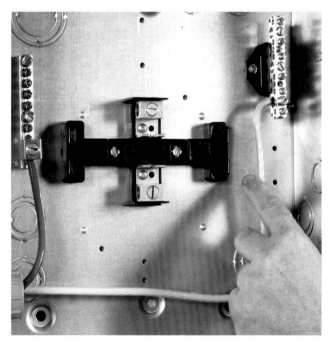

6 Next, feed a white neutral wire through the conduit and attach it to the neutral bus bar. Strip off about ½ in. of insulation from the end of the wire, and push it under one of the bus screws. Bend the wire so that it stays away from where the breakers will be installed in the middle of the box.

7 Complete the service connections by feeding a black and red wire into the subpanel and installing them on the top and the bottom of the hot bus bar. Again, bend these wires out of the way so they won't interfere with the area where the circuit breakers will be installed.

Continued on next page.

Wiring Methods

Continued from previous page.

8 Bring circuit cables into the subpanel, and attach them to the box using cable connectors. Then strip off the sheathing and the wire insulation from these cables. Install a breaker for each circuit by hooking one end in the hot bus and pushing the other into the hot bus clip.

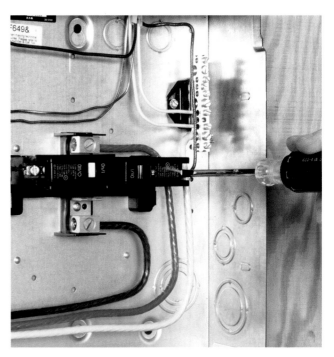

9 Attach the white circuit wires to the neutral bus bar inside the subpanel. Then attach the black hot wire from each circuit to the terminal located on the end of the breaker. Make sure all the terminal screws are tightened securely.

12 Slide the cover over the breakers, and make sure it sits flat against the box at all four corners. Attach it with the screws provided. Make sure to label where the new circuits go and what they service.

13 Install the two hot wires, red and black, to the 60-amp 240-volt breaker in the main panel. Then push the breaker onto the hot bus bar, and flip the breaker switch so it's in the ON position. Make sure to fold the hot wires out of the way.

10 Finish connecting the new circuits by installing the grounding wires in the grounding bus bar. Try to work neatly so the wires don't interfere with other wires or the breakers in the middle of the box. A good professional job can also make a good impression on your electrical inspector.

11 The subpanel cover comes with knockout plates covering all the breaker openings. Determine which slots your breakers occupy, then remove the appropriate plates using pliers.

14 Install the white neutral wire and the green grounding wire to the neutral bus bar in the main panel. Some main panels have separate neutral and grounding buses. Others, like this one, have a single bus for both white and ground wires.

15 The finished main panel shows the subpanel's wires folded neatly out of the way and the breaker installed and turned on. Finish up the service panel by removing the knockout plates for the double breaker from the cover. Then attach the cover, and mark the location and purpose of this subpanel circuit.

lighting

2

IF YOU ARE AN AVERAGE do-it-yourself homeowner, you will seldom find yourself lacking in opportunities to apply basic wiring skills. Whether you are adding new fixtures or repairing existing ones, you will use many of the basic wiring techniques learned earlier in this book—including the handling of wires, switches, receptacles, and other electrical devices. Double-check code requirements. For the fundamentals, including an explanation of the home electrical system, see Chapter 8, page 254. For more on the tools you will need, see Chapter 9, page 272; for more on essential equipment, see Chapter 10, page 286.

LIGHTING TYPES

Incandescent

Artificial lighting is the primary illumination we use to perform tasks. Lighting also provides ambient, or general, lighting and decorative, or accent, lighting. The quantity and quality of light produced will depend on the type of lightbulb you use. Incandescent, fluorescent, and high-intensity discharge bulbs (including mercury-vapor lamps) provide the three major sources of artificial light. A standard incandescent lightbulb produces light when electricity is passed through a thin wire, or filament. As a result of heating, the filament emits a visible light called incandescence. Incandescent lightbulbs come in a variety of shapes and styles to match fixtures that are freestanding, wall or ceiling mounted, or recessed. The term luminaire describes the entire assembly of lamp, fixture, housing, and attached electrical wires.

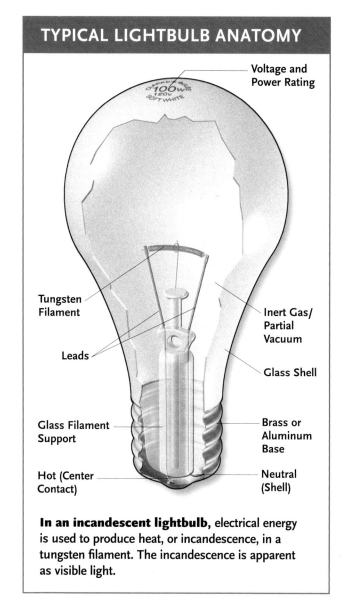

TYPICAL LIGHTBULB ANATOMY

Voltage and Power Rating

Tungsten Filament

Leads

Inert Gas/ Partial Vacuum

Glass Shell

Glass Filament Support

Brass or Aluminum Base

Hot (Center Contact)

Neutral (Shell)

In an incandescent lightbulb, electrical energy is used to produce heat, or incandescence, in a tungsten filament. The incandescence is apparent as visible light.

Lighting

LED

Any existing lamp or ceiling fixture can be retrofitted with an equal size and shape of LED bulb. The major advantages of LED over incandescent lighting are 1) lower power consumption for the same light output, 2) less heat, 3) more options in terms of brightness (incandescent bulbs are not being made any brighter than 60 watts), and 4) wide availability.

Though the LED bulb is more expensive than the incandescent bulb, the lifespan of LED versus incandescent outstrips the purchase price by far when compared to the shorter lifespan and greater wattage consumed by incandescent bulbs. (A good comparison between watts and lumens is a 100-watt incandescent bulb equals a 1600-lumen LED bulb.)

Moreover, modern LED bulbs are available in different color tones to provide that "soft white" or "daylight" that incandescent bulbs accomplished with their variety of wattages.

You can find LED light fixtures for several uses besides the recessed wafer lights mentioned on pages 80 and 81, including track lighting, flat-panel ceiling lights for utility spaces and garages, exterior lights, bathroom lights, floor lamps, and security lights, just to name a few.

Choosing the right LED fixture to meet your needs and tastes requires a search on the internet or a personal visit to your local lighting store to make your selections.

LED light fixtures may have an adjustable lumen output switch inside or outside the fixture. The light can typically be toggled between 2500, 3000, and 4000 lumens per fixture. The color of the LED fixture lens changes from yellow on low settings to bright white on the highest setting. Consult your installation instructions to pick the lumens you want for the light output before installing the fixture.

Use the circle template provided to mark the hole cut-out at the desired location in the drywall sheet.

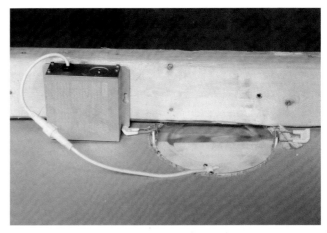

Locate the junction box as close as possible to the hole cut-out.

The LED wafer light held in place in the cut-out using spring tension tabs.

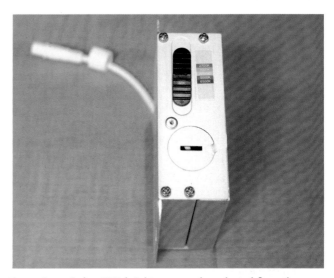

Intensity switch—LED brightness can be selected from the choices shown. Be sure all LED lights are set the same.

LED RECESSED LIGHTING

LED TECHNOLOGY MEANS that recessed ceiling lights can be more efficient and adjustable in brightness without the use of dimmer switches. Canless recessed LED lights, often called wafer lights, have been introduced to solve the problems that conventional recessed lighting can create. For one, recessed lights use incandescent or fluorescent lightbulbs, which generate heat in the space in the soffits (if installed outside) or ceiling. But because they use LED lights, wafer lights transmit minimal heat. In addition, wafer lights are designed to eliminate the vertical space requirements of recessed lighting fixtures. Some wafer light designs can even be added directly under a joist due to their thickness of less than ½ in.

The biggest difference between the two designs is in the junction box mounting method. One is the traditional metal electrical box on top of the wafer light; the other involves a separate rough-in box and low-voltage wire twist connection that can be connected after the drywall has been cut to receive the wafer light.

Wafer lights also have adjustable intensity settings, ranging from soft white to strong daylight.

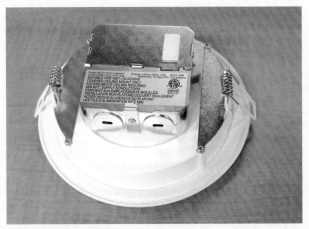

This model incorporates the junction box on top of the LED light. It costs slightly less, but its build means it will be more limited in terms of where it can be placed in both retrofit and new-work installations.

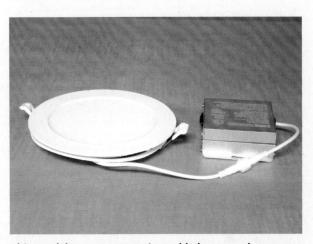

This model uses a connection cable between the separate junction box and the LED light. It costs slightly more, but is more flexible in terms of the height of the space it needs in the ceiling. This model can be installed directly under a floor or ceiling joist if necessary.

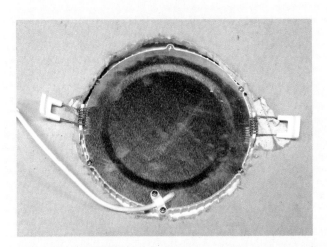

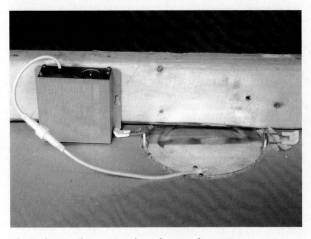

Both styles are held in place by strong spring retention clips and can be easily removed to change the LED intensity levels.

TESTING A LAMP CORD FOR BROKEN WIRES

project

If a lamp isn't working, you will usually see signs of a faulty plug, switch, or cord. A defective plug normally has visible damage, such as cracks in the plug housing or loose, broken, or bent prongs. A bad switch may feel loose when you turn it on and off, or the bulb may flicker when the switch is jiggled. Damaged cord will often look frayed or worn. Sometimes a broken wire within the cord causes problems. You can check for this, as explained below, but don't do so if the cord seems frayed or if any bare wire

is exposed. Cords in this condition should always be replaced. You can use the table, opposite, to troubleshoot some of the more-common problems encountered with incandescent light fixtures.

TOOLS & MATERIALS

■ Insulated screwdriver ■ Continuity tester
■ Multipurpose tool ■ Utility knife ■ If required: plug, socket, or cord replacement

Incandescent lightbulbs are designated by letters and numbers that represent their shapes and diameters.

1 There are several reasons that a light fixture can flicker on and off. To check the cord, turn on the light then flex the cord back and forth. If the light flickers, the cord is faulty and needs to be replaced.

2 Another way to test a cord is with a continuity tester. Hook the clip end onto one plug prong, and touch the probe end to one socket terminal screw, then the other. Do the same test with the other plug prong. The tester should light up when you touch the probe to the screws if the circuit is complete.

LIGHTBULB BURNOUT

A TYPICAL INCANDESCENT LIGHTBULB has a life span of approximately 900 to 1,000 hours. At roughly five hours per day, that's about six months. If your lightbulbs seem to have a shorter life span, the problem may be with the fixture. Some fixtures have loose contacts. A loose center contact on a lamp can overheat, melting the lead weld on the glass filament support. If the fixture does not appear to be the problem, check the lightbulb for the following:

An Overheated Lightbulb. If bulb wattage is too high and there's too little space around the fixture, the bulb will burn out due to improper air circulation.

Vibration. Bulbs can vibrate in loose fixtures or a wall that bounces.

Excessive Line Voltage. If the line voltage equals or exceeds 135 volts, have it checked out by your power company.

Lightbulbs rated 130 volts are superior to standard lightbulbs but may not last as long as a commercial-grade bulb.

The plastic coating on a rough-service lightbulb will contain the glass shards, should it explode.

If none of these is the cause of your bulb burnout, the bulb may be inferior. Be sure to purchase the best bulbs you can. Look for commercial- or industrial-grade lightbulbs because they last much longer than standard lightbulbs. Bulbs rated at 130 volts are better than standard lightbulbs but do not necessarily last longer. This is also true of rough-service bulbs that have a plastic coating on the surface and are designed to withstand vibration and will prevent shattering if the bulb explodes.

TROUBLESHOOTING INCANDESCENT LIGHT FIXTURES

Problem	Diagnosis	Solution
Bulb Doesn't Light	Plug has been pulled from receptacle.	Push plug back into receptacle.
	Bulb is loose; isn't making contact with socket.	Tighten bulb.
	Bulb is burned out.	Replace bulb.
	Cord is damaged.	Replace cord.
	Switch is defective.	Replace switch.
	Receptacle is defective.	Replace receptacle.
Bulb Flickers	Bulb is loose; barely makes contact with socket.	Tighten bulb.
	Loose wire at socket terminal.	Turn off power to circuit or unplug fixture; then secure wire.
	Switch is defective.	Replace switch.
	Receptacle is intermittent.	Replace receptacle.
	Receptacle wire is loose.	Reconnect or splice wires.
	Socket contact is dirty or corroded.	Turn off power; clean contact.
Fixture Blows a Fuse or Trips Circuit Breaker	Short circuit in cord.	Replace cord.
	Plug is defective.	Replace plug.
	Socket is defective.	Replace socket.

Problems with incandescent light fixtures can often be identified by checking a troubleshooting table and using a process of elimination.

Lighting

Fluorescent

In a fluorescent tube, electrical current jumps from an electrode at one end of the tube and flows through the tube to an electrode at the other end. This current flow causes mercury and argon gases in the tube to emit ultraviolet (UV) light, which is not visible to the human eye. To make the ultraviolet light visible, the tube is coated with a phosphor powder that glows, or fluoresces, when it is struck by the light. (See page 86.) When the fixture is turned off, the mercury/gas mixture within the tube does not conduct electricity. When power is first applied, several hundred volts are emitted from the ballast to initiate the release of electrical energy. Once this occurs, however, a much lower voltage is all that is required to maintain power—usually less than 100 volts for fluorescent tubes under 30 watts and 100 to 175 volts for tubes of 30 watts or more. When the higher voltage breaks down the gas and current begins to flow through it, the gas emits a great quantity of ultraviolet light but not much visible light. Only when the UV light hits the phosphor coating does the tube begin to glow. Different phosphors are used to achieve the light spectrum required for the fluorescent tube's intended designation—cool white, warm white, colored, or black light.

Fluorescent bulbs are about two to four times more efficient at light production than incandescent bulbs. They also last a lot longer—10,000 to 20,000 hours vs. 900 to 1,000 hours for a typical incandescent. However, this does not take into account the expense of replacing a fluorescent light ballast when one fails. Nevertheless, not all fluorescent bulbs require ballasts, and they are more energy-efficient than incandescents, providing two to four times more light per watt and using fewer watts than standard bulbs. They are also fairly maintenance-free.

FLUORESCENT TUBE TYPES

WARM WHITE

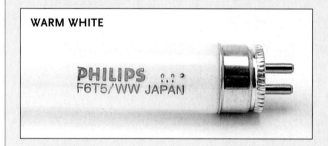

COOL WHITE

TINTED

BLACK

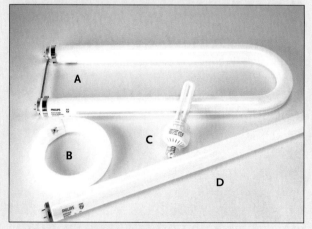

Fluorescent tubes are designated by shape and diameter, just as incandescent lightbulbs. A–T-12 medium bi-pin u-bent tube; B–4-pin circline tube; C–PL compact screw-in twin tube; D–T-12 medium bi-pin straight tube

FLUORESCENT LIGHT STARTERS

ONE WAY to start a fluorescent light is to use a starter switch, sometimes known as a glow switch. The switch turns on when it is activated by an electric current. Inside it is a contact and a bimetal strip that provides the initial current surge that warms the bulb's cathode (electron-emitting electrode). After the initial warm-up, the starter permits the electrical current to energize the gases in the tube. There are three types of starters: preheat, rapid start, and instant start. In preheat starters, the electrodes are heated before high voltage is affected to the bulb. This type of starter is a replaceable twist-in module. Rapid-start fixtures have electrodes that are constantly heated by low-voltage coiled wires (windings), and instant-start bulbs rely on step-up transformers for a short burst of high voltage to start up. The latter two types of starters are built into the ballast and cannot be independently replaced. The ballast is an enclosed component, that governs the electric current—holding it to the level required to operate a fluorescent light properly. There are two types of ballasts: choke and thermal-protected. Choke ballasts limit the amount of current flowing through the fluorescent tube. Fixtures that hold long fluorescent tubes use thermal-protected ballasts that include transformers as well as choke coils. With this type of ballast, when the light is turned on, a transformer momentarily steps up the voltage. The three types of fluorescent light starters are preheat, rapid starter, and instant start.

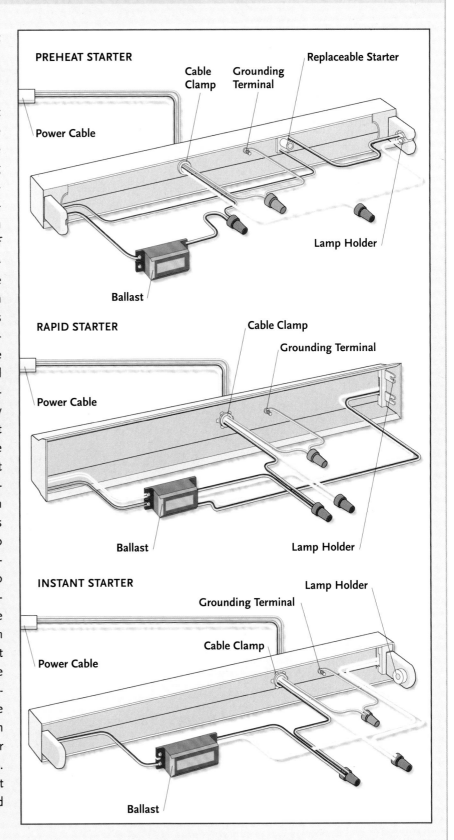

PREHEAT STARTER
Power Cable
Cable Clamp
Grounding Terminal
Replaceable Starter
Lamp Holder
Ballast

RAPID STARTER
Cable Clamp
Grounding Terminal
Power Cable
Ballast
Lamp Holder

INSTANT STARTER
Grounding Terminal
Lamp Holder
Cable Clamp
Power Cable
Ballast

TYPICAL FLUORESCENT TUBE ANATOMY

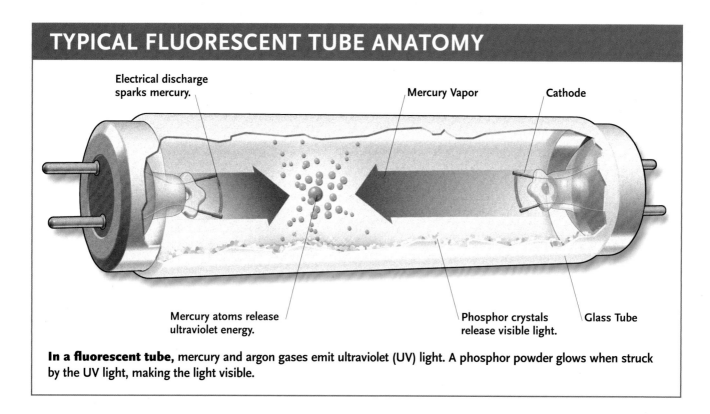

Electrical discharge sparks mercury.

Mercury Vapor

Cathode

Mercury atoms release ultraviolet energy.

Phosphor crystals release visible light.

Glass Tube

In a fluorescent tube, mercury and argon gases emit ultraviolet (UV) light. A phosphor powder glows when struck by the UV light, making the light visible.

TROUBLESHOOTING FLUORESCENT LIGHT FIXTURES

Problem	Diagnosis	Solution
Bulb Doesn't Light	Bulb is loose; pins aren't making contact with fixture terminals.	Reinstall lamp.
	Bulb is burned out.	Replace bulb.
	Terminals are corroded.	Clean terminals.
	Lamps are dirty.	Remove lamps and wash them.
	Bulb is cold.	Remove old ballast and install cold-rated ballast.
	End pins are broken or bent.	Replace bulb.
	Starter/ballast is defective.	Replace starter/ballast.
Bulb Flickers	Bulb is loose; pins aren't making contact with fixture terminals.	Reinstall lamp.
	Bulb is cold.	Allow enough time for ballast to warm up.
	Starter/ballast is defective.	Replace starter/ballast.
Bulb Discoloration	Bulb is worn out.	Replace bulb.
	Starter/ballast is defective.	Replace starter/ballast.
Humming	Loose ballast wires.	Secure wire connectors.
	Ballast is incorrect.	Replace with correct ballast type.

Though most problems with fluorescent fixtures involve loose tubes or poor contacts, consult the table above to check for problems other than these.

FLUORESCENT TUBE PIN CONFIGURATIONS

An important aspect of fluorescent tubes is their pin configuration. The pins are the protrusions on each end that hold the tube in the fixture and transfer power to the tube. Fluorescent light fixtures commonly installed in homes use 4-foot-long bi-pin (two-pin) lamps. The two narrow pins on each end make these lamps difficult to install but easy to be loosened by normal vibrations. Once the base pins become loosened, the tube contacts disconnect, causing the light to flicker or go out.

A more reliable configuration is found on 8-foot-long tubes. These have a large pin on each end, and one is spring-loaded. They are equipped with an instant starter. They are easy to install and present few problems. Having one large connection on each end of the lamp eliminates the light flickering and corrosive tendencies of the smaller bi-pin tubes. In areas needing even more light, special fixtures with high-output tubes can be used.

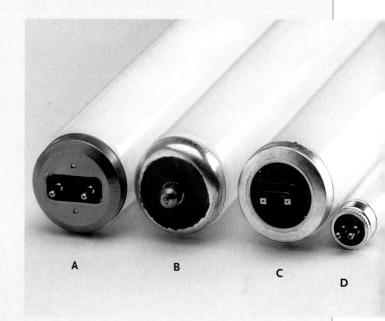

Base-pin configurations are generally: A–RDC (recessed double contact); B–single pin; C and D– bi-pin (two-pin).

ENERGY-SAVING COMPACT FLUORESCENT LAMPS

In an era when saving energy has become a top priority, many experts now recommend switching to compact fluorescent lamps (CFLs) to brighten our homes. According to the Department of Energy's Energy Star program, qualified CFLs use about 75 percent less energy and last as much as 10 times longer than standard incandescent bulbs. If each household replaced a standard bulb with a CFL, it would save enough electricity to light 3 million houses for a year.

The major difference between CFLs and other fluorescents is that CFLs are designed to be used in standard lamps and lighting fixtures, replacing incandescent bulbs. You just screw in the CFL as you would any lightbulb. They do need a bit more energy when they are first switched on, but once they get going, CFLs use only a fraction of the power gobbled by incandescent bulbs.

CFLs provide illumination comparable to incandescent bulbs but at much lower wattages. When shopping, check the lumens or look for labels with information such as "60-Watt Replacement." This means that you are getting the same brightness as a 60-watt incandescent bulb while using less wattage.

Many people find the spiral shape of most CFLs difficult to get used to, especially in fixtures and lamps where the bulb is visible. However, some CFLs have a covered spiral and look like standard bulbs. Because CFLs contain mercury, they should be recycled or treated as hazardous waste and not simply discarded in the trash.

Lighting

REPLACING A FLUORESCENT BALLAST

project

Fluorescent lighting is generally a better deal than incandescent lighting because it delivers more light per watt of electricity. Unfortunately, this efficiency doesn't tell the whole story. Fluorescent fixtures have ballasts that incandescent fixtures don't have, and when these wear out, they need to be replaced, usually at about $20 each.

TOOLS & MATERIALS

- Insulated screwdriver
- Neon circuit tester
- Diagonal cutting pliers
- Adjustable wrench
- Electrical tape
- Wire connectors
- Ballast replacement

1 First, disconnect the power to the light circuit that serves the fixture. Then remove the light diffuser, the bulbs, and the metal cover plate (top). Remove the wire connectors from the power leads, and use a circuit tester to verify that the circuit power is off.

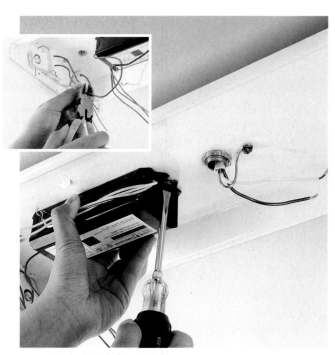

2 Cut the wires that extend from the ballast to the bulb sockets on both ends of the fixture (inset). Then remove the screw that holds the ballast in place.
Be sure to hold the ballast with your other hand when the screw is removed. This device is heavy and can do some damage if it's allowed to drop.

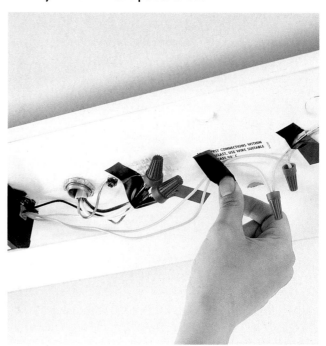

3 Install the new ballast, and make sure the mounting screw is tight. Then strip the insulation off the cut wires, and join these to the ballast wires with wire connectors. To prevent these wires from being pinched when the metal cover is installed, tape the wires to the fixture.

REPLACING A FLUORESCENT FIXTURE

project

Because fluorescent fixtures are very durable, they don't usually need to be replaced because they don't work anymore. When they are replaced, it's often because people want something that looks more residential and less industrial, which was the case here. The hardest part of this job is repairing the old-fixture mounting holes in the ceiling and touching up the paint so it's not noticeable afterwards.

TOOLS & MATERIALS

▌ Insulated screwdriver
▌ Neon circuit tester
▌ Long-nose pliers
▌ Multipurpose tool
▌ Wire connectors
▌ Fluorescent fixture replacement

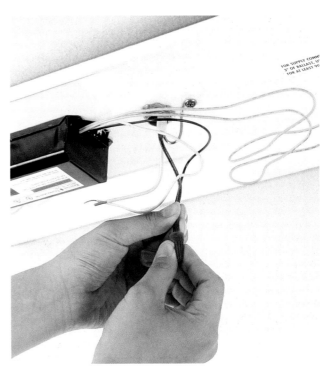

1 Turn off the power to the circuit that serves the fluorescent fixture. Then remove the light diffuser, the lamps, and the fixture cover. Remove the wire connectors from the power wires, and verify that power is off using a neon circuit tester.

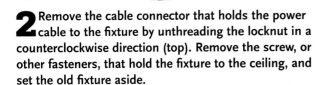

2 Remove the cable connector that holds the power cable to the fixture by unthreading the locknut in a counterclockwise direction (top). Remove the screw, or other fasteners, that hold the fixture to the ceiling, and set the old fixture aside.

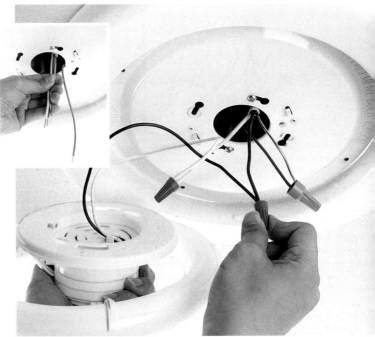

3 Install the new fixture base over the ceiling box. In this case, it just hangs from the box screws (inset). Then hold the new light next to the base, and connect the power wires to the fixture wires with wire connectors. Push the wires into the box, and install the fixture.

INSTALLING A FLUORESCENT DIMMER SWITCH

Everybody knows how convenient a dimmer switch is for standard incandescent bulbs. With a turn of a knob you can change the amount of light in any room from bright to practically dark. The same capability is available for fluorescent lights, but it costs a lot more and takes more time to install than the simple dimmer switch that we've all used. You can get a cheap incandescent dimmer for about $15. A fluorescent unit, on the other hand, will probably cost over $50, and you'll have to replace the ballast in your light unit, which is another $120 or more. Still in some situations, having the dimming capability for fluorescent units is more than worth the trouble. Installation isn't too hard, but it does require that you install a three-wire-plus-ground cable from the wall switch to the light fixture.

TOOLS & MATERIALS

■ Insulated screwdrivers ■ Fish tape
■ Multipurpose tool ■ Electrical tape
■ Wire connectors ■ 12/3 or 14/3 NM cable ■ Fluorescent dimmer switch
■ Fluorescent dimmable ballast

RECYCLING A BALLAST

THERE IS NOTHING MORE RESPONSIBLE FOR THE MESS IN THE BASEMENT OR THE GARAGE THAN THE IMPULSE TO KEEP SOMETHING FOR A RAINY DAY, ONLY TO FIND OUT 10 YEARS LATER THAT THE WEATHER NEVER GOT THAT BAD. A FLUORESCENT BALLAST, HOWEVER, IS NOT SOMETHING THAT SHOULD BE THROWN OUT. IF YOU REPLACE A STANDARD BALLAST WITH A DIMMABLE UNIT, HOLD ONTO THE OLD ONE FOR FUTURE USE.

1 Turn off the power to the fixture at the service panel; then take off the switch cover and pull out the switch. Loosen the terminal screws to free the wires, or cut them off close to the switch using wire strippers (top). Feed a fish tape into the switch box, and tape the end of a three-wire-with-ground cable onto the end of the fish tape.

4 Remove the existing ballast from the fixture housing. Ballasts are usually held in place with just a couple of screws. You can remove the ballast wires from the bulb sockets, or just cut the wires and use twist connectors to join the new ballast to the socket wires.

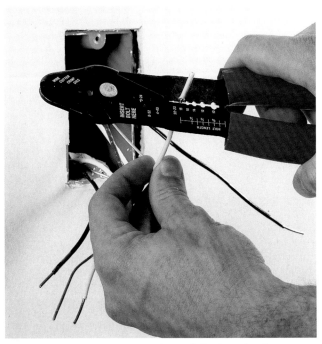

2 Once the new cable has been fished to the fluorescent fixture, prepare the wires in the switch box so the new dimmer switch can be installed. Strip the insulation off the ends of all the wires.

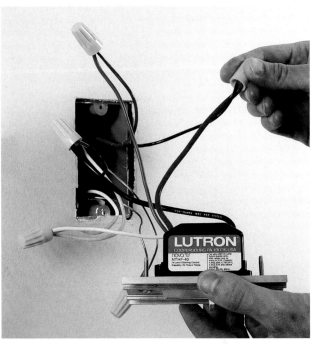

3 Join all the white wires, then all the ground wires. Next, join the black wires from the switch and the power line, the red switch lead to the black fixture wire, and the orange switch lead to the red fixture wire. Refer to directions that come with the switch.

5 Install the new dimmable ballast by driving screws into the fixture housing. The old screw holes may work. But if they are located in the wrong spot for the new unit, just drill new pilot holes, and use them for the ballast mounting screws.

6 Join the ballast wires to the switch wires with twist connectors. The white wires go together, as do the blacks and ground wires. The orange ballast wire is joined to the red switch wire.

REPLACING A QUARTZ HALOGEN BULB

Quartz Halogen

Quartz halogen lamps have become very popular in recent years. However you must be extremely careful using any light fixture that employs a quartz halogen bulb. This type of bulb gets extremely hot and can easily cause a fire. Never allow anything flammable to come near the glass covering on the bulb. Even an extension cord placed too close to the lamp can heat up and ignite. Do not use quartz halogen bulbs where children or pets may be in danger of knocking them over or coming into contact with the bulb. Exposed skin will burn immediately if it comes into contact with the glass. Though advertised as having a long life span, quartz halogen bulbs sometimes last only for minutes and have been known to explode within a fixture. Use extreme caution if you decide to use this type of bulb.

TOOLS & MATERIALS

▌ Insulated gloves
▌ Quartz halogen bulb replacement

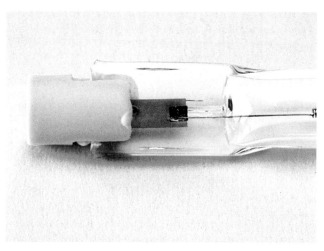

Although quartz halogen bulbs are protected by a glass tube, they must nevertheless be used with extreme caution because of the intense heat they generate.

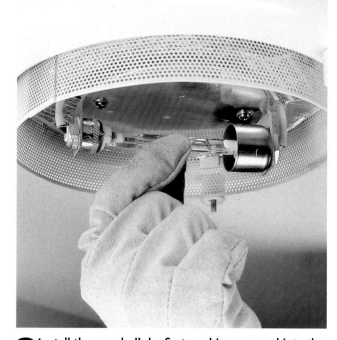

1 Turn off the power to the light fixture, and allow the bulb to cool for several minutes. Remove the diffuser, and push in the bulb toward its spring-loaded socket. Then pull it out. Wear gloves to keep oils from your skin from touching the bulb. These oils can destroy the bulb when it heats up.

2 Install the new bulb by first pushing one end into the spring-loaded socket; then push the other end up into its socket. Reinstall the fixture diffuser; turn on the circuit power; and check for proper operation.

LIGHTING FIXTURES

Recessed

Recessed lights are typically used where spot lighting is needed or low-hanging fixtures are not desirable. They are commonly used in kitchens and living areas where they provide concealed lighting over a large area. Recessed light can also illuminate a specific area, providing task lighting. Some recessed lights rotate and focus at an angle to illuminate or bathe a particular object in light.

Recessed light fixtures fall into two categories: insulated ceiling (IC) and non-insulated ceiling (NIC). It is best to opt for IC light fixtures so that you can put insulation right up against the metal fixture housing in an attic floor or cathedral ceiling. Non-insulated ceiling fixtures require, for fire safety, a minimum clearance of 3 inches between the housing and insulation, and a clearance above the fixture so as not to entrap heat (NEC Section 410.116LB). Most housings have two adjustable arms that are mounted to adjoining ceiling joists. The exposed surface of the fixture is extended below the joists just far enough to be flush with the finished ceiling. A decorative cover is snapped into place when the ceiling is finished. After the fixture has been mounted, the power branch-circuit cable is run into the electrical box attached to the housing.

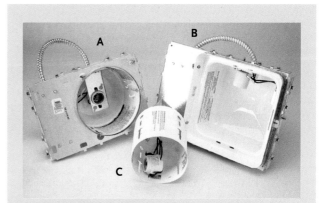

Recessed lamp housings: A–7-in. round downlight housing; B–7-in. square downlight housing; C–5-in. globe eyeball housing

A recessed ceiling fixture has its own prewired box attached. You need only bring the power cable into the box, and splice the wires.

INSULATING AROUND RECESSED LIGHTS

NIC-RATED FIXTURE

USA ONLY-WARNING **RISK OF FIRE** DO NOT INSTALL INSULATION WITHIN 3 INCHES OF FIXTURE SIDES OR WIRING COMPARTMENT NOR ABOVE FIXTURE IN SUCH A MANNER TO ENTRAP HEAT.

Min. 3" Clearance around Fixture

IC-RATED FIXTURE

USA ONLY: INSULATED CEILING TYPE IC FIXTURE. CAUTION: RISK OF FIRE. USE WITH "COMMERCIAL ELECTR WATTAGE INDICATED. NOTICE: THERMALLY PROTECTED FIXTURE. A BLINKINGLI OTHER CONDITION CAUSING OVERHEATING.

Recessed light housings are either rated for non-insulated ceilings (NIC) or insulated ceilings (IC). For fire safety, NIC housings must be at least 3 in. clear of any insulation, while IC housings are permitted to be in direct contact with insulation.

INSTALLING A RECESSED LIGHT FIXTURE

Recessed lights come in different styles. But generally, the unit has a housing mounted on sliding brackets and a separate electrical box for making the wiring connections. Start the job by installing the unit between ceiling joists. Then open up the electrical box, and install the cable that comes from the wall-mounted light switch. Join the cable wires to the fixture wires with wire connectors. Replace the box cover, and install a bulb, lens, gasket, and trim ring.

TOOLS & MATERIALS

▮ Insulated screwdrivers ▮ Hammer
▮ Long-nose pliers ▮ Power drill ▮ Cable ripper ▮ Multipurpose tool ▮ Nails or screws ▮ Cable clamps ▮ Wire connectors
▮ Recessed lamp housing

1 Begin by establishing the location of the light unit and cutting a hole in the ceiling drywall. Then take the fixture into the attic; pull back the insulation; and adjust the extension bars until the fixture is centered over the hole.

Recessed ceiling fixtures can provide general lighting to a room, or when placed properly, task lighting, such as these lights placed above this vanity.

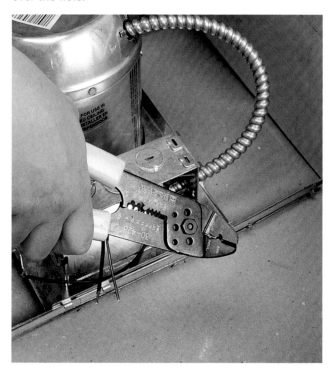

4 Install a cable connector in the knockout hole; then slide the switch cable through the connector; tighten it in place; and strip the insulation from the end of each wire.

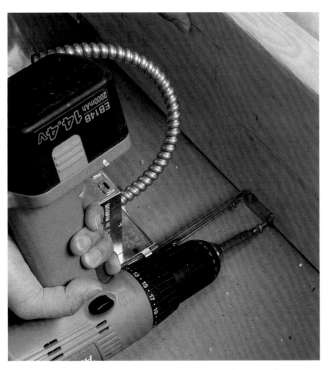

2 Make sure the mounting brackets on both sides of the fixture are positioned flat against the ceiling joists. Then screw these brackets in place using a drill/driver.

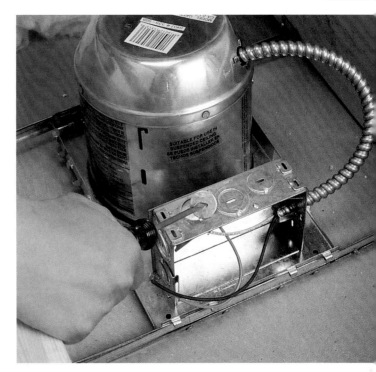

3 Take off the side cover to the electrical box, and using a flat-blade screwdriver, remove one of the box knockouts.

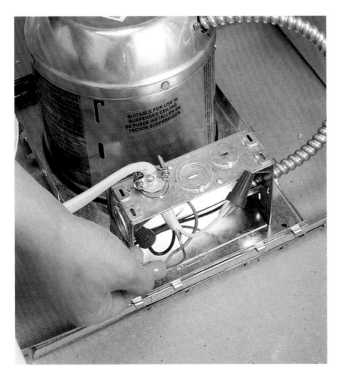

5 Join the like-colored wires from the switch cable and the fixture by hand-tightening the wire connectors. Make sure to install the proper size connector for the wire gauges you are joining. In this case the connector must be rated for at least two 14-gauge wires.

6 Carefully tuck all the wire connections into the box, and replace the side cover. Then go back to the kitchen and install the gasket, lens, and trim ring to the bottom of the fixture. Turn on the circuit, and test the performance of the fixture and switch.

95

Lighting

Surface-Mounted

Surface-mounted fixtures are usually installed on a ceiling or wall. They may use incandescent, fluorescent, or quartz halogen bulbs. Wall sconces, globe lights, above-vanity strip lighting, and ceiling fixtures are all examples of this type of lighting. Surface-mounted lights are generally attached to lighting outlet boxes.

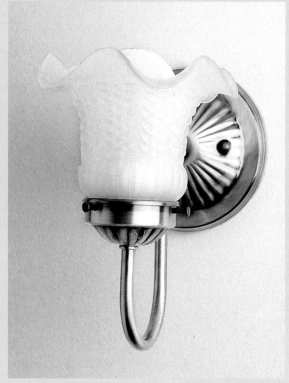

Surface-mounted fixtures come in a variety of styles appropriate for ceiling or wall installation.

INSTALLING A CEILING-MOUNTED FIXTURE

project

The hardest part of this job is getting the box and cable installed. (For help on this job see pages 28–30.) Once both are in place, strip the sheathing and wire insulation from the cable, and screw a light fixture-hanging strap to the box. Join the wires from the fixture and the cable using wire connectors. Then tighten the fixture in place; install the proper light bulb (or bulbs); and screw on the fixture globe.

TOOLS & MATERIALS

▮ Insulated screwdriver ▮ Wire stripper
▮ Long-nose pliers ▮ Cable ripper
▮ Mounting strap ▮ Cable clamps
▮ Wire connectors ▮ Electrical box
▮ Threaded nipple ▮ Surface-mounted light fixture

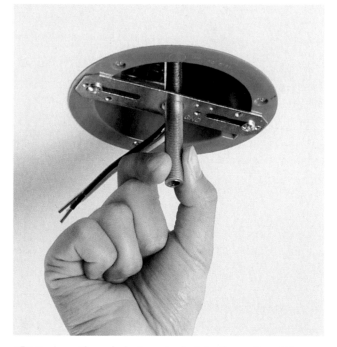

3 Screw a threaded pipe nipple into the collar of the hanging strip. After the fixture is installed, you'll thread another nut onto the bottom of this nipple that will hold the fixture securely in place. Make sure the threads are clean so the fixture nut is easy to install.

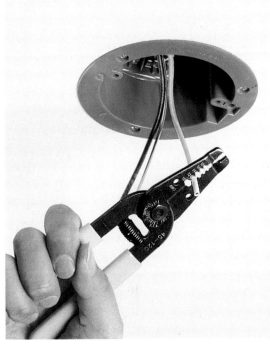

1 Begin by cutting a box hole in the ceiling and fishing new cable from the switch box into the ceiling opening. Install a retrofit ceiling box, and tighten the support wings against the drywall. Remove the cable sheathing, and strip the ends of the wires using wire strippers.

2 Screw a metal light-fixture hanging strip to the bottom of the box. This strap provides threaded holes for mounting different fixtures.

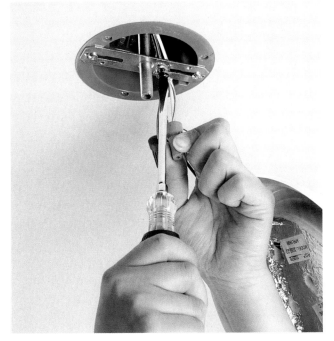

4 Join the fixture wires to the cable wires by combining like-colored wires with wire connectors. Add a short pigtail wire to the ground wires, and then tighten this pigtail wire under a green grounding screw. If possible, have someone hold the fixture while you make these connections.

5 Slide the fixture over the box, and turn the retaining nut onto the threaded nipple. Tighten the nut until the fixture is against the ceiling. Add the recommended bulbs, and install the globe that came with the fixture. Do not use bulbs with more wattage than the manufacturer recommends.

INSTALLING TRACK LIGHTING

project

Track Lighting

If you want to try some track lighting to change the look of your kitchen or to direct more task lighting where you need it, then you're in luck. Installing one of these systems is not difficult, especially if you already have a switch-operated ceiling fixture. Just remove the old fixture; install the track; and slide the light heads into place.

TOOLS & MATERIALS

■ Insulated screwdrivers ■ Pencil ■ Long-nose pliers ■ Neon circuit tester ■ Multipurpose tool ■ Measuring tape ■ Straightedge ■ Power drill ■ Wire connectors ■ Molly bolts or wood screws ■ Track lights ■ Track connectors and covers ■ Track ■ Power connector plate ■ Power box cover

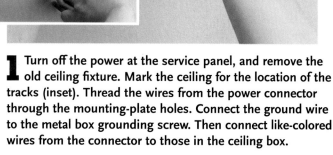

1 Turn off the power at the service panel, and remove the old ceiling fixture. Mark the ceiling for the location of the tracks (inset). Thread the wires from the power connector through the mounting-plate holes. Connect the ground wire to the metal box grounding screw. Then connect like-colored wires from the connector to those in the ceiling box.

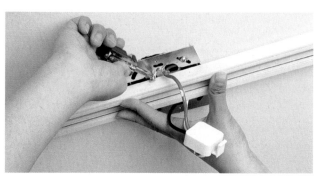

2 Screw the power connector mounting plate to the electrical box. Make sure the plate is tight and doesn't pinch any of the cable or fixture wires. Then lift up a section of track; slide it between the connector wires; and attach it temporarily to the mounting plate (top). Push the connector into the track, and twist-lock it in place.

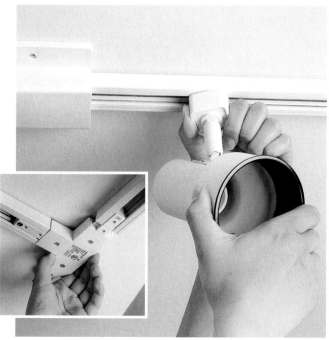

3 Install the tracks and any T- or L-connectors, and make sure they are all tight against the ceiling (inset). Slide the light fixtures onto the track, and lock them in place. Turn on the lights, and adjust the direction of the lamps if necessary.

INSTALLING A CHANDELIER

Chandeliers

Hanging a chandelier differs from installing a ceiling-mounted light fixture because of the added weight of the fixture. This requires modifying the ceiling box to accommodate the extra weight. Special chandelier-hanging hardware is used for this purpose, including a threaded stud and nipple, a hickey, and locknuts. If you're replacing an existing light fixture, you'll have to beef up the box-hanging hardware.

TOOLS & MATERIALS

▌Insulated screwdrivers ▌Adjustable wrench
▌Neon circuit tester ▌Long-nose pliers
▌Multipurpose tool ▌Wire connectors ▌Stud
▌Chandelier ▌Collar nut ▌Threaded nipple
▌Hickey ▌Escutcheon plate ▌Locknuts

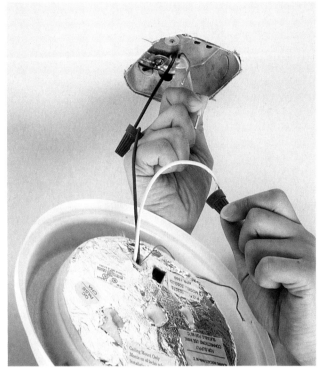

1 Turn off the circuit power to the existing light fixture at the service panel. Then remove the screws that hold the fixture in place, and unthread the wire connectors that join the circuit and fixtures wires.

2 Make sure the electrical box is securely mounted to the ceiling framing. Connect the ground wire to the metal box grounding screw. Then remove the center knockout plate; install a stud in the knockout hole; screw a hickey into the stud and a nipple into the hickey.

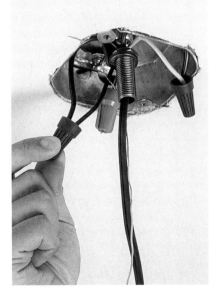

3 Have someone hold the chandelier or support it on a stepladder while you work. Thread the chandelier wires through the threaded nipple. Then connect the fixture wires to the box wires.

4 Once the wires are joined, slide the chandelier escutcheon plate up against the ceiling box. Hold it in place as you screw the collar nut onto the threaded nipple in the middle of the box.

99

Lighting

INSTALLING VANITY LIGHTING

project

Vanity Lighting

A common bathroom-wiring scheme for above a vanity calls for a light fixture over the sink, a receptacle on both sides, and a switch closer to the door to provide easy access when entering the room. Once you rough in the wiring, install and finish the drywall. Then wire the first receptacle, followed by the light fixture, the second receptacle, and the switch that operates the light.

TOOLS & MATERIALS

▌Insulated screwdrivers ▌Long-nose pliers ▌20-amp GFCI receptacle ▌15-amp standard receptacle ▌Single-pole switch ▌Lighting fixture(s) ▌Switch box ▌12/2G NM cable ▌12/3G NM cable ▌Light fixture box ▌Outlet boxes

1 Install a two-wire power cable (yellow-colored above) to the receptacle on the right and then to the light fixture. Use three-wire cable to connect the light fixture to the receptacle on the left.

ALTERNATIVE WIRING

Here's another wiring method common for vanities. In this configuration a GFCI-protected outlet is always hot and shares a box with a switch that controls the light on the vanity. The black wire from the power source is attached to the brass screw of the outlet. A jumper wire connects the outlet and the switch.

4 Attach the light fixture-mounting bracket to the wall. Then connect the white fixture wires with the white cable wire. Join the bare grounding wires together, and attach them to the grounding screws. Join the black fixture wires to the red cable wire.

2 Connect the incoming power cable wires to the line side of the GFCI receptacle. Connect the wires that run from the receptacle to the fixture to the LOAD side of the receptacle.

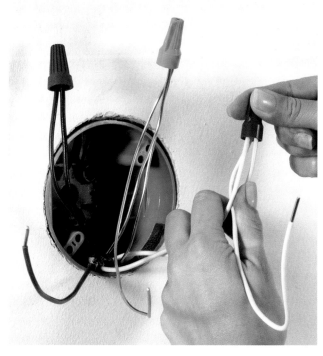

3 In the light fixture box, join the black wire from the LOAD side of the GFCI receptacle to the black wire that runs to the other outlet with a wire connector. Join the grounding wires, and add a white pigtail wire to the other two white wires.

5 Attach the black and white wires from the three-wire cable to the second receptacle. Join the red wire from the three-wire cable to the white wire from the switch cable, and code it with black tape. Screw the black switch wire to the second brass receptacle screw.

6 Finish up the wiring for this installation by attaching the white and black wires to the switch. Make sure to code the white wire with black tape to indicate that it's now a hot wire.

Lighting

INSTALLING UNDER-CABINET LIGHTING

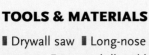

Under-Cabinet Lighting

Installing fluorescent or halogen fixtures on the bottom of wall cabinets is a great way to provide task lighting for the countertop. When either type of fixture is located near the front of the wall cabinet, it completely washes the counter with light. The fixtures are also a good choice if the walls are already finished, because you can install the switch and fixture with a minimal amount of damage to the wall. Place the fixture

toward the front of the cabinet so that its light illuminates as much of the counter as possible. If you have framed cabinets, the face frame should shield the light. Frameless cabinets, however, usually do not offer this protection.

Plan on providing fluorescent tubes that extend about two-thirds the length of the countertop. This should provide adequate working light with no dark spots.

1 Start by establishing the best location for the light switch on the kitchen wall. Then trace the outline of a cut-in box on the wall. Cut along these lines using a drywall or keyhole saw.

TOOLS & MATERIALS

▪ Drywall saw ▪ Long-nose pliers ▪ Cable stripper ▪ Power drill and bits ▪ Insulated screwdrivers ▪ Lighting fixture(s) ▪ Single-pole switch ▪ 12/2G NM cable ▪ Wire connectors

Under-cabinet lighting is not only a good source of task lighting, it also provides excellent background lighting when no one is working.

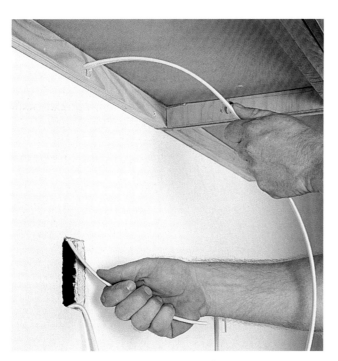

2 Once the switch-box hole is cut, fish a power cable into the hole from a close-by circuit. Make sure this circuit has enough capacity available for the lights you want to install. If it doesn't, bring a new circuit cable from the service panel. Also fish a cable from the back of a wall cabinet and into the wall opening.

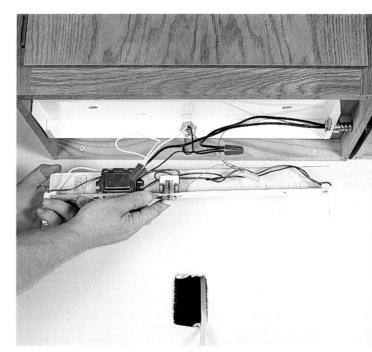

3 Attach the base of an under-cabinet fluorescent fixture to the bottom of the wall cabinet. Then pull the switch cable through a cable connector mounted in the back of the base. Tighten the connector, and join the switch wires to the fixture wires using wire connectors. Lift the light fixture onto the base, and attach it securely.

4 Install a switch box in the wall opening, and attach both black wires to the switch terminals. Join the white wires together and the ground wires together using wire connectors. Screw the switch securely to the box, and test the installation.

5 When everything works correctly, install the plastic diffusers on all the fixtures. Many under-cabinet units also have surface-mounted rotary switches just behind the diffusers so you can turn off a specific fixture while all the others stay on.

INSTALLING CABLE LIGHTS

Cable Lights

Cable lights are a clever way to add a series of small spotlights without going to the trouble of installing full-size track lighting. In this kit, the fixtures were outfitted with 20-watt halogen bulbs that supplied more than enough light to illuminate a kitchen island without adding a lot of light to the rest of the room.

TOOLS & MATERIALS

▮ Insulated screwdrivers ▮ Multipurpose tool ▮ Locking pliers ▮ Power drill and bits ▮ Wire connectors ▮ Surface-mounted receptacle, switch, and light boxes ▮ Surface-mounted conduit ▮ Duplex receptacle ▮ Single-pole switch ▮ Cable light kit with cables, lamps, transformer, and mounting hardware

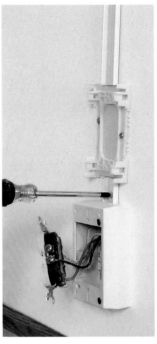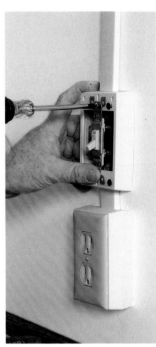

1 Begin by mounting a surface-wiring box over a standard receptacle box; then attach a switch box base and surface conduit to the wall (left). Run cable from the receptacle box to the switch box, then from the switch box to the cable lights above. Join the wires to the switch, and screw cover plates over both boxes.

4 Attach the cable to the holder using the threaded fitting. Finger tighten these fittings (top); then snug them tight with locking pliers. Install cable holders on the opposite wall. Then hang a turnbuckle adjuster onto both holders.

5 Attach the cable fittings to these turnbuckles (top), and tighten the turnbuckles until the fittings are taut. Attach the cables that go to the wall-mounted transformer to the cables using self-piercing fittings. Just tighten the screws and the electrical contact is made.

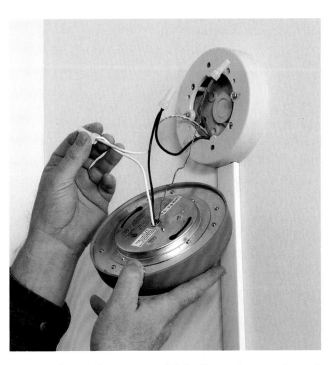

2 Install a surface-mounted light fixture box on the wall near where the cable lights will be installed. Join the cable from the switch below to the fixture transformer leads. Then attach the transformer to the box.

3 Attach the cable holders to the wall by driving the screw inside each holder into a solid base. If you don't have a good surface to screw into, install a board or use toggle bolts to hold the cable holding hardware.

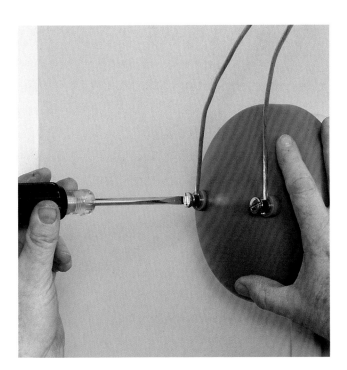

6 Attach the short cables, from the light cables above, to the terminals located on the front of the transformer. Just loosen the screws; feed each wire into its slot; and tighten the screws.

7 Mount each light on the cables using self-piercing fittings. The rods that hold the lights are hinged so the lights can be pointed in different directions.

INDOOR LIGHTING DESIGN

Use lighting the way an artist uses a brush, to downplay or highlight elements in a room. Lighting focused on an object will draw the eye to that object in contrast to its background. For example, lighting the corners in a room makes it seem larger, as the eye takes in its entirety. In comparison, a soft pool of light created around a sofa will focus attention on the piece of furniture. The remainder of the room recedes into shadow, making it seem smaller.

Not everyone reacts to light in the same way. Some people are more photosensitive than others, preferring a lower field of general lighting. To others, the toned-down lighting suitable to photosensitive people may be depressing. Consider the personal preferences of all family members when you design your lighting system.

The functions of lighting divide into three basic categories: to provide general or ambient lighting, task lighting, and accent or decorative lighting.

General Lighting. General or ambient lighting provides overall brightness for an area. Furnishing background illumination, it can vary with day and night, winter and summer, or different moods and activities.

Task Lighting. Task lighting makes it easier to see what you are doing. Individual fixtures concentrate light in specific areas for chores such as preparing food, reading, or doing crafts.

Accent Lighting. Accent or decorative lighting highlights an area or object, emphasizing that aspect of a room's character. These mood-makers of lighting, to be effective, must contrast with their background of ambient lighting.

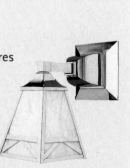

BASIC FIXTURE TYPES

Suspended. Globes, chandeliers, and other suspended fixtures can light a room or a table. Hang them 12 to 20 inches below an 8-foot ceiling or 30 to 36 inches above table height.

Surface-Mount. Attached directly to the ceiling, it distributes very even, shadowless general lighting. To minimize glare, surface-mount fixtures should be shielded. Fixtures with sockets for several smaller bulbs distribute more even lighting than those with just one or two large bulbs.

Recessed. Recessed fixtures, which mount flush with the ceiling or soffit, include fixed and aimable downlights, shielded fluorescent tubes, and totally luminous ceilings. Recessed fixtures require more wattage—up to twice as much as surface-mount and suspended types.

Track. Use a track system for general, task, or accent lighting—or any combination of the three. You can select from a broad array of modular fixtures, clip them anywhere along a track, and revise your lighting scheme any time you like. Locate tracks 12 to 24 inches out from the edges of wall cabinets to minimize shadows on countertops.

Under-Cabinet. Fluorescent or incandescent fixtures (with showcase bulbs) mounted to the undersides of wall cabinets bathe counters with efficient, inexpensive task lighting. Shield under-cabinet lights with valances and illuminate at least two-thirds of the counter's length.

Cove. Cove lights reflect upward to the ceiling, creating smooth, even general lighting or dramatic architectural effects. Consider locating custom cove lights on top of wall cabinets, in the space normally occupied by soffits.

An elegant chandelier on a dimmer switch, above, provides both ambient mood and task lighting.

Wall sconces, right, provide task lighting as well as a decorative flourish to this bathroom. [See NEC Section 210.70(A)(1).]

HOW MUCH LIGHT DO YOU NEED?

TYPE	INCANDESCENT	FLUORESCENT	LOCATION
General (ambient) Lighting	2–4 watts per square foot of area. Double this if counters, cabinets, or flooring are dark	1–1½ watts per square foot of floor area	90 inches above the floor
Task Lighting			
Cleanup Centers	150 watts	30–40 watts	25 inches above the sink
Countertops	75–100 watts for each 3 running feet of work surface	20 watts for each 3 running feet of work surface	14–22 inches above the work surface
Cooking Centers	150 watts	30–40 watts	18–25 inches above burners Most range hoods have lights.
Dining Tables	100–120 watts	Not applicable	25–30 inches above the table
Accent Lighting	Plan flexibility into accent lighting so that you can vary the mood with a flick of a switch or the twist of a dimmer. Suspended, recessed, track, and cove fixtures all work well.		

3

appliances and equipment

IF YOU ARE AN AVERAGE do-it-yourself homeowner, you will find that there are many appliances and other equipment that must be installed during a major remodeling. Some types of equipment are direct-wired, such as dishwashers. (See "Direct-Wiring a Dishwasher," page 110.) Other appliances, such as an electric range, require special receptacles that only that appliance can use. (See "Installing a Range Receptacle," page 116.)

The amount of power required for each appliance or piece of equipment you install will also vary. An electric cooktop may need a 30-amp circuit, while a ceiling fan will operate on a 15- or 20-amp circuit.

For the fundamentals, including an explanation of the home electrical system, see Chapter 8, page 254. For more on the tools you will need, see Chapter 9, page 272; for more on essential equipment, see Chapter 10, page 286.

SELECTION

Today's appliances are status symbols, and the vast selection of models and features is dazzling. With such a variety, it's important to analyze your needs carefully before you shop. New appliances will consume a considerable portion of your remodeling budget, so you've got to choose wisely. Most major kitchen appliances will last as long as 15 to 20 years. The way to get the most for your money is to purchase the model and size that's right for your lifestyle now—and for the not-too-distant future.

Manufacturers are required by law to label every appliance with certain energy-related information. That informa-

SHOPPING TIPS

ASK FOR AN IN-STORE DEMONSTRATION.
You want the appliance to perform with space-age precision, but you shouldn't have to be an engineer to use it. Also, check key pads and other controls. They should be within convenient reaching distance (on the front or side of the appliance) and easy to read, and they should accommodate any finger size—from a teenager's to an adult man's.

Don't find out after the appliance has been delivered that it's too wide for its allocated location. Always check the measurements on your plan against the manufacturer's specifications and the actual in-store model, if possible. Another measurement to check is the depth of an appliance, especially if you want the look of something that is built-in. Some "cabinet-depth" refrigerators now come 24 inches deep, for example. If you are shopping for many appliances at once, it pays to take a plan of the room with you. The layout should contain all room dimensions and available electrical power.

tion must include a description of the appliance, the model number, projected energy costs to run the appliance, a range of energy costs for similar models, and a table to estimate energy costs for running the appliance based on local utility rates. (To learn more about energy labels, see "Appliance Ratings," on page 263.)

Appliances and Equipment

APPLIANCES

Dishwasher

Before installing a dishwasher, you must first install a dedicated circuit to provide power to the appliance. In addition, you must be able to disconnect the dishwasher from the electrical system. You can either install a dedicated receptacle for the dishwasher, normally installed below a kitchen counter and near the sink, or connect the wiring to a switch. New dishwasher installations are required to have a service cord attached to the internal junction box under the front panel of the dishwasher. The service cord has to be an SJ or SJT rubber-coated, insulated cord with an integral 20 amp-rated wire and three-prong plug end. The plug end attaches to a single outlet device in a junction box in the wall behind the dishwasher.

Many dishwashers have a built-in electric dryer. The dryer is an ordinary heating element. It's a circular device made of metal that's found at the inside bottom of the dishwasher. This type of dryer draws a great deal of current because it uses the same 120-volt circuit that feeds the dishwasher. For this reason, use 12-gauge wire.

Dishwasher internal junction box with approved SJ or SJT cord connected to the dishwasher wires.

A dishwasher requires its own circuit and can be hardwired to the junction box or simply plugged into a designated receptacle.

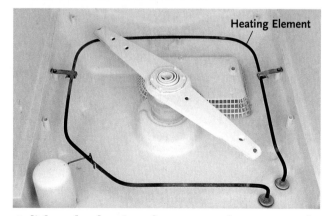

Heating Element

A dishwasher heating element uses the same 120-volt circuit as the dishwasher. For this reason, the dishwasher should be on a separate circuit.

DIRECT-WIRING A DISHWASHER

project

Bringing power to a dishwasher is one of the easier wiring jobs. Because the internal wiring of the machine terminates inside a built-in electrical box, all that's required is to bring a power cable from a switch to the box; attach it using a cable connector; and join the power wires to the fixture wires.

TOOLS & MATERIALS

▌ Insulated screwdrivers
▌ Long-nose pliers
▌ Cable ripper
▌ Multipurpose tool
▌ Wire connectors
▌ 12/2G NM cable
▌ Dishwasher

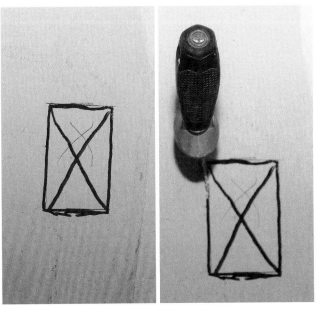

Creating an old work receptacle box in the wall behind the dishwasher.

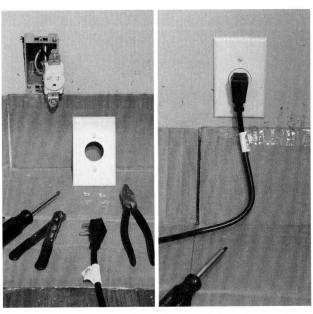

Installing a single outlet device for the dishwasher cord.

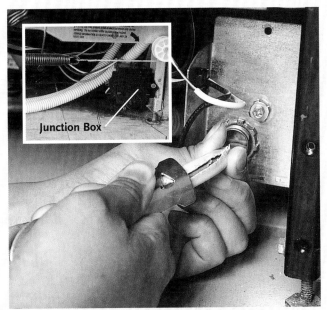

Junction Box

1 Most dishwashers have their own junction box located behind the kick panel. Gain access to it by simply removing the panel (inset). Then pull a power cable from the switch box into this box. Make sure to leave a wire loop behind the dishwasher so you can pull out the appliance without disconnecting this cable.

2 Join the black fixture wire to the black power wire using a wire connector. Do the same with the white wires. Then attach the ground wire from the power cable to the grounding screw inside the box. Finish up by reinstalling the box cover and the dishwasher's access panel.

Appliances and Equipment

RETROFITTING A DISHWASHER WITH A FLEXIBLE CORD SYSTEM

In the past it was acceptable for dishwashers to be "hardwired" to the house electrical system. Today that is not the case, due to the hazards of such wiring and the new requirement for being able to disconnect the appliance from the house electrical system when the breaker is turned off.

Retrofitting a dishwasher with a flexible cord system is relatively easy and will provide a safe and easy way to disconnect the appliance from the house electrical system.

TOOLS & MATERIALS

- 4-way screwdriver
- Wire strippers
- Old plastic work box with ears
- Single-device receptacle
- Single-device cover plate

1 Turn off the breaker that powers the dishwasher. Check to see if the power to the front panel has been eliminated: if the lights don't come on when you press the buttons, it's safe. Turn off the water supply to the dishwasher to prevent any leaks from occurring.

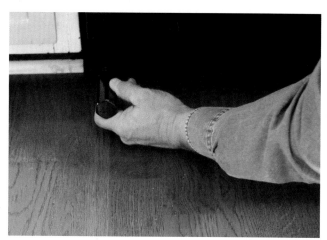

4 Use a screwdriver to remove the two front panel trim screws.

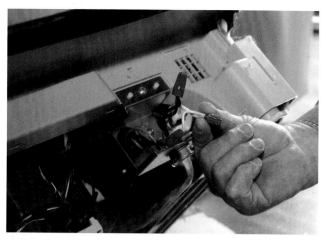

7 Remove the wire nuts for the black HOT and white NEUTRAL wires. Remove the green ground screw and the bare copper ground wire.

2 Remove the screws that attach the dishwasher to the underside of the counter.

3 Gently slide the dishwasher out from the opening. Hint: It is advisable to place a thin rug or mat of cardboard for the dishwasher feet to slide on. This prevents them from damaging the finished floor surface.

5 After removing the front trim pane, remove the screws securing the inner panel to access the electrical and water connections.

6 Remove the electrical junction box cover.

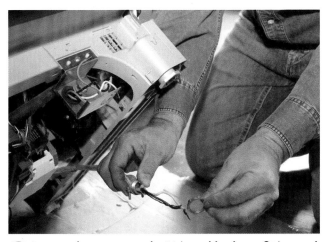

8 Loosen the screws to the ⅜-in. cable clamp fitting and slide the Romex wire cable out of the junction box.

Appliances and Equipment

9 Locate an area between two studs on the wall behind the dishwasher, then mark and cut the drywall to accept an old-work box with ears using a keyhole saw. Test fit the box in the cut opening before finishing.

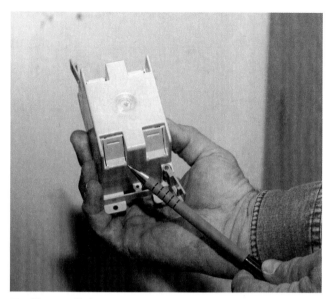

10 Install the Romex wire into the back of the box in a designated opening. Fit the box and the wire into the space cut into the wall and complete the installation of the junction box.

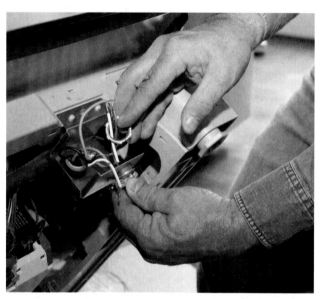

12 Install the 4-ft. minimum length three-prong SJ or SJT insulated cord rated for the circuit through the back of the dishwasher junction box where the Romex wire was removed.

13 Connect the black HOT wires together then the white NEUTRAL together using lineman pliers and yellow wire nuts.

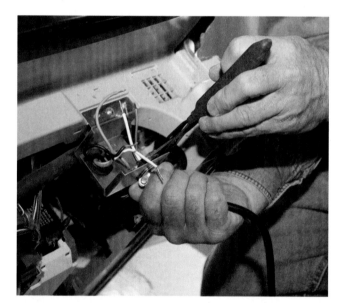

14 Using a ring terminal that matches the size of the wire gauge, crimp the green ground wire of the new cord and secure the ring terminal to the junction box housing. If the junction box of the dishwasher has a green pigtail wire attached, simply wire-nut the two ground wire ends together.

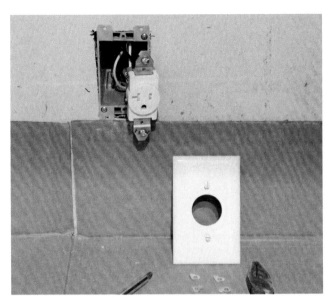

11 Install a grounded, single-device outlet rated to match the breaker for that circuit with the ears removed when using a new old work box. Example: 12 AWG size is controlled by a 20- amp circuit breaker, which requires a 20-amp rated receptacle. Turn the breaker back on and test the new receptacle with a polarized plug analyzer to be sure all connections are correct. Refer to label on the side of the analyzer to ensure this.

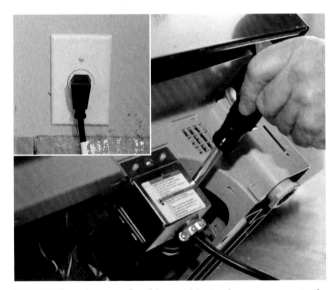

15 Plug the new flexible cord in to the new receptacle installed in the back wall and make sure power exists at the front panel. Reinstall the cover on the dishwasher junction box.

16 Carefully slide the dishwasher back into place and re-install the front panels and the two front panel screws along the bottom. Then reinstall the two screws that attach the dishwasher to the underside of the countertop. Next time the dishwasher needs servicing or replaced, it will be a simple matter of unplugging it to disconnect the dishwasher from the house wiring.

RANGE RECEPTACLE

IN THE PAST, cable for kitchen ranges included two hot wires and a stranded ground/neutral. This type of cable is called service-entrance conductor (SEU) cable. The range receptacle for this kind of cable accommodated a three-prong plug configuration. The problem with this arrangement was that the current-carrying neutral was also used as the grounding conductor for the appliance frame. Today, cables for kitchen ranges are still required to carry two hot conductors, but the neutral wire must also be insulated, and the grounding conductor can be either bare or insulated. It is a four-conductor cable containing three insulated wires and one grounding conductor. Usually, there are two hot wires, a neutral, and a ground wire that is green or bare. This category of cable is called service entrance round (SER) cable. Type NM cable with three conductors and a ground is also allowed. The size used for a kitchen range is usually 6/ 3G SER.

Of the four wires in SER cable, the two hot wires carry the 240 volts required to power the heating elements. The 120-volt power is carried across the neutral to either of the two hot wires—it doesn't matter which one. The 120-volt power is used to run the timer, clock, buzzer, etc. Drawing the neutral current away from the grounding conductor causes the return current to flow safely through an insulated conductor rather than through a bare copper grounding wire. The four-slotted female receptacle into which the SER cable is wired can be surface- or flush-mounted. When a range is not hard-wired but has a cord and plug, the plug must have four prongs to match the receptacle.

If you are installing a new circuit for a new range, remove the jumper wire or strap between the white wire terminal at the range connection box and the frame of the range. If you are using the existing circuit, make sure there is a jumper between the white wire terminal and the frame of the appliance.

INSTALLING A RANGE RECEPTACLE

First determine the location of the range receptacle so it can be reached by the built-in range pigtail. Then cut a hole in the wall, and pull a circuit cable into the room. Join the cable wires to the receptacle, and install the appropriate breaker in the service panel.

TOOLS & MATERIALS

▪ Insulated screwdrivers
▪ Long-nose pliers ▪ Fish tape
▪ Cable ripper ▪ Multipurpose tool
▪ Keyhole or saber saw
▪ Cable clamp and staples
▪ 50- or 60-amp 125/250-volt range receptacle (NEMA 14-50R or 1460R)
▪ 6/3G SER copper cable ▪ 50- or 60-amp double-pole circuit breaker

1 Cut a hole in the drywall for the receptacle cable. Then go into the basement; drill a hole up through the floor; and feed the cable from the service panel into the wall hole. Use a fish tape to pull the cable. Install solid blocking behind the drywall to securely mount the range receptacle to.

2 Strip the sheathing off the cable and the insulation off the individual wires. Then slide the wire ends under their corresponding clamps, and tighten them in place. Attach the receptacle to the wall, and install the receptacle cover.

3 Shut off the power at the main panel breaker switch. Then attach the black and red hot wires to the range breaker, and push the breaker into the bus bar. Install the white neutral wire and the bare ground wire to the neutral and grounding bus bars.

RANGE RECEPTACLES

Older range receptacles had only three slots, combining the current-carrying neutral with the appliance's frame grounding.

Modern range receptacles have four slots, for three insulated wires and a grounding conductor or wire, either bare or insulated.

DRYER RECEPTACLES

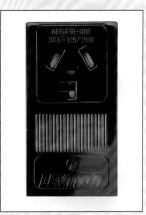 

An older-style dryer receptacle had two angled slots for hot wires and a third elbow-shaped slot for the grounding/neutral.

Newer dryer receptacles have four slots to provide independently for the two hot wires, the neutral, and the grounding wire.

Dryer Receptacle

Like an electric range, an electric dryer uses both 120- and 240-volt power and requires a four-conductor cable. The greater voltage supplies only the heating element while the lesser voltage powers the motor timer and buzzer. Also like ranges, dryers were once powered by two-conductor cable with a ground. Such dryers were fed with 10/2G NM copper cable containing a black hot wire, a white neutral wire, and a bare copper grounding wire. Ten-gauge NM cable is still used, but it must now have three conductors—red, black, and white wires—plus a bare copper grounding wire. This 10/3G NM cable must be connected to a dedicated female four-slot receptacle rated at 30 amps. The cord on the dryer must have a four-prong male plug, and the neutral must not be connected to the dryer frame. The receptacle is usually surface-mounted but can be flush-mounted. When the dryer is shipped to a distributor, the plug and cord are not sent with it. The distributor must install the cord onto the dryer. Before you have a dryer delivered to your home, ask the distributor to install an extra-long, rather than standard-length, cord. The extra cord will permit you to pull the dryer away from the wall for servicing. It is also a good idea to install the plug high enough on the wall so that you will not have to bend far to unplug it.

smart tip

CHOOSING A DRYER

PURCHASING A CLOTHES DRYER OFTEN MEANS CHOOSING BETWEEN A GAS- OR AN ELECTRIC-HEATED MODEL. GAS DRYERS ARE SLIGHTLY MORE EXPENSIVE TO PURCHASE AND MAINTAIN BUT LESS EXPENSIVE TO OPERATE. FOR SOME HOMEOWNERS, HOWEVER, GAS MAY NOT BE AN OPTION. REGARDLESS, YOU CAN CONSIDER OTHER OPTIONS. OLDER DRYERS, FOR EXAMPLE, RELY ON TIMERS OR THERMOSTATS TO SENSE WHEN CLOTHING IS DRY. NEWER MODELS GAUGE HUMIDITY IN A DRYER, ALLOWING PRECISE HEAT CONTROL TO PROTECT CLOTHING FROM DAMAGE. ANOTHER OPTION IS A WRINKLE-GUARD. WHEN HEAT TURNS OFF, THIS KEEPS CLOTHING TUMBLING UNTIL IT'S REMOVED FROM THE DRYER. IF YOU WANT CLOTHING DRIED IN A HURRY, CONSIDER A LARGER DRYER. EXTRA AIR SPACE BETWEEN CLOTHING EXPOSES MORE FABRIC SURFACE, RESULTING IN FASTER DRYING TIMES. FOR AESTHETICS, THINK ABOUT BUILT-IN UNITS. IF YOU LACK SPACE, LOOK AT COMBINATION OR STACKABLE WASHER/DRYERS.

Appliances and Equipment

INSTALLING A DRYER RECEPTACLE

Dryer receptacles must be located within easy reach of the pigtail cord that is mounted on the back of the dryer. So be sure to measure the cord before you pick a location for the receptacle. Also, pick a spot over a wall stud so you can screw the base of the receptacle directly into the stud.

TOOLS & MATERIALS

▪ Insulated screwdrivers ▪ Long-nose pliers ▪ Fish tape ▪ Cable ripper ▪ Multipurpose tool ▪ Keyhole or saber saw ▪ Cable clamp and staples ▪ 30-amp 125/250-volt dryer receptacle (NEMA 14-30R) ▪ Conduit straps ▪ Masonry screws ▪ 10/3G NM cable ▪ 30-amp double-pole breaker ▪ EMT conduit (for masonry walls)

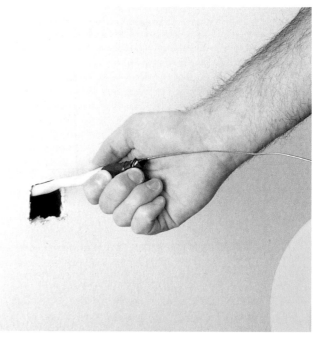

1 Establish a good location for the receptacle; then cut a hole in the wall so that you can fish the circuit cable from the service panel into the room. The standard cable for this job is 10/3G cable, and the standard breaker is a 30-amp 240-volt breaker. Install solid blocking behind the drywall to securely mount the range receptacle to.

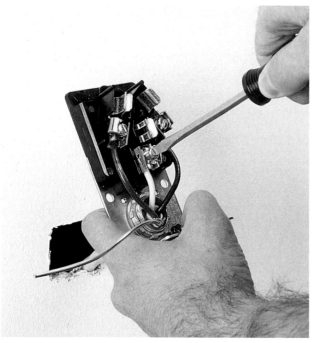

2 Strip the sheathing from the cable and the insulation from the wires. Then join the wires to the receptacle, following the instructions that came with the device. Once all the wires are connected, screw the receptacle base to the wall, and install the cover plate over the base.

3 Install the dryer cable in the service panel using a cable connector. Then strip the sheathing from the cable and the insulation from the wires. Attach the red and black wire to the breaker, and push the breaker into the hot bus. Attach the white neutral wire and the ground wire to the neutral and grounding buses.

Waste-Disposal Unit

Ordinarily, you should mount a disposal-unit switch on the wall off to one side of the kitchen sink. However, if the disposal unit is an add-on, you must choose between the expense of mounting the switch on the wall or simply placing it in the cabinet beneath the sink. Some homeowners choose the latter because it is simpler and less expensive. However, should you need to shut off the disposal unit in an emergency, having the switch readily accessible is safer and more convenient. To mount your switch on the wall, follow the instructions on the next page.

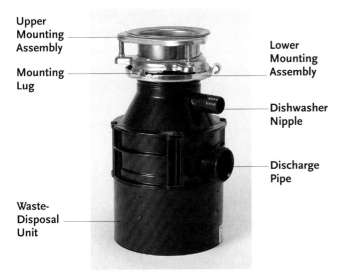

Upper Mounting Assembly

Mounting Lug

Lower Mounting Assembly

Dishwasher Nipple

Discharge Pipe

Waste-Disposal Unit

smart tip

DISPOSAL SAFETY

- Limit waste to non-fibrous foods such as meats, eggshells, coffee grounds, rinds, and peels. Avoid fibrous foods like celery, and bones over ½ inch in diameter.
- Install a ½-hp unit for light use; ¾ hp for heavy use.
- Never use chemical drain cleaners.
- Run water while grinding food to ensure that particles are properly flushed into the sewer system.
- When dismantling the unit or working on electrical connections, shut off power at the main panel.
- Never put your hands into a disposal unit; use tongs to remove objects.

Waste-Disposal-Unit Wiring

Although it may be easier to position a retrofit waste-disposal-unit switch in a sink cabinet, the best location is at the side of the sink where it can be quickly reached in an emergency. Bring a two-wire power cable into the switch box; then from the box to the disposal unit.

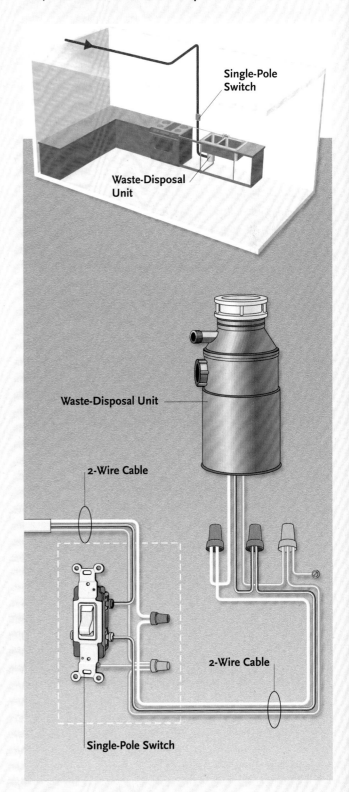

Single-Pole Switch

Waste-Disposal Unit

Waste-Disposal Unit

2-Wire Cable

2-Wire Cable

Single-Pole Switch

Appliances and Equipment

WIRING A WASTE-DISPOSAL UNIT

A waste-disposal unit can be controlled by a switch from two different locations. The first is by using a wall-mounted switch located above the countertop and close to the sink. This is the preferred location. But you can also install the switch in the sink cabinet, on the cabinet wall right next to the cabinet door. Installing this switch is much easier, but it's not as convenient or as safe as the first option.

TOOLS & MATERIALS

- Insulated screwdrivers ▍Cable clamps ▍Long-nose pliers
- Cable ripper ▍Multipurpose tool
- Wire connectors ▍12/2G NM cable
- Switch box ▍Single-pole switch
- Waste-disposal unit

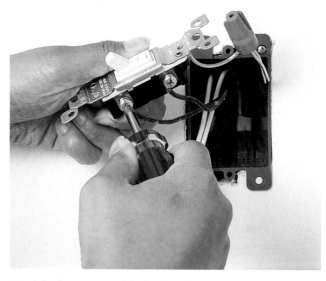

1 Fish the power cable for the disposal unit into the kitchen sink cabinet. Then cut a hole in the wall above the countertop, one below this in the back of the cabinet, and one in the wall behind the cabinet. Push the circuit and switch cables into this hole and up through the wall hole. Install a switch box and a switch.

4 Install the drain flange, which comes with the disposal unit, in the sink drain hole. Take a golf ball size lump of plumber's putty in your hands, and roll it into a ½-in.-diameter rope. Press this around the bottom of the flange. Press the drain spud into the drain hole so the putty squeezes out slightly around the flange.

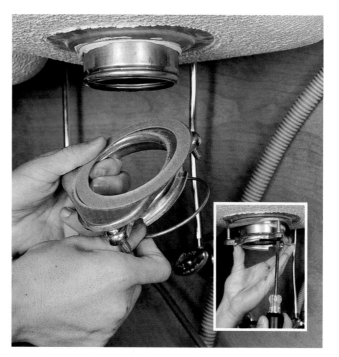

5 The mounting assembly consists of a gasket, sealing flange, mounting flange, and split ring. Lift these parts over the spud. Then install the split ring (inset) This ring fits in a depression around the bottom of the drain spud and holds the other parts in place. Tighten these by turning the flange bolts using a screwdriver.

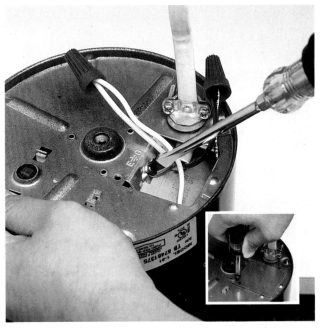

2 Remove the cover plate, and pull the lead wires from inside the unit. Most disposals have just two leads, a black and a white wire. Install the cable that comes from the switch into the bottom of the disposal using a cable connector. Strip the sheathing off this cable and the insulation off the wires. This cable will have three wires, a black, a white, and a bare ground wire.

3 Join the black circuit and appliance wires together using a wire connector. Do the same with the two white wires. Then form a hook on the end of the grounding wire, and attach it to the grounding screw in the base of the disposal unit. Tuck the wires into the disposal base, and install the cover plate (inset).

6 The disposal unit comes with a mounting ring installed at the top. This ring engages with the mounting flange in the mounting assembly that's installed on the bottom of the sink. To join these parts, lift up the disposal unit, and rotate the mounting ring until it fits over the flange.

7 Install the drain line. On single-bowl sinks, add a trap, and attach it to waste piping in the wall. For two-bowl sinks, use a tailpiece extension to connect the disposal to the main drain. For a dishwasher hookup, attach the waste line to the disposal unit (inset). Break the plug; attach the hose to the nipple with a hose clamp.

Appliances and Equipment

INSTALLING A HOT-WATER DISPENSER

Hot-Water Dispenser

Sink-mounted hot-water dispensers deliver water that's 40–60 degrees warmer than standard tap water, at a rate of about 50 cups per hour. The heater unit is mounted in the kitchen sink cabinet and gets its water from the sink's cold-water supply line. Some codes call for these units to be served with a switched receptacle, which is shown here.

TOOLS & MATERIALS

■ Insulated screwdrivers ■ Wire stripper
■ Power drill and bits ■ Adjustable wrench
■ Cable clamps ■ Wire connectors ■ Metal outlet box ■ Switched receptacle ■ Saddle valve ■ Armored cable ■ 15- or 20-amp circuit breaker ■ Hot-water dispenser

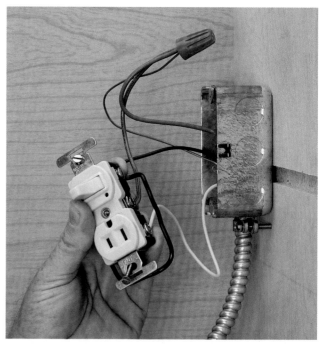

1 Install a metal outlet box on the inside wall of your sink cabinet. Bring an electrical cable, shielded with flexible conduit, to the bottom of the box, and attach it using a box connector. Join a switched receptacle to the cable wires; push the receptacle into the box; and attach it with screws. Attach the cable within 12 in. of the box.

4 Slide the supply tubes at the bottom of the dispenser faucet through the hole in the sink. Then attach the faucet from below using a mounting washer and screw.

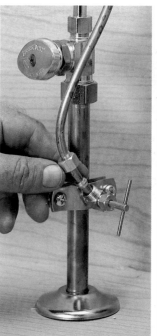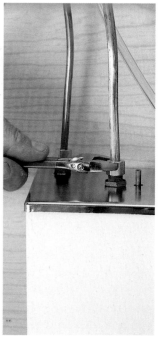

5 To join the dispenser to the saddle valve, install a flexible copper tube between the two. Attach the tube using compression ferrules and nuts (left). Install the two supply tubes that come from the faucet to the top of the dispenser tank. Use compression fittings and an adjustable wrench to attach the tubing (right).

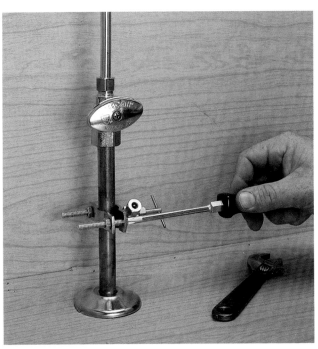

2 The water supply to the heater comes from the cold-water supply line under the sink. To gain access to the water, install a self-piercing saddle valve on the pipe. Make sure to tighten the saddle bolts evenly by alternating between the sides as you tighten.

3 Check the manufacturer's instructions to determine the best place to hang the heater unit. Then attach its mounting bracket to the sink cabinet wall. Hang the unit on the mounting bracket.

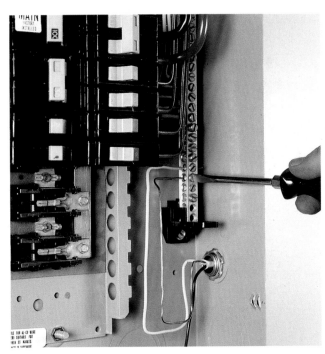

6 Turn off the power to the service panel; then remove the cover; and install the circuit cable into a connector mounted in a side knockout hole. Strip the insulation from the end of the wires; then install the wire and ground wires in the neutral/grounding bus bar.

7 Attach the black (hot) circuit wire to the circuit breaker by tightening it under the terminal screw. Then push the breaker into the hot bus. If your dispenser instructions called for 14-gauge cable, use a 15-amp breaker. If you used 12-gauge wire, use a 20-amp breaker.

INSTALLING A KITCHEN ISLAND RECEPTACLE

Island Receptacle

Kitchen islands almost define the term convenience. As a staging area, these cabinets can't be beat. And as an extra food-prep area, they can take a lot of pressure off the rest of the kitchen—if there's power available. Newer kitchens just about always have receptacles on their islands. But older ones don't. Here's how to install one.

TOOLS & MATERIALS

▌Insulated screwdrivers ▌Utility knife ▌Power drill and bits ▌Saber saw ▌Multipurpose tool ▌Wire connectors ▌12/2G NM cable ▌Electrical box ▌Duplex receptacle ▌Flexible conduit ▌Cable support bracket

1 Start by tracing a standard metal receptacle box at the preferred location. Drill a blade-access hole at all four corners of the box outline. Then, using a saber saw, slide the blade into one of the holes and start cutting. Work carefully to prevent the surface of the cabinet from splitting.

4 Slide the flexible armored conduit into the floor hole. Then feed one end of a 12/2G cable from the service panel (or another circuit) through the conduit and into the box. Attach the conduit to the cabinet wall using a support bracket.

5 Install the cable in the box using a cable connector or an internal box connector. Then, using a utility knife or a cable ripper, strip off the sheathing from the cable, and strip the insulation from the ends of the wires.

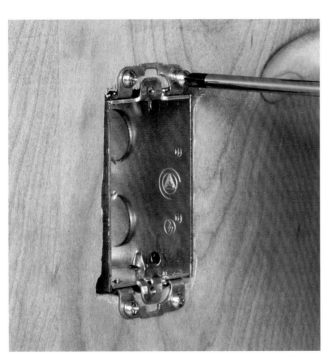

2 Slide the electrical box into the hole, and screw the support ears into the cabinet. Usually it's easier to drive the screws into the cabinet if you prebore screw pilot holes.

3 Locate the best place for the power cable to enter the cabinet; then drill an access hole through the cabinet floor. Because the cable will be exposed to possible damage when it goes through the cabinet, the code requires that it be covered with conduit from the floor to the bottom of the electrical box.

6 Attach the white circuit wire to a silver terminal screw on the receptacle. Attach the black wire to a brass-colored screw on the opposite side. Join the ground wire from the circuit cable to a grounding pigtail using a wire connector. Attach the other end of the pigtail to a grounding screw inside the box.

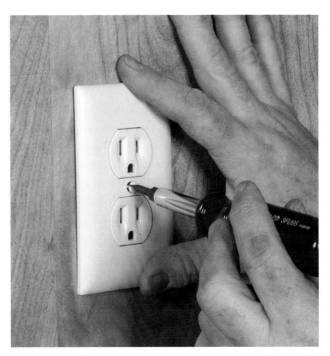

7 Carefully fold the cable wires into the box; then push the receptacle in and screw it to the box ears. Finish up by screwing the cover plate to the receptacle. Then go to the service panel; turn on the circuit power; and check your work.

VENTILATING AND HEATING EQUIPMENT

Ceiling Fans

When it comes to installing ceiling (paddle) fans, homeowners commonly assume that a fan can be suspended from an existing ceiling box. This is often not the case. A ceiling-suspended fan weighing up to 35 pounds, for example, requires an electrical box that is approved for the weight of the fixture [NEC Section 422.18]. If it does not have this approval, an existing box must be replaced with one that does. The electrical box must be firmly secured to the structural framing. If the box is not completely rigid, the fan will wobble. A fan weighing more than 35 pounds must be supported independently of the electrical box [NEC Section 314.27(D)].

Adding a light kit to a ceiling fan is a popular option among homeowners, but be aware that some light kits produce only enough illumination for general-purpose lighting and not for task lighting.

CEILING FAN SUPPORT

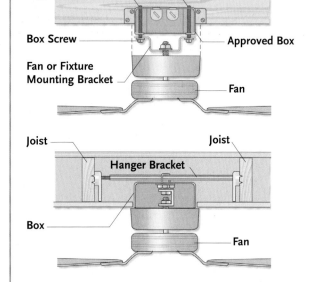

The NEC requires that a ceiling-suspended fan be supported by one of two methods, depending upon the weight of the fixture [Sections 422.18 and 314.27(D)]. If the fixture weighs up to 35 lbs., it can be supported by an electrical box listed for that purpose. If it weighs over 35 lbs., the fixture must be supported independently of the electrical box.

WIRING A CEILING FAN/ LIGHT

project

Installing a standard ceiling fan just requires cutting in a single switch box and a round fan box in the ceiling. But if you want to add a light kit to the bottom of the fan, you must add a second switch in the wall box to control the light.

TOOLS & MATERIALS

▌Insulated screwdrivers ▌Cable clamps ▌Long-nose pliers ▌Cable ripper ▌Multipurpose tool ▌Wire connectors ▌12 or 14/2G NM cable ▌12 or 14/3G NM cable ▌Ceiling an/light ▌Hanger bracket (for fans over 35 lbs.) ▌Fan switch ▌Approved ceiling-fixture box ▌Square light-switch box ▌Light switch

2 Install the mounting bracket. Join the fixture wires to the cable wires using wire connectors. The blacks go together; the whites go together; and the red wire from the switch goes with the third fixture wire—in this case, the blue wire. Join the cable and fixture grounds to a pigtail; connect the pigtail to the fixture grounding screw.

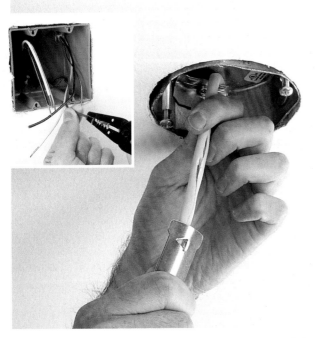

1 Install a double-wide cut-in box in the wall, and fish a power cable into the box (inset). Also fish a three-wire cable from the switch box up to a ceiling-fan box location. Slide the cable into the box, and install the box into the ceiling hole. Strip the sheathing from the cable and the insulation from the wires.

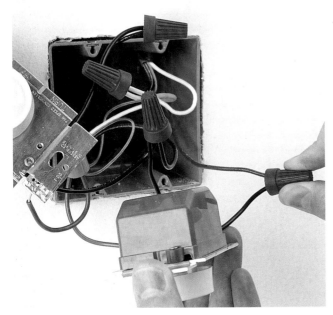

3 In the switch box, join both white wires using a wire connector; join all the ground wires under another wire connector; and hook the light dimmer switch and the fan speed-control switch together, as shown in the wiring diagram at right. (See page 128 for additional fan wiring.)

End-of-Run Ceiling Fan/Light Wiring

In this arrangement, a two-wire cable feeds power into a start-of-run double-ganged switch box. It then proceeds to the end-of-run combination ceiling fan/light along a three-wire cable. The fan/light fixture is controlled by separate speed-control and light dimmer switches.

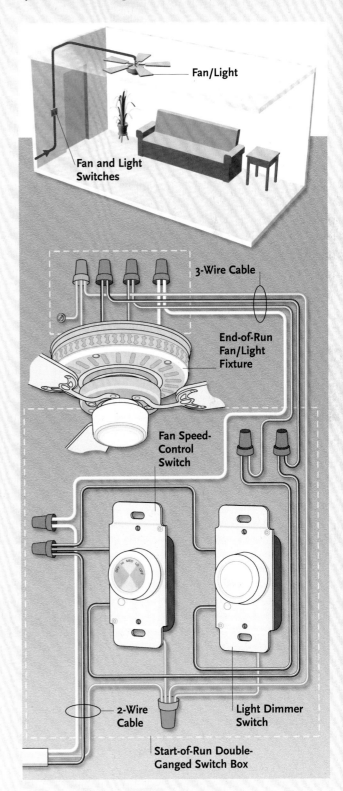

Fan/Light

Fan and Light Switches

3-Wire Cable

End-of-Run Fan/Light Fixture

Fan Speed-Control Switch

2-Wire Cable

Light Dimmer Switch

Start-of-Run Double-Ganged Switch Box

Start-of-Run Ceiling Fan/Light Wiring

Following a switch-loop configuration, in this layout power flows first to the fan/light fixture through two-wire cable. It then proceeds to the double-ganged end-of-run switch box and back to the fixture along a three-wire cable.

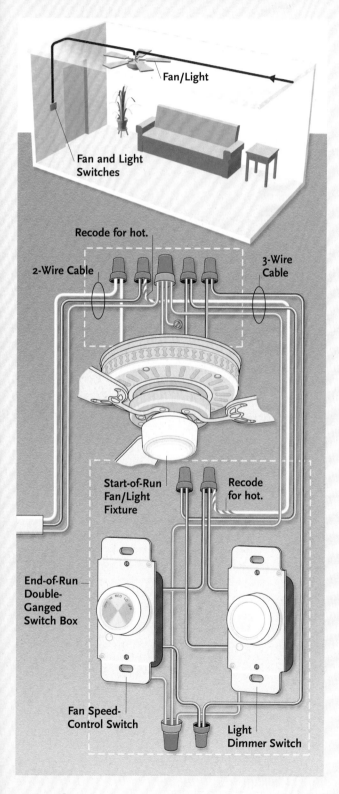

Fan/Light

Fan and Light Switches

Recode for hot.

2-Wire Cable

3-Wire Cable

Start-of-Run Fan/Light Fixture

Recode for hot.

End-of-Run Double-Ganged Switch Box

Fan Speed-Control Switch

Light Dimmer Switch

Whole-House Fans

Installing a whole-house fan in an attic floor is a great way to remove excess heat buildup in your home. The volume of air moved by a fan is measured in cubic feet per minute (CFM). The fan capacity you need is determined by the cubic volume of your home. The CFM rating of the fan also determines the amount of venting area you will need to prevent air pressure from building up in your attic space. As an alternative, a whole-house fan can be installed in an attic gable, but you will still need a louver in the attic floor. It is better to put the entire unit in the floor and use the gable ends and eaves for ventilation. In either case, the size of the fan and venting area must be calculated on the basis of the volume of space being vented. (See "Calculating Fan/Vent Sizes," opposite.) The airflow drawn through screened windows and doors must be at least equal to the airflow through the ventilation system.

A properly sized whole-house fan is capable of changing the air in your home within one to three minutes.

smart tip

USING WHOLE-HOUSE FANS

THE HOME VENTILATION INSTITUTE REC-OMMENDS THE FOLLOWING FOR GETTING THE BEST USE FROM A WHOLE-HOUSE FAN:

- IN THE EARLY EVENING WHEN THE OUT-DOOR TEMPERATURE BEGINS TO DROP, OPEN DOORS AND WINDOWS AND TURN ON THE FAN TO COOL THE HOUSE.
- AT BEDTIME, CLOSE ALL BUT THE BED-ROOM WINDOWS.

CALCULATING FAN/VENT SIZES

TO DETERMINE FAN SIZE, first calculate the total volume of all the rooms in your house. Multiply the length x width x height of each room, and add them all together. An ideal airflow would be one air change per minute. Simply divide the total room volume by 2 to obtain airflow in cubic feet per minute (CFM). A 2,000-square-foot home with an 8-foot ceiling height, for example, would have a volume of 16,000 cubic feet. Ideal airflow would be 16,000 ÷ 2 = 8,000 CFM. For such a house, you would need a fan having an airflow rate of 8,000 CFM. The venting area would be about 1 square foot of unobstructed space per 750 CFM of airflow. In this example, that would be almost 11 square feet. For ¼-inch screen multiply this by a factor of 1.00; for ⅛-inch screen, 1.25; and for 1⁄16-inch screen, 2.00.

Fan Sizes and Exhaust Ratings

Fan Size	Typical Exhaust Rating in CFM
24"	3,500–5,500
30"	4,500–8,500
36"	8,000–12,000
42"	10,000–15,000
48"	12,000–20,000

An effective fan will change the air in a house at least once a minute. Check the manufacturer's exhaust rating in cubic feet per minute (CFM) to determine whether a fan has the capacity you need.

- IN EARLY MORNING, OPEN ALL WINDOWS AND ALLOW THE FAN TO COOL DOWN THE REST OF THE HOUSE.
- AS THE OUTDOOR TEMPERATURE RISES, CLOSE ALL DOORS AND WINDOWS TO KEEP THE COOL AIR INSIDE. IT IS ALSO A GOOD IDEA TO CLOSE DRAPES ON THE SUNNY SIDE OF THE HOUSE.

Whole-House Fan Wiring

In this wiring layout, two-wire cable feeds power into a junction box mounted near the whole-house fan. Three-wire cable takes power on to the fan speed-control switch box and then returns to the junction box. A three-wire armored cable powers the fan motor.

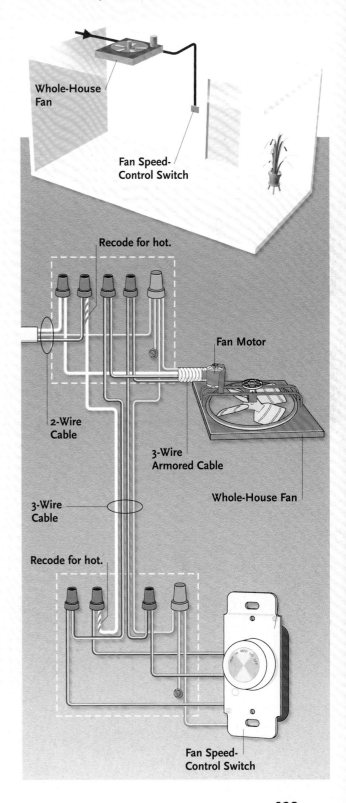

Whole-House Fan

Fan Speed-Control Switch

Recode for hot.

Fan Motor

2-Wire Cable

3-Wire Armored Cable

Whole-House Fan

3-Wire Cable

Recode for hot.

Fan Speed-Control Switch

INSTALLING A WHOLE-HOUSE FAN

A whole-house fan is a great way to keep things cooler in the summer without installing central air conditioning. The wiring on this job isn't difficult, but installing the fan can be. Just make sure, if you tackle the job, to install a fan that's the right size. (See page 129.)

TOOLS & MATERIALS

▐ Insulated screwdrivers ▐ Keyhole saw ▐ Long-nose pliers ▐ Pencil ▐ Hammer ▐ Stepladder ▐ Measuring tape ▐ Circular saw ▐ Power drill ▐ Multipurpose tool ▐ Work gloves ▐ Dust mask ▐ Safety glasses ▐ 12/2G and 12/3G NM cable ▐ Whole-house fan ▐ Joist lumber ▐ ½-inch plywood panels ▐ 1½-inch rigid foam board ▐ Bracing lumber ▐ Nails ▐ Speed-control fan switch ▐ Wire connectors ▐ Screened louver vents ▐ Junction box ▐ Switch box ▐ Wire staples

1 Establish a good location for the fan in the ceiling just below the attic. In a two-story house, just above the top of the stairs is a good choice. Mark an opening on the ceiling according to the fan manufacturer's instructions; then cut out the drywall using a drywall or keyhole saw.

4 Install the fan louver underneath the fan assembly by screwing its frame to the rough opening lumber. Make sure the louvers move freely and weren't distorted during shipping or installation.

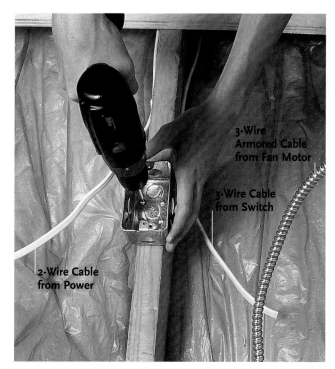

3-Wire Armored Cable from Fan Motor

3-Wire Cable from Switch

2-Wire Cable from Power

5 Install a junction box next to the fan's plywood box by screwing it to the top of a ceiling joist. The box will hold the two-wire power cable, the three-wire switch cable, and the three-wire armored cable that comes from the fan.

2 Cut away any ceiling joist segments that fall in the fan opening. Install headers on both sides of the opening to support the cut joists and to frame a rough opening to support the fan. Use the same size lumber that was used for the ceiling joists.

3 Install the fan in the opening; then build an insulated plywood box above it. Also build an insulated cover for the box for use in the winter months when the fan isn't in use. The box sides should extend about 12 in. above the top of the fan.

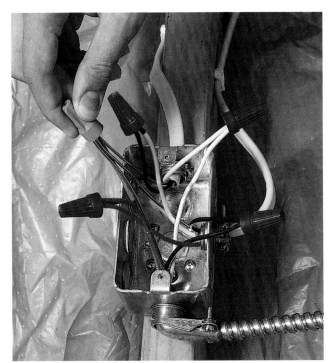

6 Install the two cables in the box using cable connectors and the armored cable using an armored-cable connector. Strip the sheathing from the cables and the insulation from the wires. Then join the wires using wire connectors, as shown above.

7 Install the switch box in the wall, and fish the three-wire cable from the fan junction box in the attic into the switch box. Strip off the cable sheathing and wire insulation, and attach the switch leads to the cable leads. Push the switch into the box, and add a cover plate (inset).

Appliances and Equipment

A range hood may be ducted or ductless. A ducted system exhausts air to the outside, while a ductless system recirculates filtered air.

project

WIRING A DUCTED RANGE HOOD

Range Hood

Range hoods come in two styles: ducted and ductless. A ducted hood removes heated air by exhausting it outside, while a ductless hood filters smoke and odor from the air and returns the air directly to the room. An average-size range hood circulates or removes 400 to 600 cubic feet of air per minute (CFM). The fan rating will determine the size duct you need for a ducted system.

TOOLS & MATERIALS

▮ Insulated screwdrivers ▮ Reciprocating saw ▮ Long-nose pliers ▮ Pencil ▮ Hammer ▮ Cable ripper ▮ Measuring tape ▮ Caulking gun ▮ Power drill ▮ Multipurpose tool ▮ Work gloves ▮ Dust mask ▮ Safety glasses ▮ Aviation snips ▮ Nonmetallic fish tape ▮ NM cable ▮ Ducted range hood ▮ Duct elbow (if needed) ▮ Ducting ▮ Cable clamp ▮ Wire connectors ▮ Silicone caulking or roofing compound ▮ Wall or roof cap ▮ TEK-head screws ▮ Aluminum flashing

RANGE HOOD DUCTING

THROUGH WALL

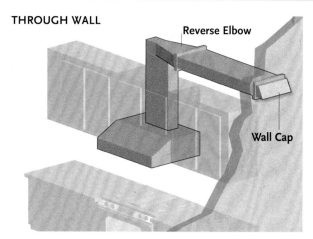

Reverse Elbow

Wall Cap

THROUGH ROOF

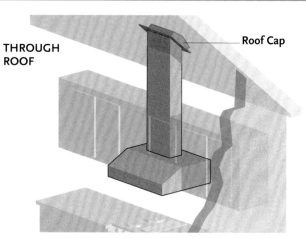

Roof Cap

If the duct comes out through the side wall of the house, install a duct cap. Make sure to seal around the perimeter of the cap with exterior caulk. If the duct goes through a soffit, you'll need a transition fitting to connect the round duct to the square grille.

1 Establish the best location for the exhaust duct on the outside wall following the range hood manufacturer's instructions. Cut the hole in the wall using a reciprocating saw (inset). Then cut a matching hole in the wall cabinet that will be above the range hood. Install the cabinet and then the ductwork.

2 Ducted range hoods can exhaust air through the roof or the wall (see facing page). The roof option requires installing a metal roof cap that is sealed to the shingles with plastic roof cement (top). The wall option requires a wall cap that is caulked against the siding to make a weatherproof seal.

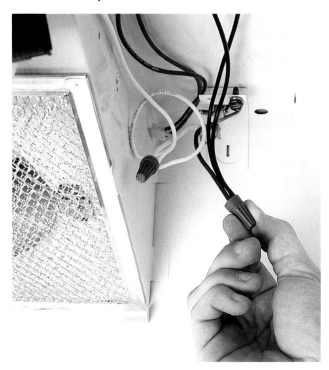

3 Lift the hood against the bottom of the wall cabinet, and attach it using the fasteners supplied by the manufacturer. Also, install the light bulbs and the grease filter panels.

4 Fish a power cable into the range-hood electrical box through an approved cable clamp connection. Then strip the sheathing from the cable and the insulation from the wires. Join the wires using wire connectors, following the wiring diagram supplied for your specific unit.

Appliances and Equipment

Ventilating Fans

To remove moist air and odors effectively from a bathroom, you need to match the fan capacity to the room's volume. Ventilating fans are sized by the number of cubic feet of air they move each minute (cfm). A fan should change all of the room's air at least eight times each hour. Use the following formula for rooms with 8-foot ceilings.

Fan capacity (cfm) =
Room Width (feet) x Room Length (feet) x 1.1

Fans are also rated in "sones" for the amount of noise they produce, from 1 to 4 sones. A fan rated at 1 sone, the quietest, is about as loud as a refrigerator.

Power to the Fan. There are a couple of code-approved ways to provide power to a fan housing. Usually the easiest approach is to bring a power cable to the fan and then run a switch leg cable down to the wall switch. In this configuration the wire connections are made as follows: the white wires from the fan and the power source are joined; the black wire from the power source and the switch cable are joined; and the black wire from the power source is joined to the white wire (wrapped with black tape) on the switch cable.

At the switch, there is a single cable. Code the white wire with black tape; then connect the black wire to one terminal and the white-with-black tape wire to the other.

Another approach is to run power to the switch box and then run a switch leg up to the fan. In this option, the white wires from the fan and the power cable are joined, and the black wires from the fan and the power source are joined.

smart tip

PLANNING AHEAD

BECAUSE VENTING AN EXHAUST FAN CAN BE DIFFICULT, IT'S TEMPTING TO OMIT THE DUCT ALTOGETHER AND JUST VENT THE EXHAUST FAN INTO THE ATTIC SPACE. NO BUILDING CODES PERMIT THIS AND THEIR MOTIVATION ISN'T BASED ON AN EXCESS OF CAUTION. BY DUMPING LARGE AMOUNTS OF WATER VAPOR INTO THE ATTIC, YOU VIRTUALLY ASSURE THAT WATER WILL CONDENSE OUT OF THE VAPOR AND COAT THE FRAMING MEMBERS. THIS GREATLY INCREASES THE LIKELIHOOD OF SERIOUS DAMAGE CAUSE BY ROT.

INSTALLING A VENTILATING FAN

project

An exhaust fan is a welcome addition to any bathroom because it takes away harmful water vapor. To install one, first locate the best position and cut a hole in the ceiling. Attach the fan housing to a framing member, and install the duct work. Then complete the job by cutting a vent hole through the roof and installing a vent hood.

TOOLS & MATERIALS

▌Insulated screwdrivers ▌Power drill and bits ▌Reciprocating saw or saber saw ▌Hammer ▌Multipurpose tool ▌Cable ripper ▌Work gloves, safety goggles, and face mask ▌Wire connectors ▌14/2 NM cable with ground ▌Switch ▌Pigtails ▌Switch box ▌Ventilating fan ▌Flexible aluminum duct and vent-cap kit ▌10-inch-long rigid aluminum duct ▌Duct tape ▌Silicone caulk and caulking gun ▌8d common nails ▌Drywall screws ▌Roofing cement

VENTILATING FAN DUCTING

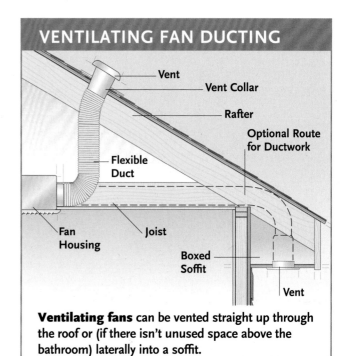

Ventilating fans can be vented straight up through the roof or (if there isn't unused space above the bathroom) laterally into a soffit.

Appliances and Equipment

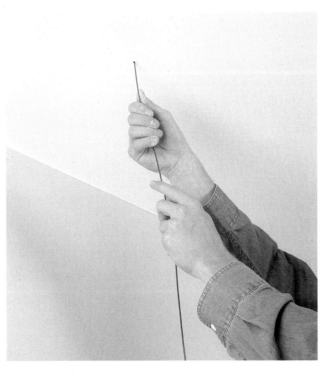

1 Establish the approximate location of the fan on the ceiling. Then drill a small hole, and feed a coat hanger wire up through the ceiling and the insulation above if any is present.

2 Pull back any insulation to find the reference wire. Then establish the fan location. It should be installed against a framing member to provide adequate support. Drill small holes through the ceiling at the corners of the fan.

3 Press the fan housing against the ceiling so its corners fall within the four holes you drilled from above. Trace around the housing to mark the ceiling.

4 Cut the drywall using a keyhole or saber saw.

Continued on next page.

Appliances and Equipment

Continued from previous page.

5 Place the fan housing over the ceiling hole, and screw it to a framing member. Then choose the best path for the vent duct, and attach it to the end of the fan housing with a screw clamp.

6 Extend the vent duct up to the point where it goes through the roof. Then attach an aluminum vent collar to the end of the duct using duct tape.

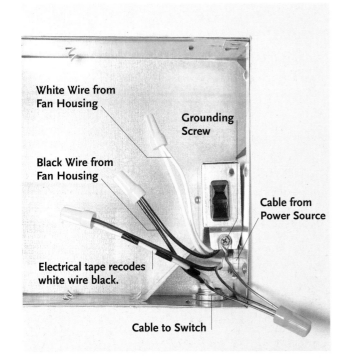

White Wire from Fan Housing

Grounding Screw

Black Wire from Fan Housing

Cable from Power Source

Electrical tape recodes white wire black.

Cable to Switch

9 Every electrical outlet has to be supplied with power either directly from a branch circuit or from a controlling switch. In the photo above, the power comes directly from a circuit into the fan motor and then is directed down to a controlling switch.

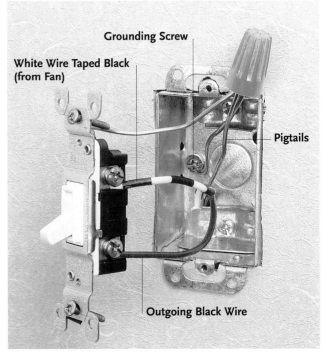

Grounding Screw

White Wire Taped Black (from Fan)

Pigtails

Outgoing Black Wire

10 When power goes to the fan first and only a single cable goes to the switch below, the wiring connections are simple. The black wire goes to one terminal. The white wire (that should be wrapped in black tape) goes to the other terminal.

7 Cut a vent hole through the roof using a saber saw. If you don't have one, use a reciprocating saw or a keyhole saw.

8 Once the hole is cut, pull up the vent duct, and attach it to the vent hood. Seal the adjacent shingles with roof cement.

White Wire from Power Source

Grounding Screw

White Wire from Fan Housing

Black Wire from Fan Housing

Black Wire from Power Source

11 When the power goes to the switch first and only a single cable goes to the fan, connect the fan by joining like-colored wires with wire connectors.

12 After installing the fan housing, put the fan into the housing and plug its pigtail extension cord into the receptacle provided in the housing. Cover the whole assembly with the fan grille.

INSTALLING AN ELECTRIC WATER HEATER

project

Electric Water Heater

The biggest trick to installing a new electric water heater is to position it as closely as possible to where the old one was so that the pipe hookups are easier. If you don't have the appropriate cable for the power supply, run a separate 240-volt circuit back to the service panel, and install a new breaker.

TOOLS & MATERIALS

■ Tubing cutter ■ Propane torch ■ Groove-joint pliers ■ Screwdrivers ■ Multipurpose tool ■ Wire connectors ■ Copper pipe and fittings ■ Pipe thread tape ■ Solder and flux ■ Steel wool ■ 10/2G cable ■ Cable clamps ■ Metal conduit and fittings ■ Foam pipe insulation ■ Temperature-and-pressure relief valve

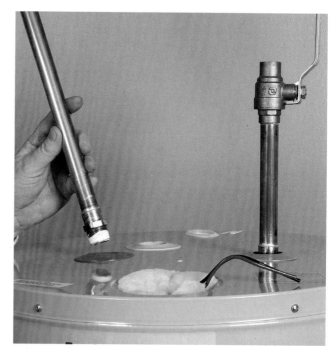

1 Begin by removing your existing water heater and rolling the new one into the space that was vacated. Putting the new one in the same place as the old one makes the plumbing hookups easier. Thread the copper pipe risers, with male adapters on the ends, into the top of the tank using dielectric pipe fittings.

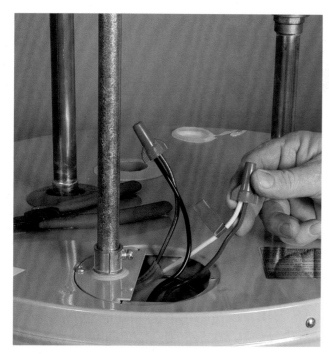

4 Join the black wires using a wire connector, and the white cable wire to the red tank wire using another wire connector. Mark the white wire using red or black tape to indicate that it's a hot wire. Attach the ground wire to the grounding screw.

5 Slide pipe insulation over the tank pipes to help reduce heat loss (inset). Install a temperature and pressure (T&P) relief valve in the side of the tank. Apply thread-sealing tape; then turn it into place in a clockwise direction. This valve protects the tank from becoming pressurized and possibly exploding.

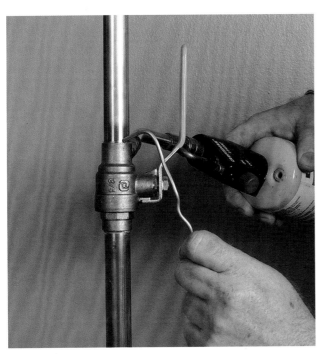

2 Join the risers at the top of the tank to the plumbing lines above with solder. To make these joints, clean the pipe and the fitting with steel wool. Then apply flux to both parts, and push them together. Heat the joint until the solder melts.

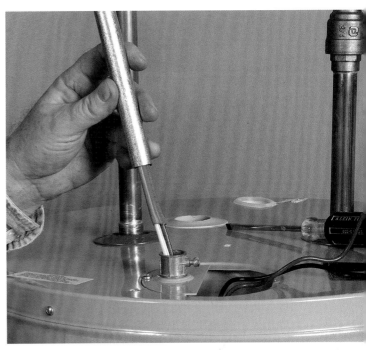

3 Bring 10/2G cable to the top of the tank inside the metal conduit. Push the wires into the tank box, and slide the conduit into its coupling on top of the tank. Tighten the setscrew to hold the conduit securely. In many cases, the heater should be connected to a disconnect switch. Check local requirements.

6 Install a drainpipe into the bottom of the T&P valve. Just cut a pipe so it falls within a couple inches of the floor; solder a male adapter onto one end. Then apply thread sealer to the threads and tighten the assembly in place.

7 Run the cable to the service panel, and turn off the main breaker. Remove one of the knockout plates; install a cable connector; then slide the cable through the connector; and tighten it in place. Strip insulation from the wires, and install them in the breaker. Mark the white wire using red or black tape.

Appliances and Equipment

EASY WATER HEATER UPGRADES

Pipes of dissimilar metals that are connected in plumbing systems will, over time, corrode each other through the process of electrolysis. In the case of copper pipes connected to a water heater, corrosion can occur in the thread area, leading to small leaks and, eventually, larger leaks. To keep this from happening, install **dielectric unions**.

A **dielectric union** is comprised of a plated female-threaded adapter that is attached to the pipes protruding from the top of the water heater, as in the photo for step 1 on page 138. The threads must be sealed using a thread sealant compound or Teflon tape before installing. Tighten by hand and use a pipe wrench to tighten an additional half or complete turn.

TOOLS & MATERIALS

- Pipe cutter or hacksaw
- Adjustable wrench
- Teflon tape
- Stainless Steel flex hoses:
  - ¾" stainless water heater flex hose (correct length required) for hot water side
  - ¾" stainless steel water heater flex hose with integral ball valve (correct length required) for cold water side

1 The plated hex nut and plastic isolation sleeve are placed over the end of the house copper water pipe with the threads and shoulder of the sleeve facing the end of the pipe.

Dielectric fittings used for copper solder pipes.

Appliances and Equipment

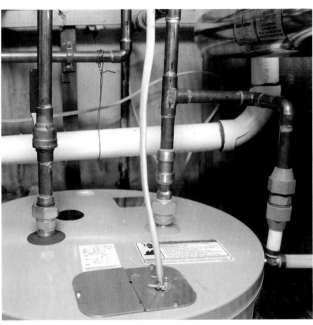

2 The brass-shouldered sleeve and copper water pipe end are cleaned, fluxed, and soldered together. Insert the flat rubber washer on top of the female threaded adapter and hand tighten the plated hex nut onto the male threads of the female adapter. Tighten by hand and use a pipe wrench to tighten an additional half to complete turn.

3 Check for leaks at the union connection and slightly tighten more to stop the leak. Overtightening can affect the corrosion resistance of the dielectric fitting through damaging the plating finish.

Stainless steel flexible hose connections with ball valve

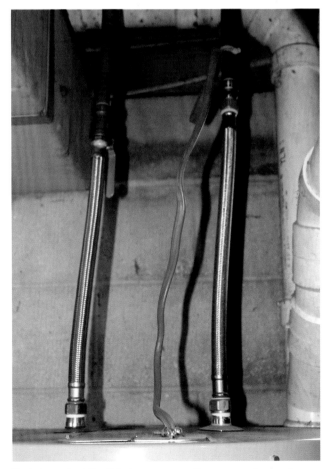

Stainless steel flexible hose connections on water heater

Appliances and Equipment

INSTALLING RADIANT FLOOR HEATING

Electric Radiant Floor Heating

Ceramic, slate, and tile floors are elegant and durable, although they often feel cold even at comfortable room temperatures. Radiant floor-heating systems are an effective and economical method of removing the chill from ceramic, marble, or stone type floors. Installed between the subfloor and the finish flooring material, these cables will heat parts of the floor to a comfortable warm temperature with a minimal use of electricity.

Heating Systems. There are a number of these products on the market, but in general they consist of an insulated, flexible resistance-type heating element with attached nonheating leads. The product shown here has the conductors contained in a fabric material. The fabric keeps the conductors spaced properly on the floor.

Where the final flooring is tile or stone, the system should have a heat density of 10 or 15 watts per square foot. The NEC requires that these systems be provided with ground-fault circuit-interrupter protection.

Floor Preparation. Heating cable may be installed over wood flooring. Drive protruding nails flush or below the flooring, and sand uneven edges where floorboards come together. Nail down any loose flooring. For concrete floor installation, remove all debris, and grind down sharp edges of small cracks. Some manufacturers recommend installing a thermal barrier or layer of insulation under the heating cables. Secure the thermal barrier to the floor using a high-temperature adhesive.

Testing Cables. Unpack the heating cable, and check the ohms, or resistance between the two conductor wires, to ensure that there is no break in the nonheating and resistance conductors. Each set of heating cables is marked with the proper ohms. Follow the manufacturer's testing procedures carefully. They are designed to keep you from tiling over a heating system that does not work.

Placing Cables. Plan the heating-cable layout. Remember that the nonheating conductors must be able to reach the control unit, which will be mounted on the wall. Don't overlap the heating cables, and do not allow the nonheating leads to overlap the heating area of the mat. Section 424.44(E) of the NEC requires nonheating conductors to be protected where they leave the floor by rigid metal conduit, intermediate metal conduit, rigid nonmetallic conduit, electrical metallic tubing, or by other approved means.

3 Spread a layer of thinset adhesive over the heating pad, and start laying tiles. Don't cover the entire floor with adhesive. Spread only as much as you can comfortably cover with tile before the thinset dries. Consult the product container for drying times. When all the tiles are laid and dry, grout the joints.

TOOLS & MATERIALS

- Insulated screwdrivers
- Scissors
- Long-nose pliers
- Multimeter
- Notched trowel
- Sponge
- Grouting float
- Duct tape
- Radiant heating kit and controls
- Ceramic tile or other suitable flooring
- Acrylic or latex thinset tile adhesive
- Mortar for tile grout

1 Determine where you want radiant heat. There's no need to cover the entire floor, just the areas where you commonly walk or stand in bare feet. Cover this part of the floor with thinset mortar; let it dry; and install the fabric and cable over the thinset.

2 Locate the best spot for the temperature sensor by following the instructions that come with the radiant heating components. Use duct tape to hold the sensor cable in place on the heating pad. Make sure the cable falls between the heating elements.

4 Mount an outlet box on the side of a stud, and bring a power cable into the box. Bring the power wires from the heating mat, through rigid conduit, into the other side of the box. Join the like-colored wires using wire connectors.

5 Once the power hookups are done, install the temperature sensor cables to special terminals on the controller thermostat. Follow the product instructions for the specific unit that you are installing.

Appliances and Equipment

INSTALLING A SCHLUTER® UNDERLAYMENT SYSTEM

project

SCHLUTER SYSTEMS has designed two different types of underlayment mat system that will work extremely well with all tile products, including floors, wall, and showers, which can include an array of heat applications to keep you warm in the bathroom.

Every job requires careful planning and decision-making on form, function, and style of the complete tile job to be installed, including which Schluter underlayment mat to choose—either the Schluter-DITRA or the Schluter-DITRA-HEAT. Both products provide uncoupling to prevent cracked tile and grout as well as waterproofing; the HEAT product also provides selective heating. In addition, consideration must be given for the type of floor substrate the system will be installed over. Is it wood, concrete, or another building material? In any case, the design parameters of the system will accommodate just about every type of material.

TOOLS & MATERIALS

- Schluter-DITRA-HEAT underlayment roll
- thin-set adhesive
- 5-inch Kerdi tape roll
- desired floor tiles
- sanded floor grout
- Schluter programmable thermostat, heat sensor, and heat wire kit
- Simpson steel stud guard screwdriver
- notched floor trowel

1 Begin over any floor substrate that is structurally sound and does not have surface defects. Use a wet mop to clean the floor prior to beginning layout of the underlayment. This will ensure the top surface is free of dust and will increase the bonding strength of the adhesive layer that must be added beneath the underlayment.

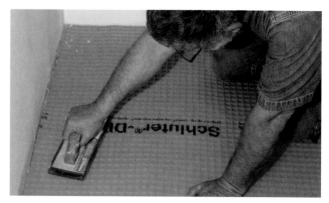

4 Using a rubber grout float or a flat wooden trowel, smooth the underlayment material from the center to the outside edges to eliminate any air pockets under it. Repeat the adhesive spreading step and this step at the opposite end of the section and on every section until the floor is covered with the underlayment.

7 You can also create a watertight perimeter around the room wherever the underlayment material meets with a finished wall surface. Just as each seam was covered and sealed previously, cover and seal at the bottom of all vertical walls that meet the floor system.

2 Burnish the adhesive layer into the top of the sub-floor surface with the straight edge of a notched floor trowel, covering the entire floor.

3 Roll the underlayment out along the entire area to be tiled. Then lift the underlayment, starting at one end, so that half of the floor is exposed. Using the notched end of the notched trowel, spread more adhesive over the floor area, then place the underlayment material back down over the notched adhesive.

5 Schluter-DITRA material will require that all the seams running the length of the material have adhesive applied over the joint with a flat trowel; usually, a 4-inch drywall taping knife works best for this.

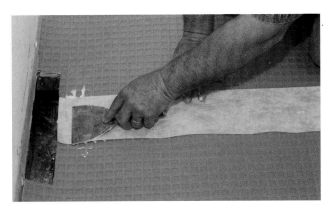

6 After spreading the adhesive along a joint, apply the 5-inch-wide Kerdi tape over the seam. Then use the drywall knife to burnish the tape into the adhesive. Complete this for every seam between the rows of the underlayment.

8 Using the drywall taping knife to embed the Kerdi tape into the floor and wall adhesive for a smooth application. When complete around the room, the Kerdi tape provides a strong watertight application, which is not achievable when using older-style, rigid underlayment boards.

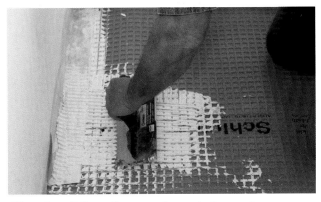

9 To install floor tiles over the underlayment, use a notched floor trowel to create an even, wide area larger than the tiles to form an adhesive bed for the tiles to set on.

10 Install the tiles according to the manufacturer's instructions. You will typically apply some adhesive to an area, install a tile or two, and then repeat, rather than applying adhesive to the entire area and installing all the tiles at once.

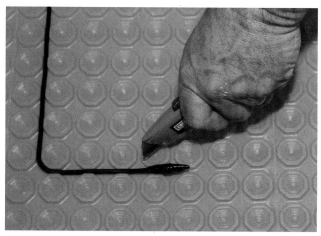

11 When using the Schluter-DITRA-HEAT underlayment, the project will require using a Schluter programmable thermostat, heat sensor, and heat wire. The floor heat sensor has to be placed over the underlayment, and the sensor's wires have to be run behind the wall to an approved junction box, typically a single gang size box. You will need to notch the underlayment so that the end of the sensor can lay unobstructed in the mat design.

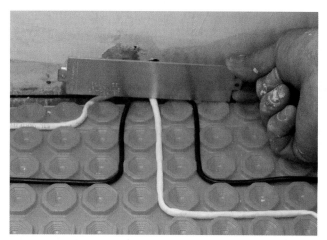

14 Install an approved stud guard plate over the opening at the bottom of the wall, below the programmable thermostat, to protect the wires running behind the wall to the junction box.

15 Inside the thermostat junction box will be 120-volt line wires (black and white), heat wire ends that create the closed loop, and heat sensor wires.

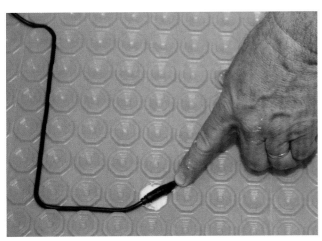

12 Cut the required notch and place the sensor flush with the mat design.

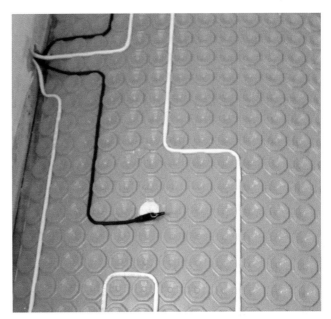

13 Run the heat wire behind a finished wall and apply it over the underlayment in a specified pattern, not crossing over the heat sensor or sensor wires.

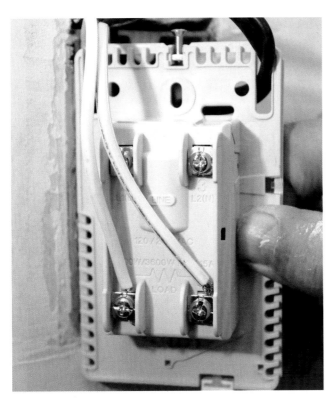

16 Connect the heat sensor wires, heat wires, and line voltage wires to the programmable thermostat as detailed in the instruction booklet provided by the manufacturer.

Fri 3:29 PM
71°

72°
On Schedule

Next Change: 74° 6:00 PM

Adjust...

17 Finish installing the programmable thermostat by mounting it to the junction box with the screws included. Follow the instruction booklet to program all of the digital functions of your new thermostat, and enjoy years of a stable, warm, watertight floor system.

Appliances and Equipment

BASEBOARD HEATING

ELECTRIC BASEBOARD HEATERS, also called resistance heaters, are extremely popular because of their low cost and ease of installation. They are manufactured in sizes ranging from 2 to 10 feet in length, 7 to 8 inches in height, and approximately 2 to 3 inches in depth. Electricity is supplied to a heating element running the length of the baseboard heater. Aluminum fins attached to the heating element absorb the heat and radiate it out into the surrounding space. Electrical current enters a baseboard heater from either end. Most units require 240 volts and draw about 1 amp or 250 watts per linear foot of baseboard. Units using 120 volts are also available. Be aware, however, that if they are wired to a 240-volt line, they will severely overheat and breakdown, and could cause a fire. They also draw twice as much current as a 240-volt heater, making them extremely inefficient and requiring larger and more expensive cable to power them.

Although baseboard-heating units can be powered separately, you do not need to run a separate cable for each heater. One cable can feed several heaters in paral-

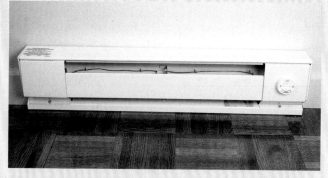

Electric baseboard heaters come in various lengths and can be installed individually or in parallel, as long as circuit capacity is not exceeded.

lel, provided that the circuit capacity is not exceeded. The branch-circuit cable connects to one heater and is then circuited to the next in line so that all the heaters are wired in parallel—not in series.

Twelve-gauge cable is most commonly used to wire baseboard heaters. However, even though 12-gauge cable can carry 20 amps of current, you cannot power 20 linear feet of baseboard heating on a wire of this size.

BASEBOARD HEATING WIRING IN PARALLEL

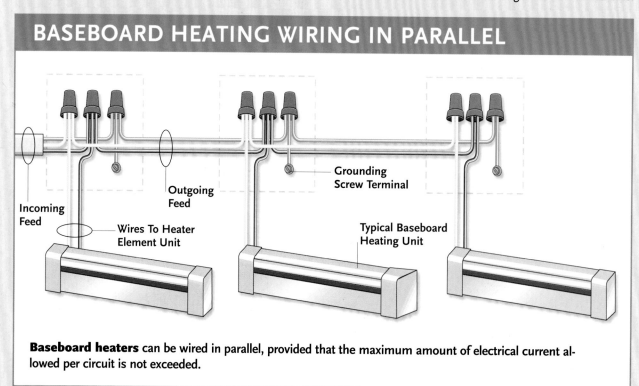

Incoming Feed

Outgoing Feed

Grounding Screw Terminal

Wires To Heater Element Unit

Typical Baseboard Heating Unit

Baseboard heaters can be wired in parallel, provided that the maximum amount of electrical current allowed per circuit is not exceeded.

Such a heater, if run continuously for three or more hours, will load the cable to its maximum capacity. It should not be loaded beyond 80% of its capacity, which would be 16 amps, or 16 linear feet of heater.

You can install baseboard heaters in virtually any room in a house. Place baseboard heating on the coldest walls in a room—usually the outside walls below window openings. However, don't locate the heating units below wall receptacles because rising heat can cause a cord hanging across a heater to become brittle, resulting in wire damage and a short-circuit. On walls that already have or require receptacles, install heaters in short sections, placing the receptacles on the wall between the heaters. An alternative is to purchase baseboard heaters that have built-in receptacles wired on a separate cable.

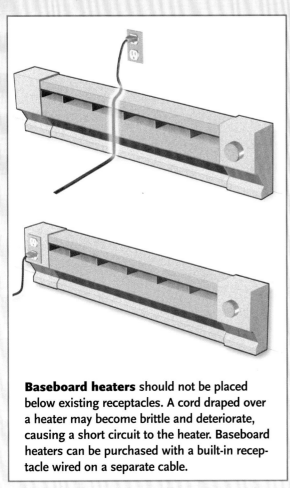

Baseboard heaters should not be placed below existing receptacles. A cord draped over a heater may become brittle and deteriorate, causing a short circuit to the heater. Baseboard heaters can be purchased with a built-in receptacle wired on a separate cable.

Baseboard Heater Wiring

In this setup, 240-volt baseboard heaters are laid out in series and controlled by a wall-mounted thermostat. Two-wire cable extends through the thermostat to power the heaters. Only one cable connects to the last heater in the series.

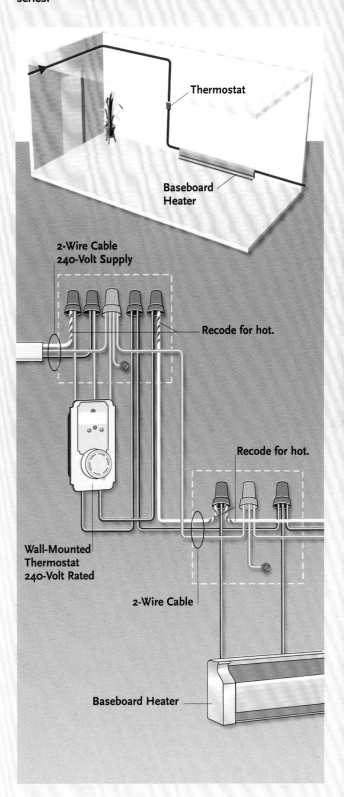

Thermostat

Baseboard Heater

2-Wire Cable 240-Volt Supply

Recode for hot.

Recode for hot.

Wall-Mounted Thermostat 240-Volt Rated

2-Wire Cable

Baseboard Heater

WIRING A BASEBOARD HEATER

Electric baseboard heaters are easy to install, especially compared to forced-air ducts or hot water pipes. Unfortunately, their power costs are generally high. But these units are a good choice for room additions in warm climates.

TOOLS & MATERIALS

- Keyhole or saber saw ■ Long-nose pliers ■ Cable ripper ■ Power drill ■ Insulated screwdrivers ■ Knockout punch ■ Wire stripper ■ 12/2G NM cable ■ Wire connectors ■ Electrical tape ■ Cable clamp ■ TEK-head screws ■ Baseboard heating unit ■ Double-pole thermostat (in-heater or wall-mounted) ■ Electrical box (for wall-mounted thermostat)

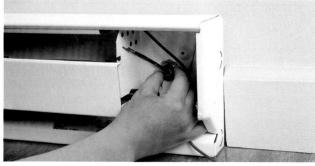

1 Establish the best wall location for the heater, and cut out the baseboard molding in this area so the heater can fit flat against the wall. Cut a cable hole in the wall, and fish a power cable from the service panel into this hole (top). Pull the cable into the heater, and secure it with a cable connector.

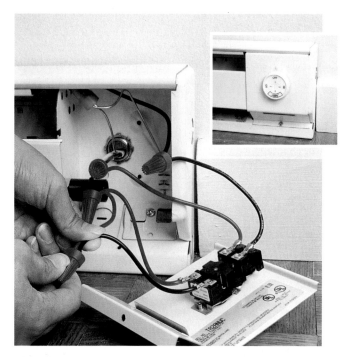

3 The heater can be controlled by either a wall-mounted thermostat or a heater-mounted unit (inset). To install a heater-mounted thermostat, join the circuit cable wires to the thermostat wires using wire connectors, following the wiring diagram that came with the heater unit.

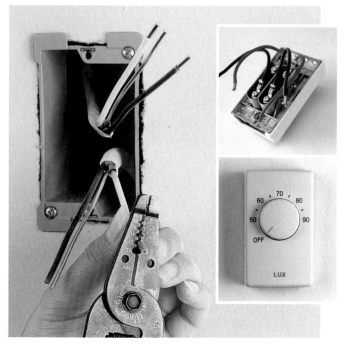

4 A wall-mounted thermostat (inset) is mounted in an electrical box. Fish a power cable and the heater cable into this box. Then strip the cable sheathing and the wire insulation. Join the thermostat wires to the cable wires according to the wiring diagram supplied by the thermostat manufacturer.

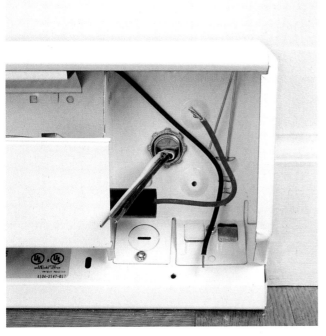

2 Push the heater against the wall, and attach it according to the manufacturer's instructions. Some units, for example, require 1 in. of clearance between the bottom of the heater and the floor.

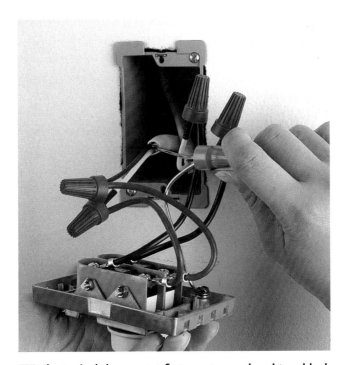

5 The typical thermostat features two red and two black wires. Join the black thermostat wires to the power wires, coding the white power wire with black tape. Then attach the red thermostat wires to the heater wires, again marking the white wire with black tape.

RECESSED WALL HEATER

A RECESSED WALL HEATER is ideal for spot-heating small areas not easily reached by other types of heaters, such as a mudroom or bathroom. This type of heater is preferred over a combination ceiling unit that includes a fan, a light, and a heater because it places the heat closer to the floor, and it can be operated by a thermostat. If desired, use a wall-mounted timer instead of a thermostat to operate the fan. It is best to install a 240-volt unit because it will draw less current than a 120-volt heater. A 120-volt heater may also short circuit, creating a fire hazard, if it is attached to a 240-volt line.

A recessed wall heater is typically mounted inside a simple metal box. The metal box is then mounted vertically or horizontally inside a stud space. Recessed wall heaters come in various sizes ranging from 750 to 1,000 watts for smaller units, to 1,500 watts for larger ones. Using 1 amp per 250 watts as a rule of thumb, you can see that a 1,500-watt heater draws about 6 amps of current. As long as the total circuit current doesn't exceed 16 amps, the heater can be added to another heater circuit. If wired by itself, the cable gauge should be No. 12 because the heat produced corresponds to the amount of voltage accessed by the heater. The less voltage the unit gets, the less heat it produces and the more inefficient it becomes. Smaller-gauge wire reduces the amount of accessible voltage, making it impossible to install a larger heating unit later on, should you want one.

Recessed wall heaters provide spot heat in small areas like bathrooms. The heaters can be operated by a thermostat or a timer.

Appliances and Equipment

INSTALLING A RECESSED WALL HEATER

A wall heater can be controlled with either a wall-mounted thermostat or by a simple dial thermostat on the front of the unit. Because wiring a remote thermostat can be difficult, we chose the on-unit option here. This choice is a good one, especially for bathrooms that are used infrequently.

TOOLS & MATERIALS

■ Insulated screwdrivers ■ Keyhole or saber saw ■ Long-nose pliers ■ Hammer ■ Measuring tape ■ Cable ripper ■ Power drill ■ Multipurpose tool ■ Cable clamp ■ Nonmetallic fish tape ■ 12/2G NM cable ■ Electrician's tape ■ Wire connectors ■ 2-by framing lumber ■ TEK-head screws ■ Recessed wall heater ■ Electrical box (for wall-mounted thermostat)

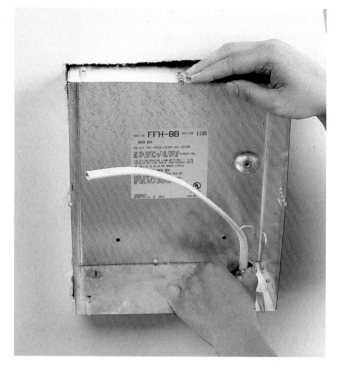

1 Establish the best location for the heater, then cut a hole in the wall, and fish a power cable from the service panel into this opening. Connect the cable to the heater housing using a cable connector, then push the housing into the wall.

2 Attach the housing to the wall studs by driving screws through the metal sides. Then strip the cable sheathing and the wire insulation using a multipurpose tool. Slide the heater into the housing, and feed the cable wires into the electrical box on the front of the heater.

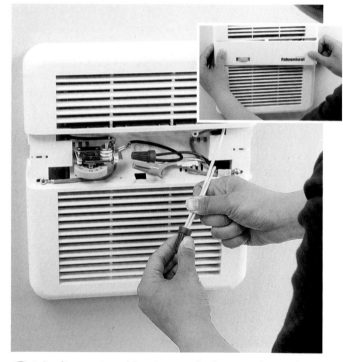

3 Join the power cable wires to the heater wires using wire connectors, keeping the whites together and the blacks together. Join the ground wires under a green connector, and mount the heater grill over the wires (inset).

Appliances and Equipment

SAFETY EQUIPMENT

Hardwired Smoke Detectors

Though battery-powered smoke detectors are widely used and readily available, most building codes now require hardwired smoke detectors (with battery backup) in a home. In addition, all hardwired residential smoke detectors must be interconnected so that when one alarm sounds, they all sound. If you purchase any smoke detectors, be certain that they have these capabilities—many don't. Continue to use your battery-powered detectors as a backup system, remembering to change the batteries at least twice a year.

Most building codes now require homes to have hardwired smoke detectors. Use battery-powered detectors only as a backup.

WIRING SMOKE DETECTORS

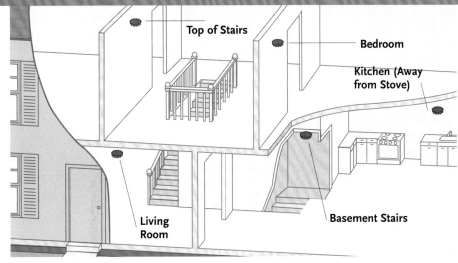

Top of Stairs

Bedroom

Kitchen (Away from Stove)

Basement Stairs

Living Room

TYPICAL DETECTOR LOCATIONS

Place smoke detectors, left, high on the walls where their mechanisms can sense rising smoke. Ideal locations include the top of stairs, bedrooms, and hallways at each bedroom door. Most codes call for at least one detector on every level of the house.

Smoke detectors, below, can be wired independently or in parallel. To wire in parallel, use a three-wire smoke detector. When one alarm sounds, they will all sound.

DETECTOR WIRED INDEPENDENTLY

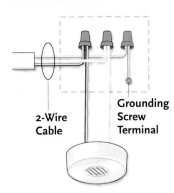

2-Wire Cable

Grounding Screw Terminal

DETECTORS WIRED IN PARALLEL

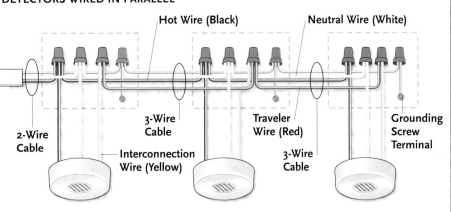

Hot Wire (Black)

Neutral Wire (White)

2-Wire Cable

3-Wire Cable

Interconnection Wire (Yellow)

Traveler Wire (Red)

3-Wire Cable

Grounding Screw Terminal

HARD-WIRING SMOKE DETECTORS

project

There's no question that hard-wired smoke detectors are worth what they cost and the time they take to install. Some detectors, such as those in bedrooms and hallways, can often be installed from the attic above. But detectors that fall on ceilings between floors are more difficult to install. (For help on fishing wires through ceilings see pages 28–30.)

TOOLS & MATERIALS

- Insulated screwdrivers ▌ Wire stripper
- Long-nose pliers ▌ Cable ripper
- Multipurpose tool ▌ Fish tape
- Cable clamps ▌ Wire connectors
- 14/2G or 12/2G NM cable z 14/3G or 12/3G NM cable ▌ Ceiling boxes ▌ Smoke detectors

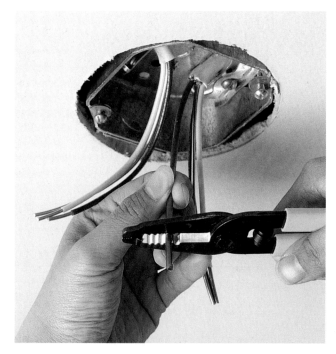

1 Establish the locations of all your smoke detectors, and cut a hole in the ceiling or wall for each one. Fish a two-wire power cable to the first hole, and a three-wire cable between the rest of the holes. Install these cables in cut-in boxes, and install the boxes. Strip away the cable sheathing and wire insulation.

2 Using wire connectors, join the black wires together, the white wires together, and the ground wires together. The red wire from the three-wire cable is attached to the yellow wire from the smoke detector.

3 Plug the fixture wires into the smoke detector wiring module. Then attach the module to a mounting plate on the ceiling box. Install the other detectors in the same way, and test the system to make sure it works well.

HARD-WIRING CARBON MONOXIDE DETECTORS

project

Carbon monoxide (CO) detectors are as important to life safety as a smoke detector. Carbon monoxide can accumulate from any number of sources, including clogged chimneys, gas or wood-burning stoves, or gas heaters—even a car left running in a garage. Like smoke detectors, carbon monoxide detectors can be battery operated or hardwired. As with smoke detectors, CO detectors can be wired in parallel.

TOOLS & MATERIALS

■ Insulated screwdrivers ■ Long-nose pliers
■ Cable ripper ■ Multipurpose tool ■ Fish tape ■ Cable clamps (if boxes are metal)
■ Wire connectors ■ 14/2G or 12/2G NM cable ■ 14/3G or 12/3G NM cable ■ Wall or ceiling boxes ■ Carbon monoxide (CO) detectors

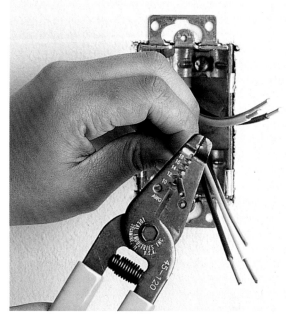

1 Locate the detectors according to the manufacturer's instructions. Then cut holes in the wall for cut-in boxes. Fish two-wire cable into the first box, and connect the first box to the other detectors with three-wire cable. Install the boxes, and strip off the sheathing and wire insulation.

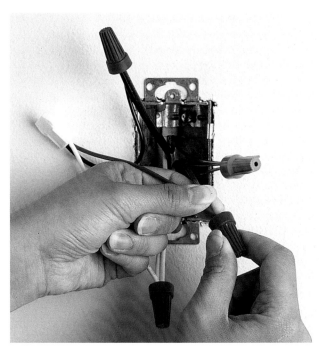

2 The detector leads are black, white, and red. Join these to like-colored wires inside the box using wire connectors. Join together the grounding wires using a grounding pigtail, and attach the pigtail to the grounding screw in the back of the box.

3 Attach the mounting bracket to the electrical box. Then plug the wiring module into the back of the detector, and attach the detector to the mounting plate. Turn on the circuit power, and test all the detectors by pressing their test buttons.

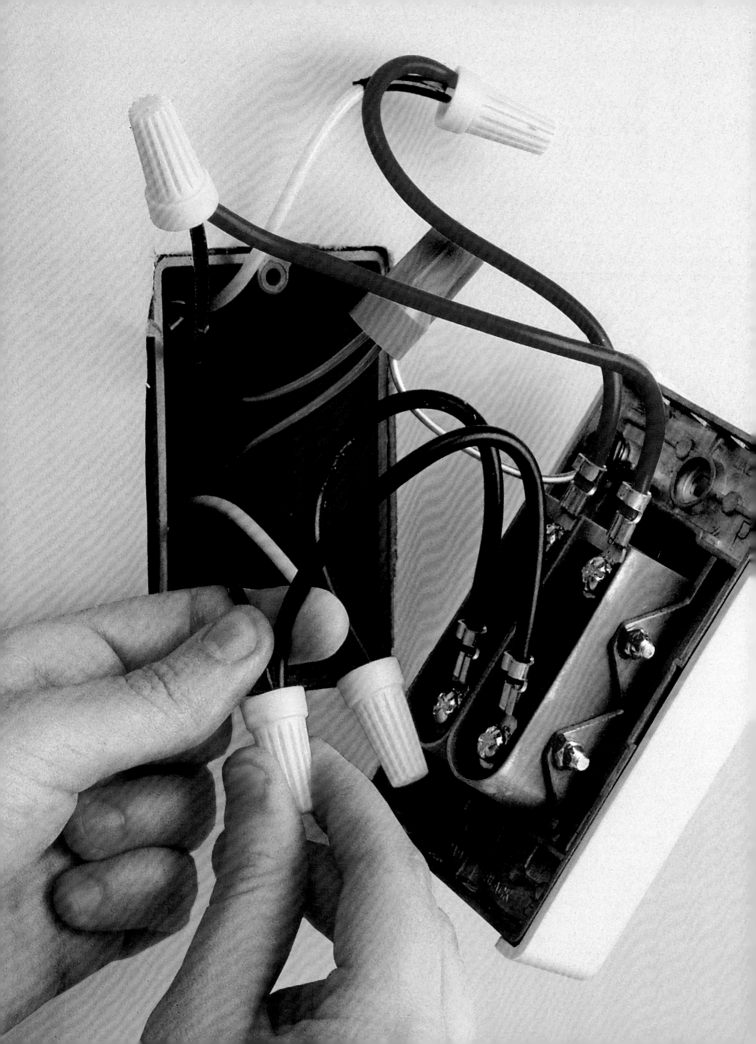

specialty wiring

SO FAR standard 120- and 240-volt residential circuits have been discussed. Many devices used in contemporary homes, however, require much less voltage to operate. Such devices include but are not limited to bells, chimes, timers, sensors, alarms, thermostats, antennas, and tele-communications equipment. Because low-voltage wiring presents few hazards, it is barely touched upon by the NEC, except as it pertains to recreational vehicles and RV parks.

LOW-VOLTAGE POWER

What It Is and How It Works

Low-voltage power is defined as 30 volts or less supplied through a transformer, a device that reduces standard 120-volt house current to the current required to power low-voltage equipment. A transformer may be mounted near or be directly attached to a junction box. In either case, the low-voltage wiring is connected to the transformer, which is in turn connected to the 120-volt wiring in the junction box. The current is converted as it passes from the box through the transformer and proceeds from the transformer to the low-voltage switch and/or device.

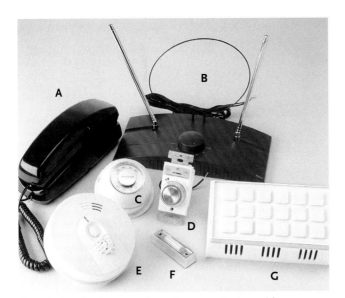

Specialty devices, such as timer controls and heat detectors, use standard 120-volt current. Low-voltage devices, such as chimes, telephones, and thermostats, use 30 volts or less. A–telephone; B–TV antenna; C–thermostat; D–timer control; E–smoke detector; F–doorbell; G–door chimes

Power is provided to low-voltage equipment by means of a step-down transformer that reduces standard 120-volt current to the lower voltage required. A–24-volt transformer; B–16-volt transformer; C–8- to 24-volt transformer

INSTALLING A LOW-VOLTAGE TRANSFORMER

Low-Voltage Transformers

Transformers are usually composed of two tightly wound coils of wire. Because the coils, known as primary and secondary windings, are close together, as a current passes through the primary winding, magnetic flow produces another current in the secondary winding. In a low-voltage or step-down transformer, the primary coil—rated at 120 volts—has more windings than the secondary coil. A reduction in windings results in a proportional reduction in voltage, with the secondary coil usually providing 8 to 24 volts.

TOOLS & MATERIALS

▮ Insulated screwdrivers
▮ Hammer ▮ Long-nose pliers
▮ Wire stripper ▮ Cable ripper
▮ Cable clamp ▮ Wire connectors
▮ Transformer with locknut
▮ 14/2G NM cable ▮ Mounting bracket ▮ Screws or nails
▮ Octagonal junction box

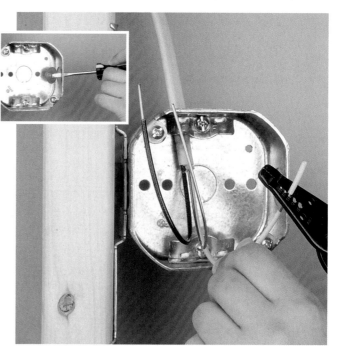

1 Start by mounting a metal octagonal box on the side of a stud or joist. Then remove the knockout plate on the side of the box (inset). Bring the circuit wire into the box, and tighten the box clamp or install a cable clamp. Strip the sheathing from the cable and the insulation from the wires.

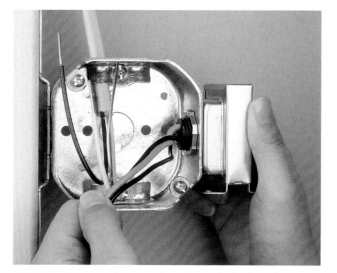

2 Slide the transformer wires through the knockout hole, and mount the transformer on the box using the nut that's provided. If the insulation hasn't been stripped from the ends of the transformer wires, do it now.

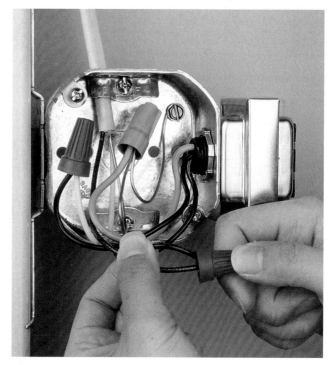

3 Join the two black transformer wires to the white and black circuit wires using connectors. Join the ground wires from the circuit and the transformer to a grounding pigtail using a wire connector. Attach the other end of the pigtail to the grounding screw inside the box.

Low-Voltage Wire

Because it carries such low secondary power, low-voltage wiring requires only a thin layer of plastic insulation. Low-voltage wiring may consist of a single conductor or multiple conductors wrapped in cable. This type of wiring encompasses a variety of uses from connecting simple bells and chimes to wiring sophisticated home theater, telecommunications, and computer networking systems. (See the table, below, "Low-Voltage Wire and Cable.") Typically, low-voltage wires extend in size from 14 gauge down to 24 gauge (AWG) and even smaller. The NEC does not permit this type of wiring to run in the same raceways, conduits, or cables as wires carrying normal voltage (Article 725). In addition, low-voltage wires may not occupy any electrical box containing higher voltage wiring, unless the box is properly partitioned. Low-voltage wires must generally be separated from higher-voltage wiring by 2 inches or more.

Low-voltage wires can be fished, stapled, and spliced the same way as conventional wiring. In some ways, more care should be taken with low-voltage wires because most of them are small gauge and more fragile. Just as full-voltage wire must be joined at screw terminals or be spliced inside a junction box, low-voltage wires must be connected or spliced inside a terminal jack or other type of specialized coupling device. Today, most electronic equipment comes with its own specialized wiring and terminal connectors to make properly insulated splices. Common connectors are also available and are usually color-coded red for 22- to 18-gauge wire and blue for 16- to 14-gauge wire.

LOW-VOLTAGE WIRE AND CABLE

Wire Type	Description	Gauge	Typical Usage
Lamp Cord *Zip Cord*	Two insulated wires that can be pulled or "zipped" apart	18	Lamps, small appliances, cords
Flat Ribbon Cable	Several insulated, color-coded wires that can be "zipped" apart	24	Computer circuit/ serial bus connections for keyboards, scanners, printers
Bell Wire	Single or multistranded, insulated, color coded	18	Bells, chimes, thermostats, timers, control circuits
Video Co-axial Cable	A single insulated wire wrapped by a foil and braided shield	RG-59 *22-Gauge Core*	Television antenna connections, home entertainment
	Quad-shielded cable containing 2 foil shields, 2 braided shields	RG-6 *18-Gauge Core*	Cable, satellite television antenna connections, home entertainment
D-Station Cable	Cable containing four insulated, color-coded wires	24–28	Permanent, indoor, home-telephone wiring
Category 5 Cable	Cable containing four pairs of insulated, color-coded wires	24	Increased circuit capacity for home computer, telecommunications

Low-voltage wires and cables are available in a variety of types and gauges that are suitable for different purposes, including wiring bells and chimes, telecommunications equipment, and home theaters.

Specialty Wiring

WIRING APPLICATIONS

Bells and Chimes

Although modern homes are more likely to have chimes than doorbells or buzzers, their wiring systems are essentially the same. Because a doorbell or chime needs less than 120 volts of power to operate, you will have to install a step-down transformer to reduce house voltage to 24 volts. Some systems, however, may need as little as 15 volts. (See "Installing a Low-Voltage Transformer," on page 158.) Be sure to use a transformer that is right for the signal system you are installing.

Once a low-voltage transformer is in place, you must make three separate connections to complete the doorbell or chime circuit. The push button is the switch that, when pressed, completes the circuit by ringing the signal.

DOORBELL CIRCUITS

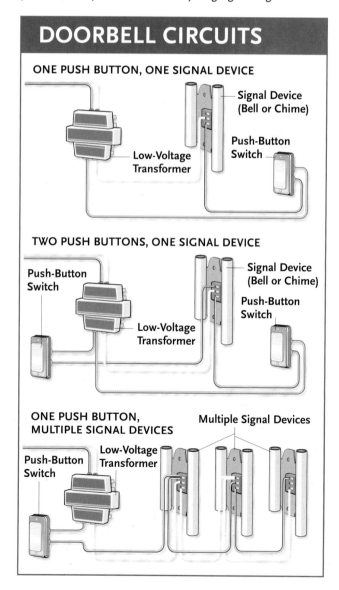

ONE PUSH BUTTON, ONE SIGNAL DEVICE

Signal Device (Bell or Chime)
Push-Button Switch
Low-Voltage Transformer

TWO PUSH BUTTONS, ONE SIGNAL DEVICE

Push-Button Switch
Signal Device (Bell or Chime)
Push-Button Switch
Low-Voltage Transformer

ONE PUSH BUTTON, MULTIPLE SIGNAL DEVICES

Multiple Signal Devices
Low-Voltage Transformer
Push-Button Switch

project

INSTALLING DOOR CHIMES

The busier your house is, the more you need door chimes. A simple door knocker may have worked when you were a kid, but it doesn't stand a chance against a home theater system or any number of kitchen appliances. Fortunately, installing chimes isn't very hard and requires only common tools.

TOOLS & MATERIALS

▌Insulated screwdrivers ▌Long-nose pliers ▌Continuity tester ▌Multi-tester ▌Multipurpose tool ▌Fish tape ▌Power drill and ⅜-inch bit ▌Caulking gun and silicone caulk ▌Toggle or molly bolts ▌Two doorbell push-button switches ▌Door chimes ▌Low-voltage bell wire

smart tip

TESTING DOOR CHIMES

AFTER INSTALLATION, PRESS EACH BUTTON. IF THE CHIMES SOUND, THE INSTALLATION IS COMPLETE. IF THE PUSH-BUTTON SWITCHES DON'T WORK, THE PROBLEM IS WITH EITHER THE TRANSFORMER OR THE WIRING BETWEEN THE TRANSFORMER AND THE CHIMES. IF ONE BUTTON WORKS BUT THE OTHER DOES NOT, THE TROUBLE IS IN THE SWITCH OR THE WIRING CONNECTING THE SWITCH TO THE CHIMES UNIT. IF THE TRANSFORMER MAKES NO HUMMING SOUND, IT MAY BE FAULTY OR THE CIRCUIT MAY BE DEAD. TO TEST THE CIRCUIT, TOUCH THE PROBES ON A MULTI-TESTER TO THE ENDS OF THE CIRCUIT WIRES WHEN THE CIRCUIT IS ON. IF THE MULTI-TESTER DOES NOT DETECT POWER WITHIN 2 VOLTS OF ITS RATING, REPLACE THE TRANSFORMER; IF IT DOES, HAVE AN ELECTRICIAN INSPECT THE CIRCUIT.

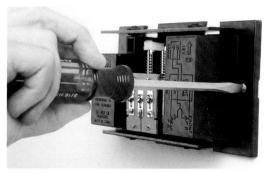

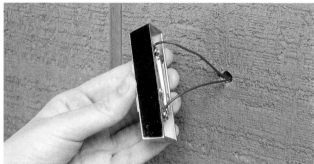

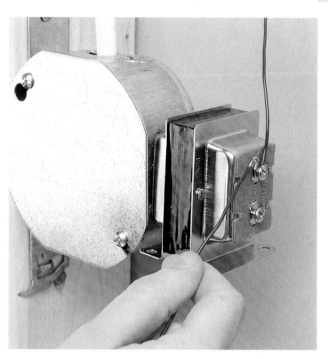

1 Begin by choosing a good location for the chimes unit. The goal is to be able to hear the signal throughout the house, which usually means mounting it near the center of the house. Once the site is located, attach the chimes unit to the wall (top). Then mount a push-button switch at each entrance to the house.

2 Strip the wire insulation from the ends of all the wires that connect the push-button switches with the low-voltage transformer and chimes. Then attach one red wire from each switch to one of the terminal screws on the transformer.

3 When running the wires from the switches to the chimes, label which wire goes to the front of the house and which goes to the back. Then connect the front wire to the FRONT chimes terminal, and the back-door switch wire to the REAR terminal.

4 Once the switch wires are attached to the transformer, run another wire from the second terminal on the transformer to the terminal marked TRANS on the chimes. Tighten it securely in place. Then install the chimes cover to the chimes base (inset), and test the installation.

Specialty Wiring

WIRING A CLOCK-TIMER SWITCH

Timers

Timers can turn on your porch light at dusk or control your thermostat when you're not home during the day. Also, timers operate electrical devices for a set length of time—turning off a heat lamp or exhaust fan when its task is completed. State-of-the-art digital timers can be programmed to perform even more sophisticated automation tasks, such as random security switching—turning several lights and other devices on and off during the course of a day to simulate your presence while you're away from home. Clock-type switches operate by trippers that rotate on an electronically motorized dial. When the tripper reaches a preset time, a set-pin switches the circuit on or off. A digital timer does essentially the same thing, switching on and off electronically at the time set by using push-button controls. When installing a clock-timer switch you wire the device you wish to control into the switch box. A clock-timer switch must be wired in the middle of a run.

TOOLS & MATERIALS

- Insulated screwdrivers
- Long-nose pliers
- Wire stripper
- Cable ripper
- Red and green wire connectors
- Switch box
- Clock-timer switch
- 14/2G NM cable

smart tip

EASY SECURITY

SPECIALTY SWITCHES ARE A GREAT WAY TO CONTROL THINGS THAT ARE OTHERWISE DIFFICULT, OR ANNOYING, TO CONTROL, SUCH AS TURNING LIGHTS ON AND OFF IN A RANDOM PATTERN WHILE YOU'RE AWAY ON VACATION.

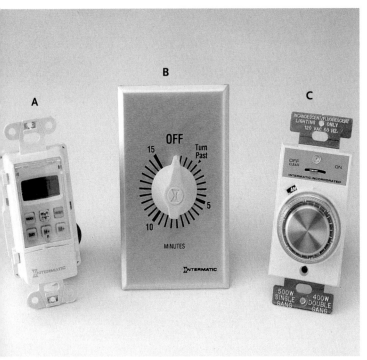

Many types of switching devices perform specialized functions. A–programmable-timer switch; B–time-delay switch; C–clock-timer switch

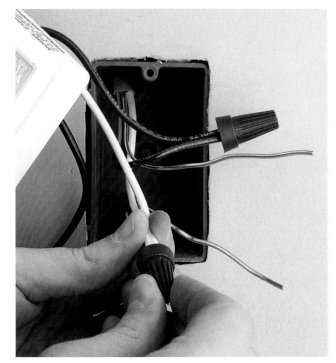

3 Join the white wires from both cables and the switch using another wire connector. Make sure all the wire connectors are as tight as possible. These connectors can become loose and the wires come apart if they aren't tightened properly.

1 Cut a box hole in the wall where you want the switch to be located. Then fish cables from the power source and the fixture into this hole. Feed the cables into a cut-in switch box, and install the box in the hole. Strip the sheathing from both cables and the insulation from all the wires.

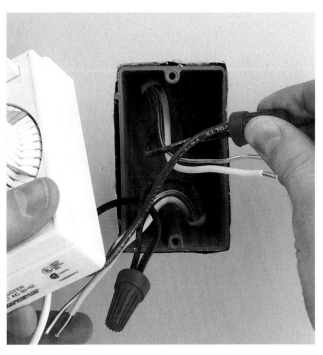

2 This switch came with three leads on the back: one red, one black, and one white. Join the red and black switch wires to the black wires from the power cable and the fixture cable using wire connectors.

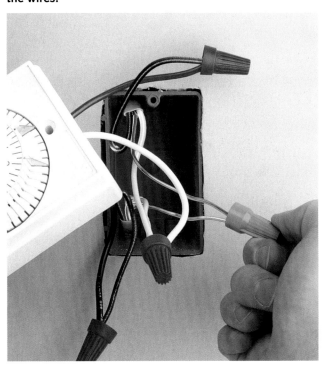

4 Join the ground wires from the two cables together using a wire connector. Because a plastic box is being used here, no grounding pigtail is required. The box doesn't have a grounding screw to receive the end of the pigtail.

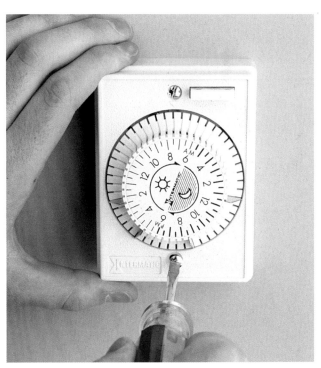

5 Carefully push the wires back into the box so none will be pinched when the switch is installed. Then screw the switch to the box; turn on the circuit power at the service panel; and test the operation of the switch.

Specialty Wiring

TIME-CONTROL SWITCHES

BECAUSE A TIME-DELAY SWITCH, unlike a clock-timer switch, does not require a neutral connection, it can be installed either in the middle or at the end of a wire run. Instead of three wires coming off the switch, there will only be two. Connect the black lead wires from the timer to the black hot wires from the circuit and fixture cables; then splice the two neutral circuit wires. Pigtail the bare copper grounding wires from the cables to the grounding screw in the switch box, if the box is metal. A digital-control switch is typically installed in the same way.

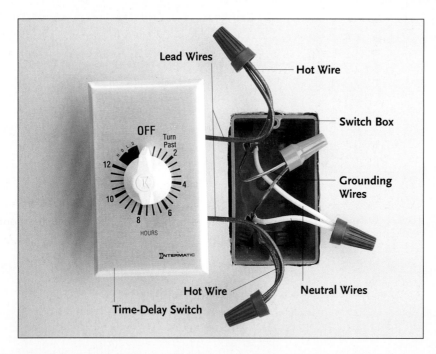

A time-delay switch operates a device for a given period of time, as opposed to operating it at a specified time.

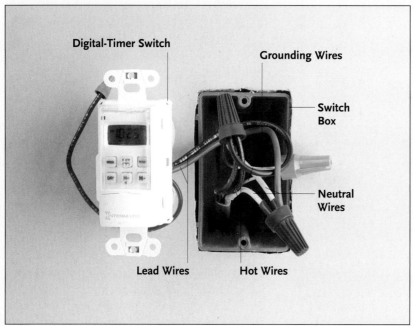

A digital timer switch is programmable, allowing you to set multiple on/off cycles during the day. Cycles may be set at either regular or random intervals.

SENSORS & ALARMS

THE SAME TYPE of low-voltage circuiting that is used to wire bells and chimes is also used to wire various types of sensors and alarm systems. Low-voltage wiring has the advantages of being relatively hazard-free and easy to install—making it ideal for the homeowner who wants to set up his or her own security or alarm system.

Different types of sensors are available that can detect motion, smoke, flame, heat, gas, and even human occupancy. A passive infrared (PIR) motion detector, for example, can sense the heat emitted from a human body. Such devices are often used to detect intruders moving through a security zone. When motion is detected, a light will turn on and remain on until the motion stops. The light will stay on for a set length of time; then it will turn itself off.

Smoke detectors are designed to set off an alarm before smoke and fire become intense enough to overwhelm the occupants of a home. Ionization smoke detectors contain electrically charged molecules that cause a flow of current within the detection chamber. Smoke particles

attracted to the ions reduce the current flow, thereby triggering the alarm. Photoelectric smoke detectors, on the other hand, use a photocell that is sensitive to light. When smoke interrupts the source light, a broken signal causes an alarm to sound. Infrared flame detectors respond to high-frequency radiant energy emissions that are characteristic of flickering flames. Fixed-temperature heat detectors set off alarms when either a metal having a low melting point reaches the temperature at which it will melt, breaking a circuit; or a metal that expands in heat touches a terminal to complete a circuit. Rate-of-temperature heat detectors can measure a minute rise in temperature by calibrating the expansion of air.

An occupancy detector uses either a passive infrared or an ultrasonic sensor. Ultrasonic sensors emit high-frequency sounds—setting off an alarm when they sense a change in the frequency of reflected sound. Several different types of sensors are combined to create a comprehensive home security system.

A–ionization smoke detector;
B–fixed-temperature heat
detector; C–photoelectric
smoke detector

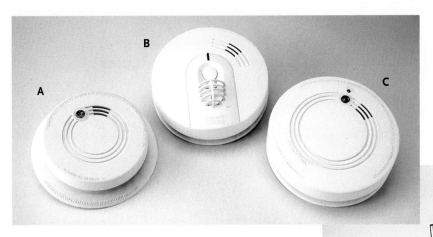

A–photoelectric
water-tight
sensor; B–motion
sensor with
weatherproof
plate; C–wireless
motion sensor

Photoelectric Cell

Specialty Wiring

WIRING A MOTION SENSOR

As is the case with many wiring projects, the hardest part of this job is installing the cut-in switch box and fishing the power and fixture cables into this box. If you work carefully, you can avoid damaging surrounding surfaces, which will minimize the amount of touch-up work required once the switch is installed.

TOOLS & MATERIALS

▮ Insulated screwdrivers
▮ Long-nose pliers
▮ Wire stripper
▮ Cable ripper
▮ Red and green wire connectors
▮ Switch box
▮ Motion sensor
▮ 14/2G NM cable

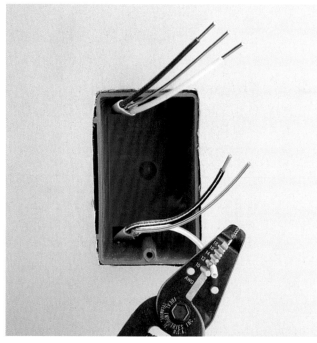

1 Locate the motion sensor where it will strategically detect the passage of an intruder. Cut a hole in the wall; fish the power and fixture cables into a cut-in box; and strip the wires.

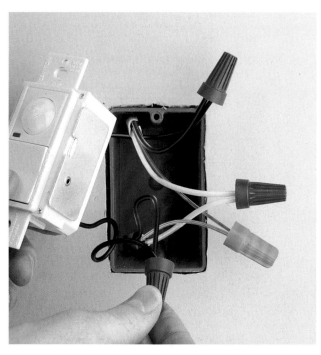

2 Join the black switch leads to the black cable wires using wire connectors. Also join the white wires and the bare ground wires from the cables using wire connectors.

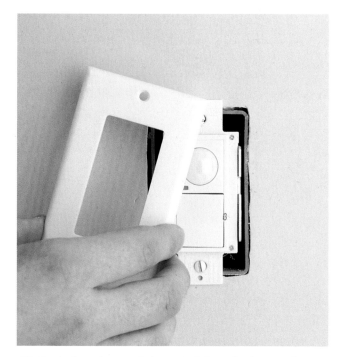

3 Push the wires and the switch into the box, and attach the switch using screws. Add the cover plate; turn on the circuit power; and check for proper operation of the switch.

WIRING A LOW-VOLTAGE HVAC THERMOSTAT

project

Thermostats

Thermostatic controls work off low-voltage or line-voltage wiring, depending on the type of heating, ventilating, and air-conditioning system (HVAC) you have in your home. Low-voltage thermostats typically control central HVAC systems, while line-voltage thermostats control multi-zone systems. As a thermostat senses a temperature change, it signals the HVAC equipment to kick on or off. A low-voltage thermostat, powered by a transformer that reduces 120-volt current to 24 volts, may require up to six wires to transmit this signal. A line-voltage system typically has four wires and is powered by a 240-volt circuit. Today, most thermostats are programmable, allowing you to raise or lower the temperature in your home at preset times.

TOOLS & MATERIALS

▌ Insulated screwdrivers ▌ Long-nose pliers
▌ Wire stripper ▌ Circuit cable ▌ Low-voltage transformer ▌ Cable clamps ▌ Red and green wire connectors ▌ Low-voltage programmable thermostat ▌ Octagonal electrical box

1 First determine where to locate the thermostat. Usually a spot near the middle of the house on an interior wall is best. Install the box on the side of the stud; then bring a power cable to the box; and tighten it in place using a cable clamp. Strip off the cable sheathing and the wire insulation.

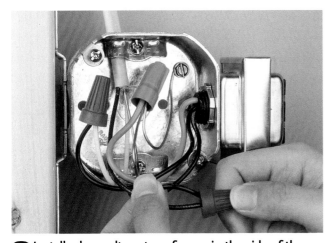

2 Install a low-voltage transformer in the side of the box. (See page 158.) Join the black wires from the transformer to the white and black wires from the power cable. Then join the grounding wires to a grounding pigtail using a wire connector, and attach the other end of the pigtail to the grounding screw in the box.

3 Bring wires from the transformer and the HVAC device through the back of the thermostat, and attach the wires to the proper terminals. The thermostat installation instructions explain which wires go where. Add the thermostat and cover; turn on the power; and test the equipment.

Specialty Wiring

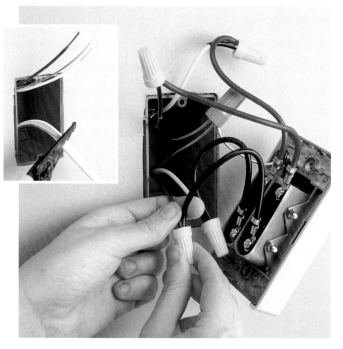

WIRING A LINE-VOLTAGE HEATER THERMOSTAT

project

Many electric wall heaters and baseboard heaters have a thermostat installed directly on the unit. While this arrangement makes for an easy installation—when the heater is installed the thermostat is also installed—using this type of thermostat isn't very convenient. In most cases, you have to bend down to adjust it. The better approach is to control electric heaters with a wall-mounted thermostat, just like other HVAC equipment.

TOOLS & MATERIALS

▌ Insulated screwdrivers ▌ Long-nose pliers ▌ Wire stripper ▌ Cable ripper ▌ Electrical tape ▌ 14/2G NM cable ▌ Line-voltage thermostat ▌ Yellow and green wire connectors ▌ Rectangular electrical box

Cut a hole in the wall, and fish a power cable and a heater cable through the hole and into the box. Then push the box into the wall, and strip the sheathing and wire insulation from both cables (inset). Attach the thermostat LINE wires to the power cable wires and the LOAD wires to the heater cable wires (above).

ANTENNAS

ANTENNAS ARE USED to transmit and receive electromagnetic waves. When a transmitted wave is received by a television antenna, for example, a current is produced in the antenna. This current travels through the lead-in wires to your television set where it provides enhanced signal reception. The quality of that reception depends largely upon the type of antenna used and the strength of the signal received. Older, mast-style antennas, commonly seen on residential rooftops, have many technical limitations and code restraints. The NEC specifies what materials are used to construct antennas and lead-in wires, as well as their size and how they are spliced and supported (Article 810). Most importantly, mast antennas must be located and installed to avoid potential contact with live wires. These radio and television antennas must also be grounded to protect against lightning. Poor mast antenna performance is only one of the reasons that cable and satellite television systems are so popular today.

Keep mast antennas a safe distance from overhead wires, and be sure that they are connected to a grounding rod driven into the earth at least 8 ft.

TIME FOR A THERMOSTAT UPGRADE

THE COST TO HEAT AND COOL A HOME is rising every year. Along with their help with conserving energy, both saving you money and reducing your fossil fuel use, many modern thermostats can be controlled by app, as long as the thermostat is connected to the house Wi-Fi. This makes them far more user friendly than the analog thermostats of old.

Installing these programmable thermostats is fairly straightforward: they can connect directly to your existing low voltage thermostat wires, which are already connected to your heating and cooling appliances. Be sure to have a look at what's available at your local home centers to see if it's time for a "smart" thermostat upgrade for your home.

Analog thermostat, not programmable

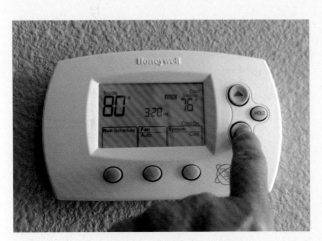

Honeywell programmable digital thermostat

Nest digital thermostat linked by Wi-Fi to control by app—in regular mode

Nest digital thermostat linked by Wi-Fi to control by app—in energy-saving mode

Nest digital thermostat wire connections

Specialty Wiring

MODERN TRENDS

BECAUSE SO MANY VARIABLES determine the quality of signal received by a conventional mast antenna, improvements to this system are often employed. Today, many antenna systems use coaxial-cable lead-in wires to improve reception. Other choices include preamplifiers, high-sensitivity receivers, and directional antennas that can be rotated by remote-control motors. A rotating antenna is commonly operated by a simple low-voltage plug-in transformer that reduces 120-volt power to 24 volts—enough power to control the rotational motor.

Where available, most homes today have cable television connections that provide direct-wired reception through a cable company antenna. This type of antenna typically uses RG6 quad-shielded coaxial cable, which consists of two foil shields, each covered with a second braided shield. The shielding helps to prevent loss or degradation of the signal at higher electromagnetic frequencies.

Many homeowners who don't have access to cable television or who simply prefer another option now use satellite systems to receive television programming. Satellite television offers a wider selection of programming than cable and often provides better-quality reception. A home satellite television (HSTV) system consists of a transmitter that beams microwaves at a communications satellite, the satellite itself, a receiving antenna dish, and a satellite television receiver, known as a TVRO (Television Receive Only).

Once it receives a signal, the satellite responds by transmitting it back to earth (transponding), where it may be received by any digital satellite antenna aimed toward the satellite and tuned to the right frequency. A device called a feedhorn at the focal point of the parabolic (bowl-shaped) antenna dish focuses imprecise satellite signals and conveys them to a low-noise block converter (LNB). (See the illustration on page 171.) The signals are then greatly magnified and sent to the digital satellite system (DSS) receiver that sits on your television set. Audio/video tuning is handled by an A/V receiver that sits on or near your television set.

INSTALLING A SATELLITE TV SYSTEM

project

In many rural areas where cable isn't available, and the reception of broadcast television is poor or nonexistent, satellite dishes are a real blessing. Their cost and service are comparable to cable systems, and the digital picture is very high quality. Most satellite companies offer installation as part of their initial purchase package. But not everyone wants to be available when the installer is available. Doing the job isn't difficult, but it will probably take most of a day to complete. If you had to install a second system right away, it would take just a couple of hours.

TOOLS & MATERIALS

■ Insulated screwdrivers ■ Multipurpose tool ■ Fish tape ■ Satellite dish ■ Low-noise amplifier/blocker/connector ■ RG-6 quad-shielded coaxial cable ■ DSS receiver ■ AV receiver ■ *For a large dish antenna you will also need an antenna positioner, antenna motor cable, and polarization motor cable.*

DIGITAL CONNECTIONS

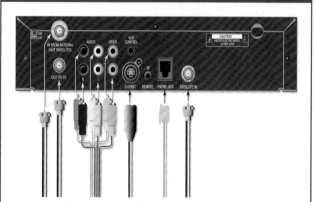

For a digital-satellite-system television receiver, color-coded wiring connections are made between the receiver, a low-noise amplifier or blocker, and an antenna. These are connected, in turn, to the satellite dish antenna.

1 Bowl-shaped (parabolic) antenna dishes must be precisely aimed at a satellite that is positioned in a fixed orbit around the earth. The satellite provider will explain the best places on your house to install the dish. Begin by attaching the mounting bracket; then slide the dish onto this bracket.

2 Different dish systems may have different ways to join the dish antenna to the back of your TV, but all systems use coaxial cable to connect the two. Follow the manufacturer's instructions on what type of cable to use, where to route the cable through the house wall, and how to staple it to the floor framing inside the house.

3 Attach the satellite cable to the back of the system receiver. The back of the receiver also has jacks for TV audio and video, as well as a phone line and an S-video cable.

4 Once the antenna and the receiver are connected, turn on the TV and adjust the position of the dish antenna for the best reception. The goal is to get the strongest signal that's possible from your location.

Specialty Wiring

TELECOMMUNICATIONS

Telecommunications wiring includes both conventional telephone and data transmission wiring for computers. In this chapter, discussion is limited to telephone wiring. (See Chapter 7, pages 228–253, "Home Automation," for more information.) Before you attempt to do any telephone wiring in your home, be sure to check with your state public service commission and local telephone company concerning rules and regulations that may apply to your work. National regula-

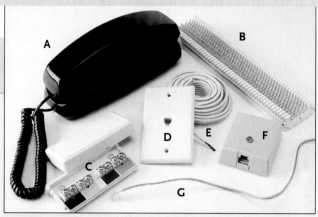

Basic telephone system: A–telephone; B–punch-down block; C–wire junction; D–flush-mounted wall jack; E–D-station cable; F–surface-mounted wall jack; G–flat cable

SATELLITE/LOCAL TELEVISION RECEPTION

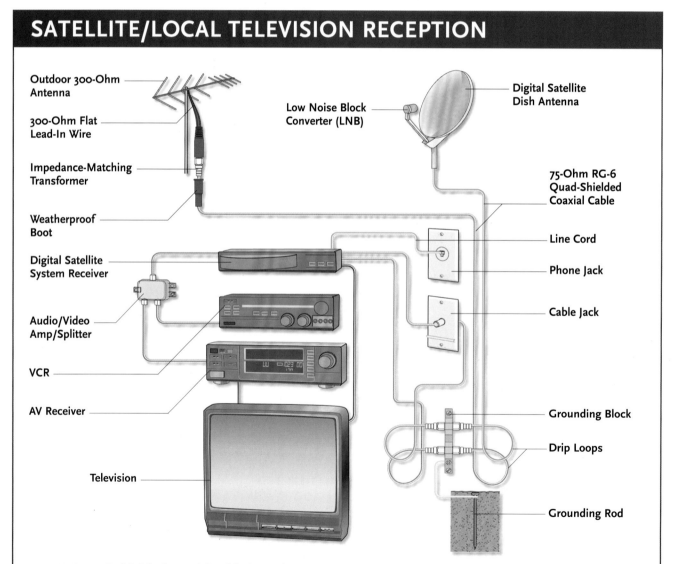

An RG-6 quad-shielded coaxial cable is used to connect a twin-lead flat antenna wire, through an impedance-matching transformer, to a digital satellite receiver. Reception from a 300-ohm flat lead-in antenna may be enhanced by connecting a 75-ohm RG-59 coaxial lead-in cable between a matching transformer and your TV receiver.

tions, set by the Federal Communications Commission (FCC), also define your responsibilities with regard to system maintenance and hookup. For example, the telephone company may be responsible for central wiring to your home, while you are responsible for all of the wiring beyond the point of entrance, commonly called the point of demarcation. A modular wiring jack must also be provided. It allows you to disconnect everything on your side of the demarcation point from everything on the other, public side of the telephone network.

Telephone wiring is commonly available as four-conductor line cord and telephone station cable. Line cord is the flat cord that connects your telephone equipment to a telephone jack. It should not be used for anything else. Telephone station cable for residential use typically consists of D-station wire that is color-coded for easy identification. Most home telephone systems require only four conducting wires (two-pair wire), with one pair for the phone and the remaining pair for a secondary line for a fax machine or modem. Color codes for telephone wire may consist of solid colors or two-color banding. The standard solid colors are red, green, yellow, and black. Banded colors are more varied. The telephone station cable variations shown in the phone-jack illustration below consist of alternating bands of green and white, orange and white, and blue and white.

The diagram below shows how to wire two- or three-pair telephone jacks. Each pair includes a tip and a ring wire. The tip wire on a single-phone line is usually green, while the ring wire is usually red. In any case, it is important to connect like-color wires together throughout any telephone wiring system.

smart tip

HOW MANY PHONES?

ALTHOUGH LOCAL TELEPHONE COMPANIES GENERALLY PROVIDE YOU WITH ENOUGH POWER TO RING FIVE TELEPHONES ON A SINGLE LINE, THE ACTUAL NUMBER YOU CAN INSTALL IS DETERMINED BY THE AMOUNT OF POWER REQUIRED BY THE PARTICULAR TELEPHONE—SOME PHONES REQUIRE MORE POWER THAN OTHERS. THE POWER REQUIRED IS REPRESENTED BY A NUMBER, CALLED A RINGER EQUIVALENCY NUMBER (REN). THE TOTAL NUMBER OF TELEPHONES THAT YOU CAN INSTALL ON YOUR LINE IS DETERMINED BY ADDING UP THE RENs ON YOUR PHONES. IF THE NUMBER IS LESS THAN FIVE, YOU WILL NOT HAVE ANY PROBLEMS.

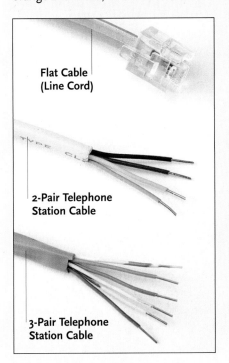

Flat Cable (Line Cord)

2-Pair Telephone Station Cable

3-Pair Telephone Station Cable

Use telephone station wire, left, between wire junctions and modular telephone jacks. Use flat cable to connect telephone or data transmission equipment.

This phone-jack diagram at right illustrates a standard 3-pair color scheme for telephone wiring. A 4-pair scheme would also have a white wire with brown banding and a brown wire with white banding. The slot numbers apply to 4- and 6-terminal telephone jacks only and would not apply to a fourth pair of wires. In a pair of telephone wires, each wire is identified by a tip (+) or a ring (-) polarity, as well as being coded by primary color or a primary and secondary color.

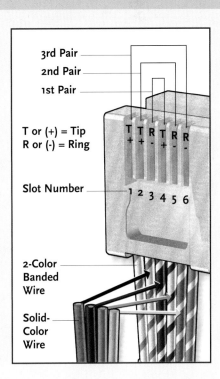

3rd Pair
2nd Pair
1st Pair

T or (+) = Tip
R or (-) = Ring

Slot Number

2-Color Banded Wire

Solid-Color Wire

Specialty Wiring

TELEPHONE WIRING

STRAIGHT HOME-RUN WIRING SYSTEM

To Network Interface

Wire Junction

Modular Phone Jacks

Telephone Station Cable

OPEN-LOOP WIRING SYSTEM

To Network Interface

Wire Junction

Modular Phone Jacks

Telephone Station Cable

CLOSED-LOOP WIRING SYSTEM

To Network Interface

Wire Junction

Modular Phone Jacks

Telephone Station Cable

Telephone wiring can be run using either a home-run system, in which each telephone jack is directly wired to a wire junction, or a loop system, in which wiring runs from jack to jack in an open or closed loop that returns to the wire junction and provides a second wiring path. Up to three jacks may be wired to one wire junction. A wire break to an independent jack will only cut service to the phone on that one line. A break in an open-loop system cuts service to any phones beyond the break. But a break in a closed-loop system won't stop a signal from traveling to the break point from either direction.

WIRING A TELEPHONE JACK

project

As with most other wiring projects, the hardest part of the procedure is fishing the telephone cable to the location of the phone jack. This type of project has the added disadvantage of using very small wires, so working with them can become frustrating at times. Begin by running the cable from the junction box to the new jack. Strip the wires, and attach them to the color-coded terminals. Mount the jack on the wall, and you are finished.

TOOLS & MATERIALS

▪ Insulated screwdrivers ▪ Long-nose pliers ▪ Wire stripper ▪ Telephone line tester ▪ Fish tape ▪ Telephone jack ▪ D-station telephone cable ▪ Cable staples ▪ Telephone wire junction

PUNCH-DOWN BLOCKS

Newer phone systems, instead of screw-terminal junction blocks, use punch-down, or connection, blocks. They are also known as insulation displacement connectors (IDCs). A standard M, or 66, block has connections for 25 pairs of wires. Additional blocks can be added if needed. A special punch-down tool presses the telephone wires into a 66 block, eliminating the need to strip the wires before connecting them to the block.

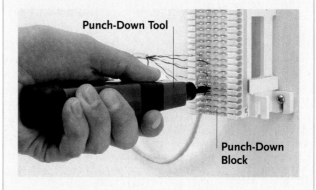

Punch-Down Tool

Punch-Down Block

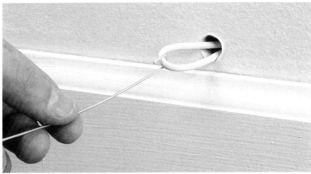

1 Start installing a new phone jack by removing the cover to the wire junction box and stripping 2 in. of sheathing from the end of a D-station cable. Strip the insulation from the ends of the wires, and attach each colored wire to its matching-colored terminal.

2 Choose a good location for the jack, and drill a hole through the drywall for cable access. Then fish the phone cable into this hole (top). Strip off about 2 in. of cable sheathing; then remove the insulation from the end of each wire.

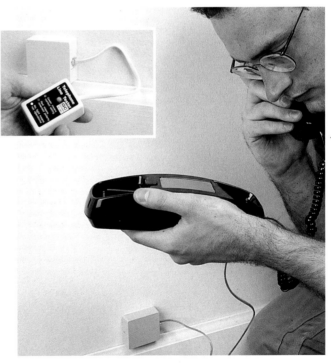

3 Bring the stripped cable into the bottom of the phone jack, and attach like-colored wires to the same terminals. Tighten the screws securely; mount the jack on the wall; and screw the jack cover to the jack.

4 Using a telephone line tester, test the polarity of the telephone jack wiring. A green light indicates correct wiring (inset). Plug a telephone cord into the jack, and listen for a dial tone. If you get one, make a call, and check that the line sounds clear.

5

outdoor wiring and low-voltage lighting

OUTDOOR POWER AND LIGHTING enables you to light walkways, driveways, pools, patios, and yards to maintain the safety and security of your home. You will need exterior receptacles to power outdoor appliances, tools, and equipment. Before providing this power and lighting, however, you must be aware of how it differs from interior power. (See Chapter 8 "Understanding Electricity," page 254.) Some communities require a licensed electrician to do outdoor wiring, while others simply demand that the work be inspected by one before you use it. The strictest localities require inspections by a licensed electrical inspector.

WHAT MAKES IT DIFFERENT

Circuiting

Underground or overhead outdoor wiring needs protection from the elements. It's subjected to wet and icy conditions, frost heaves, yard tools, and excavation equipment. Overhead cable must be kept high enough not to pose a hazard to anyone beneath it. Generally, a height of 12 feet is adequate for residential work, but does nothing to guard against falling tree limbs and swinging ladders. To avoid these risks, burying the cable is usually a better option.

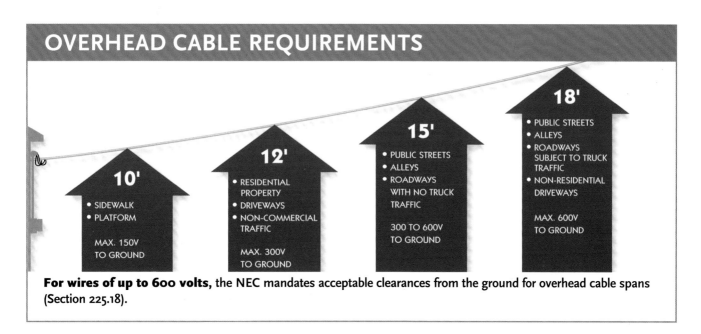

OVERHEAD CABLE REQUIREMENTS

10' • SIDEWALK • PLATFORM MAX. 150V TO GROUND

12' • RESIDENTIAL PROPERTY • DRIVEWAYS • NON-COMMERCIAL TRAFFIC MAX. 300V TO GROUND

15' • PUBLIC STREETS • ALLEYS • ROADWAYS WITH NO TRUCK TRAFFIC 300 TO 600V TO GROUND

18' • PUBLIC STREETS • ALLEYS • ROADWAYS SUBJECT TO TRUCK TRAFFIC • NON-RESIDENTIAL DRIVEWAYS MAX. 600V TO GROUND

For wires of up to 600 volts, the NEC mandates acceptable clearances from the ground for overhead cable spans (Section 225.18).

OUTDOOR CONDUIT AND CABLE TYPES

TO AVOID THE WORRY of maintaining overhead wire, you'll probably to want bury your outdoor cable or conduit underground. Burying underground cable in a protective conduit is one choice. Or, if identified for such use, cable can be buried directly in the ground.

ENT (Electrical Nonmetallic Tubing)

Flexible nonmetallic conduit offers limited protection for underground cable or conductors.

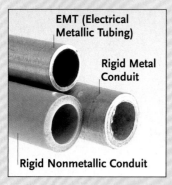

EMT (Electrical Metallic Tubing)

Rigid Metal Conduit

Rigid Nonmetallic Conduit

Rigid conduit affords extra protection for underground cable, but water penetration and eventual corrosion remain an inevitable problem.

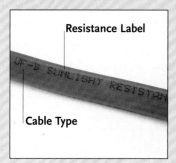

Resistance Label

Cable Type

Type UF (underground feeder) cable is designed for direct burial underground. The sheathing label indicates whether it is also sunlight and corrosion resistant.

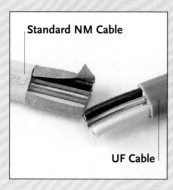

Standard NM Cable

UF Cable

UF cable doesn't have paper insulation between the wires and outer sheathing. A thermoplastic coating encases the wires, making them water resistant but difficult to strip.

Underground feeder and branch-circuit cable, known as UF cable, is designated for outdoor wiring because it is weatherproof and suitable for direct burial. UF cable looks somewhat like ordinary NM cable, so be sure that the UF designation is clearly written on the sheathing. The wires are molded into plastic rather than wrapped in paper and then sheathed in plastic, like NM cable wires. Aboveground UF cable must be protected with conduit.

Direct-burial cable must be buried deeply enough to be protected from routine digging, yet not so deeply that trenching may interfere with existing water or power lines. The NEC specifies minimum depth requirements for underground cable: 24 inches for direct-burial cable; 18 inches for rigid nonmetallic conduit; 6 inches for rigid and intermediate metal conduit (NEC Table 300.5). If your cable is powered from a ground-fault breaker, you may be permitted to trench less deeply, but this is not recommended—you might someday plant a tree or shrub over the cable and risk cutting it while digging.

Any special characteristics of newer types of cable insulation will be identified on the sheathing, such as sunlight and corrosion resistance. Note that the plastic sheathing on UF cable encases the insulated conductors inside it, making the individual wires somewhat difficult to strip, even using a utility knife.

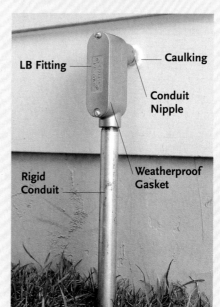

LB Fitting

Caulking

Conduit Nipple

Rigid Conduit

Weatherproof Gasket

Outdoor cable run underground must be protected in rigid conduit where it enters or emerges from the trench.

UNDERGROUND CABLE DEPTH REQUIREMENTS

Condition	Direct-Burial Cable	Rigid Nonmetallic Conduit (PVC)	Rigid and IMC Conduit
In open soil-pedestrian traffic only	24"	18"	6"
In trenches below 2" of concrete	18"	12"	6"
Under streets, highways, roads, alleys, driveways, and parking lots	24"	24"	24"
1- & 2-family dwelling driveways and outdoor areas; used for dwelling related purposes only	18"	18"	18"

The NEC requires that there be a minimum distance between the topmost surface of an underground cable or conduit and the top surface of the finished grade or other cover above the cable or conduit (NEC Table 300.5).

Outdoor Wiring & Low-Voltage Lighting

MATERIALS AND EQUIPMENT

Outdoor Electrical Boxes

Outdoor electrical boxes are either rain-tight or watertight. Rain-tight boxes typically have spring-loaded, self-closing covers, but they are not waterproof. This type of box has a gasket seal and is rated for wet locations as long as the cover is kept closed. It is best to mount a rain-tight box where it cannot be penetrated by driving rains or flooding. Watertight boxes, on the other hand, are sealed with a waterproof gasket and can withstand a soaking rain or temporary saturation. These boxes are rated for wet locations.

smart tip

WEATHERPROOFING

OUTDOOR ELECTRICAL MATERIALS AND EQUIPMENT, SUCH AS FIXTURES, ELECTRICAL BOXES, RECEPTACLES, CONNECTORS, AND FITTINGS MUST BE MANUFACTURED NOT ONLY TO MEET CODE REQUIREMENTS BUT TO RESIST THE ELEMENTS. OUTDOOR ELECTRICAL EQUIPMENT MUST BE WEATHERPROOF AND, IN SOME CASES, WATERTIGHT. FOR THESE REASONS, YOU USE DIFFERENT MATERIALS AND EQUIPMENT FOR OUTDOOR ELECTRICAL WORK THAN FOR INDOOR WORK.

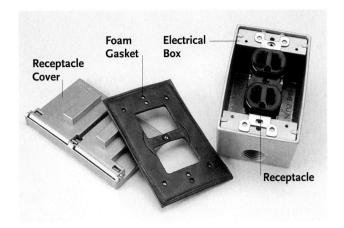

Self-Closing Covers

Receptacle Cover | Foam Gasket | Electrical Box | Receptacle

A rain-tight electrical box is not waterproof. It is rated for wet locations only if the cover remains closed.

Watertight receptacle boxes are sealed with waterproof foam gaskets. Receptacle covers snap shut. Switch covers have watertight levers.

179

RECEPTACLES AND SWITCHES

ANY RECEPTACLES that provide outdoor power for a residential dwelling, even if they are in an outbuilding, must have ground-fault-circuit-interrupter protection [NEC Section 210.8(A)]. Although GFCI receptacles may be used, they tend to nuisance-trip when exposed to the weather. It is better to have your outdoor branch circuit powered by a cable connected directly to a GFCI circuit breaker.

Every residence must have at least one receptacle installed at the front and back of the house. These receptacles must be within 6½ feet of the finished grade [Section 210.52(E)]. In addition, any outdoor receptacle that will be in unattended use, such as one that supplies power to a pump motor, must have a weatherproof box and a cover that protects the box even when the plug is in the receptacle [Section 406.8(B)]. Receptacle covers are available for both vertical and horizontal installations and are either on the device in the box or attached to the box itself.

An outdoor receptacle may be mounted on a wall, post, or any secure location. If you choose to screw a receptacle box onto a wooden post, then be sure that the post is pressure-treated to inhibit rotting. You can also mount a weatherproof electrical box on the end of two ½-inch-diameter sections of galvanized rigid metal conduit that are threaded on one end and anchored in concrete at the other. A two-gallon bucket can be filled with concrete to form the anchor. Burial depths vary across the country.

Weatherproof boxes and covers are also required to protect outdoor switches from exposure to the elements. Covers to single-, double-, and triple-gang boxes operated by toggle levers are available for outdoor switches, and there is also a cover for a combination single-pole switch with a duplex receptacle.

A freestanding receptacle box supported by rigid metal conduit must be mounted at least 12 inches, but no more than 18 inches, above the ground. It should have secondary support, such as a second conduit.

Receptacle coverplates for vertical or horizontal boxes may be box-mounted (A) or device-mounted (B). Cover types can be snap-shut (C), screw-cap, or flip-top (D).

Weatherproof boxes and cover plates are available for single-pole, double-pole, and three-way switches. Covers also exist for switch/pilot lights. A–double-gang cover plate; B–switch/receptacle cover plate; C–single-gang cover plate

MOUNTING REQUIREMENTS

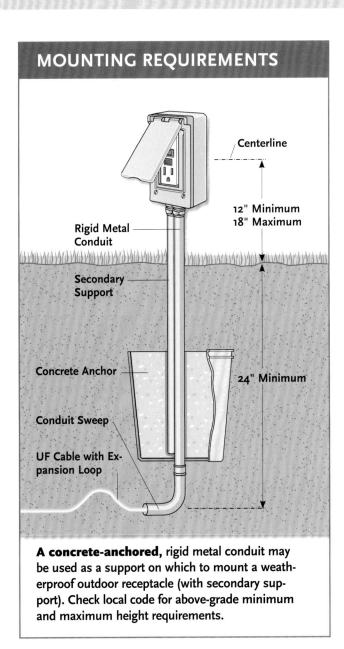

A concrete-anchored, rigid metal conduit may be used as a support on which to mount a weatherproof outdoor receptacle (with secondary support). Check local code for above-grade minimum and maximum height requirements.

WET-RATED WEATHERPROOF BOXES

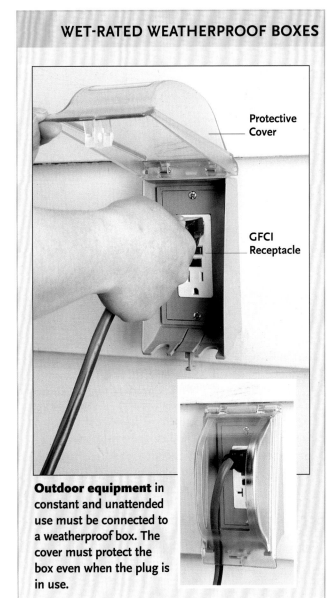

Outdoor equipment in constant and unattended use must be connected to a weatherproof box. The cover must protect the box even when the plug is in use.

Conduit, Connectors, and Fittings

As mentioned above, under "Circuiting" (page 177), outdoor wiring is typically protected by rigid conduit—both aboveground and wherever it enters or emerges from underground trenching. Rigid and intermediate metallic conduit (IMC) are most commonly used, but most local codes permit the use of rigid nonmetallic conduit, which is made of Schedule 80 polyvinyl chloride (PVC). Regardless of which type of rigid conduit you are permitted to use, you will have to make a variety of connections. To do this, you will need special connectors. These are available for metal and nonmetallic conduit, including bushings for straight pieces and elbow connections, locknuts, offsets, and various couplings. Be sure that the connectors you select

match the material and category of conduit you are using.

At the point where cable runs through the exterior wall of your home, you will need a special L-shaped connector called an LB conduit body. An LB encloses the joint between your indoor cable and the outdoor UF cable running down the side of your house and into an underground trench. LB conduit bodies are fitted with a gasket that seals the cable connection against the weather.

Another type of fitting that you may find useful is a box extension, or extender, which is used to increase the volume of an existing outdoor receptacle or junction box when you need to tap into it to bring power where it is required. This is often done to avoid extensive rewiring and/or renovation work. (See page 182 for more examples.)

Outdoor Wiring & Low-Voltage Lighting

CONDUIT, CONNECTORS, AND FITTINGS

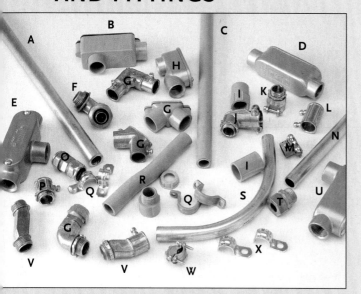

Outdoor wiring can be protected in rigid or intermediate metal conduit. Some local codes may not permit rigid nonmetallic conduit. A–rigid metallic conduit; B–plastic LB fitting; C–rigid nonmetallic conduit; D–C fitting; E–T fitting; F–multi-piece liquid-tight connector; G–elbow connectors; H–SLB fitting; I–plastic coupling; J–90-deg. connector; K–squeeze connector; L–setscrew coupling; M–NM cable clamp; N–electrical metallic tubing; O–compression coupling; P–setscrew connector; Q–conduit straps; R–offset NM connector; S–conduit sweep; T–watertight cable connector; U–LB fitting; V–offset couplings; W–cable connector; X–cable straps

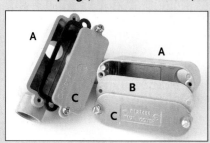

LB fitting: A–conduit body; B–gasket; C–cover plate

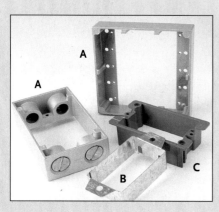

Extension boxes: A–outdoor box extensions; B–depth ring; C–plastic box extension

LAMPS & YARD LIGHTS

THE NEC REQUIRES that all residential dwellings have switch-controlled exterior lighting outlets to provide illumination at outdoor entrances or exits accessible from grade level, at attached garages, and at detached garages with electrical power (Section 210.70). In addition to such required lighting, you may wish to highlight a pond, garden, flower bed, or other feature in your yard. Whatever your purpose, you should be familiar with currently available types of outdoor lighting.

For general-purpose outdoor lighting, either type R (reflector) or type PAR (parabolic aluminized reflector) lamps are suitable. These long-lasting lamps have a reflective interior surface that maintains a bright light and resists weathering. Although PAR lamps are not affected by inclement weather, not all type R lamps are acceptable for outdoor use, so check the package labeling carefully. To mount lamps of this kind, you must install weatherproof lamp sockets. Outdoor lamp sockets for single-, double-, and triple-lamp installations are available on both rectangular and round electrical-box lamp mounts. Some mounts can also accommodate a motion-sensor control switch.

For accent or yard lighting, both 120-volt and low-voltage lighting can be used, depending upon your purpose. You can mount a 120-volt light fixture on a post or on a ground spike containing a built-in extension cord. If you choose low-voltage lighting, then you will also need to install a 120- to 12-volt outdoor step-down transformer on the exterior wall of the house.

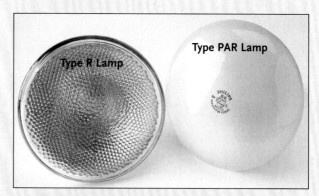

Type R (reflector) and **PAR** (parabolic aluminized reflector) lamps are typically used for general purpose outdoor illumination and floodlighting.

Outdoor Wiring & Low-Voltage Lighting

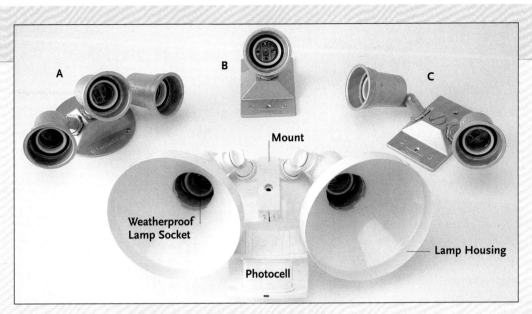

Mount

Weatherproof
Lamp Socket

Lamp Housing

Photocell

A

B

C

Outdoor lamps must be installed in mounts having weatherproof lamp sockets. The mounts accommodate one, two, or three lamps, or two lamps and a motion sensor.
A–triple mount;
B–single mount;
C–double mount

Fixture-Mounting Spike

120-Volt Extension Cord

Outdoor 120-volt lights are available that can be spiked into the ground as far from an outdoor receptacle as the length of the pre-attached extension cord.

120- to 12-Volt Outdoor Transformer

Fixture-Mounting Spike

Low-voltage lights, powered by outdoor step-down transformers, are commonly strung along a path or drive to provide safe low-level accent or guide lighting.

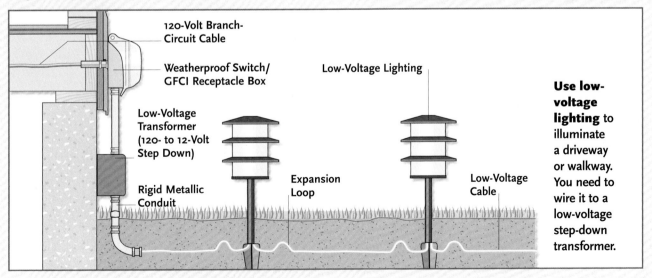

120-Volt Branch-Circuit Cable

Weatherproof Switch/ GFCI Receptacle Box

Low-Voltage Lighting

Low-Voltage Transformer (120- to 12-Volt Step Down)

Rigid Metallic Conduit

Expansion Loop

Low-Voltage Cable

Use low-voltage lighting to illuminate a driveway or walkway. You need to wire it to a low-voltage step-down transformer.

SENSORS & TIMERS

As an added security measure, you can combine outdoor lighting with devices that sense motion or operate off a timer-switch. Infrared motion detectors trip on the lights whenever an object passes within a given field of vision. The detector is usually attached to a special socket on an outdoor lamp mount that also houses sockets for type R or PAR lamps. A photocell prevents the device from tripping during daylight hours, and a timing mechanism determines the length of light operation in the absence of continued motion. You can use a manually operated indoor switch to override the automatic control.

You can also control outdoor lighting by using an indoor timer-switch in place of a conventional switch. There is a drawback to this, however: you must be aware of which types of lamps are permitted for use with a particular timer switch. Some switches can only be used with incandescent lamps. Timer switches using type R and PAR lamps may be unable to prevent potential damage to the timer in the event of an overload and should be limited to 150 watts.

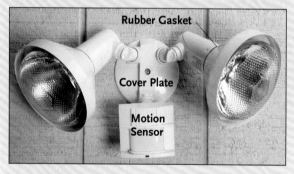

Rubber Gasket

Cover Plate

Motion Sensor

An exterior lamp mount having an extra socket for a motion sensor can play an important part in any home-security system.

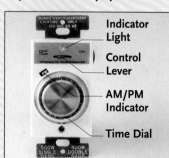

Indicator Light

Control Lever

AM/PM Indicator

Time Dial

Setting your exterior lights to work on a timer is a good way to enhance your security system.

OUTDOOR LIGHTING DESIGN

Outdoor lighting is an essential part of any home lighting system, whether it is used to add interest to a landscape, accent design elements on and around the house, or provide illumination for the safe movement and security of a homeowner or guest.

Strategically placed uplighting, above, invites the viewer to enter this tree-lined walkway.

Simple porch lights near an entryway, below, provide a warm welcome to visitors.

5

Outdoor Wiring & Low-Voltage Lighting

Low-voltage lighting, above, lends interest to this home and accentuates its pathways, outdoor areas, and landscaping.

Strings of mini-lights, left, set off these exterior steps, emphasizing their presence to the unwary walker.

Decorative bollards, below, highlight these deck walks, while the individual step lights provide additional safety.

WIRING PREPARATION

Planning

Whatever your intentions are for outdoor power and lighting, you should first plan your work; then follow certain precautions before you actually begin it. As with interior wiring, it is a good idea to make a diagram indicating where and how you want to locate receptacles, switches, lighting fixtures, pump and sprinkler motors, trenches, and cable runs. Your plan should also show the location of major elements like pools or ponds, outbuildings, patios, and yard equipment. It should also include other important items, especially known hazards, such as large trees, boulders, and rock outcroppings, and underground hazards like pipes, cables, and septic systems. In fact, you should contact your utility company and municipal government to get help in locating underground utilities before you even sketch out your final plan. To avoid potentially dangerous consequences and unnecessary expenses, it is better to be forewarned than to be surprised.

EXTENDING SERVICE

EXTEND POWER from your interior service entrance panel to the outside either through a basement/crawl space or a roof overhang. Exiting from a basement or crawl space requires mounting an LB conduit body on the side of your house. Run a rigid-metal conduit nipple through the wall to link the interior junction box to the LB fitting. For power exiting through an eave, mount an outdoor junction box on the surface of your soffit; then run Schedule 80 PVC or rigid metallic conduit from there down to a ground trench. If possible, run your conduit alongside a downspout so that it will be less conspicuous.

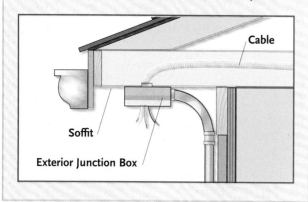

Cable

Soffit

Exterior Junction Box

project

EXTENDING POWER OUTDOORS

Extending power from your house to another building, such as a garage or storage shed, is best done by burying waterproof cable in a trench. Cables installed above ground can be critically damaged by falling branches during a storm.

TOOLS & MATERIALS

■ Insulated screwdrivers ■ Cable clamps ■ Measuring tape ■ Power drill and bits ■ Long-nose pliers ■ Cable ripper ■ Star drill ■ Small sledgehammer ■ Electrician's hammer ■ Safety glasses and work gloves ■ Caulking gun and caulk ■ 14/2G NM cable ■ Mounting bracket ■ Rigid conduit ■ Conduit compression connector (if metal) ■ Masonry anchors ■ Cable staples ■ Junction box ■ LB fitting ■ Conduit sweep bend ■ Conduit nipple ■ Pipe straps

3 Measure the distance from the junction box inside the house to the back of the LB fitting on the outside of the house. Then install a threaded conduit nipple to connect the two. Tighten this nipple into the back of the LB fitting, and thread a box nut on the other end of the nipple inside the junction box.

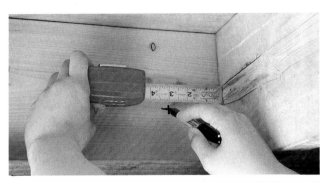

1 To extend power to the outside of the house, a cable hole must be drilled through the rim joist. Drill a small pilot hole to ensure the desired location on the other side. Make sure it's at least 3 in. away from any other joist (top). Drill the hole using a spade bit, and once the point starts to break through the other side, go outside and finish the hole from there.

2 Remove the knockout plate in the back of a junction box; then mount the box over the cable access hole. Bring a power cable from the service panel or another circuit, and attach it to the box using a cable connector.

4 Connect a piece of conduit to the bottom of the LB fitting and the top of a conduit sweep bend inside the trench. Fasten this conduit to the building using a conduit strap that's attached to the siding or the foundation wall.

5 Attach a sweep bend to the bottom of the conduit, and cover the open end with a plastic bushing to keep the conduit from chafing the cable. Then slide the end of the buried cable into the conduit and up through the hole in the LB fitting.

Outdoor Wiring & Low-Voltage Lighting

TRENCHING

DIGGING A TRENCH without first knowing what is underneath can be extremely dangerous. If you excavate randomly, you may unwittingly cut into a sewer or water pipe, or a telephone, cable TV, or electrical power line. Before you do any digging, be sure to check with your local utility company and have it mark the location of any underground utility lines where you plan to dig. In most areas, you are required by law to inform your utility company and secure its approval before you do any excavating. Once you are cleared to excavate, you can dig your trench using a shovel, mattock, backhoe, trencher, or any other suitable equipment. Keep your trenches as short and narrow as possible to reduce expenses and keep landscaping damage to a minimum. Also, when you run UF cable in a trench, always be sure to leave a slack loop for expansion wherever the cable enters or leaves the pipe (conduit). (See table, "Underground Cable Depth Requirements," page 179.) Pulling the cable tight will result in damage or even a complete break because of the soil pressure against the cable.

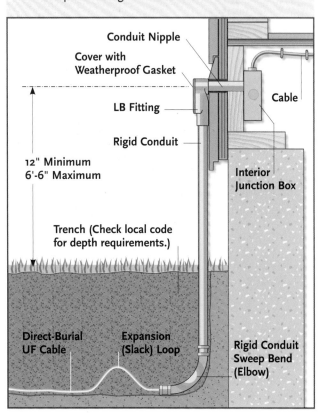

Conduit Nipple

Cover with
Weatherproof Gasket

LB Fitting

Rigid Conduit

12" Minimum
6'-6" Maximum

Cable

Interior
Junction Box

Trench (Check local code
for depth requirements.)

Direct-Burial
UF Cable

Expansion
(Slack) Loop

Rigid Conduit
Sweep Bend
(Elbow)

INSTALLING UF CABLE

project

UF cable is waterproof and specifically designed to be installed underground. The insulation that encapsulates the wires is very rugged. But it still needs some protection when it's exposed to possible damage. That's why the code calls for rigid conduit protection above grade and where the cable enters or leaves a building.

TOOLS & MATERIALS

▮ Round-head shovel ▮ Backhoe (optional)
▮ Adjustable pliers ▮ Small sledgehammer
▮ Chalk-line box ▮ Mason's string ▮ 6-mil plastic sheeting ▮ Work gloves ▮ Conduit compression connectors and bushings
▮ Wooden stakes ▮ UF direct-burial cable
▮ LB fitting ▮ Rigid conduit

3 Inside the junction box, attach the NM power cable from the service panel to the UF cable coming from the trench outside. Join the white wires, the black wires, and the ground wires (using a grounding pigtail) under separate wire connectors. Attach the free end of the pigtail to the grounding screw inside the box.

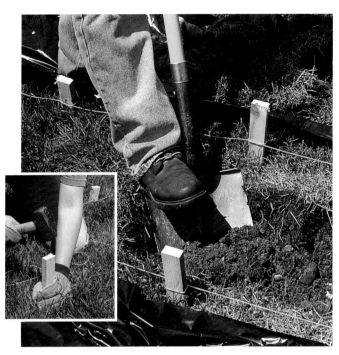

1 Lay out the path of your trench from the LB fitting on the house to the cable's destination point, using wooden stakes and mason's string (inset). Then dig the trench by hand, using a shovel, or rent a backhoe for the job. Set aside the sod so it can be put on top when the trench is refilled.

2 Attach a conduit sweep to the conduit coming out of the bottom of the LB fitting. And make sure to install a plastic bushing on the open end to protect the cable from damage. Then feed the cable into the sweep, up through the conduit, into the LB fitting, through the house wall, and into the junction box.

4 Once the cables are attached in the junction box, continue laying the UF cable. Form an expansion loop in the cable next to the conduit sweep, and at any point where the cable enters or leaves rigid conduit, to prevent it from being stretched tight with changes in temperature.

5 When the cable installation is complete, carefully refill the trench with the soil that was excavated. When all the loose soil is back in place, cover it with the pieces of sod that were set aside earlier. Tamp them down using a tamping tool, garden rake, or the back of a shovel.

OUTDOOR WIRING METHODS

Receptacles

Standard metal or plastic boxes are not acceptable outdoors because they aren't watertight. Watertight receptacle boxes are made of plastic, aluminum, bronze, or zinc-coated steel. If the cable is direct-burial type UF, it can be run directly in a trench at the code-specified depth. Wherever cable is exposed it must be protected in rigid conduit. Check your local code for variations.

smart tip

TRENCHING UNDER SIDEWALKS

IF UNDERGROUND (UF) CABLE MUST BE RUN BENEATH A SIDEWALK OR A DRIVEWAY, THEN THE CABLE MUST BE PROTECTED IN RIGID CONDUIT. RUN THE TRENCH FOR YOUR DIRECT-BURIAL CABLE RIGHT UP TO THE SIDEWALK OR DRIVEWAY; THEN CONTINUE IT ON THE OPPOSITE SIDE. TO BRIDGE THE GAP BETWEEN THE TWO

TRENCHES, CUT A LENGTH OF RIGID METAL CONDUIT APPROXIMATELY 12 INCHES LONGER THAN THE WIDTH TO BE SPANNED. YOU HAVE A COUPLE OF OPTIONS. ONE WAY IS TO FLATTEN THE END OF THE PIPE, AND DRIVE IT BENEATH THE SLAB USING A SLEDGEHAMMER. ANOTHER, PREFERRED, WAY IS TO PUT A CAP ON THE END OF THE PIPE, AND POUND IT THROUGH. IF YOU CRIMPED THE END OF THE PIPE, CUT OFF THE DAMAGED SECTION. IF YOU USED THE CAP METHOD, REMOVE THE CAP; THEN PUSH THE CABLE THROUGH THE PIPE.

project

INSTALLING AN OUTDOOR RECEPTACLE

Outdoor receptacles must be protected with a GFCI. Like the inside of your house, you can provide this protection by installing a GFCI receptacle or a GFCI circuit breaker. Because these receptacles tend to trip periodically without cause, most people think it makes more sense to use the breakers. They may cost more, but they're less troublesome.

TOOLS & MATERIALS

■ Insulated screwdrivers ■ Multipurpose tool ■ Long-nose pliers ■ Utility knife ■ Adjustable pliers ■ UF direct-burial cable ■ Receptacle (GFCI if needed) ■ Weatherproof box ■ Rigid conduit ■ Conduit compression connectors (if metal) ■ Mounting ears ■ Conduit sweep bend

3 Strip the thermoplastic coating from the wires. This can be difficult to do. Start by cutting the plastic with a utility knife. Then pull the plastic off the ends of the wire using pliers. When all this coating is gone, strip the insulation off the individual wires.

1 Begin by mounting an outdoor receptacle box on the side wall of a building, a porch, a deck, or a freestanding post. Screw the mounting ears securely to the surface (left). Or mount the receptacle on the top of some rigid metal conduit that is anchored in concrete (right). Check local requirements.

2 Once the receptacle is mounted, install a plastic bushing in the end of the conduit to prevent the cable from chafing against any sharp edges. Then pull the cable up through the conduit so about 8 in. extends into the box.

4 Connect the ground wire to the metal box grounding screw. Attach the black wire to the brass screw terminal and the white wire to the silver screw terminal. Attach the grounding wire to the grounding screw on the side of the receptacle.

5 Push the wires inside the box; then screw the receptacle in place. Seal the perimeter of the receptacle with the foam gasket that came with box. Keep the gasket aligned as you install the box cover so that it doesn't become distorted and possibly leak as a result.

Switches

Just like their receptacle counterparts, outdoor switch boxes are waterproof and sealed with foam gaskets. A control lever mounted on the surface of a switch box cover plate operates a conventional-style switch screwed to the inside face of the plate. UF cable is brought into a switch box through a rigid conduit by means of a watertight compression fitting.

Install the Switch Box. Attach mounting ears to the back of the switch box; then screw the box in place. Using a fitting, connect a vertical section of rigid conduit to the bottom of the switch box. Then couple a conduit sweep bend (if metal) beneath the vertical section of conduit running down into the end of your underground cable trench. Anchor the conduit in concrete. (See "Receptacles and Switches," page 180.)

WATERPROOF SWITCH ANATOMY

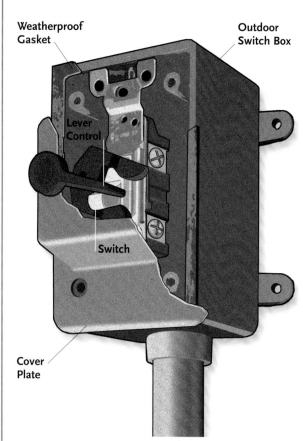

Weatherproof Gasket

Outdoor Switch Box

Lever Control

Switch

Cover Plate

An outdoor waterproof switch box is sealed with a foam gasket. A lever on the cover controls a switch mounted on the box. A flip of the outside lever moves the switch inside.

INSTALLING AN OUTDOOR SWITCH

project

Having access to power outside the house isn't just limited to receptacles or lights that you control from inside the house. Sometimes it's convenient to have outdoor switches close to things, such as floodlights, so you don't always have to go back to the house to turn the power ON or OFF. Fortunately, installing a switch is pretty easy.

TOOLS & MATERIALS

▌Insulated screwdrivers ▌Multipurpose tool ▌Long-nose pliers ▌Utility knife ▌Adjustable pliers ▌UF direct-burial cable ▌Weatherproof switch box and cover ▌Conduit compression fittings and connectors ▌Standard switch ▌Mounting ears ▌Rigid conduit

3 Strip the thermoplastic coating off the UF cable and the sheathing off the NM cable. Then strip the insulation off all the wires using a multipurpose tool.

1 To install an outdoor switch to control something like an overhead floor light, start by mounting an outdoor switch box on top of the conduit that comes from the buried cable trench. Then install conduit that runs from the box up to the fixture.

2 Pull underground UF cable into the box from the trench, and bring NM cable from the light fixture above into the box. Pull at least 8 in. of each into the box so you have enough wire to make the switch connections comfortably.

4 Attach the two black (hot) wires to the two terminal screws on the switch. Then join the two white (neutral) wires with a wire connector. Finish up by joining the ground wires to a pigtail with a wire connector and attaching the other end of the pigtail to the grounding screw on the switch.

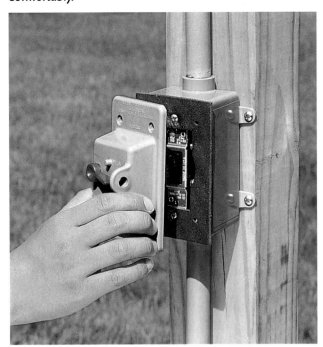

5 Carefully fold the circuit wires into the box; then push the switch in place; and screw it to the box. Cover the switch with a foam gasket, and install the box cover over the switch. Make sure that the outside lever mechanism fits properly over the switch lever inside.

INSTALLING A MOTION-SENSOR LIGHT

project

Lights

Employ exterior lighting to provide required illumination and task lighting, or go further by providing decorative and accent lighting. Combined with motion sensors, you can even use exterior lighting as a part of your home security system. All outdoor lighting, whether practical or decorative, must be weatherproof. You can mount an exterior light on a porch ceiling, building wall, or freestanding post. Pipe-mounted fixtures are secured by a threaded compression fitting, while floodlights require special lamp-socket fittings having movable heads that can be adjusted in any direction. An additional movable head is often furnished for attaching a motion sensor. (See "Lamps and Yard Lights," page 182 and "Sensors and Timers," page 184.)

TOOLS & MATERIALS

- Insulated screwdrivers ▌ Fish tape
- Multipurpose tool ▌ Saber saw
- Wire connectors ▌14/2G NM cable
- Rectangular weatherproof light fixture box ▌ Indoor switch box ▌ Outdoor light fixture with motion sensor

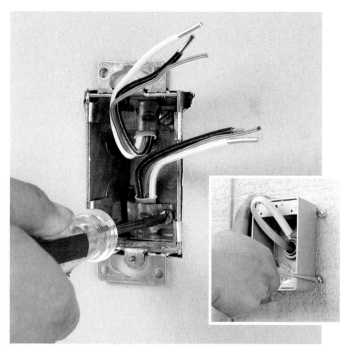

1 To install an outdoor light fixture that has a built-in motion sensor, first install a switch box on the inside of the house. Fish a power cable and a cable from the light fixture into this box. Then mount an outdoor box on the exterior wall, and fish the cable from the switch into this box (inset).

4 Slide a foam gasket over the fixture wires and against the base of the fixture. Then join all the white wires with a wire connector and all the ground wires with another wire connector. Join the hot leads from the box, the two lights, and the sensor unit according to the manufacturer's directions.

3 Assemble the light fixture according to the manufacturer's directions. Usually, the two light sockets and the single motion-detector unit are held to the fixture base with retaining nuts tightened from inside using pliers. Untangle all the lead wires.

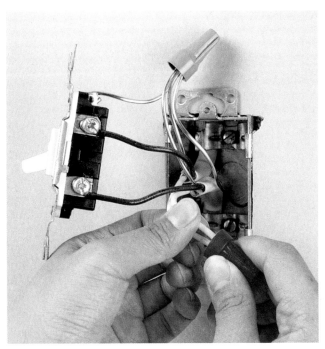

2 Attach the two black (hot) wires to the switch termi-nals, and join the two white (neutral) wires with a wire connector. Use another connector to join the ground wires to a pigtail. Then attach the free end of the pigtail to the grounding screw in the fixture box, if it's metal, or to the ground screw on the switch.

5 Carefully tuck the wires into the box, and press the fixture into place. Make sure the gasket remains properly aligned to ensure a weatherproof fit. Then screw the fixture to the box. Install the bulbs; turn on the power; and test for proper operation.

Outdoor Receptacle, Switch and Fixture Circuit

A GFCI receptacle protects the circuit wires as well as the switch and fixture from shock damage in this outdoor cir-cuit. Two-wire cable feeds power to the line screw terminal on the receptacle and proceeds to the switch and fixture from the load terminal.

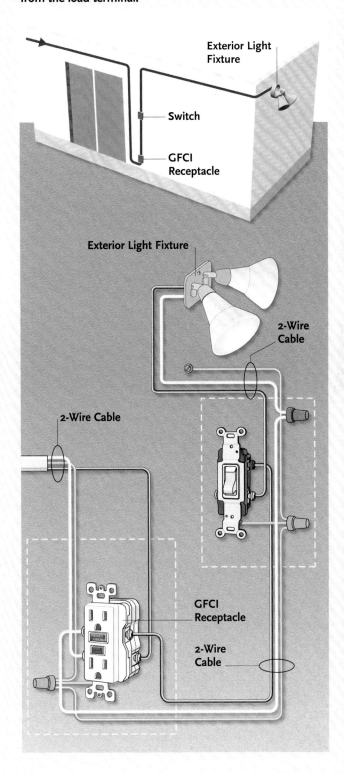

INSTALLING A LAMPPOST

Lampposts

Many different lamppost designs are available, but most are installed in a similar way. First, a concrete base is poured, with conduit in the middle that carries wiring from the house to the lamp fixture. This wiring is buried in an 18-inch-deep trench. You can control the light from an interior switch, or install an outdoor switch as shown here.

TOOLS & MATERIALS

▪ Shovel ▪ Post-hole digger ▪ 2-foot level
▪ Mason's trowel ▪ Adjustable pliers
▪ Ready-mix concrete ▪ Concrete form tube
▪ Plastic conduit and fittings ▪ 14-gauge insulated wires ▪ Anchor bolts ▪ Lamppost ▪ Extension box for outdoor receptacle
▪ Outdoor switch box ▪ Metal conduit and fittings ▪ Wire connectors

1 Start by digging a hole about 14 in. wide x 2 ft. deep so that a 12-in. form tube will fit in the hole. Cut plastic conduit to run from the bottom of the hole to about 12 in. above the top of the form. Join the bottom of this conduit to conduit going back to the house. Fill the form with concrete (top). Install the attachment bracket that comes with the lamppost.

4 Join the fixture head to the lamppost according to the instructions that came with the product. The heads also need to be wired to the main fixture's wires.

5 Pull the electrical wires through the conduit, and join them to the fixture lead wires. Then lift the post onto the base, and screw it to the mounting bracket that was installed earlier.

2 The conduit that runs from the base of the post to the house should be buried 18 in. deep to prevent any damage to the wires. Any necessary turns are made using stock elbows of different turning radii.

3 A good place to access power is at an outdoor receptacle. To use one, remove the cover, and install a metal extension box over the existing receptacle box.

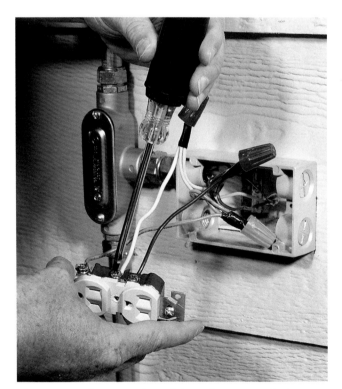

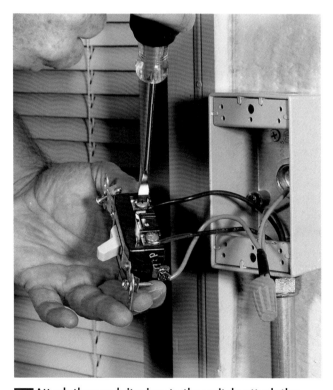

6 Connect the ground conduit to the receptacle box using metal conduit. Also run conduit up the wall to a switch box. Attach the conduit wires to the receptacle terminals.

7 Attach the conduit wires to the switch; attach the ground pigtail wire to the metal box grounding screw, then install the switch in the box, and protect it with a waterproof cover. (See "Installing an Outdoor Switch," page 192.)

Outdoor Wiring & Low-Voltage Lighting

197

LOW-VOLTAGE LIGHTING BASICS

Installing low-voltage lighting is one of the most popular do-it-yourself projects. Since the systems operate on only 12 volts of power as opposed to the 120 volts of standard line voltage, installing a low-voltage system is much safer than working on house wiring. Some manufacturers recommend turning on the power to connect the lights, so you can see the results right away. (Always follow the manufacturer's directions.)

Installation is easier, too. For most systems, plug in a step-down transformer to a standard GFCI-protected outdoor outlet, and run the wires to the light fixtures. Working with low voltage wiring means there is no need to bury wires in conduit or as deeply as standard wiring. Requirements vary, but most manufacturers call for direct burial of a few inches.

The quick installation also means it is easy to change the system by adding new fixtures or moving fixtures to new locations. That is a real plus because landscapes tend to change over time, and a low-voltage system can change with the environment.

Small pools of light cast by these path fixtures, above, light the way and provide a decorative accent to the yard.

When choosing fixtures, below, keep in mind that aboveground fixtures should be attractive in daylight.

DESIGN BASICS

SURVEY YOUR PROPERTY to identify the best locations for low-voltage lights. Note how moonlight affects your landscape, keeping in mind how you plan to use the property at night. Most homeowners use low-voltage lights to achieve a variety of design goals.

• **Highlighting Focal Points.** Use lights to up-light a distinctive tree or shrub. Or train a flood light on garden statuary or a water feature. It is best to choose no more than one or two focal points. Choosing too many will make the yard look chaotic.

• **Safety Lighting.** Fixtures installed along paths and driveways and on stairs add a measure of safety to your yard and outdoor living areas.

• **Decks and Patios.** Low-voltage fixtures installed in deck railings or along the perimeter of patios provide good ambient lighting. They help extend the time these areas can be used.

smart tip

BUYING THE RIGHT WIRING

Wire Gauge	Length of System	Maximum Wattage
16	100 feet	150 watts
14	150	200
12	200	250

Design Mistakes. Don't over-light. Many homeowners make the mistake of installing too many lights, especially along walkways and driveways. Over-lighting these areas creates an airport runway look, which is something to be avoided. Place fixtures so that they do not produce glare or shine into your home's windows or the windows of your neighbors.

Create a balanced lighting plan by varying the lighting techniques. For example, try teaming a dramatically up-lighted tree with subtle walkway lighting that casts small pools of light.

Pick a System. You will find it helpful to sketch your lighting plan on paper. The perspective a scaled drawing affords you makes it easy to make changes quickly.

Once you have a plan, choose the fixtures you want to use. Home centers and lighting dealers usually have a selection of fixtures and low-voltage systems in stock. Lighting kits usually contain everything you will need. The disadvantage is that you are limited in fixture selection. Fixtures that will be visible should look as good during the day as they do when illuminated at night.

Wiring. When assembling components for low-voltage lighting, determine the length of the necessary wiring runs. The length will tell you what gauge wiring to buy. Unlike line-voltage lights, low-voltage lights experience a drop-off in power the farther away the light fixture is from the transformer, so matching the right wiring to the system is important. Follow manufacturer's recommendations. (See the Smart Tip, "Buying the Right Wiring," on page 198.)

Accessories. One of the most practical accessories for a low-voltage system is a mechanism for switching the lights on and off. Many systems are light sensitive, meaning that they turn on at dusk and off at dawn. An alternative is a system that switches on at dusk and then remains on for a predetermined number of hours.

Create focal points with light, above left. Use lighting to draw attention to specific areas of your yard.

Light fixtures installed in steps make the deck safer, left. Direct lights so that they do not cause glare.

Low-voltage walkway lighting, below, produces a soft glow that welcomes visitors to your home.

INSTALLING LOW-VOLTAGE LIGHTING

Low-Voltage Lighting

The most popular type of outdoor lighting is low-voltage lighting. Because of the low voltage needed to power this type of lighting, it is much safer to use outdoors than lighting powered by a conventional 120-volt line. It is so low, in fact, that a short-circuit in low-voltage underwater lighting would not even be felt by a swimmer. For this reason, it is the ideal type of lighting for in-ground pools. More often, though, low-voltage lighting is employed to light a drive or pathway or to accent landscaping. Lamps for low-voltage lighting commonly range between 25 to 50 watts. To get these lower voltages, you install a transformer to step down standard 120-volt service. Lighting controlled from a transformer can be strung together and connected to fixtures that can then be spiked into the ground along the length of the low-voltage wiring. Because there is little hazard associated with this kind of wiring, it doesn't need to be buried any deeper than 6 inches.

TOOLS & MATERIALS

▪ Insulated screwdrivers ▪ Hammer ▪ Multipurpose tool ▪ Saber saw ▪ Adjustable pliers ▪ Fish tape ▪ Wire connectors ▪ 14/2G NM cable ▪ UF direct-burial cable ▪ Plastic or metal retrofit receptacle box ▪ GFCI receptacle ▪ 14/2 cable staples ▪ Watertight low-voltage transformer ▪ Low-voltage lighting fixtures with spikes

Low-Profile Well Light

Hanging Solar Light

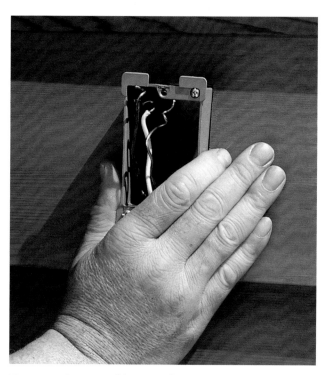

1 Determine a good location for an outdoor receptacle; then trace the perimeter of a box on the siding; and drill saw-blade access holes in the corners. Cut out the waste using a saber saw or a reciprocating saw. Then fish a power cable into the box, and attach the box to the wall.

4 Once the light heads are positioned in the soil, dig a 6-in.-deep trench between the lights, and lay the low-voltage cable in the bottom of the trench. Join the leads from the light heads to the cable using their self-piercing clips.

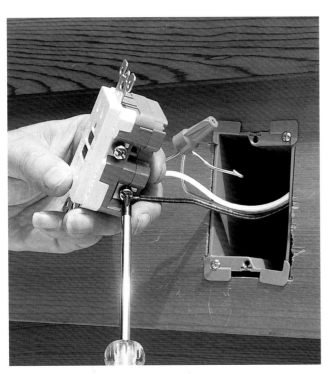

2 Attach the black (hot) and white (neutral) wires to the terminals on a GFCI receptacle. Then join the bare ground wire to a grounding pigtail that attaches either to the ground screw on the receptacle or a grounding screw in a metal box.

3 Position the light heads along the walkway, driveway, or other feature that you want to illuminate. Follow the manufacturer's recommendations to get the best light coverage from the units.

5 Connect the underground power cables to the back of the transformer, following the manufacturer's instructions. Usually all that's required to make a good connection is to slide the cable wires under self-piercing terminal screws and to tighten the screws.

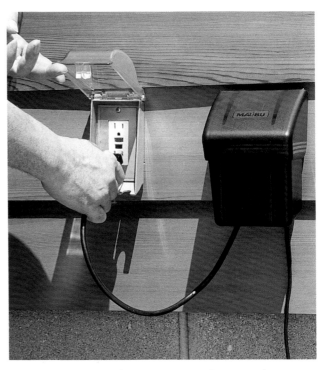

6 Mount the transformer on the wall next to the GFCI receptacle. Then plug the power pigtail cord from the transformer into the receptacle. Close the weatherproof cover; turn on the power to the circuit; and check for proper operation.

SWIMMING POOLS AND SPAS

Swimming pools and spas are becoming increasingly popular among homeowners. One reason for this popularity is the wide variety of products available in the pool and spa area—everything from small wading pools to in-ground, Olympic-size pools to spas that can hold up to 8 people. Because many of these products include electric pumps, filters, and heaters, some wiring is required.

For large inground pools, a licensed electrician should handle the electrical installation. In fact, many local codes will have this as a requirement because the process involves bonding all metal used in the structure to a common bonding grid. The process is different for smaller pools and spas. In most of these cases, the electrical installations are no more difficult than installing the switches and receptacles described throughout this book. If local code authorities prohibit anyone but a licensed electrician to make the connections, you can run the cable, dig the trenches, etc. that are part of the installation.

Overhead electrical wiring, below, must be at least 22½ ft. above water level.

Electrical and telecommunications clearances governing pools apply to portable spas as well, opposite top.

Aboveground pools, opposite bottom, rely on pumps and filters that operate on GFCI-protected 20-amp circuits.

CODE REQUIREMENTS

AS DISCUSSED BELOW, the type and size of pool or spa you will be installing will determine the wiring requirements. But there are some common code requirements as specified by the NEC.

- Overhead electrical wiring and network powered broadband communications systems must be kept at least 22½ feet above the pool water level, and not less than 14½ feet above any diving boards or platforms. The same requirements apply to spas as well.
- Wiring for communications systems, such as those used for telephone and cable service, must be kept at least 10 feet above the water in a swimming pool or spa or 10 feet above a permanent diving platform or diving board.
- Underground wiring must be at least 5 feet away from the inside wall of the pool or spa unless the wiring supplies power to the pool or spa.
- Receptacles supplying power to pumps and other pool and spa-related equipment must incorporate ground-fault circuit interrupter (GFCI) protection, or the circuit must be protected by a GFCI type circuit breaker.
- Where a power disconnect is required by code, the disconnect switch or breaker must be in sight of someone using the pool or spa but not closer than 5 feet to the pool or spa.

Aboveground Swimming Pools

The size of the pool determines how the wiring is installed and the type wiring used. Many aboveground pools are sold as packages where the pool is sold along with a pump and filtering system designed to handle that size pool. In other cases, you will need to buy the pump and filter separate. Your pool dealer can help you select the proper equipment.

A 20-amp circuit usually powers a pump of this type. In most cases, simply plugging the pump into a GFCI-protected receptacle is all that is required. The pool filter pump must be listed by a recognized testing laboratory, such as Underwriters Laboratories. It must be identified as "double insulated" and have provisions for the connection of an equipment-grounding conductor that is an integral part of the flexible supply cord. Listed pump filters have a 25-foot-long, grounded cord.

Outdoor Wiring & Low-Voltage Lighting

project

INSTALLING 120-VOLT STORABLE-POOL WIRING

An extension cord should never be used with this type of equipment, so it may be necessary to install an outdoor receptacle to power the pool equipment. You have two options: either install a circuit supplied by a GFCI circuit breaker, or install a standard circuit with a GFCI receptacle. Buried cable supplied by a GFCI circuit breaker must be buried no less than 12 inches deep; cable supplied by a standard breaker, even with a GFCI receptacle, must be buried no less than 18 inches deep. The reason for the difference lies in the fact that a GFCI receptacle will not protect the wiring that runs between it and the panel.

Determine the Location of the Receptacle. If the pump's cord is long enough to reach an existing receptacle, there is no need to install a new one. But if you are performing the installation, install a combination receptacle and switch. It is not called for in the current version of the NEC, but it is safer to use a switch to shut off the power before removing the plug from the receptacle.

Extend Power to the Outdoors. This installation can be performed in two ways. One method is the same as shown in "Extending Power Outdoors," page 186. In this method you

TOOLS & MATERIALS

▐ Round-head shovel ▐ Insulated screwdriver ▐ Adjustable pliers ▐ Multipurpose tool ▐ Long-nose pliers ▐ Cable ripper ▐ Portable drill ▐ Wood and masonry bits ▐ Trowel ▐ Ready-mix concrete ▐ Conduit clips ▐ Cable staples ▐ NM cable ▐ Junction box ▐ 20-amp GFCI circuit breaker ▐ 12/2G, type UF direct-burial cable ▐ Rigid conduit ▐ LB fitting ▐ Two-gang weatherproof box ▐ 90-degree conduit sweep elbows ▐ Conduit compression connectors ▐ Switch and single receptacle ▐ Locknuts and plastic bushings ▐ ½-inch cable box connector

smart tip

POOL LIGHTING REQUIREMENTS

LIGHTING FIXTURES (LUMINAIRES) FOR STORABLE POOLS MUST BE INSTALLED IN OR ON THE WALL OF THE POOL. LOW-VOLTAGE LIGHTING MUST BE LISTED AS AN ASSEMBLY. IN OTHER WORDS, YOU CANNOT PURCHASE SEPARATE FIXTURES AND TRANSFORMERS AND ASSUME THEY SATISFY THE CODE REQUIREMENTS. THE COMPONENTS MUST BE TESTED AS A COMPLETE ASSEMBLY AND IDENTIFIED TO BE USED WITH A STORABLE POOL.

install a junction box inside the house where the cable exits the building. The junction box allows you to switch from cable rated for indoor use to cable rated for outdoor use.

The method suggested here calls for running Type UF cable (the type suitable for buried applications) all the way from the distribution panel board to the outdoor receptacle outlet.

3 Install two lengths of conduit to the bottom of an outdoor receptacle. Then push the end of the power cable through one of the conduits and into the box. Dig a hole; fill it with concrete; and embed the conduit supports in the concrete. (See page 181.) Trowel the concrete surface smooth.

1 Begin by drilling a hole through the first floor rim joist and installing a LB fitting on the outside of the house. Attach the LB nipple by installing an oversize washer and a locknut on the inside of the joist. Add a plastic bushing to the end of the nipple to protect the cable; then install a cable from the service panel.

2 Push the cable out through the opening in the LB fitting. Then bend the cable and push it down through the LB fitting, the conduit under it, and the conduit sweep elbow inside the trench. Pull the cable until all the slack is removed and the cover to the LB fitting can be reattached.

4 Connect the black power wire to one switch terminal, and a black jumper wire from the other switch terminal to one side of the receptacle. Attach the white power wire to the other side of the receptacle. Attach the power cable ground wire to the switch and receptacle grounding pigtails with a wire connector.

5 Push the wires into the box, and screw the receptacle and switch units into place. Install the cover on both units, and turn on the power. Plug in the pool pump; turn on the switch; and check for proper performance.

Spas

Spas come in a variety of shapes and sizes. The power requirements may vary from 15 amperes at 120 volts to 50 amperes at 240 volts, depending on the size of the tub and the number of jets supplied by the pump. As with swimming pools, smaller units are simply plugged into a GFCI receptacle. Larger units must be hardwired. Some have two motors, one for the water pumping system and the other for the blower. Larger systems are available with two water pumps and one blower motor. The entire packaged unit should be listed by a recognized testing laboratory. Install these units in accordance with the manufacturer's instructions, as the instructions themselves are part of the laboratory's listing.

Spas and hot tubs are required to have a service disconnect switch to shut off the power to the recirculation and jet pump motors. This switch must be accessible to the users of the spa—but not within 5 feet of the spa or hot tub, not more than 50 feet away from the spa, and visible to anyone using the spa. Check with the local electrical inspector before attempting this type of installation. The code may call for all connections to be made by a licensed electrician.

SPA ANATOMY

Air Control — Jets — Jets — Control Panel — Insulation — Filters — Pump — Auxiliary Pump — Controls for Water, Air Pressure, Filtration, and Temperature

Products vary, but in many cases, you can run the conduit under the outer skirt and bring it up close to the control panel.

INSTALLING A 50-AMP SPA DISCONNECT

project

Follow manufacturer's instructions for placing and supporting the spa or hot tub. Underground and overhead electrical wiring clearances are the same as those required for swimming pools. Be sure to apply for building and wiring permits; it's a frustrating experience to have to dig up the wiring and move the spa a few feet due to a code violation.

Bringing Power Outdoors. Dig a trench at least 18 inches deep from the house to the switch and then on to the spa. Run type NM cable from the panel to a junction box located at the exterior wall of the house. From there, run individual wires in buried conduit from the junction box to the disconnect switch and then to the control panel in the spa. This installation uses a combination of metal and nonmetal conduit. But you could use all nonmetal conduit, or if you think the conduit might be damaged, all metal conduit. In many cases, the local code will dictate the type of material to use.

TOOLS & MATERIALS

■ Round-head shovel ■ Insulated screwdriver ■ Adjustable pliers ■ Multipurpose tool ■ Long-nose pliers ■ Cable ripper ■ Portable drill ■ Wood and masonry bits ■ Trowel ■ Ready-mix concrete ■ Fish tape ■ Hacksaw ■ Cable staples ■ Conduit coupling and clips ■ ¾-inch rigid conduit ■ ¾-inch nonmetallic conduit ■ ¾-inch LB fitting ■ ¾-inch cable box connectors ■ ¾-inch 90-degree conduit sweep elbow ■ ¾-inch locknuts and plastic bushings ■ No.6 awg, black wire ■ 6/3G NM cable ■ No. 10 awg, green and white wires ■ 50-amp, 250-volt, 2-pole waterproof switch

1 Attach a standard LB fitting to the outside of the house wall, and add enough metal conduit to reach into the trench. Attach a sweep elbow to the end of this conduit. Then glue a male adapter to the end of some plastic conduit. Thread this conduit assembly into the threaded end of the sweep elbow.

2 Install a 4x4 pressure-treated post in a hole, and dig a trench from the house to the post and to the spa. Attach a disconnect box to the post (inset); then install sweep elbows and straight conduit to the bottom of the box. Attach the conduit using straps or clips.

3 Fish the individual power wires from the house to the disconnect box and from the box to the spa. Follow the wiring diagram supplied with the switch and the spa to make the wire connections. Usually the black and red-coded power wires go to the LINE side of the switch, while the spa wires go to the LOAD side.

4 Once all the wires are connected, install the waterproof cover according to the manufacturer's instructions (inset). Then turn on the circuit power, and check the performance of the switch.

Outdoor Wiring & Low-Voltage Lighting

smart tip

ELECTRICITY AND WATER

ELECTRICITY AND WATER CAN BE A DEADLY COMBINATION. ALWAYS FOLLOW ALL SAFETY PROCEDURES COMPLETELY. AN ELECTRIFIED POOL CAN BE THE DIRECT RESULT OF A JOB DONE CARELESSLY.

- IF A FIXTURE, GASKET, OR LENS LOOKS OLD OR WORN, REPLACE IT.
- ALWAYS USE A REPLACEMENT LENS, BULB, OR GASKET MADE SPECIFICALLY FOR THE FIXTURE. USE THE SAME MANUFACTURER OR A GENERIC BRAND DESIGNED FOR THE SPECIFIC MAKE AND MODEL.
- EACH FIXTURE IS DESIGNED TO TAKE A SPECIFIC BULB. IF THE WRITING ON THE BULB IS NOT READABLE, NEVER REPLACE THE BULB WITH ONE THAT IS HIGHER THAN 400 WATTS. HEAT CAN MELT THE RESIN THAT MAKES THE FIXTURE WATERPROOF.

REPLACING AN UNDERWATER BULB

project

Underwater Pool Lighting

Install underwater pool lighting in conformance with code requirements. Use wiring suitable for wet locations, and make all splice connections above water. All electrical components below water must be watertight. In addition, the entire lighting system must be grounded.

Underwater lighting can be standard 120-volt or low-voltage (12 volts). Low-voltage systems are highly recommended because the current is so low that it will not endanger a swimmer.

TOOLS & MATERIALS

- Bulb and gasket replacements
- Insulated screwdriver

UNDERWATER LIGHTING CIRCUITS

FOR SAFETY, electrical wiring in and around swimming pools must be on a separate circuit. The wiring must also be suitable for wet locations. There are specific NEC requirements regarding underwater light fixtures [Section 680.23(B)] and the transformers and ground-fault circuit interrupters [Section 680.23(A)(3)] that power them. Although 120-volt lighting systems are available, a 12-volt low-voltage system is advantageous. This type of system uses a weatherproof step-down transformer specifically designed to supply underwater systems. The voltage supplied is so low that a short circuit in the lighting system would be imperceptible to a swimmer and GFCI protection is not required. Low-voltage underwater lights are installed in either wet or dry niches on the interior sides of a pool. A wet niche is a waterproof, standard-size lamp housing connected by conduit to a junction box located above the water and away from the pool. A dry niche isn't waterproof.

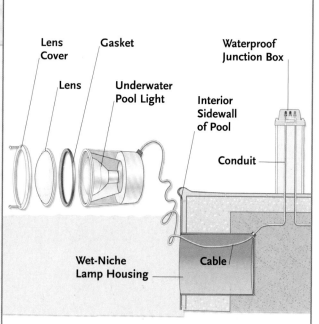

Underwater pool lights can be installed in either wet- or dry-niche lamp housings. Unlike a dry niche, however, a wet niche is waterproof. This way you can replace a lamp without having to first lower the level of the water.

1 Turn off the circuit power at the main service panel. Then lean down into the pool, and use a screwdriver to remove the lock screw that holds the face frame rim in place.

2 Pull the light fixture from its pool housing. The extra cable, attached to the unit, is usually long enough to place the light on the edge of the pool without disconnecting anything. Loosen the lens-cap screws, and carefully pry the lens from the body of the fixture.

3 Remove the burned-out bulb, and replace it with a new bulb. Before reinstalling the fixture, turn on the circuit power to make sure the bulb works. If it does, turn off the power again; reinstall the lens and the face frame rim.

4 Hold the assembled fixture under water to check for an air leak. If you see air bubbles, pull the light up and remove the face frame rim and lens cap. Dry the surfaces, and reinstall the parts making sure that all screws are snug. If another test for air bubbles is negative, install the light unit, and turn on the circuit power.

6

emergency power equipment

TODAY'S HOME needs some kind of protection against the possibility of property damage caused by lightning strikes and power surges, not to mention the threat of injury to you and your family and the inconvenience of power outages. A single lightning strike, for example, can contain 30,000 amps of electrical current—2,000 times more than a typical 15-amp residential circuit.

Electronic equipment is sensitive to lightning, which can destroy your expensive computer system and digital big-screen television. Anything with microcircuits is at risk, including security systems and portable phones. Lightning traveling through phone lines can melt your modem. To make matters worse, a single flash of lightning can consist of several discharges, increasing the odds for damage.

A well-designed lightning protection system will carry a lightning charge through lightning rods and cables on your home down to the ground and safely dissipate it. An effective system should even extend to nearby trees, outbuildings, and other structures that might attract a lightning strike. Another concern, however, is the possibility of damage caused by a power surge through your utility lines. A power surge from a lightning strike miles away can still damage your electronic equipment and telephone system.

To protect against a power surge, it is necessary to stop the surge from entering the house wiring at the main panel. This can be accomplished by installing a whole-house surge arrestor at the main panel and using individual surge arrestors, or suppressors, at points of use that protect each device or appliance at its outlet. To work properly, a surge protection system must also be well grounded be-cause excess current is diverted back through your home's grounding system and into the earth. (See "Grounding Systems," page 267.) A good lightning and surge suppression system will offer little comfort, though, if you're hit by a major power outage lasting for days. For this, it is wise to have an optional standby generator as a backup source of emergency power. (See "Optional Standby Generators," page 220.)

A single strike of lightning can easily damage your home unless you have an effective system in place to carry the current safely to ground.

Emergency Power Equipment

LIGHTNING PROTECTION

Understanding Lightning

A lightning strike occurs after a buildup of negative charges of electrical energy in a cloud and positive charges of electrical energy in the earth. As the dry air between the cloud and the ground becomes moist, negative charges move downward to meet positive charges moving upward, creating a lightning bolt. Lightning, and the thunderstorms that create lightning, occur most frequently in the spring and summer months because they thrive on high air-moisture and ground temperature levels. Lightning can be extremely hot, in some cases hotter than the surface of the sun.

Lightning Rods

Lightning descends to earth in 150-foot steps. When a negatively charged strike is within 150 feet of a lightning rod, the positive charges in the earth surge upward through the lightning protection system to meet and neutralize the strike. An effective lightning protection system creates a cone of protection around a house. The positive charges flow safely from the ground through the cable to the lightning rod, then jump to the negatively charged lightning strike from the rod, not the surface of the house. Lightning rods are usually from 10 to 12 inches long, and contrary to myth, don't attract lightning to your home because they're not much higher than the roofline.

CONE OF PROTECTION

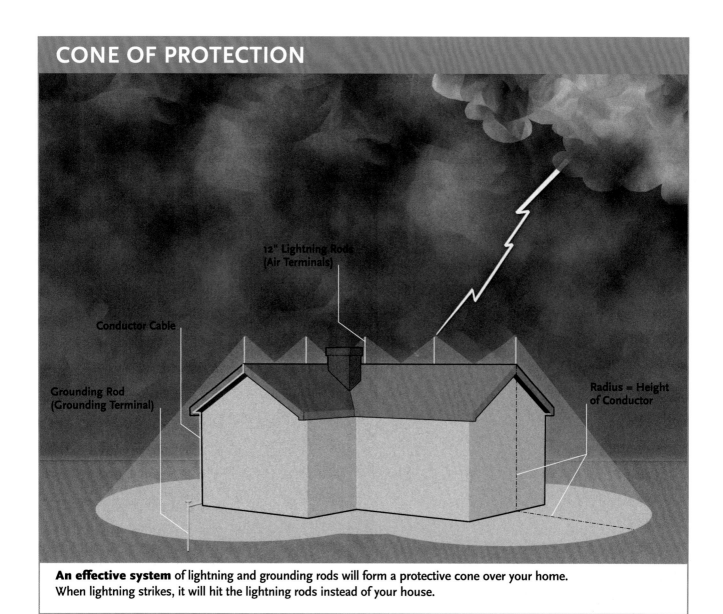

An effective system of lightning and grounding rods will form a protective cone over your home. When lightning strikes, it will hit the lightning rods instead of your house.

LIGHTNING PROTECTION SYSTEMS

A LIGHTNING PROTECTION SYSTEM provides a clear path for lightning to travel directly to the ground without causing injury or destruction to life or property. It consists of three major components: (1) lightning rods, or air terminals; (2) grounding rods, or grounding terminals; and (3) copper or aluminum low-resistance conductor cable to connect the terminals. Copper and aluminum components are used not only because they are excellent conductors of electricity, but also because they are highly resistant to corrosion. Copper is preferred because it conducts electricity better than aluminum and less is needed to carry the same amount of current. However, aluminum is necessary on an aluminum or steel roof because copper coming into contact with aluminum or steel can cause corrosion. Nevertheless, even where aluminum is used, the grounding system must be copper. Aluminum cannot be used underground and must be spliced into the grounding wire at least 18 inches above the ground [NEC Section 250.64(A)].

Before beginning any work, check your local and regional building codes to see whether you must satisfy any special requirements. Also, be certain that all of the lightning protection components you install are listed by Underwriters Laboratories.

Lightning Protection Standards

Various standards for product specifications and installation methods are published regarding lightning protection systems. The National Fire Protection Association (NFPA) publishes "NFPA 780: Standard for Installation of Lightning Protection Systems" (2004). This 45-page document provides requirements for the protection of people, buildings, and property against lightning damage. The Lightning Protection Institute (LPI) publishes "Standard of Practice LPI.175," which establishes requirements for design, materials, workmanship, and inspection of professionally installed lightning protection systems. Underwriters Laboratories (UL) sets guidelines for the certification of systems materials and components in its publication, "Standard UL96A."

When designing a lightning protection system, always include a minimum of two grounding rods as widely separated as possible. To calculate the total number of grounding rods, first measure the perimeter of your home, totaling the length of each exterior wall. If the perimeter is 250 linear feet or less, use two grounding rods; between 250 and 350 linear feet, use three grounding rods; and between 350 and 450 linear feet, use four grounding rods, and so on. Keep all conductor cable running horizontally or angled downward, and avoid sharp turns and U-turns.

To calculate the number of required lightning rods, measure the cumulative length of all roof ridges, including the garage roof and dormers. Antennas, chimneys, weather vanes, cupolas, gables, and other roof projections must all be connected to the main cable using bonding lugs or cable connectors. Most importantly, make certain that the entire lightning protection system is well grounded. If only part of a system is grounded, lightning may flash sideways between grounded metal components on the roof or within the building, setting fire to flammable materials.

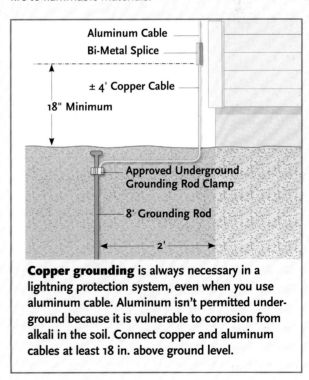

Copper grounding is always necessary in a lightning protection system, even when you use aluminum cable. Aluminum isn't permitted underground because it is vulnerable to corrosion from alkali in the soil. Connect copper and aluminum cables at least 18 in. above ground level.

Emergency Power Equipment

LIGHTNING PROTECTION SYSTEM COMPONENTS

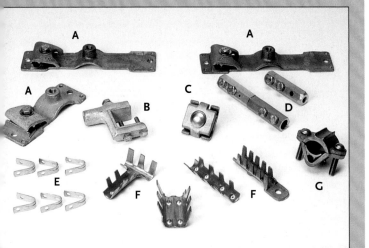

Various clips, clamps, and splicers are used to secure cable, mount lightning rods, clamp cable to lightning and grounding rods, and connect cable runs and tie-ins. A–mounting saddle with clamp; B–flue-tile mount; C–multipurpose clamp; D–cable connectors; E–cable clips; F–cable splicers; G–grounding-rod clamp

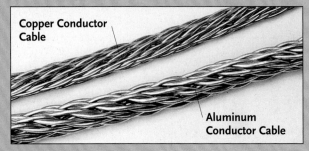

Copper Conductor Cable

Aluminum Conductor Cable

Low-resistance conductor cables carry the lightning current from the rods on your home and other structures safely down to the grounding rods.

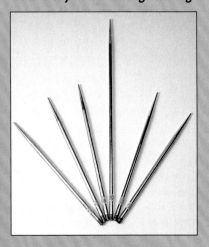

Lightning rods, or air terminals, are vital components of any lightning protection system, detouring current away from your home into grounded conductor cables and, further, to grounding terminals.

INSTALLING A LIGHTNING PROTECTION SYSTEM

project

Once you have determined whether your system will be copper or aluminum (these instructions are for copper only—do not use copper with aluminum), measure the length and width of the roof on your home; then sketch the roof plan to scale on graph paper. Indicate the location and size of all elements on your roof, including chimneys, vents, exhaust fans, antennas, and other equipment. Also note on your plan the height of roof ridges and eaves. This information will be used to lay out the components of your lightning protection system.

TOOLS & MATERIALS

- Round-head shovel ▪ Sledgehammer
- Extension ladder ▪ Measuring tape
- Hammer ▪ Graph paper ▪ Pencil and drafting tools ▪ Work gloves ▪ Safety glasses ▪ ⅝ x 12-inch copper lightning rods with mounting saddles ▪ 8-foot copper-clad ½-inch grounding rods
- ⅜-inch-diameter 20-gauge one-nail copper clips (loop type) ▪ 2½ x 2¾-inch copper flue-tile mount with ⅝ x 18-inch chimney rod ▪ ½-inch-diameter bronze grounding rod clamps ▪ ¹⁵⁄₃₂-inch-diameter smooth-twist 32-strand 17-gauge copper conductor cable
- Bonding lugs and connectors
- Crimp straight and tee cable connectors

Grounding rods, or grounding terminals, take the lightning current from the conductor cables and safely dissipate it into the ground.

Plan the Layout. Plan and sketch the location of each lightning and grounding rod, cable run, chimney rod, bonding lug, splicer, and connector. Locate a lightning rod within 18 inches of each ridge end and spaced no more than 20 feet apart along the remainder of each ridge. On a flat or low-sloped roof, place lightning rods within 18 inches of the corners, at 20-foot intervals along the roof edges, and at 50-foot intervals across the flat or low-sloped area of the roof. Bond all antennas, vents, flues, stacks, and metal objects on the roof to the main ridge cable. Avoid unnecessary turns and bends when laying out your cable runs. Remember that every system requires at least two widely separated grounding rods. One should be located as close as possible and bonded (connected) to your service entrance grounding rod using a bonding jumper cable. The other should be located diagonally across at the opposite side of the house or as far from the first as possible. However, the distance between them should not exceed 100 feet along the perimeter of the house. If it does, add a third grounding rod somewhere between the first two. Use your finished layout to make a list of materials needed; then purchase them. Allow extra conductor cable for turns, branch runs, and terminal connections.

1 Before designing a lightning protection system, take measurements to sketch an accurate plan of your roof. Measure the location of all the roof elements, including dormers, chimneys, antennas and all the HVAC venting equipment.

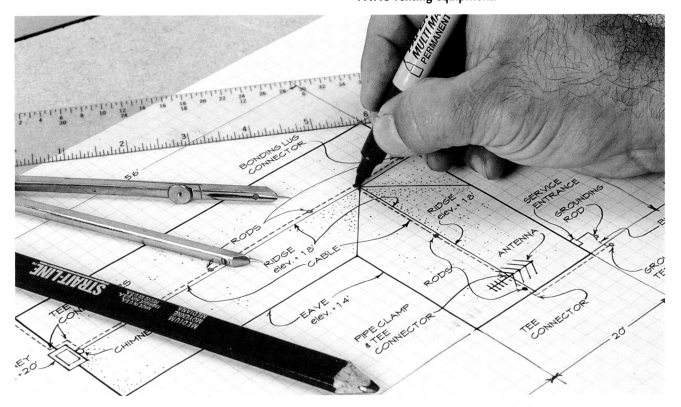

2 Working with the dimensions laid out on your roof plan, determine the optimal location for lightning and grounding rods, cable runs, and connectors. Using this information, compile a list of materials needed for your system.

Continued on next page.

Emergency Power Equipment

Continued from previous page.

3 Begin installing the system by positioning the lightning rods. Be sure to follow local code requirements and the manufacturer's instructions. At each location, attach a mounting saddle on the ridge. Then thread a lightning rod into the saddle, and tighten it using an adjustable wrench.

4 Connect all the lightning rods using conductor cables, and connect this cable system to at least 2 grounding rods on opposite corners of the house. Avoid making sharp turns and bends in the cable.

5 Install a minimum of two 8-ft.-long copper grounding rods located at least 2 ft. away from the house foundation. Drive them straight into the ground using a sledgehammer. Then attach the conductor cable to the rod using grounding rod clamps.

6 One of the grounding rods has to be installed near the service panel grounding rod, so the two can be joined with a jumper cable. Attach one end to the old cable using a grounding clamp. Slide the other end under the grounding clamp on the new rod. Tighten both clamps.

SURGE PROTECTION

Electrical Surges

The major drawback to a lightning protection system is that lightning rods cannot stop electrical surges from coming into a house through utility lines, which is the most common way that lightning damages homes. Transient electrical currents from telephone, cable, and telecommunications lines can cause undesirable surges in voltage. The magnetic field created by a lightning bolt can cause voltage to flow through any conducting material such as the wiring or metal piping in your home. Therefore, an effective surge protection system is a necessity in every home—if it is to be safeguarded against these kinds of potential disruptions.

Whole-House Protection

Many people install low-cost surge arresters, or suppressors, that plug directly into an outlet, believing they are providing themselves with whole-house protection. Unfortunately, this is not the case. Surge suppression must be accomplished on two levels. First is at the main panel, where the surge can be prevented from entering the house wiring, and the second is at the point-of-use, where any surge remaining on a line can be removed just before it enters an appliance or other electrical device. Clearly, it makes sense to use a surge arrester to eliminate heavy surges before they enter your home, rather than after. A surge arrester will divert heavy electrical surges into your grounding system, permitting your point-of-use devices to serve as sensitive electronic filters, shutting down noise on the line, as well as stopping any remaining line surges. If your home has a subpanel located 20 feet or more from the main panel, you should install a second device to protect it, too.

Surge arresters may be directly wired to the main panel and mounted either on the inside or outside of the panel box. The type that mounts inside the panel box is usually preferred because it will keep the arrester safely contained should it explode, preventing a fire. A better system for containing lightning surges, and the easiest to install, is a whole-house protection system in which the surge arrester replaces a circuit breaker in the main panel. Because you have to have a circuit breaker anyway, it makes sense to build the protection directly into it. This type of breaker has a red light that indicates whether or not the surge arrester is functional. Once you install the device, whatever it is wired to will be automatically protected. Though the protection system is contained within the device for a particular circuit, the entire house will be protected—not just that circuit.

Point-of-Use Protection

Providing surge protection directly at an electrical outlet is common practice because it is easy to do—you simply purchase the device and plug it in. No wiring needs to be done. This is called point-of-use protection. These types of surge protectors perform several layers of filtering to eliminate the noise on house wiring and prevent damage to highly sensitive circuitry. They are often used to protect personal computers and home audio-video equipment. Some point-of-use surge protectors electrically isolate their connected plug-ins so that the noise generated by a printer, for example, will not cross over to the computer. Be sure to buy a surge protector that has receptacles arranged in such a way that a plugged-in transformer will not block any of the unused outlets. Also look for one that provides telephone or modem protection.

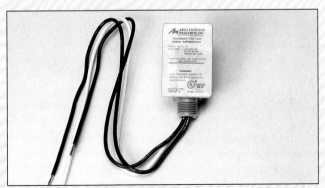

A surge arrester is an essential part of any whole-house protection system, diverting power surges away from your house wiring and into the ground.

Point-of-use surge protectors prevent damage to sensitive equipment, such as computer circuits, and filter out noise on house wiring.

Emergency Power Equipment

GROUNDING

REGARDLESS OF THE QUALITY of your surge protector, it cannot be effective unless it is connected to a good grounding system. An ideal grounding system will typically consist of one or more approved grounding rods and clamps. As a rule, the more grounding rods you have, the better the system. Be certain that the grounding wires are buried deeply enough not to be cut by your lawn mower or otherwise disconnected from the grounding system. Check local code for grounding wire depths.

A lightning strike produces a tremendous amount of power in the form of magnetic flux—lines of force moving through the atmosphere. These lines of force combine to induce a massive voltage and current pulse (fluctuation) in the utility lines. This pulse rides the line until it reaches and enters the electrical system within your home.

Mounted in your main panel, a whole-house surge arrester acts to remove lightning pulses from the line, diverting them to the house grounding system (grounding rods), transforming large pulses into smaller, easily managed pulses. Point-of-use protection devices then carry off the smaller pulses and any others generated within a house that might be able to damage sensitive electronic equipment.

A main-panel surge arrester takes the space of a conventional circuit breaker. Though connected through one circuit, the device protects the entire house.

SURGE OF PROTECTION

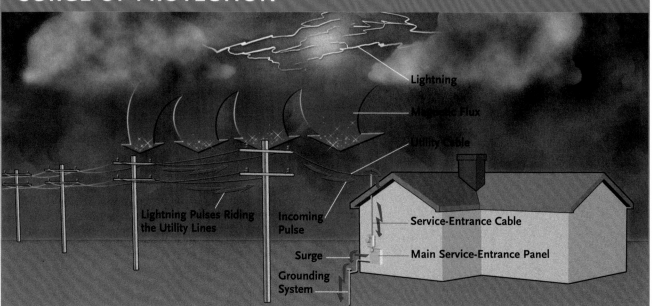

Lightning

Magnetic Flux

Utility Cable

Lightning Pulses Riding the Utility Lines

Incoming Pulse

Service-Entrance Cable

Surge

Main Service-Entrance Panel

Grounding System

Lightning strikes produce a massive amount of power in the form of magnetic fluctuations traveling through the atmosphere. These forces cut into metal wire in power and telephone utility lines, generating a surge or fluctuation in voltage. Incoming surges from a lightning strike are diverted to a grounding system by a whole-house surge arrester. A point-of-use device plugged into an outlet prevents damage to sensitive microcircuits in computers and other equipment. Individual surge arresters give additional protection to phone lines, keeping your modem from meltdown, for instance.

INSTALLING A WHOLE-HOUSE SURGE ARRESTER

Lightning rods, with a properly installed grounding system, go a long way to protect your house from lightning damage. But they can't do much for power surges that reach your house from lightning strikes that happen else-where and are carried to your home by utility lines. A whole-house surge arrestor can neutral-ize these power spikes. Some are designed as circuit breakers to be installed in the main ser-vice panel, as shown here. Others are installed in separate subpanels.

TOOLS & MATERIALS

▪ Insulated screwdrivers
▪ Long-nose pliers
▪ Multipurpose tool
▪ Whole-house surge arrester

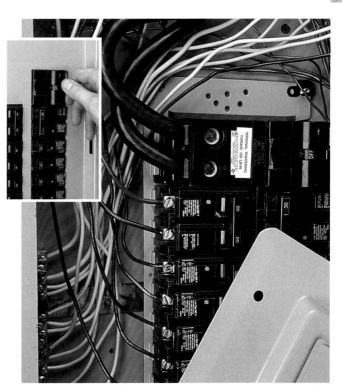

1 Begin installing a whole-house surge protector by turning off the main breaker in the service panel (inset). Then remove the panel cover, and decide where to put the new arrestor breaker.

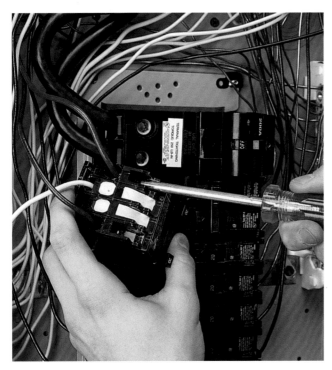

2 Remove two single breakers or one double breaker to make room for the arrestor. Attach the circuit wires to the arrestor according to the manufacturer's instructions. Then push the arrestor into the panel's hot bus.

3 Replace the panel cover, and tighten the mounting screws. Turn on the main breaker to restore power to the whole panel. The surge arrestor's light should be on, which indicates that the device is operating properly.

Emergency Power Equipment

OPTIONAL STANDBY GENERATORS

What They Are and How They Work

In many areas of the country, both winter and summer storms can frequently cause power outages that may last for several days. Homeowners in isolated areas must not only be aware of, but must be prepared for the possibility that storms may bring down power lines. It takes just one extended power outage to convince a homeowner of the benefits of owning an optional standby generator. This differs from a required system and is termed optional because it is intended for use where one's life doesn't depend on the system (NEC Section 702.2). An optional system, for instance, is ideal for a private residence but not for a hospital.

An important concern for the homeowner interested in installing a generator is hooking it up in accordance with legal requirements. Check your local code before starting work. You cannot, for example, connect a generator to your house unless it has a particular type of switch called a double-pole, double-throw switch. This switch has an off position that lies between two on positions. One of the on positions controls the utility power, and the other controls the standby generator power. Some switches made for this purpose may be labeled LINE (utility power), OFF, and GEN (generator power). Hooking a standby generator into a home using any other type of switch will place at risk anyone who works on the power lines.

Temporary Relief. An optional standby generator is basically a small gasoline-powered motor that generates a limited amount of electrical power. The main advantage of owning a generator is to provide temporary power to your home for essential appliances such as a freezer

The safest way to provide temporary power for your home during a power outage is by using a properly connected optional standby generator.

or refrigerator to keep food from spoiling, to power a few lights, to run a well pump, or to keep your house warm. It would not be practical to provide power to an entire house because of the expense and limitations of operating such a system. Gasoline is usually used to operate standby generators because, in most parts of the country, it is not cost-effective to install diesel, propane, or natural-gas generators.

Standby generators are heavy and noisy and require air to "breathe." Because of its great weight, you will need a dolly to move one if it doesn't have wheels. The generated noise and exhaust require a location outside the house or in a vented garage. Another possibility is to put the generator in a small shed or lean-to built just for it. In any case, ventilation must be provided for the generator. Some generators come with a silencer for the exhaust system, as well as a kit for directing the exhaust safely outdoors.

Operation Schedule. How long your generator will run depends on the amount of time you need to draw power from it and the size of its fuel tank. If you have plenty of spare gasoline, you may choose to run the generator all day and then turn it off at night, weather permitting. Or if you must

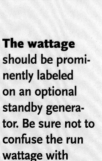

The wattage should be prominently labeled on an optional standby generator. Be sure not to confuse the run wattage with short-lived surge wattage.

A high-end generator motor should be easier to start and more reliable than a low- to mid-range engine. It should also be able to go as long as a year without maintenance.

conserve gasoline, you can run the generator for just one hour out of every four to keep your refrigerator and/or freezer cool or only when you need water or lights. If you choose to use it intermittently, run the generator for at least two to three hours just before you go to bed and again when you get up in the morning. Be sure to read the manufacturer's manual to determine whether you must add oil to the generator motor before starting it.

As an alternative to using a standby generator, homeowners sometimes consider powering a house with batteries. This isn't logical, unless you use solar-powered batteries. Also, batteries provide direct current (DC), while your house uses alternating current (AC). Running a house on batteries during a power outage would require a large investment in a power converter to transform one type electric power into the other.

Selection

Several factors will determine your selection of a home generator. You must consider the wattage, the type of generator motor, whether it is electric or pull-start, and its plug configuration (pattern).

Wattage. A generator has both surge and run wattage. Surge wattage is the power needed to start a device, such as a sump pump, while run wattage is the power needed to keep it running. Because surge wattage lasts for only a few seconds, you will need enough run wattage to satisfy the total wattage of the circuits you want to power. One or two lighting and power circuits, a refrigerator, and hot water and heating controls, for example, require at least a 4,500-watt generator. Preferably, a standby generator should be 6,300 watts or more. The larger the run wattage, the more circuits can be powered at once. Lower-wattage generators may not supply enough wattage to start several appliances at once.

They can be used effectively, however, by operating only one or two appliances at the same time.

Type of Motor. The type, manufacturer, and quality of the generator motor you purchase will largely determine whether or not the engine will start without difficulty when the time comes to use it. Standby generators are often taken for granted until there is a power outage. Many low- to mid-range generators have engines that pull-start like lawn mower engines, and they are just as difficult to start. High-end generator engines are typically easier to start, even when they are not maintained for up to a year. The best engines usually have a key-operated ignition. Generators can be purchased at home centers.

Electric or Pull-Start. Because starting an engine by simply turning a key is a lot easier than pull-starting it, electric-start generators are widely preferred over the pull-start variety. Electric-start engines are also more reliable. Nevertheless, for best performance, it is a good idea to start your generator motor at least once or twice a year to verify that the battery works.

Plug Configuration. Low-power generators have a standard 120-volt ground-fault receptacle on their housings, into which you can plug appliances or extension cords. Mid-power generators characteristically have an additional 240-volt receptacle that looks like a standard receptacle with two horizontal, rather than vertical, slots. Also commonly used is a three-slot twist-lock receptacle that supplies 120 volts. If your generator must supply an entire house with power, though, it must have a female round twist-lock receptacle with four slots. This type of receptacle supplies both 120- and 240-volt power—exactly what is required to power a home.

An electric-start motor is usually superior to a manual pull-start engine. This type of motor starts with a simple turn of a key, just like an automobile. The pull-cord is a backup.

Only receptacles labeled GFCI are ground-fault circuit protected. Only a four-slotted twist-lock receptacle labeled 120V/240V can be used to power an entire house.

Emergency Power Equipment

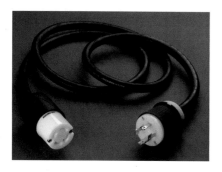

A **twist-lock** extension cord using a three-conductor with ground cable is required to connect power from a generator to a house.

Placement and Hookup

An optional standby generator should be located as close as possible to the main panel. The longer the extension cord, the more voltage-drop will occur across the distance, reducing power available to your home. For ease of hookup, you can run an extension cord through a window or other opening, through a wall, or into wall-mounted male and female receptacles.

It is not permitted by code to connect an optional standby generator directly to your house wiring by plugging it into a dryer or range receptacle. When a generator is hooked directly to a house circuit, it can send electricity back to the utility—a process called back-feeding. Not only is back-feeding a code violation, it is extremely dangerous to utility workers because it can cause electrocution, not to mention the possibility of burning down your house. Power surging up and down the lines can even burn up the source generator. The standby generator must be installed using a transfer switch suitable for the intended use, and designed and installed so as to prevent the inadvertent interconnection of normal and alternate sources of supply.

smart tip

BUILT-IN BACKUP POWER

PORTABLE GENERATORS CAN BE HARD TO FIND DURING A POWER OUTAGE. AN ALTERNATIVE EMERGING ON THE HOME IMPROVEMENT MARKET IS THE STATIONARY EMERGENCY POWER GENERATOR. THIS TYPE IS BUILT INTO A HOME IN MUCH THE SAME WAY AS CENTRAL AIR CONDITIONING. LIKE A PORTABLE GENERATOR, THE SYSTEM AUTOMATICALLY KICKS IN MOMENTS AFTER AN INITIAL LOSS OF POWER. CONNECTED TO A NATURAL-GAS LINE OR PROPANE TANK, IT ELIMINATES THE NEED FOR GASOLINE.

INSTALLING AN OPTIONAL STANDBY GENERATOR

project

Being without power for a few hours, or even a day, can be aggravating but tolerable. Having no power for a couple of days is another matter, especially if you have a freezer full of food getting warmer by the hour. A standby generator can make problems like these go away.

TOOLS & MATERIALS

▮ Insulated screwdrivers ▮ Knockout punch ▮ Cable ripper ▮ Long-nose pliers ▮ Multipurpose tool ▮ Power drill with 11/16-inch spade bit ▮ Caulking gun and caulk ▮ Electrical tape ▮ Wire connectors ▮ Cable clamps ▮ Standby generator ▮ Transfer-switch panel box with manual transfer switch ▮ ¾-inch-diameter conduit nipple ▮ Wood or masonry screws ▮ 10/4G rubber, water-resistant cord with stranded wires ▮ 4-prong motor receptacle ▮ Panel grounding bus ▮ 30-amp, 240-volt breaker ▮ 1-inch-diameter conduit or threaded nipple ▮ 10/3G NM cable ▮ ¾-inch cable staples ▮ Outdoor receptacle box and weatherproof cover ▮ 240-volt 3-wire with ground twist-lock extension cord

4 Determine which circuits you want to be powered by the standby generator, and identify which breakers service these circuits. Then remove the black (hot) wire from each of these breakers.

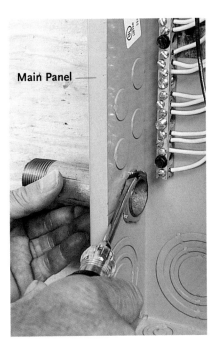

Main Panel

1 Begin the installation by turning off the main breaker, unscrewing the panel cover, and removing a knockout plate from the side of the box. Then install a conduit nipple that's threaded on both ends.

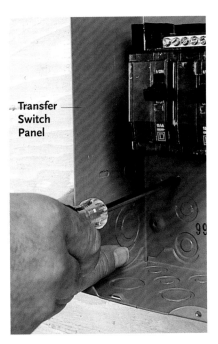

Transfer Switch Panel

2 Remove a knockout plate on the side of the transfer switch box, and slide the box over the end of the conduit nipple. Attach the switch box to the wall.

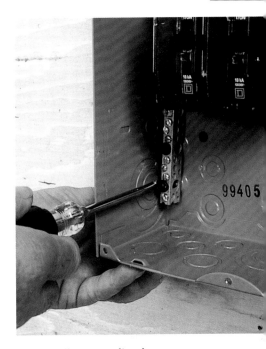

3 Install a grounding bus on the back panel of the transfer switch box. The box has threaded holes to accept the screws used to mount the bus bar.

5 Once all the black wires are removed from the relevant breakers, pull these breakers from the hot bus, and set them aside.

6 Each circuit also has a white (neutral) wire and a bare ground wire that are attached to the neutral and/or grounding bus bars. Remove these wires from the bus bars.

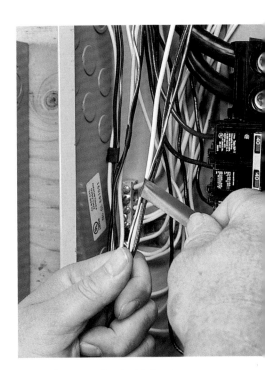

7 To keep track of which wires go together, identify the black, white, and ground wire for each circuit, and wrap them with tape.

Continued on next page.

Emergency Power Equipment

Continued from previous page.

8 Transfer power from the main service panel to the transfer switch with 10/3G NM cable. Then cut a length to size, and strip the sheathing from both ends of the cable. Feed this cable through the conduit nipple.

9 Strip the insulation off the wires that join the two boxes. Then attach an end of the white wire and the ground wire to the neutral/grounding bus bar. Tighten the lugs that hold these wires securely, and fold any extra wire out of the way at the bottom of the box.

12 Attach the two hot wires (red and black) from the main panel to the 240-volt circuit breakers in the transfer switch panel. Attach the white wire to the neutral bus bar and the ground wire to the grounding bus bar.

13 The circuits that are going to be controlled with the transfer switch need their wires extended so they reach into the switch box. Cut pieces of proper-gauge cable to length, strip off a couple inches of sheathing and the insulation off the wire. Join these wires to the circuit wires with wire connectors.

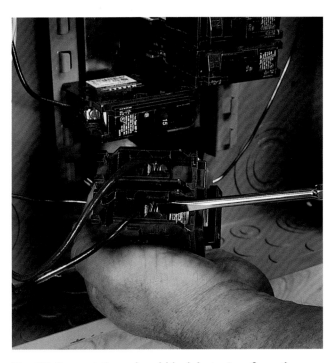

10 Connect the red and black hot wires from the cable that joins the two boxes to the hot terminals on a 30-amp, 240-volt circuit breaker. Make sure these screws are tightened securely.

11 Push the new breaker into the hot bus bar using any available empty space. Make sure the breaker is pushed all the way in. If its outside surface is flush with the other breakers, it's installed properly.

14 Attach the other ends of the wire extensions to the bus bars in the transfer switch. The white wires go to the neutral bus, and the ground wires go to the grounding bus. Tighten the lugs securely over all these wires.

15 Attach the black (hot) wire from each extended circuit cable to the screw clamp on one of the transfer switch circuit breakers. Once the wire is attached, push the breaker in the switch panel's hot bus.

Continued on next page.

Emergency Power Equipment

Continued from previous page.

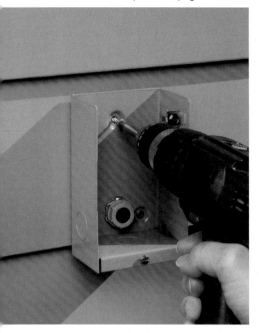

16 To make the exterior connections to the generator, first mount a weatherproof box on the outside of the house. Choose a spot close to the service panel.

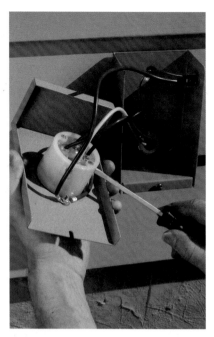

17 Fish 10/3G cable into the back of the receptacle box. Then join these wires to the back of the receptacle.

18 Bring the other end of the cable that goes to the exterior receptacle into the transfer switch box. Attach the white and ground wires to their bus bars and the hot wires to the breaker.

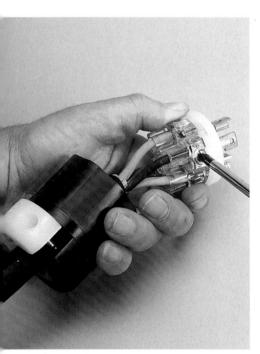

19 Create the extension cord that connects the receptacle to the generator by installing a male plug on one end and a female plug on the other.

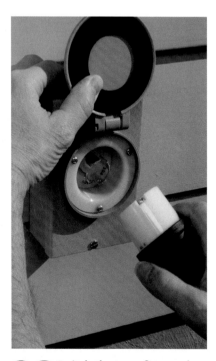

20 Switch the transfer panel to the generator supply, and plug the female end of the extension cord into the receptacle.

21 Plug the other end of the extension cord into the generator, and start the engine. Check that all the breakers in the switch and main panel are working properly.

smart tip

GENERATOR SAFETY

- Because they are powered by gasoline, standby generators emit carbon-monoxide fumes. For this reason, locate your generator outdoors in a well-ventilated area or in a vented garage or shed.
- If no electricity is generated after a long period of storage, follow the manufacturer's directions for reset-ting the generator polarity (positive or negative state).
- Ground the generator to the proper connection provided on the motor base.
- If it must be stored, leave oil in the generator but do not store it with gasoline in the lines.
- Do not make any modifications to a generator. Use only in accordance with the manufacturer's instructions.

TRANSFER-SWITCH PANELS

SOME TRANSFER SWITCHES come prewired and self-contained in their own panel box. The panel box has an already attached flexible conduit lead. You simply need to turn off the power; attach the conduit lead to the main panel box; pull the lead extension wires from the switch panel into the main box; disconnect the black wires going to the breakers you want powered by the generator; and splice them into the black lead wires from the switch panel. Connect the red wires to the breakers and the white wire to the neutral bus of the main panel. If there is a green wire, attach it to the grounding bus in the main panel. On many panels, the grounding and neutral bus will be combined into one grounding/neutral bus. Connect the generator power to the transfer-switch panel by inserting a female, four-prong, 240-volt, twist-lock plug into the receptacle on the face of the prewired switch panel.

1 Some transfer-switch systems are prewired out-of-the-box, simplifying their connection to the main panel. Attach the conduit lead from the switch panel to the main panel; then pull the lead wires into the main panel.

2 Splice the hot black wires to the breakers; attach the hot red wires to the empty slots; and connect the neutral and ground to the grounding/neutral bus.

3 Connect the standby generator to the newly installed transfer-switch panel using a female, four-prong, 240-volt twist-lock plug.

7
home automation

HOME AUTOMATION has been growing steadily in the building industry since its inception during the 1970s. In the past, low-quality cable and poor connections resulted in noise and interference on communication lines. Today, structured wiring systems eliminate this problem. A structured wiring system is one that uses a wider bandwidth, allowing more information to pass through the wire. Structured wiring, such as Category 5 (CAT 5) wiring, is critical for phone, fax, and high-speed digital computer transmissions. It is being installed in many new homes; and new buzzwords such as "power-line carrier controls," "design protocols," "home networking," and "smart house" are rapidly entering our vocabulary. Originally, individual appliances were automated for the sake of cutting down on energy use, creating built-in security, and providing simple convenience. Today's systems go much further—integrating all functions in a house and controlling them directly and remotely. All the electricity, heating, cooling, plumbing, lighting, and even communications, computer, security, and audio-video equipment are united by a single control system. Appliances merge with this system and can monitor themselves to schedule repairs and maintenance. Through various internet connections, appliances will soon be able to download their own software upgrades or make purchases for you. Such systems may be controlled from a master console located in your home, programmed and run by your personal computer, or even controlled remotely from an outside location. Currently emerging systems even act as a residential gateway, or central entry point, through which outside data and services may enter your home and be distributed.

SMART HOME BASICS

Power-Line Carrier Control

Depending on the type, home-automation systems may be hardwired using special structured cable or conventional residential cable. Alternatively, they may be remotely controlled by radio-frequency signals. Running wires to connect light switches, thermostats, home theaters, and other devices to a microprocessor is extremely difficult to do in an existing home and is usually reserved for new construction. Surface wiring is an alternative, if you are determined to have a hardwired system. Some homeowners may choose this method because hardwired systems are extremely reliable. It is simpler and more cost-effective to install a system that transmits commands to your electronic devices through existing house wiring and/or radio waves.

A power-line carrier (PLC) is any automation controller that permits one-way command signals to be transmitted over a standard electrical system without needing to run additional wires. Coded digital pulses sent over wires control designated electrical circuits. The transmitter can be a simple wall-mounted keypad or a key-chain remote. With a remote wireless transmitter, you can sit in your favorite armchair, lounge out in your yard, or even pull into your driveway and still be able to turn any device in the house on or off. If you want to turn off your upstairs lights while you're watching television downstairs, you can do it with a single push of a button. Today, you can control virtually any electrical device using keypads, touch panels, handheld remotes, or even your voice.

Home Automation

TYPES OF SIGNAL CONTROLLERS

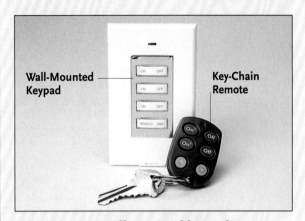

Wall-Mounted Keypad

Key-Chain Remote

You can use a wall-mounted keypad to control any function from a single location inside your house, while a key-chain remote extends this control outdoors.

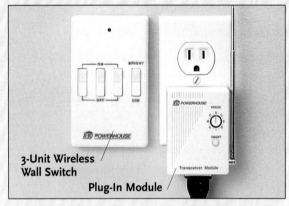

3-Unit Wireless Wall Switch

Plug-In Module

A remote switch transmits control signals to any number of plug-in receivers or control units (modules) within a house.

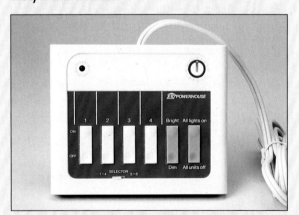

A plug-in master controller transmits signals onto a conventional alternating current (AC) line to control X-10 plug-in modules from any location you choose.

Timer Control

In the past, one mechanical timer could control only one device. Today, standard home-automation timer controls can independently or in combination perform multiple tasks throughout your house. Advanced timer controls operate directly or remotely and can even turn security switching on and off randomly. If power is interrupted, they have a battery backup.

Computer Control

Current automation standards, or protocols, provide for interaction between computers and home-automation devices. Such systems allow the homeowner to download automation schedules into their personal computers. Currently, you can use available software to control devices at specific times and locations with the simple click of a mouse. You can even dial-up your computer by telephone and control any device in your house. Call home from the office, and your whirlpool can be running, the outside security lights turned on, and your food cooked by the time you get home.

Wireless Remote Control

Remote-control devices rely on radio-frequency transmissions to operate lights and appliances from a remote location within a limited distance of your home, such as from your yard, driveway, or garage. As mentioned earlier, these controls take the form of key chains, wall switches, or handheld remotes like the one you use to operate your television set. The transceiver, whether mounted on the wall or plugged into a receptacle, receives and transmits radio signals through your existing house wiring to control a specified appliance, fixture, or other device.

Home Networking

Home networking is entering the marketplace fast on the heels of home automation. Virtually every appliance used in the home today is available with some type of independently operated electronic processor. Home networking is a system of connecting circuitry to share information electronically. Such networking enables all of your appliances to work together under one brain or control system. There are three basic types of networks: computer, entertainment, and control. A computer network links personal computers (PCs) and peripheral devices, such as printers, scanners, and fax machines. An entertainment network connects equipment like TVs, VCRs, stereos, and DVD

Home Automation

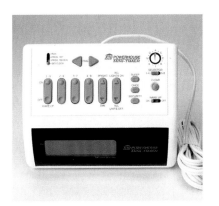

A remote timer control can command multiple modules to turn on or off at different times and even set intensity levels or work in conjunction with an alarm.

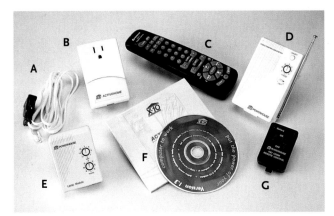

For the ultimate in home automation, install a computer software control system that operates everything from lights and appliances to home theater. A–computer cable; B–computer interface; C–handheld remote; D–transceiver module; E–lamp module; F–software CD; G–key-chain remote

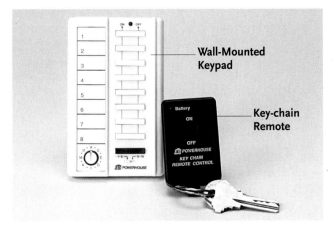

Wall-Mounted Keypad

Key-chain Remote

Wireless controls use radio frequencies, in-home or away from home, to remotely operate anything connected to your home-automation system.

players. A control network (the brains of the system) joins lighting, switching, security, sprinkler, heating, ventilating, air-conditioning, plumbing, and other mechanical and electronic equipment to one command center.

SURGE CONTROL

SOME HOME-AUTOMATION SYSTEMS use power lines to transmit their signals. Unfortunately, many appliances, such as TVs and computer printers, can create noise on a wiring network, reducing the clarity of signals. When an automation system unintentionally turns itself on and off or occasionally doesn't work at all, this may be the reason. If you suspect it is, unplug the appliance to see whether the system will then work properly. If an appliance is causing a problem, you must plug it into a high-end surge suppressor to filter out the noise. This type of suppressor is similar to the multiple-outlet adapter that you plug your computer into to protect it from power surges—but it must be premium quality and labeled "filter" on the box.

High-powered surges (lightning pulses) must be stopped before they enter the house wiring—not after. You cannot depend solely upon the multiple outlet suppressor to protect your system. Electronic devices are extremely sensitive, and home automation products are no exception. Systems can turn on and off by themselves if a surge, or spike, from a thunderstorm or other cause travels down the power line. A power reduction, or brownout, made by a utility company can also affect electronic devices. However, major surges can be minimized by installing a special type of surge arrester (suppressor) in the main service panel. The unit takes the space of a standard circuit breaker.

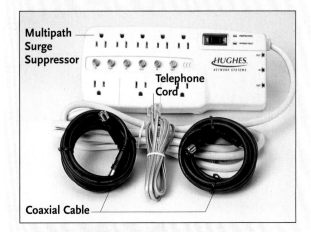

Multipath Surge Suppressor

Telephone Cord

Coaxial Cable

A multipath surge suppressor can eliminate noise on wiring that may interfere with home-automation signal transmission.

Home Automation

DATA-TRANSMISSION STANDARDS

Design Protocols

Every home-automation system consists of transmitters, receivers, and the signals transmitted between them. As one might think, any company can develop its own system of design standards, or protocols, and use them to receive and send signals along the wiring in your home to control their own automation products. The best known and most popular protocols are X-10, CEBus, and LonWorks.

X-10

X-10 technology controls circuits by sending signals from one point to another, eliminating the need to run wires. This makes X-10 especially suitable for existing homes. Not having to cut drywall and fish wires saves on labor and materials, reducing the installation cost of a complete home-automation system.

In an X-10 system, signals are transmitted by modulating radio-frequency (RF) bursts of 120-kilohertz (kHz) power. These RF bursts consist of a start code and a house code, along with function and unit codes. These are superimposed over the voltage on your house wiring.

Simply put, a burst of power is equivalent to a digital one (1), and a lack of a burst is equivalent to a digital zero (0). A combination of ones and zeros (binary system) represents a particular command. X-10 systems provide 32 codes, known as address groups. There are 16 house codes and 16 unit codes that, in combination, provide up to 256 unique addresses to assign to individual devices.

Each receiver in the system will respond to only one of up to six commands given for a set address: ON, OFF, DIM, BRIGHT, ALL LIGHTS ON, or ALL LIGHTS OFF. For example, an appliance module may receive a signal to turn on, while a wall switch is commanded to dim a light, and a wall receptacle is directed to cut power to whatever device is plugged into it. Modules are available for light switches and dimmers, occupancy sensors, timers, etc. Place a master controller by your bedside or armchair. For ultimate control, your computer can take charge.

CEBus

Consumer Electronic Bus (CEBus) is a communications protocol for home-automation networks developed by the Electronics Industry Association (EIA) and the Consumer Electronics Manufacturers Association (CEMA). CEBus signals can be transmitted across AC power lines, low-voltage wires, category 5 cable, coaxial cable, radio and infrared frequencies, and fiber optics. CEBus standards were designed to augment the remote control and monitoring

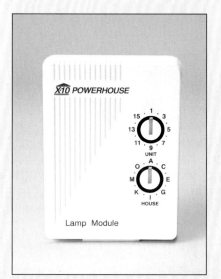

A lamp or appliance module can be programmed to any one of 16 house codes in combination with any one of 16 unit codes. The codes can control up to 256 devices.

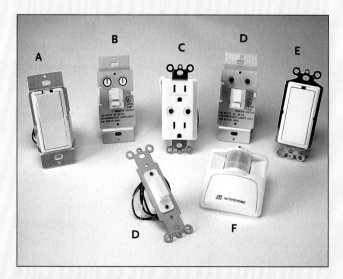

Automation components: A–master remote-control dimmer; B–wall switch module; C–wall receptacle module; D–3-way wall switch modules; E–companion remote-control dimmer; F–occupancy/motion sensor

of mechanical, electrical, home entertainment, security, and other systems. CEBus devices communicate using an electronic command language, called Common Application Language (CAL), which includes device-specific commands such as fast forward, rewind, volume up, temperature down, etc. This differs from the X-10 system in that it uses variable signals to change the intensity of each radio-frequency burst. The length of the burst determines whether the digital number created is a one or a zero. CEBus standards also make communications more reliable because they require that a system be able to recover from signaling errors.

LonWorks

LonWorks is a leading standard for home networking that provides a vehicle for communication between control products and systems. The protocol proposes design guidelines for LonWorks compatible products and systems, as well as certifies and promotes them. The latest LonWorks-based standard, known as EIA-709, was developed by CEMA. It is now a widely supported industry standard, considered by some to be the best choice for automating lighting, heating, ventilation, air-conditioning, and other systems because of its compatibility with other formats. In addition to home automation, its systems are used commercially in transportation, energy management in major buildings, and industrial equipment control.

Smart House

Smart House is a limited partnership formed by the National Association of Home Builders (NAHB) that invites competing home-automation manufacturers to develop products and applications for Smart House technology to be used for control of security, utility, home entertainment, lighting, and other residential systems. The intention is to unify the wiring of such systems to simplify installation and reduce costs and not add much to the overall cost of a house.

Smart House wiring consists of branch cabling for conventional power and digital data transmission, applications cable to transmit digital data and direct current (DC) voltage to operate control sensors, and communications cable for video and telecommunications wiring. These cables control appliances, monitor their status, and transmit information. The drawback to the Smart House system is that it is privately owned and requires custom wiring and service.

Regardless of which data-transmission standard you use—X-10, CEBus, LonWorks, or Smart House—remember that power-line communications are seldom enough. To control the multitude of electronic devices and equipment commonly found in today's homes, other types of communication methods must also be supported, including wireless systems like infrared (IR) and radio frequency (RF) transmission.

METHODS OF SIGNAL TRANSMISSION

Transmission Standard	Transmission Method	Relative Cost
X-10	Power line	Low
CEBus	Power line, twisted pair, coaxial cable, radio frequency, infrared, fiber optics	Low to moderate
LonWorks	Power line, twisted pair, radio frequency, additional types supported by third-party transceivers	Low to moderate
Smart House	Custom wiring only	Moderate to high

The standards listed above provide for data transmission using a variety of signaling methods, each with its own cost relative to the others.

Home Automation

USES FOR HOME AUTOMATION

Lighting Systems and Appliances

Uses for home automation are as varied as the users. You may, for example, wish to operate outside house lights using a key-chain remote. This comes in handy when you need to carry in groceries after dark or fumble with keys to unlock the door. If you're tired of reminding children to turn off the bathroom lights, zap them off using your chair-side remote. If you wish to turn lights on or off or dim them from your bedroom, hit your bedside remote. You can control a single device, such as dimming a bedroom light, or an entire lighting system. Lighting is commonly automated. Initially, automation wiring let people turn lights on in different rooms at varied times for security. Automation has evolved to include outside security and walkway lights, among other things. Every member of a household can possess his or her own key-chain transmitter—providing complete home control, including activation of emergency systems. If someone with a health problem is in the garden, unable to get to the house for assistance, help can be summoned using a key-chain transmitter. A button sounds an alarm or transmits a call to the police or emergency medical service. You can control all of the lights and appliances in your home by connecting each to its own transceiver, plugging modules into standard receptacles, or replacing switches and receptacles with ones that are automated. Such equipment can be controlled by a computer or timing device or activated by a heat, motion, passive infrared (light), or ultrasonic (sound) sensor.

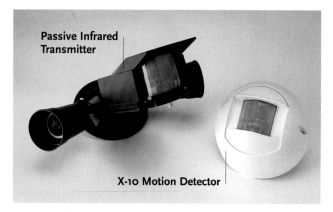

Outdoor transmitters, such as passive infrared and photocell controllers, can command both indoor and outdoor devices to switch on or off at a preset time.

PLUMBING

BOTH WATER AND NATURAL-GAS plumbing systems can be automated for user convenience and safety. Gas shutoff valves can now be electronically controlled to turn off when a fire is detected or at predetermined times. Likewise, water pipes can be turned off in an emergency or sprinkler systems set to start using a remote controller. Photoelectric sensors can even be used to automatically turn your water faucets on and off or to flush your toilet as you step away. Other possibilities include water softeners, pools, spas, clothes washers, clothes dryers, and water heaters—all of which can be tied into sensors, timers, and/or security systems. These systems usually have manual overrides or battery backup in case of power outages or malfunctions.

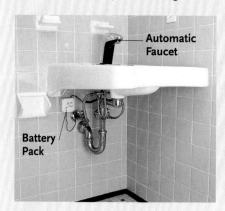

Use an automatic faucet to turn water on or off without having to touch a faucet handle, enhancing personal hygiene in your bathroom or kitchen.

Heating, Ventilating, and Air Conditioning

Energy management has become a major element in home automation. Heating, ventilating, and air-conditioning (HVAC) systems are easily programmed into a household computer system. With a click of a mouse, you can independently control the temperature in each room or zone in your house, resulting in significant energy and cost savings. You can program different temperatures for night and day and even have a temperature setting for when you go on vacation. Zone controls allow a homeowner to compensate for variable conditions in spaces exposed to different degrees of heat gain or loss. For example, conditions in a south-facing room with lots of glass will be significantly different from those in a north-facing room with a fireplace. If computers aren't your thing, you may decide to use another type of sys-

Home Automation

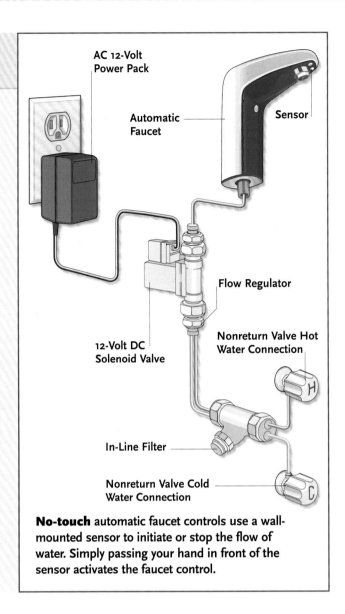

AC 12-Volt Power Pack

Automatic Faucet

Sensor

Flow Regulator

12-Volt DC Solenoid Valve

Nonreturn Valve Hot Water Connection

In-Line Filter

Nonreturn Valve Cold Water Connection

No-touch automatic faucet controls use a wall-mounted sensor to initiate or stop the flow of water. Simply passing your hand in front of the sensor activates the faucet control.

HOME SECURITY

PROBABLY THE MOST IMPORTANT ASPECT of home automation is its impact on home security—the enhanced ability to deter and prevent, or detect and apprehend intruders; to warn of smoke, fire, and carbon monoxide gases; and to signal for emergency assistance. Home automation systems take self-contained components and tie them into a single, centrally controlled network for comprehensive protection. Such a network may consist of perimeter alarms, lights, detection sensors, communications devices, and system controllers. Motion detectors can warn of someone's presence on your property. Gateways can be remotely controlled and monitored by closed-circuit television. Windows and doors may be fitted with alarms. You can install magnetic switches that sense the opening of a window or door, or screens that sound an alarm when being cut. In the home, many types of detectors can be used to warn of smoke, fire, heat, or gas. These devices may all be circuited to sound an alarm in the home while simultaneously signaling an emergency service miles away. Your entire home-security system can be connected by an automatic telephone-dialing system that sends a prerecorded message directly to security monitoring stations, police and fire departments, and emergency medical services.

tem, such as direct-wired X-10 signals or thermostats that work by sensing changes in outdoor temperatures. Such communicating thermostats may have multiple indoor and outdoor sensors. Ports, known as contact closures, allow you to remotely select temperature and time settings.

Communicating thermostats can control and monitor the heating, ventilating, and air-conditioning systems in your home, either independently or by zone.

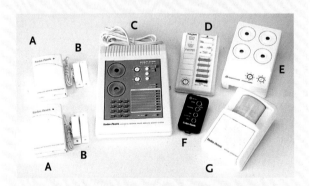

Wireless systems can monitor multiple security zones, be programmed remotely, indicate alarm status, and trigger a silent alarm. A–window/door sensors; B–magnetic switches; C–security console; D–security remote; E–power horn; F–key-chain remote; G–motion detector

Home Automation

TYPES OF AUTOMATED CONTROLS

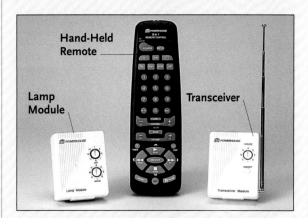

Hand-Held Remote

Lamp Module

Transceiver

Use a transceiver, lamp module, and universal remote to set up a home theater system to control your A/V equipment and switches, and even dim your lights.

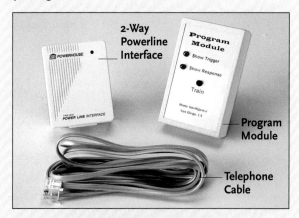

2-Way Powerline Interface

Program Module

Program Module

Telephone Cable

Dial in control commands to X-10 devices with telephone controllers. They also work with answering machines and voice mail. Security codes deter unauthorized access.

Macro controllers allow you to develop and automatically transmit complex sequences of commands for multiple devices.

OUTDOOR SYSTEMS

ASIDE FROM LIGHTING and home security, you can automate your home to meet different outdoor needs. Lawn and garden watering are most commonly automated. A sprinkler system, whether above or inground, can easily be tied to a timer set to turn the water on or off at a preset time. A controller can be programmed to set, change, or cancel watering times and even to actuate multiple spray zones at different times. Many lesser-known uses exist for outdoor automation. A hot tub or pool, for example, can be wired to fill automatically or sense when it is occupied. An occupancy sensor can be connected to an alarm that lets you know if someone, like a playing child, has fallen into the pool. Another use might be a de-icing system on your roof or under your driveway that can be activated remotely or by a temperature sensor. With rapid changes in technology, the choices available to homeowners in the future will be limited only by the bounds of their imagination.

An aboveground or underground watering system is an ideal candidate for automation, providing a homeowner with convenience and reliability. You can program automatic sprinkler controls to operate multiple valve zones and to independently set or alter watering times for each zone.

A sprinkler valve connected to an irrigation controller will automatically activate your sprinkler system.

TELECOMMUNICATIONS AND NETWORKING

SCIENCE AND TECHNOLOGY have expanded telecommunications way beyond the simple exchange of voices over telephone wire. Today, telecommunications includes fax transmission, teleconferencing, multiple-line phone systems, online data transmission, message recording and retrieval, and even video exchange. As we have illustrated throughout this chapter, the telephone is itself an important part in many home-automation systems, serving as the vehicle for remote signaling and automatic security dialing.

One of the most important aspects of telecommunications today is the ability to network (connect) computer systems, including peripheral equipment and communications devices. This is especially valuable in a world where more and more people are working at home. Being connected to a network allows you to share computer files and equipment with anyone else who also happens to be connected to the same network. These local-area networks, or LANs, may be limited to one

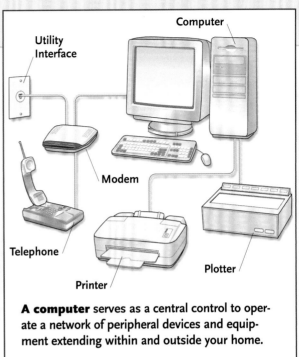

A **computer** serves as a central control to operate a network of peripheral devices and equipment extending within and outside your home.

building or an entire neighborhood. Wide-area networks (WANs) may extend over greater distances. Clearly, an automated control system connected to a network could easily be shared over multiple locations.

With the advent of fiber optics, which uses laser-generated light to transmit signals through glass fibers, the scope of telecommunications promises to become even greater. In the near future, fiber-optic signals will carry vocal, musical, and computer-generated sounds; graphic, photographic, and video images; and data transmissions to every household.

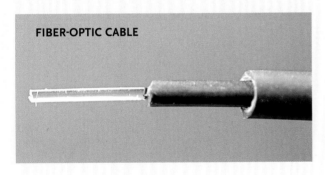

FIBER-OPTIC CABLE

Entertainment Systems

Another popular use for indoor automation is control of a home theater or entertainment center. Technological advances constantly bring new products onto the market, such laserdisc players, digital versatile disc (DVD) players, digital satellite systems (DSS), and interactive television. Add these to conventional devices, such as television sets, telephones, stereo receivers, videotape recorders, video game players, and countless other electronic gadgets that are designed to make life more enjoyable, and you have a recipe for a tangled web of wiring in your home. These systems must be carefully planned even when installed independently. They can be integrated into one system,

however, using home automation. Controllers can be programmed to command sound, vibration, power switches, and communications between devices. You can, for example, install a device to remotely control a home entertainment center. You can program a system to turn on or off when you dial your telephone by letting it ring a set number of times. Or you may set the volume to automatically lower when the phone rings and resume when it is hung up. Automation controls can be programmed to operate everything from lighting levels to curtain closers, channel switching to equipment selection—all at the push of a button. Such custom programs are called macros.

X-10 PROJECTS

Sprinkler System

An automated sprinkler system is a great convenience. You can control one or several sprinkler zones at preset times and adjust water-pressure levels for each zone, according to terrain and microclimate characteristics—all without the worry of remembering to turn the system off before going to bed. A moisture sensor can even be included to override the system settings on rainy days. Such a system can also be tied into weather monitoring instruments to automatically adjust for wind, humidity, and other weather conditions.

Optional Power-Line Interface. You may opt to add a two-way power line interface to your system to convert X-10 signals from the sprinkler controller onto the power line or relay X-10 transmissions on the line to the device. If there is one provided for this purpose, this device plugs into a jack in the automatic-sprinkler controller panel, using a standard RJ11 telephone connector and cable. This allows you to operate the system remotely.

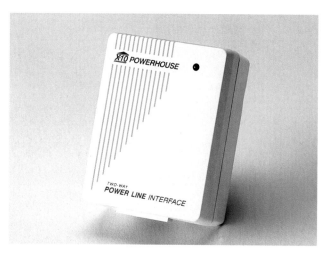

A two-way power-line interface can be added to your automated sprinkler system to transmit messages between the system and your remote control.

smart tip

SPRINKLER WIRING

AS AN ALTERNATIVE TO USING ONE MULTI-WIRE CABLE, USE TWO. CONNECT ONE TO THE FRONT YARD SPRINKLER ZONE AND THE OTHER TO THE BACKYARD SPRINKLER ZONE.

project

INSTALLING A SPRINKLER CONTROLLER

Watering a lawn (or garden) by hand can take a lot of time and can waste a lot of water unless you pay very close attention to where you place the hose and for how long. A better idea is to control your watering by establishing an automatic sprinkler controller.

TOOLS & MATERIALS

For standard 24-volt automatic sprinkler valves
▌ Insulated screwdrivers ▌ Multipurpose tool ▌ Long-nose pliers ▌ Watertight wire connectors ▌ No. 10 x 1¼-inch screws or masonry screws ▌ Pigtail connectors ▌ Automatic irrigation (sprinkler) controller ▌ 9-volt alkaline battery ▌ 18-gauge, color-coded, multistrand, direct burial (14-gauge for runs over 800 feet)

SPRINKLER ANATOMY

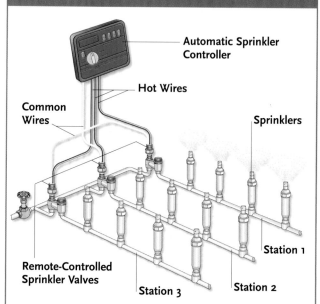

Each sprinkler station must be connected to its own station terminal in the automatic sprinkler controller. A valve opens when it receives a signal from the controller, turning the sprinkler on. After duration setting is reached, the controller closes the valve and opens the next one in the sequence.

Home Automation

1 Establish a location for the automatic-sprinkler controller unit (and install the mounting screws) on an indoor wall near a standard duplex receptacle. This location should be shielded from intense sunlight, dampness, and temperatures over 120 deg. and under 32 deg. F.

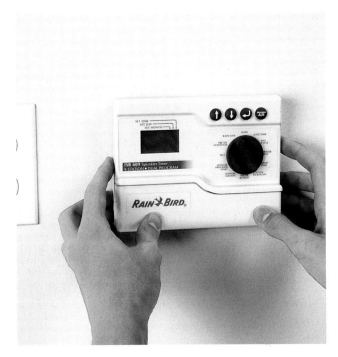

2 Hang the controller unit on the mounting screws, and make sure it fits tightly against the wall. If it's loose, remove the unit; tighten the screws slightly; and replace the controller.

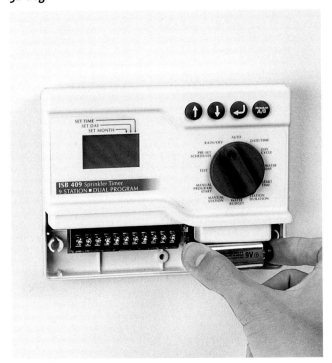

3 Before installing the sprinkler wiring or programming the controller, install the back-up battery that operates the unit's memory. Without this battery backup, you can't program the timer.

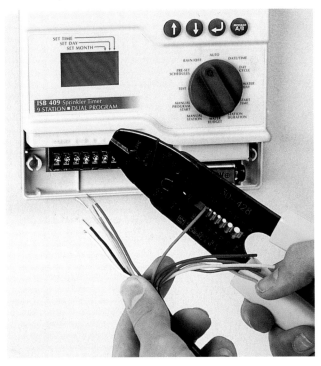

4 Connect the controller to the sprinkler valves using 18-gauge, direct-burial, color-coded, multiwire cable. Strip the insulation off all the wires using a multipurpose tool. If the valves are more than 800 ft. away, use 14-gauge cable.

Continued on next page.

Home Automation

Continued from previous page.

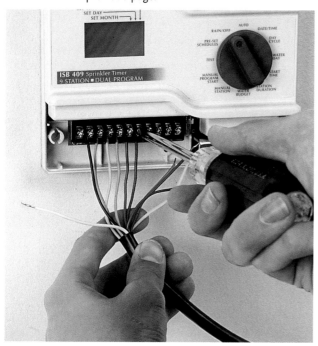

5 Each sprinkler valve must be connected to a controller unit terminal. The color-coded wire insulation is an easy way to keep track of what wire is going to what valve. Make sure that each terminal screw is firmly tightened.

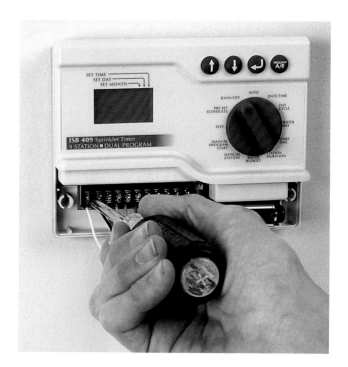

6 Usually all of the colored wires are hot, and the single white wire is a common wire that goes to its own terminal. The white wires from all the valves are joined together, along with a white pigtail wire, under a single waterproof wire connecter. Then the pigtail is screwed to the controller terminal.

7 The controller is powered by a transformer that has a pigtail connector on its lead wire. Install this connector to the 24-volt AC terminal in the controller panel. Then, make sure the controller is turned off, and plug the transformer into the nearby receptacle.

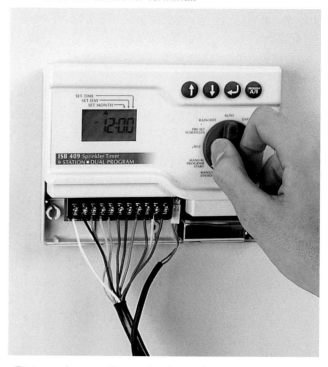

8 Once the transformer is plugged in, turn on the controller, and select a preset watering schedule recommended by the manufacturer. Or create a program of your own. The owner's manual will explain how to do this.

HOME AUTOMATION ANATOMY

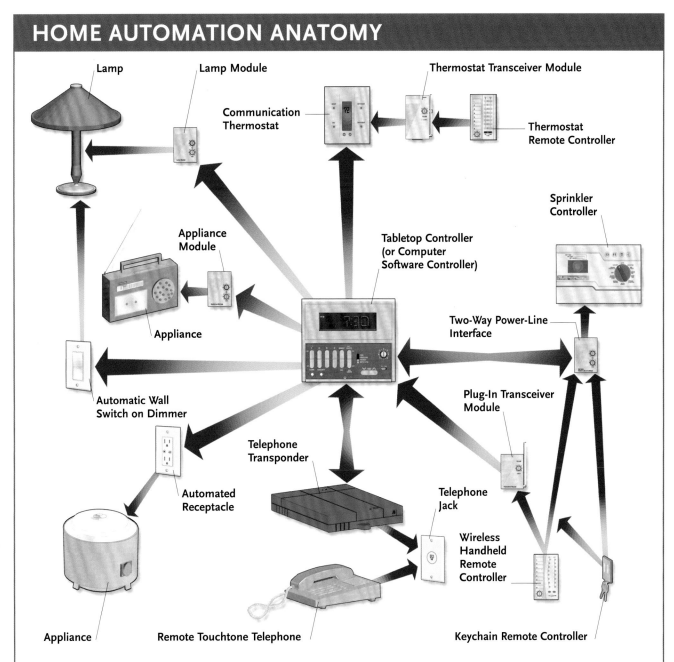

Lamp

Lamp Module

Thermostat Transceiver Module

Communication Thermostat

Thermostat Remote Controller

Sprinkler Controller

Appliance Module

Tabletop Controller (or Computer Software Controller)

Appliance

Two-Way Power-Line Interface

Automatic Wall Switch on Dimmer

Plug-In Transceiver Module

Telephone Transponder

Automated Receptacle

Telephone Jack

Wireless Handheld Remote Controller

Appliance

Remote Touchtone Telephone

Keychain Remote Controller

A typical home-automation system would most likely include a combination of devices such as wall switches, dimmers, lamp modules, timer controls, transceivers, remote controls, motion detectors, magnetic switch sensors, thermostat controls, and other devices. These are just a few of the many possible applications for an automated home-living system.

Voice-Dial Home Security System

A simple voice-dial home security system will automatically dial up to four preprogrammed emergency numbers and transmit a digital recording over the connected lines when it is triggered by a connected device such as a motion sensor or magnetic door switch. Once activated, it will send commands to flash lights on and off and sound

power horns (sirens). In most cases, these systems will contact a security company that will contact the police.

Once you have mastered installing a few X-10 projects, you will have the confidence and skills required to set up an entire automated home-living system. Simply add components in any configuration you desire to custom-design the system of your dreams.

Home Automation

INSTALLING A VOICE-DIAL HOME SECURITY SYSTEM

project

There's no question that automation products make one thing easier: home security. From a simple randomly controlled light up to a house full of sensors and motion detectors, homeowners can make their lives safer with just a little work and a couple hundred dollars.

TOOLS & MATERIALS

❚ Insulated screwdrivers ❚ Multipurpose tool ❚ Master control panel console ❚ Master remote ❚ Lamp modules ❚ Plastic anchors ❚ RJ11 telephone connector ❚ Magnetic switch connectors ❚ Motion sensors ❚ Key-chain remote ❚ Power horns (sirens) ❚ Mounting bracket and screws ❚ Cat 5 low-voltage wire ❚ Alkaline batteries, as required

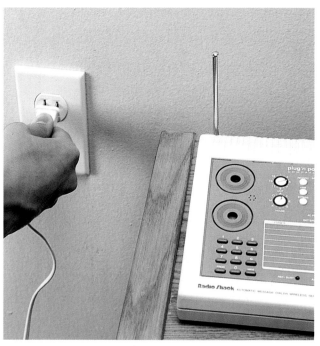

1 Set up the master control panel in a central spot in the house close to a standard phone jack and duplex receptacle. Most of these consoles can be mounted on the wall if you don't want to sacrifice any tabletop space. To mount the unit on the wall, just follow the manufacturer's directions.

4 Install motion sensor modules near entry doors and in hallways that connect various parts of the house. This will increase the chance of detecting the presence of an intruder and turn on lights, call a security service, or both.

5 Make sure to program at least one security light so it will be controlled by the master console. By doing this, you can always turn on one light by just pushing a button on your remote control.

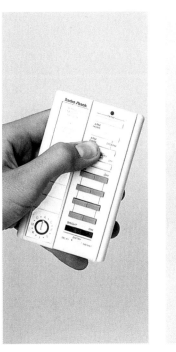

2 Set the dial on the master console to a convenient house code. Then program the remote control to match this house code (left). Then install batteries in the key-chain remote control, and test it by pressing the ARM button. If it turns on the controller, it's working properly (right).

3 Remote sensors can monitor every window and exterior door in your house. One side of the sensor mounts on the casing trim, while the other half attaches to the door (top) or window. When the door opens (bottom), the magnetic switches are separated and send a signal to the transmitter mounted on the wall.

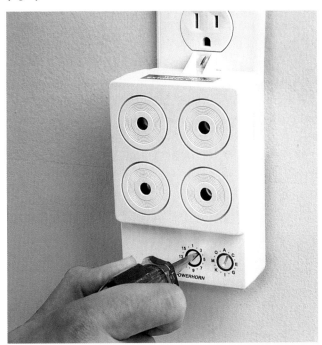

6 A power horn is a great deterrent to intruders. By hooking the horn to a motion detector module, it will be activated by any movement. It will continue to sound until a preset time passes, or until it's turned off manually at the unit.

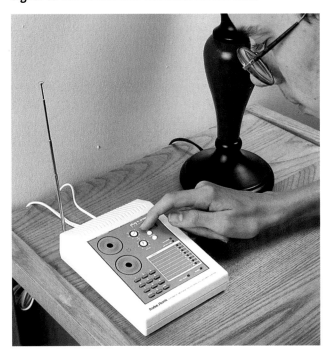

7 A combination of light and siren alarms will scare off most intruders. But these security control units can also be programmed to immediately contact a security service or any other individual. Generally, the security service will contact the police instead of your system doing this directly.

HOME NETWORKING

IN THE PAST, the term home networking meant different things to different people. To many, it was a way to link two or more computers together to share files, e-mail, internet access, and other equipment, such as printers. To others, the term described how video and sound could be piped throughout the house.

Today, home networking is called structured cabling, and it includes all of the above and more. Each system is different and depends on the needs of the user. Some want structured cabling in every room of the house. That's a good choice for new construction, but most of those systems are installed by trained professionals. For retrofit applications, it may make more sense to wire selected rooms. This section will show you how to make some of the basic connections for a structured cabling system.

Structured Cabling

Structured cabling provides efficiency and organization to the communications lines in your home. Every system is different and depends on the layout of the house and the needs of the people who live there.

The best way to understand structured cabling is to compare it to your home's electrical system. The local electric utility provides electricity to your home's fuse or panel box. From there it is distributed to the receptacles through individual circuits. Much the same happens in a structured cabling system. The providers, which in this case could be the cable and phone company, provide service to a central hub in your home. From there it is distributed throughout the house.

The Major Differences. Unlike line-voltage wiring, which consists of receptacles wired in sequence, structured cabling uses a home run or star topology wiring layout; see page 174. Each outlet, whether it be for voice, data, a computer network, video, or combinations of services, is normally connected directly to the main junction or distribution box.

Unlike your panel box or fuse box, which handles only line-voltage electricity, a structured cabling distribution panel serves as the hub for a variety of home services. It contains modules for all of the above services, creating a true home network.

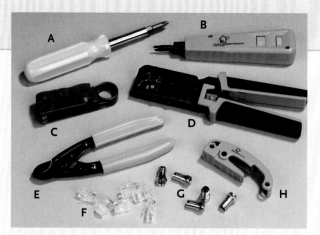

Structured cabling tools: A–screwdriver; B–punch-down tool; C–coaxial-cable stripper; D–RJ45 crimp tool; E–wire cutter; F–Cat-5 plugs; G–F-connectors; H–cable-crimp tool

Making Connections

Structured cabling systems rely on two types of cable. Unshielded twisted pair cable (UTP) consists of four pairs of twisted wires. Category 5 and Category 5e are the most common types of UTP used in homes. RG-6 coaxial cable is the other type of cable used. Coaxial cables carry video and data signals.

Plugs and Connectors. In most cases, you will be pulling home network cable using the same techniques used for pulling electrical cable, although there are differences. (See the Smart Tip, page 246.) But unlike electrical wiring, where the installer attaches wires to terminal screws, installers make connections by attaching modular plugs to the end of the cable. You will use RJ45 plugs for Category 5 cable. These look like standard phone plugs, but they are larger. You will use F-connectors for coaxial cable. To make these connections correctly, you will need special tools. (See above.)

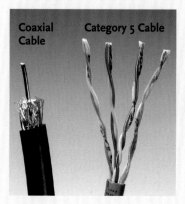

Coaxial Cable   Category 5 Cable

Structured cabling systems rely primarily on two types of cabling. Coaxial cable carries video and data signals throughout the house. Category 5 cable transmits voice and data signals.

Home Automation

ATTACHING A PLUG TO CATEGORY 5 CABLE

■ Wire stripper ■ RJ45 crimp tool ■ Category 5 or 5e cable ■ Modular plugs

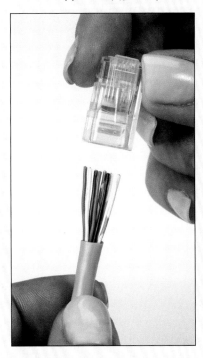

1 Remove the amount of sheathing from the outside of the cable that's recommended by the plug manufacturer. Carefully separate the individual wires, and fan them out so they are flat. Follow the guide that comes with the plug to learn how to insert the wires into the correct channels. This takes some practice to get right.

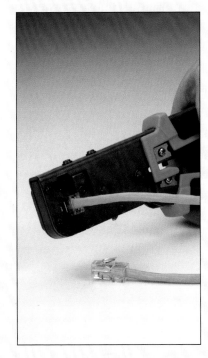

2 Once the wires are pushed all the way into the plug, the cable sheathing should be covered by the plug too. If some of the wires are exposed, take off the plug, or cut it off, trim the wires, and try again. Place the plug in a crimp tool, and squeeze the handles to permanently attach the plug to the wires.

ATTACHING AN F-CONNECTOR TO COAXIAL CABLE

■ Coaxial cable cutter and stripper ■ Crimping tool ■ Utility knife ■ F-connectors ■ Coaxial cable

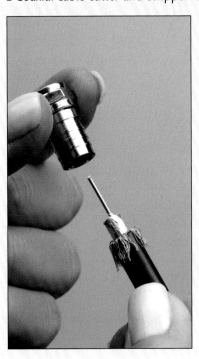

1 To attach an F-connector to the end of a coaxial cable, first use a coaxial cable stripper to remove the cable insulation. Pull the wire braid away from the middle of the cable, and bend it over the outside of the insulation. The resulting cable end should look like the photo at left.

2 Slide the F-connector over the end of the cable. Push it onto the cable insulation until the center conductor wire extends about $\frac{1}{16}$ in. beyond the end of the connector. Use an F-connector crimping tool to squeeze the barrel of the connector against the jacket of the cable.

INSTALLING CABLING OUTLETS

project

Structured Cabling Outlets

You will need to run cable, either Category 5 or coaxial or both, from the structured media center to the different rooms in your house. (See "Running Cable through Framing," page 22 and "Structured Cabling," below.)

It may pay to simply run Category 5 and co-axial cable from the media panel to every room. Structured cabling can accommodate lines for voice, fax, and computer networking. The structured cabling outlets connect your equipment with the structured media panel. An outlet can contain multiple connections.

TOOLS & MATERIALS

▌Drywall saw ▌Screwdrivers ▌Punch-down tool ▌Crimping tool ▌Hollow-back boxes ▌UTP cable ▌Coaxial cable ▌Wall plates ▌Terminal jacks and caps as needed

smart tip

STRUCTURED CABLING

INSTALLING STRUCTURED CABLING IS SIMILAR TO INSTALLING ELECTRICAL CABLES AND WIRES. BUT THERE ARE SOME DIFFERENCES.

- DO NOT BEND THE CABLE OR NICK THE PROTECTIVE COVERING.
- DO NOT RUN STRUCTURED CABLING PARALLEL WITH ELECTRICAL WIRING. IF STRUCTURED CABLES AND ELECTRICAL CABLES MUST CROSS, THEY SHOULD CROSS AT A 90-DEGREE ANGLE.
- STRUCTURED CABLING WALL OUTLETS SHOULD NOT SHARE A STUD WITH ELECTRICAL OUTLETS.
- STRUCTURED CABLING SHOULD NOT SHARE STUD BORE HOLES OR CONDUIT WITH ELECTRICAL CABLES.
- USE PLASTIC STAPLES FOR SECURING CABLES. CABLES SHOULD BE LOOSE UNDER STAPLES.

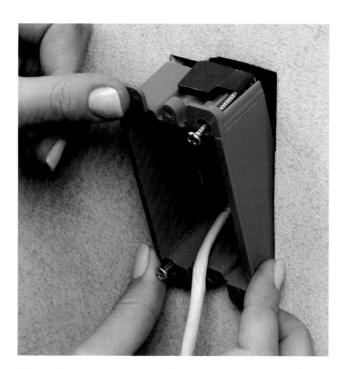

1 Begin by locating the outlet opening, tracing the box on the wall, and cutting a hole in the drywall. Fish some cable into the box; then push a cut-in box into the hole; and tighten its support wings by turning the corner screws.

4 Push the wall jack into the back side of the wall plate. This is a simple snap connection that makes it easy to change things later. For example, if you want the outlet to carry coaxial cable, you can just pull out the Cat 5 jack and put in the new cable jack.

2 Carefully strip off the sheathing from the outside of a Category 5 cable. Separate the pairs of wires; then gently separate the pairs so that each individual wire is free from the others.

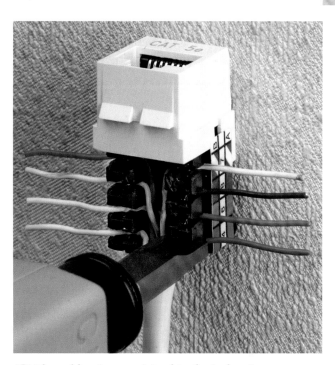

3 The cable wires are joined to the jack using a punch-down tool. The outside of the jack has color-coded panels that show where each wire color goes. The tool forces the wires into the jack where the insulation is pierced to make the proper electrical contact between the two.

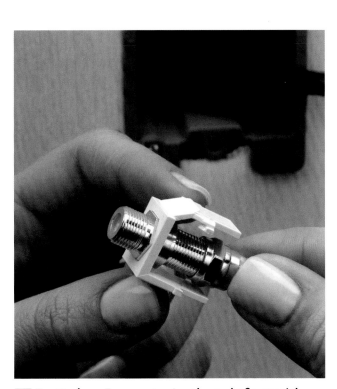

5 To attach an F-connector (on the end of a coaxial cable) to the back of a cable box wall plate, install a special fitting on the end of the connector. Then snap the connector into the plate opening.

6 Finish up by screwing the wall plate to the box. In this plate, the Cat 5 cable jack occupies the top opening. But the same plate can be used for a coaxial cable jack, too. Just break out the bottom opening that's plugged with a thin piece of plastic.

INSTALLING A STRUCTURED MEDIA CENTER

project

Structured Media Center

The structured media center, or main distribution panel, is the nerve center of the home network. It serves as the distribution point for the system.

Types of Modules. Modules are the working parts of the media center. They come in dozens of configurations. For example, the center shown here contains one preassembled module

TOOLS & MATERIALS

■ Cable stripper ■ Cable crimper ■ Coaxial-cable crimper ■ Power drill-driver ■ Punch-down tool ■ Screws ■ Distribution modules ■ Structured media panel box

that has the ability to route up to four phone lines to six different locations throughout the house. There is also a security-system hookup and a video splitter that can route a cable feed to up to six locations.

smart tip

TROUBLESHOOTING

SOMETIMES THINGS GO WRONG, AND YOU HAVE TO CHECK EACH CIRCUIT IN THE MEDIA CENTER. IF YOU CAN'T FIND THE SOURCE, ASK YOUR LOCAL SERVICE PROVIDER TO CHECK THE BOX ON THE OUTSIDE OF YOUR HOUSE, WHERE THE PROBLEM IS THEIR RESPONSIBILITY.

COMPUTER NETWORKS

ESTABLISHING A COMPUTER NETWORK in your home will allow two or more computers to share printers, files, scanners, and an internet connection. There are four ways to establish a network: ethernet cable, which is the type of system discussed under Home Networking; telephone lines that are already in your house; the electrical system already in your house; and wireless systems. They all require a network interface card (NIC), which is the hardware that allows you to connect one computer to the others; software that allows the computers to talk with one another; and in some cases, a hub or router for linking multiple computers on the network.

The Fastest. Ethernet is one of the fastest networking options, exchanging data at the rate of up to 100 megabits per second (Mbps). A megabit is a million pulses per second. The existing phone-line and electrical-system networks work at speeds under 10 Mbps. There are a number of different types of wireless systems. The fastest work at about 25 to 50 Mbps, but a number of factors can interfere with reception.

A wireless system consists of a router (the silver box) that sends data from the host computer or the signal from a high-speed internet connection to another computer, such as this laptop.

1 Most panel boxes are designed so they can be surface mounted or mounted between studs, as shown here. Just slide the box between studs; locate it at a comfortable height; and screw it through the sides and into the studs.

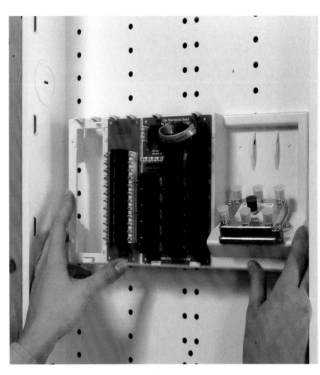

2 Individual modules, designed to handle different situations, just snap into the pegboard panel holes. This relatively simple unit can handle phone, cable, and security wiring.

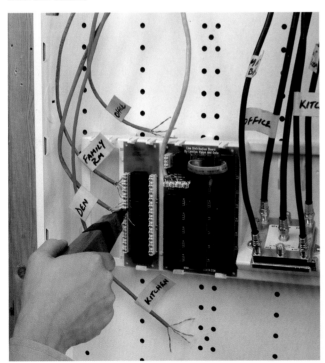

3 As you bring different cables into the panel, make sure to label where each is coming from. Cat 5 cable wires are joined to their terminals with a punch-down tool. Coaxial cable are threaded onto their terminals and tightened using an adjustable wrench.

4 Structured media panels such as this have a lot of capability. For just one example, by using small lengths of phone cable, called patch cords, you can direct incoming telephone service to different rooms in the house by simply plugging the wires into a different panel jack.

SMART HOME TECHNOLOGY AND APPS: THE WAY OF THE FUTURE

Digital applications (apps) have made our high-demand, fast-paced life easier to manage. We can successfully multitask by managing everything from our smartphones, tablets, and computers more than ever before. There now is an app for virtually every convenience we use in our lives thanks to this technology. Even more access has been added, even including smart technology in new cars to allow us to access and control these devices while driving.

To better understand this technology, separating these digital conveniences into daily functions is the best way to begin understanding how they can assist us to make life easier and more enjoyable.

Smart Home Speakers and Assistants—These devices can be used to find quick answers by asking them simple questions like: "What is today's weather forecast?" or "Who scored the tying run in the 1966 World Series game?" These digital home assistants can create shopping lists, play music, list recipe ingredients, and provide information about anything a person at home might need. They require a device service subscription and a Wi-Fi connection.

Smart Outlets—These can be used in place of any regular outlet and can be controlled remotely through an app on any digital device to turn the outlet on and off. This adds significant convenience for operating a crock pot, coffee maker, toaster, or air fryer to start and stop cooking in the kitchen. This outlet can also control any other electronic device you choose, since the app controls the power running through the outlet.

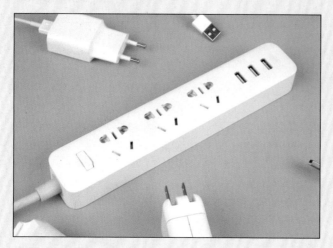

Smart Power Strips—These can control up to six devices and can be used to program the operation of individual devices one at a time for custom select uses. An example would be living room floor lamps, a smart TV, and a floor fan to circulate air. By using the app on your digital device, you can remotely turn on or off any of these devices based on your needs. You can also monitor the power consumption of each device to better control your electricity consumption.

Home Automation

Smart Locks—Home safety starts with any entry and garage doors to the home. You can use digital smart technology that can be controlled using an app from your digital device to lock, unlock, and even monitor when the lock was last set or unlocked. Additionally, these devices can be programmed to allow multiple users to have access through passwords using their individual digital devices. This technology is also being used to allow trusted repair and delivery companies to have limited access to the home while the owners are not there.

Smart Doorbell and Camera—These can allow the user to see, listen to, and talk to the person that rang their doorbell while safely in their home or from any remote location. This is accomplished by using the linked app and motion detection, which sends an alert to the user's digital device.

Wireless Security Cameras and Complete Systems—These can be set up to surveille a targeted area or multiple cameras can be used to cover the entire home. This technology allows the user to select the view from each camera location one at a time or view what all the cameras are seeing on one screen simultaneously. These cameras and motion sensors can be controlled from the user's digital device or can be set to be motion activated to send an alert to the user.

Home Automation

Smart Smoke and Carbon Monoxide Detection Alarms—Digital smoke and carbon monoxide detection alarms can be controlled and monitored from the user's digital device. They can also send alerts indicating which detection alarm has activated. These detection alarms can save lives and property.

Water Leak Detectors—To protect homes from water leaks and floods after rainstorms, waterproof sensors can be placed in areas of where known leaks have occurred to alert the user regarding any leaks inside or outside the home via alerts sent to the user's digital device.

Smart Hub Devices— Managing multiple smart devices and their apps in a home can be confusing, so a smart hub device can be incorporated into your system to control up to eight home entertainment devices simultaneously through your digital device or home assistant subscription.

Home Automation

Smart Sprinkler Controller—Watering the lawn has become easier than ever using this technology, which controls when the lawn receives water through the sprinkler system. The weather component can also detect when rain, wind, or frost occurs to activate the skip mode and conserve water. This whole thing is controlled by apps on the user's digital device.

Smart Cleaning Devices—Smart vacuum cleaners and mops use digital technology to map the house for cleaning. Using the supplied app or other home assistant subscriptions, the user can program the vacuum to schedule cleaning and sensors can detect higher levels of dirt in a home.

Robotic Lawn Mower—Creating that perfect manicured lawn is possible by using a robotic lawn mower that can do the work rain or shine. The technology provides extremely fine lawn clippings for fertilizer and eliminates the need for raking or bagging the cut grass.

PART II:
Fundamentals

8

understanding electricity

POSSESSING A BASIC KNOWLEDGE of electricity may not seem essential to doing electrical work, especially if you are using a "how-to" book with simple step-by-step instructions. However, nothing could be farther from the truth. Not every step in a process may be obvious, and very often knowing the basic theory behind a practice may enable you to figure out how to do something you have never done before. The purpose of this chapter is to give you a basic understanding of electricity—what it is, how it is provided, how it works, and how you can work with it safely.

FUNDAMENTALS OF ELECTRICITY

Electricity Defined

Electricity is nothing more than an organized flow of electrons and protons behaving in response to the attraction of oppositely charged particles and the repulsion of like-charged particles. If you can get enough electrons to break free of their orbits and start flowing in one direction or another, you have a flow of current. This current, or power, is defined as electricity. The device that frees the electrons from their orbit is called a power generator. To create vast amounts of electrical power, large generators must be turned on a massive scale. (See "How Electricity is Provided," page 258.)

Terminology of Electricity

As with most subjects, electricity has its own vocabulary. For this book, however, it is important to know the mean-

ing of only four key terms: ampere (amperage), volt (voltage), watt (wattage), and ohms (resistance). By mastering these terms, you will better understand electricity.

Ampere: An *ampere*, or *amp*, measures the rate, or quantity, of electrical flow. A typical contemporary home, for example, might have an electrical system of 150 to 200 amps. Amperage, in contrast, is the actual measure of current flowing in a circuit to an appliance. Although this can be measured only when the circuit is turned on, the rating of an electric appliance, in volts and amperes, or volts and watts, is required by the National Electrical Code (Section 422.60) to be marked on the identifying nameplate of the appliance. Amperes are designated by the letter A.

Ampacity is the amount of current in amperes a wire can safely conduct. Determining the correct ampacity of a wire is important because using an incorrect-size wire can create a fire hazard. Each wire carries a limited amount of current before it will heat to the point of damaging its insulation. For example, a 14-gauge wire can take a maximum current of 15 amps, a 12-gauge wire 20 amps, and so on. If a wire is too small for a job, generated heat can destroy its insulation, causing a fire. Amperage ratings are also important when you buy fuses or circuit breakers. Amperage of fuses or breakers, circuits, and appliances must match. Too little fuse or circuit-breaker amperage will cause these protection devices to blow or trip. Too much will permit a dangerous amount of overcurrent, or flow, which occurs when too many appliances are used on the same circuit or during a power surge. The result is overheating of the circuit, which will create a potential for fire.

Understanding Electricity

AMERICAN WIRE GAUGES

Wire Diameter (Gauge)		Ampacity (Current Capacity)	Volts (Power Capacity)	Typical Usage
○	18	7 Amps	24 Volts (134 Watts) Continuous load	**Low-Voltage Wiring** Bells, chimes, timers, thermostats, etc.
○	16	10 Amps	24 Volts (192 Watts) Continuous load	**Light-Duty Wiring** Low-voltage lighting, etc.
○	14	15 Amps	120 Volts (1,440 Watts) Continuous load	**Common House Wiring** Receptacles, lights, some A/Cs
○	12	20 Amps	120 Volts (1,920 Watts) 240 Volts (3,840 Watts) Continuous load	**Common House Wiring** Receptacles, lights, small appliances
○	10	30 Amps	120 Volts (2,880 Watts) 240 Volts (5,760 Watts) Continuous load	**Large Appliances** Clothes dryers, room A/Cs
○	8	40 Amps	240 Volts (7,680 Watts) Continuous load	**Large Appliances** Central A/Cs, electric ranges
○	6	55 Amps	240 Volts (10,560 Watts) Continuous load	**Large Appliances** Central A/Cs, electric ranges, furnaces

The NEC requires that all conductors and cables be marked, to indicate their AWG size, at intervals not to exceed 24 inches (Section 310.11). Each wire size can carry a limited amount of current under continuous load (80 percent of its maximum), which is defined as operating for 3 hours or more. The measure of how much current a wire can safely conduct is called its ampacity.

Volt: A *volt* measures the pressure exerted by electrical power. *Voltage* is the moving (electromotive) force that causes current to flow in an electrical circuit. A generator creates the pressure that keeps the electrical current flowing through conductors, known as wires.

Voltage, designated by the letter V, pushes a current that alternates between positive and negative values. This is known as an *alternating current* (AC). It periodically reverses, or alternates, direction in cycles, called *Hertz*. One cycle takes 1/60 second to complete. This is usually expressed as a rate of 60 cycles per second. The average voltage on this cycle is measured at 120 volts on the return, or neutral, wire and 240 volts across both of the two hot utility wires entering a home.

Contemporary three-wire residential wiring carries both 120- and 240-volt power. Large appliances like air conditioners, electric ranges, and clothes dryers typically use 240-volt wiring. Electrical devices must be labeled with their operating voltage level. This means that the product has been designed to operate at the listed voltage only. Do not, for example, hook up an electrical device rated at 125 volts to a circuit that supplies 220 to 240 volts. You'll burn it out.

Watt, Wattage: In practical terms, *wattage* is the amount of energy used to run a particular appliance. The wattage rating of a circuit is the amount of power the circuit can deliver safely, which is determined by the current-carrying capacity of the wires or cables. Wattage also indicates the amount of power a fixture or appliance needs to work properly.

CALCULATING THE AMPACITY OF AN ELECTRIC WATER HEATER

IF YOU WANT TO INSTALL a new electric water heater in your home, you must first determine its capacity. Let's assume that you have a family of four in a home with two tubs/showers, one dishwasher, and one clothes washer. Referring to the table below, "Usage Points," this gives you a total of 8 points. An adequately sized water heater for your home would have a 65-gallon capacity. A standard 65-gallon water heater has heating elements rated at 4,500 watts and 240-volt AC wiring. From this information, you can calculate how much current the water heater will use so that you can determine the correct-size wire to use when you install the heater. Because power (wattage) equals voltage (volts) multiplied by current (amps), and you know power and voltage, you can calculate the current:

**4,500 watts divided by 240 volts
equals 18.75 amps**

The wire-gauge table on page 256 indicates that a 12-gauge wire would be adequate to carry 20 amps. However, NEC Section 422.10 requires that the wires supplying the water heater have a capacity of 125 percent of the appliance (1.25 x 18.75A = 23.4 amperes). The wire-gauge table shows that the maximum continuous safe carrying capacity for a 12-gauge wire at 240 volts is 20 amps. The water heater exceeds this, so you must use the next-larger-size wire, which is a 10-gauge wire having an ampacity of 30 amps.

CALCULATING CURRENT

A QUICK WAY OF CALCULATING 240-VOLT CURRENT IS TO FIGURE 4 AMPS PER 1,000 WATTS OF POWER (8 AMPS FOR 120-VOLT). IN THIS WATER-HEATER EXAMPLE, YOU WOULD DIVIDE 4,500 WATTS BY 1,000, GETTING 4.5. MULTIPLYING THIS BY 4 AMPS YIELDS 18 AMPS, WHICH IS CLOSE TO THE FORMULA ANSWER.

USAGE POINTS

If your usage points equal	*Then you need a*
4 or less	40-gal. water heater
5 or 6	50-gal. water heater
7 or 8	65-gal. water heater
9 or more	80-gal. water heater

To select the proper size electric water heater for your home, calculate one usage point for each person, bathtub/shower, dishwasher, and clothes washer in your household, and consult the table to determine the capacity water heater that you need.

To calculate the wattage, or *power*, available in a circuit, first determine its amperage (amp rating). It will be marked on the circuit breaker or fuse for that circuit in the service-entrance, or main, panel—15 or 20 amps for most room circuits, 30 to 50 amps for most heavy-duty circuits. Then, **Watts = Volts x Amps.** A 15-amp circuit with 120 volts carries 1,800 watts (15 x 120); a 20-amp circuit carries 2,400 watts (but not under continuous load).

Resistance: Electrical *resistance*, measured in *ohms*, restricts the flow of current. The higher the resistance, the lower the current. This resistance causes a change of electrical energy into some other form of energy, usually heat. It is this heat, for example, that is used to warm the water in your water heater.

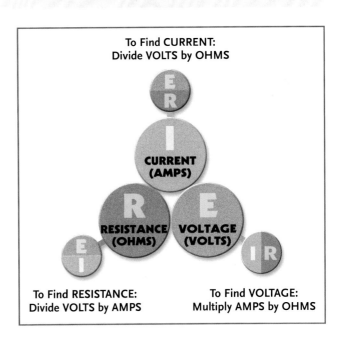

To Find CURRENT:
Divide VOLTS by OHMS

CURRENT (AMPS)

RESISTANCE (OHMS)

VOLTAGE (VOLTS)

To Find RESISTANCE:
Divide VOLTS by AMPS

To Find VOLTAGE:
Multiply AMPS by OHMS

Understanding Electricity

HOW ELECTRICITY IS PROVIDED

Generation

Utility companies generate electricity in a variety of ways. One of the most common methods uses the energy of running water to power a generator. Electrical power created in this way is termed hydroelectricity. To harness the energy of flowing water on a scale this enormous, a dam may be built across a narrow gorge in a river or at the head of a man-made lake. Water backed up behind this dam, in what is called the forebay, is then allowed to flow through a submerged passage, or penstock, in a controlled release. The massive force of this elevated water spins the generator's giant turbines as it falls, producing electricity. Electrical power produced in this way is called AC power, or alternating current.

Transmission

Once a utility company produces electricity, it must then transmit it through a distribution system for use by its customers. For ease of transmission, the electrical power is raised to many thousands of volts and conducted over high-voltage transmission lines to the utility company's regional switching stations. At the regional stations, the utility company steps down the power to a lower voltage for transmission to local substations. The utility company continues this procedure until the power reaches your home. A typical transmission starts at 230,000 volts, is stepped down to 69,000 volts at a switching station, then is stepped down further at a substation to 13,800 volts. Once at your home, this is reduced to 240 volts.

POWER GENERATION   POWER TRANSMISSION

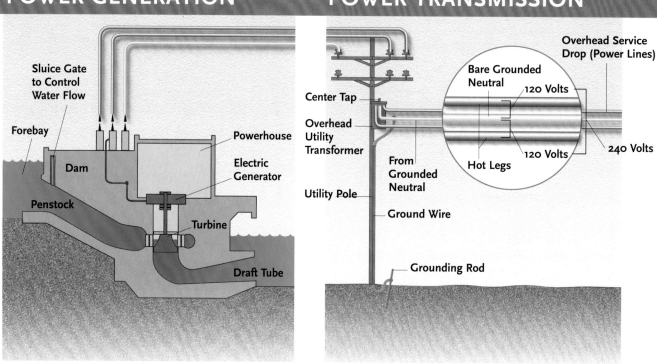

At a hydroelectric plant, the massive kinetic force of elevated water that drops down through a dam penstock in a controlled release turns giant turbines that generate electricity. Electrical current travels over high-voltage power lines to a step-down utility transformer near your house. The current then leaves the transformer, enters your home as available voltage for use (120-volt and 240-volt), and then returns to the transformer. It is transmitted to your main service-entrance panel (SEP) by means of two insulated hot conductors and a bare grounded neutral wire.

Point of Use

To be stepped down, the electricity that arrives at your home must first pass through a utility transformer. It then leaves this transformer via three terminals, mounted on its side, which are connected to three wires. These wires constitute the service drop that leads to your house service entrance. They include two insulated hot wires, or legs, and a grounded neutral. The two hot wires can each provide 120 volts or supply 240 volts of power between the two hot legs. The neutral conductor is usually bare on overhead and insulated in underground service laterals.

A glass-domed meter is connected to the two hot wires leading from the utility transformer. This meter is provided by your utility company to measure the amount of electrical energy in kilowatt hours consumed by your household. This is the rate of energy consumption in kilowatts multiplied by usage in hours.

Service-Entrance Panel

The wires from the electric meter continue on to the service-entrance panel. The panel contains circuit breakers or, in older homes, fuses and controls the flow of power to individual circuits within your home. These circuits may be 120-volt, 240-volt, or both (120/ 240-volt). At any given moment, electricity is exiting from one terminal on the utility transformer and returning by the other. Current flows from one terminal, travels through the service drop to the house, and then down the service-entrance conduit or cable into the meter base. From here it flows through the meter into the main panel and is then distributed to each of the circuits within your home. The current returns to the panel via another insulated wire, traveling back to the transformer. The final result is that you never actually "consume" electricity—you just borrow it (although you transform much of its energy, which is what you pay for).

HOUSE ENTRANCE

SERVICE-ENTRANCE PANEL

Power that enters your home must first flow through the utility company's electric meter to be measured. The electricity then goes to your service panel, where it is distributed to the various electrical circuits in your home. A 120/240-volt appliance, like a clothes dryer, needs two insulated hot wires, one insulated grounded wire, and one grounding conductor. A 120-volt duplex outlet needs an insulated hot wire, an insulated neutral wire, and a bare or green grounding wire. A 240-volt-only appliance needs just two insulated hot wires and a grounding wire.

Understanding Electricity

Hydroelectric dams, top, take advantage of the kinetic energy in falling water to drive immense turbines that in turn generate usable electrical energy. Electric utility meters, above, measure the amount of electricity that flows through your service-entrance panel.

Step-down utility transformers can be either overhead on a utility pole, top, or pad-mounted on the ground, above. Before electricity can enter your home, a transformer must lower the voltage from several thousand volts to a level appropriate for residential use.

CIRCUIT ANATOMY

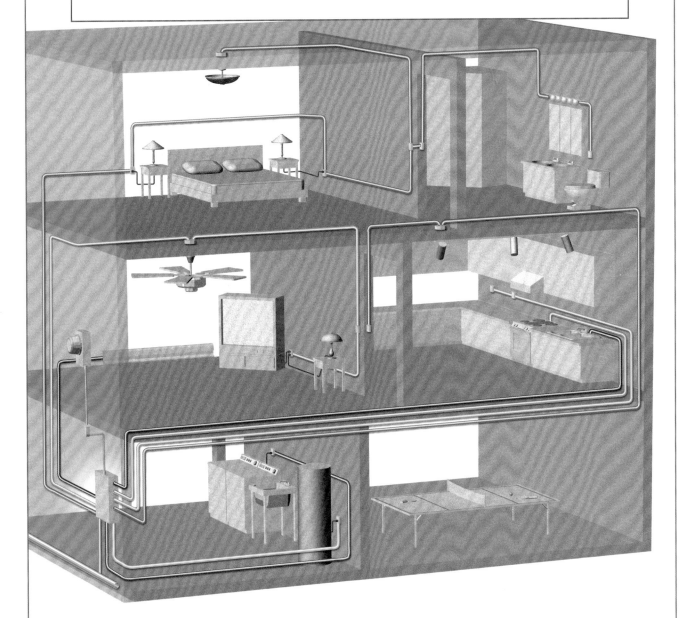

120 volts, 20 amps – disposal		240 volts, 20 amps – baseboard heater
120/240 volts, 60 amps – range		120/240 volts, 30 amps – dryer
120 volts, 20 amps – small appliances		240 volts, 30 amps – water heater
120 volts, 15 amps – lights		ground

This simplification of a house wiring system shows power split into 120- and 240-volt circuits at the service-entrance panel (SEP). Black or red wires in the branch-circuit cables are always hot (power present). White wires are neutral (no power present) when no current is flowing; they are hot whenever the circuit is turned on. Circuit breakers or fuses in the panel protect the branch circuits from overload. The grounding system (not shown) for metal switch and outlet boxes uses bare or green wires, or metal raceway. The system ground connects to the grounding electrode.

Understanding Electricity

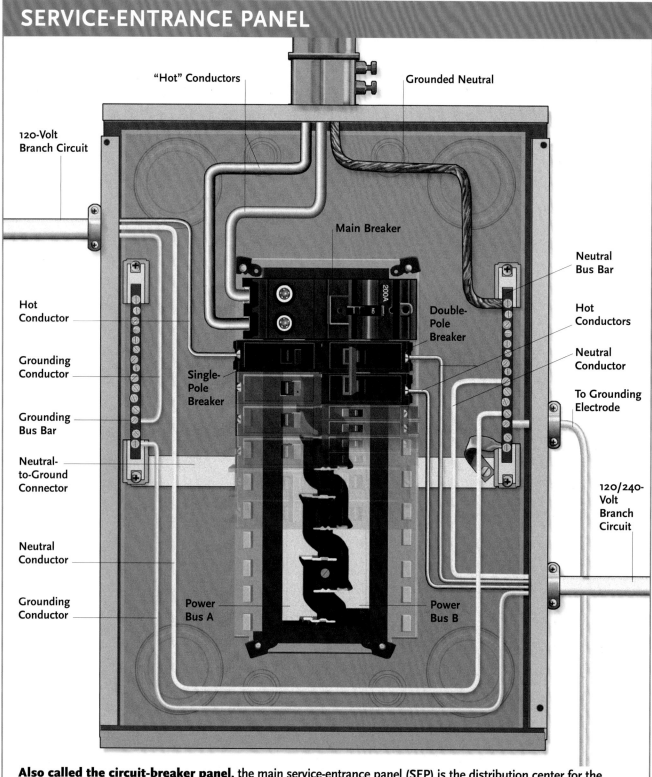

SERVICE-ENTRANCE PANEL

"Hot" Conductors

Grounded Neutral

120-Volt Branch Circuit

Main Breaker

Neutral Bus Bar

Hot Conductor

200A

Double-Pole Breaker

Hot Conductors

Grounding Conductor

Single-Pole Breaker

Neutral Conductor

Grounding Bus Bar

To Grounding Electrode

Neutral-to-Ground Connector

120/240-Volt Branch Circuit

Neutral Conductor

Grounding Conductor

Power Bus A

Power Bus B

Also called the circuit-breaker panel, the main service-entrance panel (SEP) is the distribution center for the electricity you use in your home. Incoming red and black hot wires connect to the main breaker and energize the other circuit breakers that are snapped into place. Hot (black or red) wires connected to the various circuit breakers carry electricity to appliances, fixtures, and receptacles throughout the house. White and bare-copper wires connect to the neutral and grounding bus bars, respectively. (Representative 120-volt and 120/240-volt circuits are shown.)

smart tip

APPLIANCE RATINGS

TODAY, MAJOR APPLIANCES SUCH AS FREEZERS, REFRIGERATORS, AND WATER HEATERS ARE ENERGY-RATED FOR THE AMOUNT OF POWER (WATTAGE) THEY USE. THIS INFORMATION APPEARS ON A LARGE YELLOW "ENERGY GUIDE LABEL" AFFIXED TO EACH DEVICE. SMALLER APPLIANCES MAY NOT BE SO LABELED, BUT THEIR WATTAGE RATING SHOULD BE LISTED ON THEIR PACKAGING. THE WATTAGE RATING CAN BE USED TO CALCULATE THE ACTUAL OPERATING COST OF THE APPLIANCE. THE HIGHER THE WATTAGE RATING OF THE APPLIANCE, THE MORE YOU WILL HAVE TO PAY TO OPERATE IT. FOR EXAMPLE, IF A 4-FOOT LONG BASEBOARD HEATER USES 250 WATTS PER FOOT, IT WILL REQUIRE 1,000 WATTS TO RUN. AT 10¢ PER KILOWATT-HOUR (1,000 WATTS USED BY AN APPLIANCE IN ONE HOUR), IT WILL COST 10¢ PER HOUR TO RUN THE HEATER. IF THE WATTAGE IS NOT LISTED ON THE APPLIANCE, LOOK FOR THE VOLTAGE AND CURRENT. MULTIPLY THE THE TWO TOGETHER TO FIND THE WATTAGE.

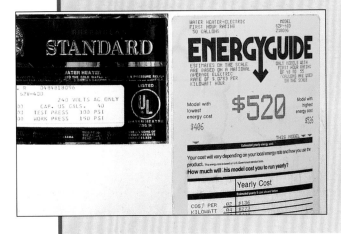

The energy-rating sticker on the side of this 4,500-watt water heater tells the prospective buyer approximately what he or she will be paying per year for the use of the appliance. Running a 4,500-watt water heater for one hour, at 10¢ per kilowatt-hour, would cost 4.5 x 10¢, or 45¢ per hour.

APPLIANCE WATTAGE

Appliance	Average Wattage	Appliance	Average Wattage
Attic fan	400	Frost-free refrigerator	400–600
Blender	400–1,000	Frying pan	1,000–1,200
Broiler	1,400–1,500	Gas furnace	800
Can opener	150	Garbage disposal	500–900
Central air conditioner	2,500–6,000	Hair dryer	400–1,500
Clock	2–3	Hot plate	600–1,000
Clothes dryer	4,000–5,600	Iron	600–1,200
Clothes washer	500–1,000	Laser printer	1,000
Computer with monitor	565	Microwave oven	1,000–1,500
Coffee maker	600–1,500	Oil furnace	600–1,200
Crock pot	200–275	Portable heater	1,000–1,500
Deep fat fryer	1,200–1,600	Radio	40–150
Dehumidifier	500	Range	4,000–8,000
Dishwasher	1,000–1,500	Range oven	3,500–5,000
Electric blanket	150–500	Refrigerator	800
Electric water heater	2,000–5,500	Roaster	1,200–1,650
Exhaust fan	75–200	Room air conditioner	800–2,500
Floor polisher	300	Sewing machine	60–90
Food freezer	300–600	Stereo/CD player	50–140
Food mixer	150–250	Television	50–450
		Toaster oven	500–1,450
		Waffle iron	600–1,200

Today, appliances are typically rated for how much power (wattage) that they draw. Because your utility bill states how much you pay per kilowatt-hour of electricity, this information can be used to calculate the actual operating cost of any appliance.

HOW ELECTRICITY WORKS

Electric Current Flow

Electric current flow can be defined as the flow of electrons through a conductor (wire) or circuit. This passage of electrons is often described as being analogous to the flow of water in a pipe or hose. For example, water flows through a pipe or hose because it is under pressure. Similarly, electric current surges through a wire because it is under pressure. Earlier, voltage was defined as the pressure, or moving (electromotive) force, that causes current (electrons) to flow in an electrical circuit. Furthermore, just as the size of a hose or pipe can affect the degree of water pressure, the size of an electrical wire can affect the flow of current passing through it. The maximum current-carrying capacity of a particular-size wire is called its ampacity. (See page 256.)

As electric current passes through your electrical system, it reaches your receptacles and switches where it becomes available for use when you flip the switch on your wall or appliance. And like the water, once the electric current is used, it exits the system. The current exits (or returns to the utility) by means of a grounded conductor.

Flow Resistance

The passage of electric current through a wire is not only restricted by the size of the wire and the amount of voltage pressure but also by the material of which it is made. Imagine water trying to flow along an incline; if the incline is downward, the flow will be unrestricted; if the incline is upward, the flow will be resisted. The steepness of the incline affects the speed of the flow. Obstacles in the incline, like rocks in a stream, also slow the flow. The chemical composition of a material determines its resistance to the flow of electricity.

Materials that allow electric current to pass through them fairly easily are electrical conductors, while materials that prevent the passage of electric current are insulators. Common conductors include copper and aluminum, which are used in the manufacture of electrical wiring. Most metals are good electrical conductors, yet even these offer some resistance to the flow of electric current. This property can be measured in units of resistance called ohms. Materials commonly used as insulators include glass, various plastics, and rubber.

CURRENT FLOW VS. WIRE SIZE	CURRENT FLOW VS. MATERIAL RESISTANCE

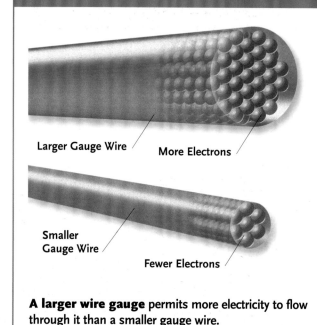

Larger Gauge Wire — More Electrons

Smaller Gauge Wire — Fewer Electrons

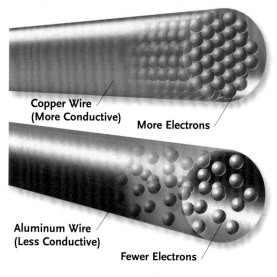

Copper Wire (More Conductive) — More Electrons

Aluminum Wire (Less Conductive) — Fewer Electrons

A larger wire gauge permits more electricity to flow through it than a smaller gauge wire.

Conductive materials allow more current than less conductive materials of the same size.

WORKING SAFELY WITH ELECTRICITY

Basic Rules of Safety

Safety is, without question, the most important aspect of any electrical work. One split-second mistake can result in serious injury or even death. Many errors are made because of impatience, ignorance, or unnecessary risk-taking. If you consider the potential cost of not following simple, common-sense rules of safety when you are working with electricity, then you will certainly realize the importance of avoiding such mistakes.

The first rule of working with electricity is to shut off the power at your main service-entrance panel before working on a circuit. Always keep a well-maintained flashlight near the panel so that when power is cut off you will not be left standing in the dark. Also, be sure to stand on a rubber mat or dry boards, especially if your utility room is damp, and use only one hand to remove or replace a fuse or flip a circuit-breaker switch. After shutting off the power, secure the panel so that no one else will accidentally turn the circuit back on while you are working on it. All circuits should be clearly marked to avoid confusion as to which circuit to shut off. Nevertheless, whenever you do work on a circuit, be doubly sure that it is not hot by testing it, using a circuit tester.

Second, be absolutely positive that you have carefully planned your work, that you know every step you'll take, and that you are not in over your head. For this reason, it is probably best to limit yourself to doing work outside your electrical panel. Leave adding circuits and making panel repairs to a licensed electrician.

Keep a well-maintained flashlight near your service-entrance panel, and always stand on a rubber mat or dry boards when working on the panel.

Before working on any circuit, test it to be sure that the power has been turned off. Test both receptacles on an outlet. It may be a split circuit.

To prevent a ladder from slipping out from under you when working outside, swivel the feet into a vertical position; then dig them into the ground.

Third, when doing actual wiring and electrical repairs, take precautions to use the correct tools, equipment, and techniques. For example, use a wooden or fiberglass ladder, never one that is made of metal; always wear safety glasses to protect yourself against sparks and flying debris; and make sure that all of your tools are properly insulated for electrical work. Be conscious of details, like properly wrapping wire terminals with electrical tape and using the correct-size electrical boxes for the work you are doing. And, especially if you are working with power equipment outside, be certain that the electrical circuit is thoroughly protected by a ground-fault circuit interrupter (GFCI), or use a GFCI extension cord. (See bottom right.) If a tool malfunctions and has a fault to ground, this type of protection can save your life. For portable power tools, be sure to use heavy-duty 12-gauge extension cords. Under-sized cords are a potential fire hazard. In addition, all electrical supplies should be UL-listed—which means that they carry the symbol of the Underwriters Laboratories, your assurance that the product meets the minimum safety standards set by this and other governing agencies.

Lastly, observe the rules and regulations established by your local, state, or regional building and electrical codes. Some codes may prohibit you from doing certain types of electrical work or using a particular type of electrical cable. Most local requirements are based on the National Electrical Code.

SHORT CIRCUITS

WHEN AN ACCIDENTAL CONNECTION is made between two hot wires or one hot wire and a grounded wire, and excess current flows across the connection, this is known as a short circuit. A short-circuited device can be life-threatening if you come into physical contact with it. Because electrical current travels along the path of least resistance, you can literally become part of the electric circuit—the part through which the current attempts to flow back to its original source. Normally, this is done through a neutral wire in the circuit. However, for safety's sake, an alternative low-resistance route is usually provided by a green or bare grounding wire leading back to the panel box. The short causes the circuit breaker to shut off.

The grounding circuit typically connects all of the electrical devices, including fixtures, switches, receptacles, electrical boxes, and so on, to a terminal, or bus bar, in the main panel. The bus bar is in turn connected to a metal cold-water pipe and a grounding rod driven into the earth "such that at least 8 feet of length is in contact with the soil" [NEC Section 250.53(G)]. (See illustration, "Grounding Rods," page 268.) Individual appliances or tools that are metal-clad are connected to this grounding system through the third prong on a three-prong plug.

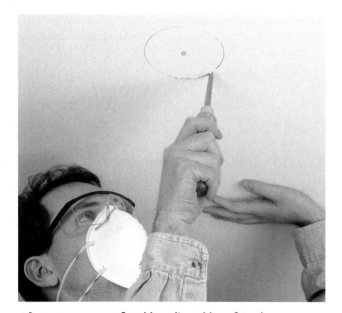

Always wear comfortable, adjustable safety glasses when doing electrical work, to protect yourself from flying debris or sparking wires.

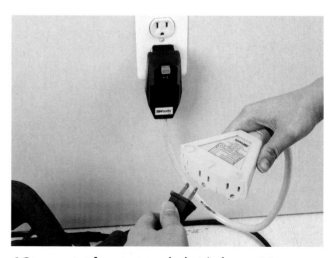

AC power tools carry enough electrical current to cause electrocution. To be safe, use a heavy-duty extension cord that has a GFCI built directly into it.

Understanding Electricity

GROUNDING SYSTEMS

Main Panel Ground

The main service-entrance ground is the principal ground in a home. It is a requirement of the NEC for all 120- and 240-volt circuits (Article 250). It is an easily seen copper grounding wire, known as the grounding electrode conductor, attached to a bus bar in the main service panel. Two such wires are visible if your water pipes are metal. One service ground runs from the terminal bus bar to the grounding-rod system, while the other goes to the main metal plumbing pipe. (Be aware that the metal plumbing pipes beyond the first 5 feet of entrance are not part of the grounding system but are, rather, grounded to the system by the grounding rod.) Minimum size requirements for grounding electrode conductors are specified by the NEC (Section 250.66).

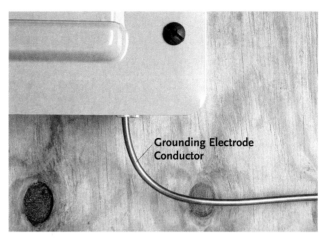

Grounding Electrode Conductor

The main service-entrance ground, known as the grounding electrode conductor, is a copper grounding wire attached to a bus bar in the main service panel. If your water pipes are metal, there will be two wires—one running from the terminal bus bar to the grounding rod, and another running to the main metal cold-water pipe.

OVERLOAD PROTECTION

THE EXCESSIVE CURRENT that is created by a short circuit, or by connecting equipment that overloads the circuit, can easily cause irreparable damage to electrical equipment. An electrical system must have some type of overload protection. This type of protection is provided by fuses or circuit breakers. (See "Service Panels," page 295.) A fuse guards against overload by melting when too much heat is caused by excessive current in the line. Once the metal wire in the fuse melts, the circuit is ef-

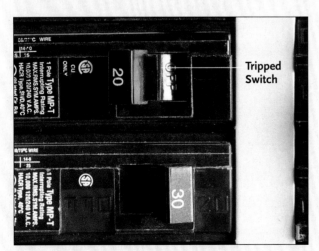

Tripped Switch

A circuit breaker switches off (trips) when the flow of current exceeds the breaker's capacity.

fectively broken. A circuit breaker, on the other hand, is an automatic switch designed to cut off the flow of electric current in a circuit that exceeds its rated capacity. Unlike a fuse, it doesn't have to be replaced; the switch, once "tripped," simply needs to be reset.

Ground-Fault Circuit Interrupters (GFCI)

Although a powerful current surging through a grounding system will melt (blow) a fuse or switch off (trip) a circuit breaker, a less powerful current may not be sufficient to do this. Nonetheless, such a current may be forceful enough to cause serious injury, or worse. The risk of this happening is especially great in moisture-prone locations, such as outdoors or in bathrooms. A way to protect against the danger of this type of electric shock is by using what is called a ground-fault circuit interrupter, or GFCI. This device can detect minute amounts of current leakage in a circuit. If the amperage flowing through the black and white wires is equal, then the circuit is operating properly. But if the GFCI detects as little as a 0.005-amp difference between the two wires, then leakage is presumed and device breaks the circuit—rapidly enough to prevent a hazardous shock.

GROUNDING RODS

GROUNDING RODS are usually composed of galvanized or copper-clad metal ⅝ inch in diameter and typically 8 feet long or longer. A good grounding system may include several grounding rods. A single grounding electrode composed of a rod or pipe must have a resistance to ground not to exceed 25 ohms (NEC Section 250.56), otherwise one or more additional grounding rods must be used. Multiple rods or pipes must be placed at least 6 feet apart and be connected to the neutral bus bar with a continuous copper conductor. Never overlook these code requirements. Note, for example, that effective grounding is essential for the proper functioning of a surge arrester. Unless low ground resistance is available, a surge arrester will not be able to draw the spikes, or massive intermittent increases in voltage or amperage, coming into a circuit during a power surge.

Because of their length and awkwardness, it is best to drive grounding rods using a borrowed or rented rotary hammer. This tool enables the rods to vibrate through soil and past small rocks with little or no difficulty.

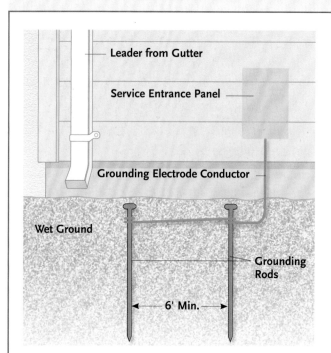

Typical Grounding-Rod System. Grounding rods conduct electricity from the grounding electrode conductors directly into the earth, where it is harmlessly dissipated. Some grounding systems may require more than one rod, in which case they must be spaced at least 6 ft. apart. Rainwater directed near grounding rods helps to lower the ground resistance.

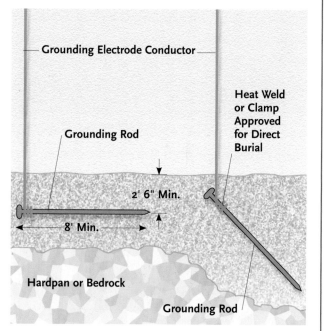

Grounding-Rod Installation. If a grounding rod cannot be driven directly into the earth because of boulders or bedrock, the NEC requires (Section 250.52) that it still must have at least 8 ft. of length in contact with the soil. To accomplish this, a rod may either be driven at an angle not less than 45 deg. or placed horizontally in a trench at least 2½ ft. deep.

GROUND FAULTS ON APPLIANCES

Equipment Grounding

Equipment that is capable of becoming electrically powered, such as an appliance, fixture, or other device, is also required by the NEC to be connected to a grounding system (Sections 250.110). Such devices use equipment grounding conductors. These bare wires, included in the nonmetallic (NM) cable typically found in modern homes, connect to the grounding (green) terminals of receptacles. They run back to the neutral/grounding bus bar in the main service-entrance panel and serve as the grounding wires that bring an electrical appliance to zero voltage. An equipment grounding conductor can either end (terminate) at a receptacle grounding screw

and connect to the appliance by means of a plug and cord connector, or it can connect directly to the appliance. Take precautions when working with bare copper and green wires such as these because you can never be sure whether or not the installation was done properly.

A ground fault can occur in an appliance any time that excess or misdirected current (a short circuit as shown below) causes the appliance to become electrically energized. A grounding system, including an equipment grounding conductor, is intended to provide a low-resistance path for current back to its source to prevent an electric shock or possible electrocution.

SAFE SETUP

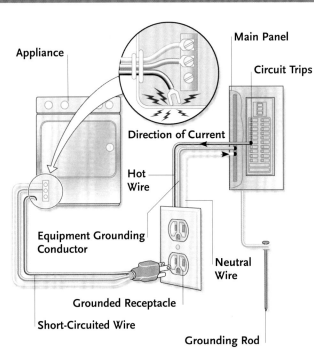

DANGEROUS SETUP

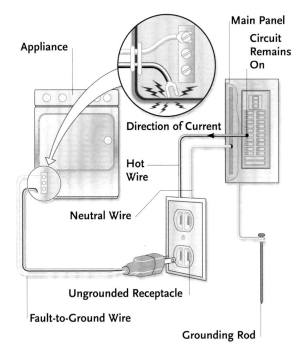

Grounded Appliance. If the metal framework of a grounded appliance becomes electrically energized, the ground-fault current will return to the service-entrance panel through the equipment grounding conductor. In this system, the current remains within the wiring system and trips the affected circuit breaker at the panel, rather than being directed to a grounding rod.

Ungrounded Appliance. If the metal framework of an ungrounded appliance becomes energized, then the ground-fault current will not be sufficient to trip the affected circuit breaker at the panel. As a result, the appliance frame will remain electrically powered, and anyone touching it and a grounded surface may be electrocuted.

IMPORTANCE OF TESTING FOR GROUND

IF YOU WISH TO CHECK whether or not your home is properly grounded, begin by testing the receptacles. Check whether they have two or three wires. If a receptacle is missing a grounding terminal, it clearly is not grounded. If a two- or three-wire plug adapter is employed, unless the house has armored cable and metal boxes, the appliance is probably still not grounded. In this case, the receptacle won't be grounded unless it is an automatic grounding receptacle, which has a spring clip on one of its attachment screws. This clip grounds the receptacle to any grounded metal electrical box. Standard receptacles are not approved for such automatic grounding. However, if the electrical box is grounded back to the main panel by means of armored cable, then you can install a standard three-pronged receptacle and connect its grounding terminal to the metal box.

To test whether an existing three-pronged terminal is grounded, use a plug-in circuit tester. Never assume that a three-pronged receptacle is grounded. If the ground is missing, the light sequence on the tester will indicate as much. The ground may even be properly connected at the receptacle but disconnected farther down the line.

Common grounding problems that occur at or near the main electrical panel include grounding connections made to rusted rebar or pipe, cut or loose grounding wires, or improper connectors on a grounding rod. Be sure that the clamp used on your rod is a listed (approved) connector, which must be cast bronze, brass, or plain or malleable iron. A heat-welded connection is also acceptable (NEC Section 250.70). The grounding rod itself, if iron or steel, must be at least ⅝ inch in diameter. Stainless-steel and nonferrous metal rods must be at least ½ inch in diameter [Section 250.52(A)(5)]. The use of improper materials may lead to corrosion and result in a high-resistance connection.

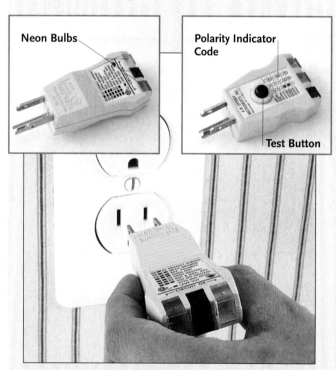

Neon Bulbs

Polarity Indicator Code

Test Button

A plug-in receptacle analyzer checks grounded outlets for correct/incorrect wiring. Three neon bulbs light up in various combinations to indicate correct wiring, open ground, open neutral, open/hot, hot/ground reversed, or hot/neutral reversed.

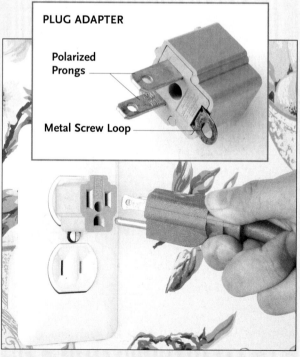

PLUG ADAPTER

Polarized Prongs

Metal Screw Loop

A two- or three-wire plug adapter cannot ground an appliance if there is no grounding path back to the main panel; it merely permits the appliance to be plugged in. A short to the appliance may still cause a severe shock or electrocution.

Higher-quality receptacles feature an automatic grounding clip on one of their attachment screws, which provides a grounding path through any grounded metal electrical box.

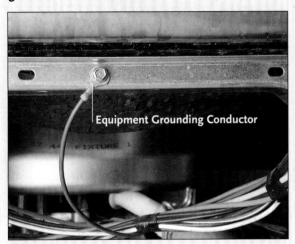

In many instances, an equipment grounding conductor may be directly connected to an appliance.

The inside of this ungrounded receptacle box reveals the lack of a grounding wire to connect the grounding circuit back to the main panel.

BONDING JUMPER

HOMEOWNERS FREQUENTLY make the mistake of thinking that they can ground an electrical system or appliance by connecting it to metal plumbing pipes. Nothing could be further from the truth! All metal pipes must themselves be connected to the grounding system. If the water pipes are connected to the grounding system by means of a clamp and bonding wire to the service panel grounding/neutral bus bar, then the circuit breaker will trip off whenever a bare wire touches the metal pipes. Where there's a break in pipe continuity, such as when a water heater is not made of metal, for instance, a bypass, or bonding jumper, must be made to connect the incoming and outgoing pipes to ensure electrical continuity. The main service panel itself must be bonded by a connection from the neutral bus bar to a bonding screw on the metal frame of the panel, and the panel in turn connected to the grounding (electrode) rod.

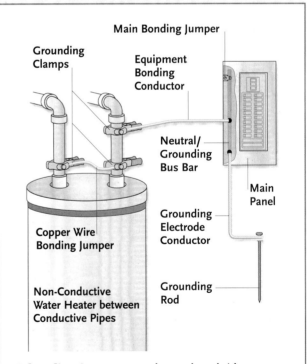

A bonding jumper must be made to bridge any potential break in a ground circuit. Bonding jumpers are required to ensure electrical continuity, as well as the ability of a grounding system to safely direct any ground fault that might be imposed on it.

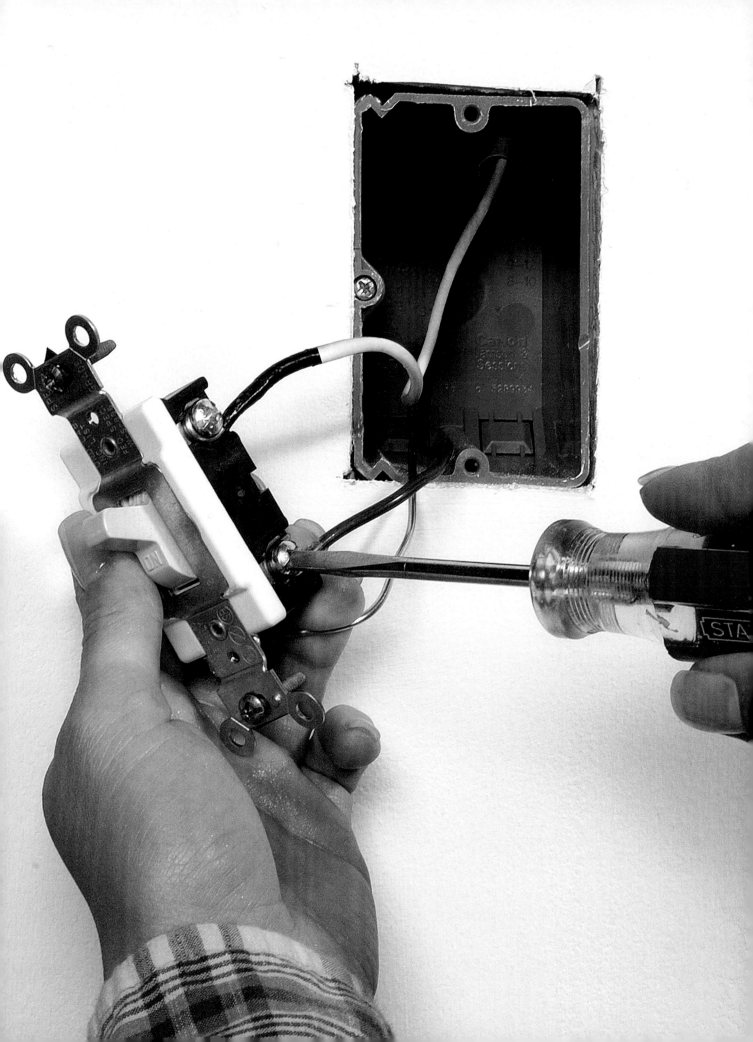

9
tools and their uses

SOME ELECTRICAL WORK can be done using standard tools, many of which you may already have in your tool kit or workshop. Most tools used in electrical work, however, are specifically designed to perform a given task. These tools make work easier and safer. More importantly, even if you already own common tools—like hammers, chisels, utility knives, measuring tapes, screwdrivers, etc.—not all of these can be used safely. For example, screwdrivers and hammers, as well as other metal tools, must be insulated to prevent current from flowing into the user's hand, causing a shock. As for specialized work, the right tool is necessary to do the job properly, whether it's cutting and stripping wire or measuring current and voltage in a line.

While safe electrical work requires the use of specific tools, it depends even more on the use of high-quality tools. Such tools are best purchased from a reputable home center or distributor of electrical supplies and equipment, rather than from a discount store. In the long run, a bargain is seldom a bargain if it endangers your life or property. Besides, well-maintained, high-quality tools will add to the versatility and reliability of your tool collection, and they can last a lifetime.

PULLING WIRES & FUSES

Fish Tape. Also known as fish wire, fish tape is a flexible wire used by electricians to snake electrical cable through walls, ceilings, and other inaccessible spaces. Various wire "fishing" techniques use either one or two fish tapes to hook and pull wire. (See "Fishing Cable Across a Ceiling," page 28.) Fish tapes come in lengths from 25 to 250 feet and widths of ⅛ to ¼ inch. Usually, the tape, or wire, is wound inside a self-tensioning winder case with a handle grip for better control and ease of use. The tape is made either of steel, flexible steel, nylon, or fiberglass. Some flexible steel tapes, rather than consisting of a solid strand of steel wire, consist of multiple strands, while others are constructed of a solid spring-like steel. The drawback to steel tape is, of course, that it is conductive. Nylon tape is nonconductive and somewhat safer to use except for the tip and leader, which are made of steel. Fiberglass tape, though expensive, is superior because it is nonconductive and has a low-friction coating that makes it the fastest fish tape available. Friction-reducing lubricants can be purchased separately, however, and applied to any fish tape.

FISH TAPE AND LUBRICANT

Tools and Their Uses

Fuse Puller. A fuse puller is specially designed for the removal of cartridge type fuses. (See "Fuses," page 300.) The grips on one end of the puller enable you to remove cartridge fuses up to 60 amps in size, while those on the other end can pull fuses of greater capacity. You clamp the puller tightly around the center of a blown cartridge fuse, and then wrench the cylinder firmly out of its fuse box. The fuse puller is also used to insert the new or replacement fuse between the fuse box spring clips. This tool must be made of a nonconductive material, such as plastic, because the spring clips that hold the cartridge fuses are metal and can carry deadly current. Always be sure that the fuse box has been switched off before you pull a fuse, and take care never to touch the spring clips with steel pliers or any other metal tools.

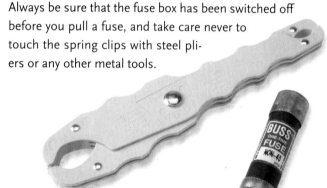

FUSE PULLER

To remove a cartridge fuse, grasp it firmly with a fuse puller, and pull it straight out.

CUTTING AND TWISTING WIRES

Lineman's Pliers. You'll use heavy-duty lineman's pliers to shape, bend, and twist wires, as well as to pull cable into electrical boxes. In a pinch, use it in place of a punch to remove knockout plates from electrical boxes. Although hardware stores rarely carry high-quality lineman's pliers, you can easily obtain a pair at any electrical supply shop.

Long-Nose Pliers. Long-nose, or needle-nose, pliers are well suited for getting into tight spaces and twisting wire ends into loops for hooking under screw terminals. They are also good for pulling out wire staples, and they have a cutting edge for snipping wires.

Diagonal-Cutting Pliers. These pliers are used for getting into tight spaces like receptacle and switch boxes to snip small wires. The angled and tapered blades enable you to reach and cut wires not accessible to conventional wire cutters. It is more sensible, as well as cost-effective, to buy a multipurpose or combination tool that can also notch, strip, and crimp wires of various types and sizes.

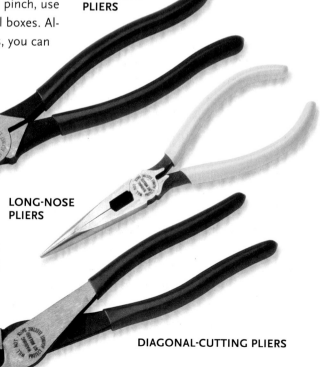

LINEMAN'S PLIERS

LONG-NOSE PLIERS

DIAGONAL-CUTTING PLIERS

STRIPPING AND CRIMPING WIRES

Wire Stripper. This is an absolute necessity when removing insulation from wire ends, although a utility knife can be used to cut the sheathing away from larger cable wires. A wire stripper is designed with precision blades to both cut and strip wires. They have depth-of-cut gauges for stripping just the right amount of insulation from a wire of a given size without cutting into the wire. Different models are sold for stripping solid wire, stranded wire, or small-gauge wire.

Automatic Wire Stripper. An automatic wire stripper is designed to simultaneously cut and strip both solid and stranded wire insulation. One pair of jaws holds the wire while the other cuts and removes the insulation, exposing the bare wire inside.

Crimper. Crimpers are used with special connectors that are designed to connect wires together. Some examples include spade connectors, ring connectors, and splices, sometimes called crimping ferrules. (See "Using Crimping Ferrules," page 278.) After you've twisted the wires using a pair of pliers, you crimp them together inside the ferrule by squeezing the jaws on the crimper together. This clinches the wires and ferrule into a permanent connection. Note that aluminum wires are rarely spliced this way.

Multipurpose (or Combination) Tool. A multipurpose tool, as its name implies, can be used for many different purposes: it can crimp; cut and strip wire; and in some cases even cut and rethread bolts. Like a conventional wire stripper, it has a depth-of-cut gauge for stripping wire. A multipurpose tool usually handles 22- to 10-gauge wires.

Cable Ripper. When multiple wires are cabled together in a protective nonmetallic sheathing, it becomes necessary to expose the wire ends so that you can splice them to other wires or connect them to wire terminals. It is important that you be able to cut back the protective plastic sheathing without damaging the insulation on the individual wires inside the cable. You can easily do this using a cable ripper, which has an internal tooth that bites into the sheathing when the tool is clamped over the cable and squeezed. Once the sheathing is punctured by this tooth, you pull the cable ripper toward the end of the cable, ripping the sheathing open along the length of the pull. You can then draw back the split sheathing to expose the wires inside—wires that can now be stripped individually, using a wire stripper or multipurpose tool.

Use these holes for looping wire.

WIRE STRIPPER

Wire Cutter

Numbers next to holes indicate wire size.

Blades cut and strip wire in one action.

AUTOMATIC WIRE STRIPPER

CRIMPER

MULTIPURPOSE TOOL

Numbers next to holes indicate wire size.

Screw and Small-Bolt Cutters

CABLE RIPPER

Wire Gauge Sizes

Ripping Tooth

Tools and Their Uses

"Stripping and Crimping Wires," continued from page 275.

Aviation Snips. Though not a specialized electrical tool, aviation snips often come in handy. After you've split and drawn back the protective sheathing around the cable, for example, you can use aviation snips (or diagonal-cutting pliers) to cut away the excess sheathing. They are also good for cutting metal lath, when trying to establish access for wiring in plaster and lath walls, and for cutting through other metal materials you may encounter or use, such as electrical boxes or fixtures.

AVIATION SNIPS

CONNECTING, SUPPORTING, AND PROTECTING WIRES

Insulated Screwdrivers and Nut Drivers. Screwdrivers are needed to do many things, from installing receptacle covers to tightening terminal screws. Needless to say, a screwdriver handle must be insulated to protect you against electric shock in case the blade accidentally comes in contact with a live wire or circuit. Screwdrivers come in several types, including flat blade, Phillips (cross-blade), and Robertson (square-blade). Some screwdrivers have offset shafts and handles that allow you to get into tight or difficult-to-reach spaces to loosen or fasten screws. For hex-head screws commonly encountered on metal fixtures and appliances, you will need a nut driver, which is really nothing more than a socket wrench with a screwdriver handle.

Cable Staples. You'll need cable staples to secure wires safely to framing members inside walls, floors, ceilings, and other concealed spaces. Various types of staples are made in metal with plastic coatings for different sizes and numbers of wires. The NEC (Section 334.30) requires that nonmetallic sheathed cable be supported at intervals not to exceed 4½ feet and must be fastened within 1 foot of any electrical box or fitting.

FLAT-BLADE SCREWDRIVER

PHILLIPS SCREWDRIVER

ROBERTSON SCREWDRIVERS

OFFSET SCREWDRIVERS

Offset in shank allows handle to be quickly rotated around the shaft.

NUT DRIVERS

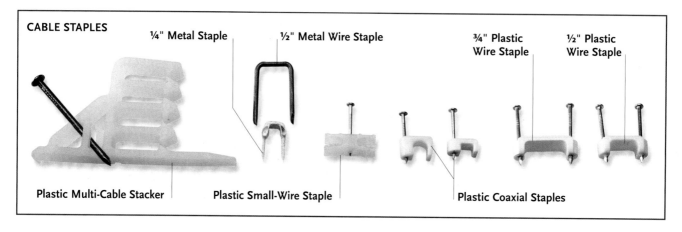

CABLE STAPLES

¼" Metal Staple

½" Metal Wire Staple

¾" Plastic Wire Staple

½" Plastic Wire Staple

Plastic Multi-Cable Stacker

Plastic Small-Wire Staple

Plastic Coaxial Staples

Tools and Their Uses

Wire Shields. Even after a job is finished, wiring still can be subject to unintentional damage. Someone nailing into a wall stud could inadvertently hit a hot wire and receive a deadly shock. For this reason, when wires are run through framing members and are subject to penetration by nails or screws, you must place wire shields on the edges of the studs along the path of the wire (NEC Section 300.4).

Wire Brush and Antioxidant Paste. You can use a wire brush to remove corrosion from wires or simply to clean wires. Aluminum wires should be treated with an antioxidant paste to prevent corrosion from recurring.

Electrical Tape. Use tape for temporary emergency wire splices; color-coding circuit wires; and attaching cables to fish tape for secure wire-pulling.

ANTIOXIDANT PASTE AND WIRE BRUSH

WIRE SHIELDS

To Clean Outer Surfaces of Wire and Conduit

GROUNDING AND TERMINAL SCREWS

GROUNDING AND TERMINAL SCREWS can be thought of as tools for safely securing grounding and circuit wires. Grounding wires must be pigtailed to the grounding screw in an electrical box that is grounded, for example, in order to connect the circuit to the grounding system.

Terminal screws connect wires to receptacles, switches, and other electrical equipment. They are generally coded by color or material to reduce the chance of mismatching wires. Brass-color screws indicate hot terminals; white or silver screws are for neutral terminals; and the grounding screw is always green. In a three-way switch, for example, a dark-color screw designates the common screw terminal connecting paired switches; the connecting wire should not be moved to either of the other two lighter-color terminal screws. Make all connections in accordance with NEC guidelines and requirements.

Some devices have terminal connections that allow you to simply push a wire into a hole rather than wrapping it around a screw. In this type of connection the bare wire must be totally pushed into the opening—no bare wire may be exposed. This type of screwless pressure connection can only be made with 14-gauge copper wire (NEC Section 110.14). These connections can be problematic and are not recommended. Use screw terminals wherever possible.

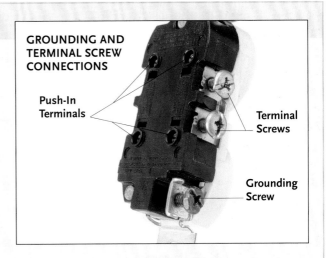

GROUNDING AND TERMINAL SCREW CONNECTIONS

Push-In Terminals

Terminal Screws

Grounding Screw

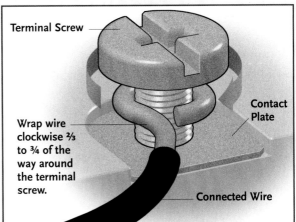

Terminal Screw

Wrap wire clockwise ⅔ to ¾ of the way around the terminal screw.

Contact Plate

Connected Wire

To properly connect a wire, first strip the wire; then wrap it clockwise two-thirds of the way around the terminal screw. Tighten the screw until the wire is firmly and fully in contact with the contact plate.

CRIMPING FERRULES

WIRES CAN LOOSEN from twist-on wire connectors. Crimping ferrules make a more permanent connection, especially when splicing together bare grounding wires. After twisting the wires together, you slide the crimping ferrule, or compression ring, over the wires and crimp them together using a crimping tool. (See below right.) For insulated wire, the ferrule must be covered with a special wire cap.

USING CRIMPING FERRULES

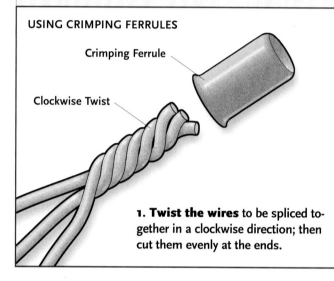

Crimping Ferrule

Clockwise Twist

1. Twist the wires to be spliced together in a clockwise direction; then cut them evenly at the ends.

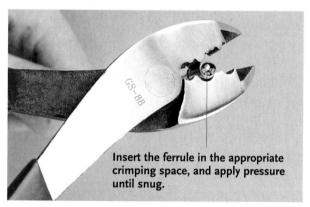

Insert the ferrule in the appropriate crimping space, and apply pressure until snug.

2. Use a wire crimper to compress the crimping ferrule around the twisted wires.

Straps. Conduit straps, which are screwed into place, are used to support metal conduit where wiring is exposed, such as in a basement. Metal conduit must be supported at intervals not to exceed 10 feet and must be fastened within 3 feet of any electrical box or other conduit termination (NEC Sections 342.30, 344.30, and 358.30).

Clamps. Grounding and acorn clamps connect ground wires to ground rods; split-bolt connectors splice together larger wire sizes; and cable connectors with locknuts are used to secure insulated wire cable to electrical boxes. This way, the unsheathed wires from the cable are protected from fraying against the metal box.

Punch-Down Tool. A punch-down, or impact, tool is used to push unstripped telephone or data communications wire down into a connecting block. A terminal post or clip pierces the insulation to complete the connection between the post and the wire. Blade tips can be obtained for either 66 or 110 punch-down wire connecting blocks. Never use ordinary pliers or other tools in place of a punch-down tool because they may cause severe damage to the connectors.

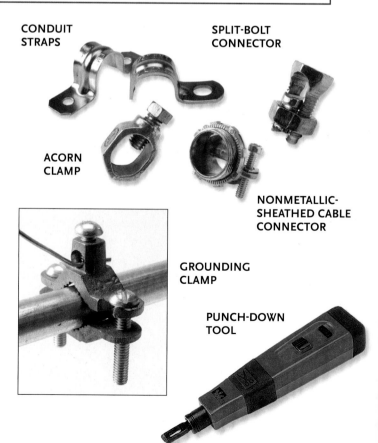

CONDUIT STRAPS

SPLIT-BOLT CONNECTOR

ACORN CLAMP

NONMETALLIC-SHEATHED CABLE CONNECTOR

GROUNDING CLAMP

PUNCH-DOWN TOOL

WIRE CONNECTORS

WHENEVER TWO OR MORE WIRES are stripped to be spliced together, bare wires become exposed. They must be protected and prevented from coming into contact with other wires, connections, and metal surfaces that may cause a dangerous fault or short circuit. This is typically done using wire connectors or crimping ferrules.

When connecting wires using twist-on wire connectors, be aware of several things. Although the color schemes may vary from one manufacturer to the next, wire connectors are color-coded by size according to the minimum and maximum number of wires they can safely connect. Wire connectors should not be used to connect wires of dissimilar materials, unless so rated, and must completely encase the bare ends of the wires joined within the connector. Green wire connectors should always and only be used for connecting grounding wires.

Use a wire connector to splice two or more wires securely together, adhering to the minimum and maximum wire capacity rating for the connector you are using. Hold the wires tightly; slip the connector over the stripped ends; and turn the connector clockwise to secure the wires together.

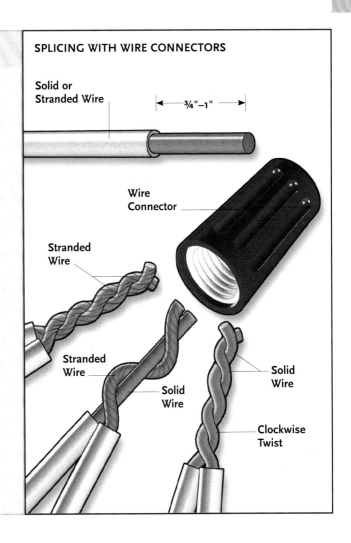

SPLICING WITH WIRE CONNECTORS

Solid or Stranded Wire

¾"–1"

Wire Connector

Stranded Wire

Stranded Wire

Solid Wire

Solid Wire

Clockwise Twist

WIRE CONNECTOR RATINGS

Wire Connector	Color	Minimum		Maximum	
		Gauge	No. Wires	Gauge	No. Wires
	Orange	18	2	14	2
	Yellow	16	2	14	4
	Red	14	2	12	4
				10	3
	Green	Green wire connectors are used for grounding wires only.			

Although they vary from manufacturer to manufacturer, wire connectors are generally color-coded according to the minimum and maximum number of wires they connect. All wire connectors can be used for either conducting or grounding wires, but green wire connectors should only be used for grounding wires.

Tools and Their Uses

"Connecting, Supporting, and Protecting Wires," continued from page 278.

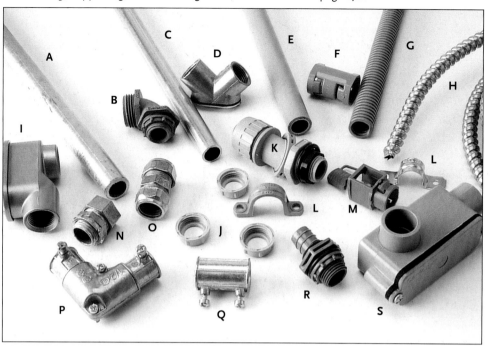

A–rigid metal conduit; B–90-deg. liquid-tight connector; C–electrical metal tubing (EMT); D–metal elbow connector; E–rigid nonmetallic conduit; F–plastic ENT coupling; G–electrical nonmetallic tubing (ENT); H–flexible metal conduit; I–SLB fitting; J–plastic bushings; K–multiposition liquid-tight connector; L–pipe straps; M–NM cable and cord connection; N–raintight compression connector; O–compression coupling; P–metal elbow connector; Q–setscrew coupling; R–plastic screw-in connector; S–plastic LBL-fitting

Conduit and Accessories. Metal conduit, or tubing, is typically used to protect wires from damage and moisture in an exposed location, such as a basement. If exposed to harsh atmospheric conditions, the tubing itself must be corrosion-resistant. There are five basic types of metal conduit: EMT (electrical metallic tubing), and the similar IMC (intermediate metallic conduit) not shown, rigid metal conduit, flexible metal conduit in a nonmetallic PVC cover (liquid-tight) not shown, and flexible metal conduit (helically wound). There are also two types of nonmetallic conduit used in residential work—electrical nonmetallic tubing (ENT) and rigid nonmetallic conduit (Schedule 40). These are made of polyvinyl chloride (PVC). Conduit sizes permitted by the NEC range from ½ inch to a maximum of 6 inches in diameter. Connection accessories include bends, couplings, compression and screw connectors, conduit bodies, and pipe supports. Check codes carefully before doing electrical work involving conduit. For example, wire splices are not permitted within conduit itself but only in electrical boxes or wherever wires remain accessible. There's also a limit on the size and number of wires permitted in conduit. (See the table at left.)

WIRE CAPACITIES OF ELECTRICAL METALLIC TUBING (EMT)

Wire Type	Gauge	Maximum No. of Wires Permitted in EMT				
		½ Inch	¾ Inch	1 Inch	1¼ Inch	1½ Inch
TW	14	8	15	25	43	58
	12	6	11	19	33	45
	10	5	8	14	24	33
	8	2	5	8	13	18
THW THHW THW-2	14	6	10	16	28	39
	12	4	8	13	23	31
	10	3	6	10	18	24
	8	1	4	6	10	14
THHN THWN	6	2	4	7	12	16
	4	1	2	4	7	10
	3	1	1	3	6	8
	2	1	1	3	5	7
	1	1	1	1	4	5

The NEC limits the total number of individual wires of the same gauge in a conduit. (See NEC 2005, Annex C, Table C1.)

Tools and Their Uses

LOCATING, MEASURING, AND MARKING

Electronic Stud Finder. When you want to locate wood framing inside a wall, you should use an electronic stud finder. Locating concealed framing makes it easier to plan wire runs and to be sure that fasteners applied to the wall will be secured to the framing—not just the drywall. Knowing where framing is located will allow you to avoid drilling and cutting holes in the wrong place or locating electrical boxes where framing will interfere with installation. You can also use a stud finder to determine the location of hidden pipes and existing wiring runs.

Measuring Tape. A heavy-duty 30-foot measuring tape is adequate for most indoor work, whether you are measuring the length of a wire run or the dimensions of a room.

Range Finder. If you want to take a high-tech approach, use an electronic range finder to sonically measure the distance between walls. Then you can use the dimensions to calculate power usage requirements.

Pencils/Felt-Tip Marker. A graphite-lead No. 2 or carpenter's pencil is useful for marking accurate measurements of any kind, whether on framing members, drywall, or any other surface on which you can write. A medium-weight black or blue felt-tip marker or grease pencil may do for surfaces that are hard to mark with a lead pencil. Markers are especially handy for labeling wires and circuits to prevent hazardous mistakes. It is important that you switch off the appropriate circuit breaker and connect the right wires whenever you are doing electrical work.

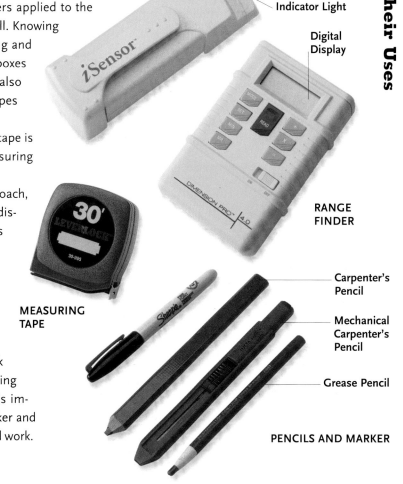

ELECTRONIC STUD FINDER

Indicator Light

Digital Display

RANGE FINDER

Carpenter's Pencil

Mechanical Carpenter's Pencil

Grease Pencil

MEASURING TAPE

PENCILS AND MARKER

HOLE-MAKING, CUTTING, AND STRIKING

Wood and Masonry Chisels. A wood chisel can be used to notch through the outer edge of a top plate or across the face of a stud in a wood-framed wall to make a pathway for fishing wires between a ceiling and a wall or across a wall. A cold chisel is helpful when you must notch, chip, and punch holes in masonry, though a star drill may be more useful for hole-making. A star drill is a hardened-steel chisel with a star-shaped tip. It is an impact tool that can be easily used with a handheld sledgehammer to punch holes through concrete block or other masonry.

WOOD CHISELS

COLD CHISEL

STAR DRILL

Tools and Their Uses

CORDLESS DRILLS AND ACCESSORIES

IT'S ESSENTIAL that you have a drill with enough torque and power to drill holes for running wires through wood framing. Even a simple task such as installing a screw into wood can be made easier by predrilling the screw holes. If you have a standard corded electric drill, using it safely requires that you must always power it through a ground-fault protection device. A cordless drill is safer and more convenient. Today's better battery-operated drills are powerful enough to handle almost any situation you'll face in a wiring project, and they reduce the potential risk of electric shock from tool wires being dragged through moist areas. They are also handy when working on a ladder. It is difficult and dangerous to haul an electric drill with a long extension cord up a tall ladder. The cord may get in your way, trip you, or catch on something. Maintaining enough balance to drill a hole while holding onto a ladder, a cord, and a drill at the same time can be extremely difficult, if not impossible.

Purchasing a battery-operated drill of 12 volts or more with a charger and second battery will make your work much easier. These drills come in two different chuck sizes— ⅜ inch and ½ inch. The ½-inch chuck is a better choice if you will make larger-diameter holes.

Drill Bits. Whether you use a conventional or a cordless drill, a variety of drill bits will come in handy. A masonry bit is a necessity when you need to drill a hole for conduit through poured-concrete or block walls. Likewise, Forstner and spade bits are convenient for drilling holes through wood studs when you need to fish wires through a framed wall.

Hole Saws. A set of hole saws (hole-cutter attachments) will make easy work of cutting holes to run wire or conduit. Hole saws are also available with carbide tips, which stay sharp under extreme use.

CORDLESS DRILL

Forstner Bit

Masonry Bit

High-Speed Steel Bit

Spade Bit

Flexbits

BATTERY CHARGERS

Battery-operated tools are safer and a lot more convenient to use than standard electric tools. The new cordless tools have plenty of torque and power to perform almost any task. It is no longer necessary for you to hunt for an outlet or extension cord or to worry about the gauge of the extension cord.

Specialty battery-operated tools are increasingly popular and available, from battery-operated screwdrivers and circular saws to reciprocating saws and drills. Of course, to keep these new tools powered, you need to have a high-quality battery charger as a permanent part of your tool collection.

Bit and mandrel section is unbolted for use with other cutter heads.

HOLE SAWS

BATTERY AND CHARGER

"Hole-Making, Cutting, and Striking," continued from page 281.

Cordless Reciprocating Saw. You can quickly rough-cut through virtually any material, from wood to metal, using a reciprocating saw. Battery-operated models are perfect for doing electrical work safely without having to drag around tool wires. Be sure to have on hand appropriate blades for cutting through different materials.

Electrician's Hammer. An electrician's hammer differs from a conventional curved-claw hammer in four important ways. First, the shaft is constructed of fiberglass to insulate against electric shock; second, the head is narrower and longer for better reach; third, the claw is flatter and longer, like that of a straight-claw or ripping hammer; and fourth, the head is designed to be non-sparking.

Knockout Punch. For twisting the slugs off of electrical boxes, a lineman's pliers will do in a pinch, but a standard round knockout punch will do a better, cleaner job of slug-splitting and removal. A heavy-duty model will also enable you to punch holes in thick sheet metal, stainless steel, plastic, fiberglass, and other similar materials.

Utility Saw and Utility Knife. Utility saws and utility knives are ideally suited for cutting into or through drywall. You'll find a utility knife especially useful for slicing through drywall to reach stud framing that must be notched for wire-pulling behind a wall.

RECIPROCATING SAW

ELECTRICIAN'S HAMMER

Insulated Handle

Extended Non-sparking Head

Sharpened edge cuts a new hole.

KNOCKOUT PUNCH

UTILITY SAW AND UTILITY KNIFE

WORKING WITH CONDUIT

Manual Tubing Bender. A manual pipe or electrical metallic tubing bender is used for bending tubing smoothly and efficiently. You can operate a pipe bender by hand or by using foot pressure to bend conduit to a 10-, 22½-, 30-, 45-, 60-, or 90-degree angle as marked on the conduit bender. This tool is essential for making accurate saddle bends, stub-ups, and back-to-back bends, as well as simple up and down bends, without crimping the pipe.

Hacksaw. You'll need a hacksaw to cut through metal pipe or conduit or metal-sheathed cable. The number of teeth in the blade determines the thickness of metal that can be cut. In general, thicker metals require coarser-toothed blades. A wing nut on the hacksaw handle allows you to remove the blade or adjust its cutting angle and tightness.

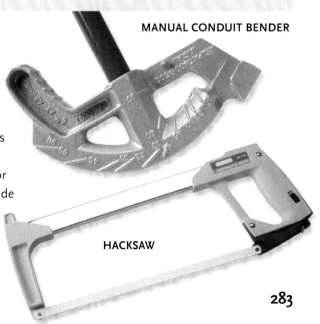

MANUAL CONDUIT BENDER

HACKSAW

Tools and Their Uses

"Working with Conduit," continued from page 283.

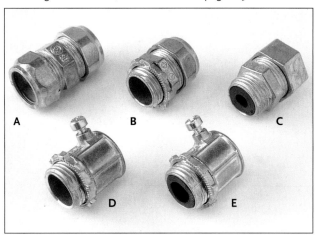

Conduit Connectors. Special types of connectors are needed to secure conduit at junctions and connection points. Above are examples of straight conduit connectors for rigid and intermediate metallic conduit.
A–straight compression coupling; B–concrete-tight straight compression; C–straight compression with insulated throat; D–concrete-tight setscrew; and E–setscrew with insulated throat.

Combination Wrench

Open-End Wrench

Groove-Joint Pliers

Adjustable Wrench

Locking Pliers

Wrenches and Pliers. Many conduit connections, as with conventional plumbing pipes, consist of compression fittings. You will need pliers and sized or adjustable wrenches to properly secure these connections.

SAFETY

Electrician's Gloves. For electrical work you should use a pair of insulated electrician's gloves, rather than using ordinary work gloves. Some high-voltage gloves can protect you up to 20,000 volts, while low-voltage gloves are sufficient for up to 1,000 volts.

   Safety Glasses. When doing electrical work of any kind, you should always wear safety glasses or goggles. A sudden spark or a bit of clipped wire could shoot out and burn or scratch your eye. When drilling overhead, it is important to wear safety goggles to protect your eyes from falling debris.

   Extension Cords. Because you should never plug a power tool into an electrical circuit unless it is ground-fault protected, a GFCI extension cord can literally be a lifesaver if a tool malfunctions and short-circuits to the housing while you are using it. A 3-foot extension cord with GFCI protection built in is ideal because of its portability. It is sold at most electrical wholesalers and retailers. Use, at minimum, a 12-gauge heavy-duty extension cord to allow your high-voltage tools to obtain maximum voltage, which prolongs their life. Under-gauged extension cords can be a fire hazard.

smart tip

USING LADDERS

ALWAYS USE NONCONDUCTIVE WOOD OR FIBERGLASS LADDERS. ALUMINUM LADDERS CAN BE AN ELECTRICIAN'S NIGHTMARE. SHOULD YOU ACCIDENTALLY CUT INTO A HOT WIRE, YOU MUST BE INSULATED FROM GROUND—NOT CONNECTED TO IT. ALWAYS WEAR RUBBER-SOLED SHOES AND ELECTRICIAN'S GLOVES TO SERVE AS ADDITIONAL INSULATORS. BRACE THE LADDER BY HAMMERING STAKES INTO THE GROUND.

SAFETY GLASSES

GFCI EXTENSION CORD

TESTING CIRCUITS

Neon Circuit Tester. Use the two probes on a circuit tester to check for live voltage in a circuit. The neon bulb will light if the circuit is live. You can also use the tester to verify that the power to a circuit has been turned off before you work on it.

Receptacle Analyzer. Use a receptacle analyzer to identify faults in receptacle wiring: simply plug the device into the outlet being tested; then read the lighting pattern made by the three bulbs on the analyzer. Different combinations of lighted and unlighted bulbs indicate specific problems with the wiring, such as hot and neutral wires connected in reverse.

Multi-tester. An analog or digital multi-tester, or multimeter, is required to measure voltage and current, as well as to make continuity and resistance checks in switches, fixtures, low-voltage transformers, and other electrical devices.

Continuity Tester. A continuity tester is powered by its own battery, which is used to generate an electrical current through an attached wire and clamp. It must only be used when the power to a circuit is turned off. The tester is especially useful for determining whether or not a cartridge fuse has blown. You can test this type of fuse by touching the tester clamp and probe to the opposite end caps of the fuse. A lighted bulb indicates a working fuse, an unlighted bulb means that the fuse has blown and is in need of replacement. The tester can also be used to detect faults and current interruptions in switches and other types of electrical equipment.

Low-Voltage Circuit Tester. A low-voltage circuit tester looks similar to a neon circuit tester, but it is strictly limited to testing circuits less than 50 volts such as door-bells, transformers, low-voltage lamps, and outlets, etc.

Telephone Line Tester. Use a telephone line tester to resolve problems with standard telephone wiring. A telephone line tester has a phone-jack plug on one end and an LED on the other. Some testers come with a splitter that enables you to strip as well as test telephone wires. Plugging the tester into a modular jack allows you to test whether any of the circuit wires have been reversed or are loose or disconnected. You can also use a telephone line tester used to check the telephone itself for dial-tone and wiring function.

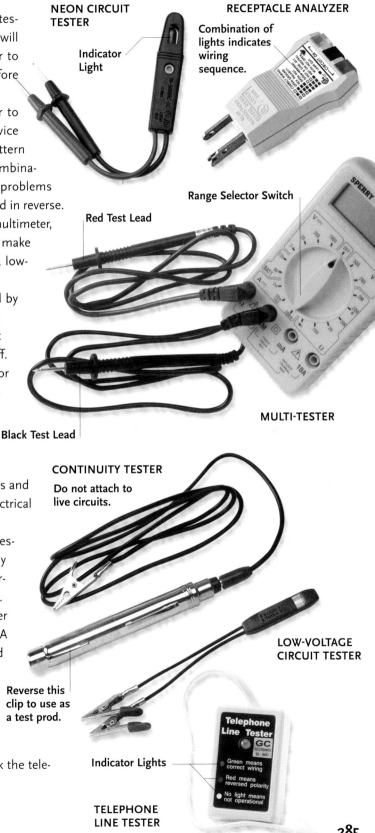

NEON CIRCUIT
TESTER

Indicator
Light

RECEPTACLE ANALYZER

Combination of
lights indicates
wiring
sequence.

Range Selector Switch

Red Test Lead

MULTI-TESTER

Black Test Lead

CONTINUITY TESTER
**Do not attach to
live circuits.**

LOW-VOLTAGE
CIRCUIT TESTER

Reverse this
clip to use as
a test prod.

Indicator Lights

TELEPHONE
LINE TESTER

285

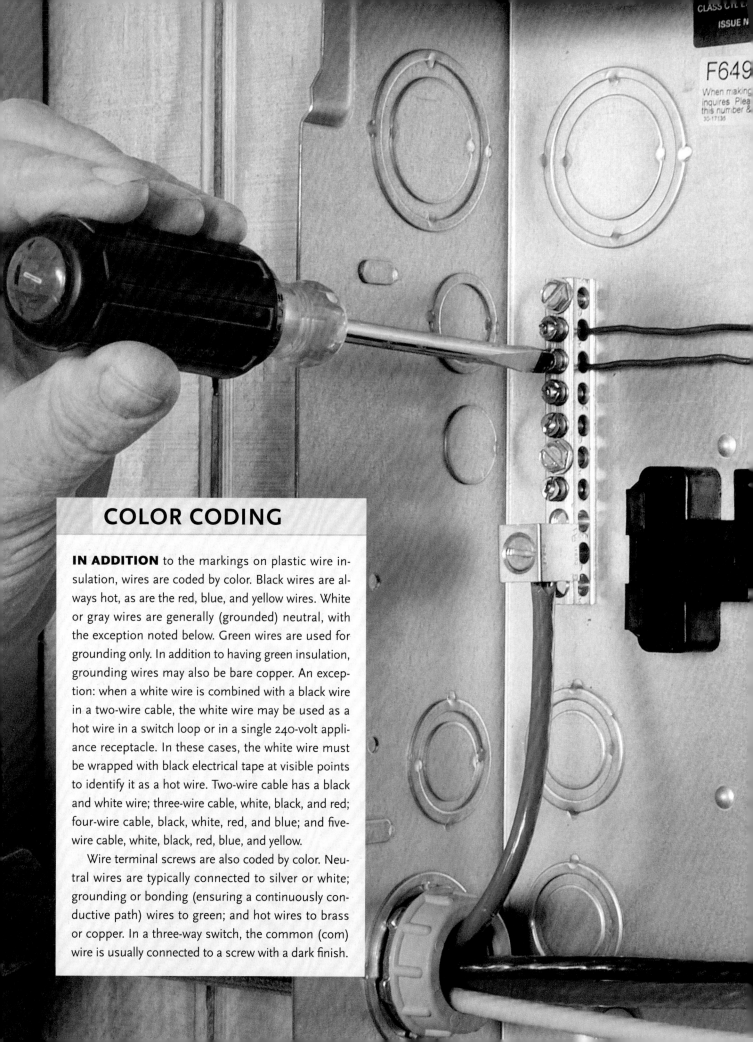

CLASS C1L L

ISSUE N

F649

When making
inquires Plea
this number &
3C-17135

COLOR CODING

IN ADDITION to the markings on plastic wire insulation, wires are coded by color. Black wires are always hot, as are the red, blue, and yellow wires. White or gray wires are generally (grounded) neutral, with the exception noted below. Green wires are used for grounding only. In addition to having green insulation, grounding wires may also be bare copper. An exception: when a white wire is combined with a black wire in a two-wire cable, the white wire may be used as a hot wire in a switch loop or in a single 240-volt appliance receptacle. In these cases, the white wire must be wrapped with black electrical tape at visible points to identify it as a hot wire. Two-wire cable has a black and white wire; three-wire cable, white, black, and red; four-wire cable, black, white, red, and blue; and five-wire cable, white, black, red, blue, and yellow.

Wire terminal screws are also coded by color. Neutral wires are typically connected to silver or white; grounding or bonding (ensuring a continuously conductive path) wires to green; and hot wires to brass or copper. In a three-way switch, the common (com) wire is usually connected to a screw with a dark finish.

materials and equipment

EVEN IF YOU HAVE THE PROPER TOOLS to do your own electrical work, you are only half-prepared for the task. You must also have the right materials and equipment. Plan your electrical work on paper so that you will know exactly what to purchase—from the service panel and electrical boxes to the receptacles, switches, and fixtures. First, you must determine what you're installing and how much power it requires. Then you can decide what categories and quantities of wire to buy; how many circuit breakers and at what amperage; whether or not conduit or cable will be used, and what type; and the accessories needed to connect and fasten wires, conduit, cable, and other materials. Carefully identifying everything you need in advance saves time, money, and effort.

MATERIAL COSTS AND AVAILABILITY—A PROBLEM OF OUR TIME

PRIOR TO THE SPRING OF 2020, electrical material supplies were abundant and prices were stable. But since then the supply of electrical materials—especially wire, panel breakers, and other major components of electrical systems—have seen a dramatic decrease in availability. And they have gotten more expensive.

What does this mean to the DIY homeowner who wants to undertake a small to mid-size electrical project? The following guidelines may be helpful.

- Do your research: check pricing and availability from multiple local home centers and online resources.
- Know exactly how much of each item you require. Estimating 300 feet of a given wire when only 250 feet is on the shelf, and you really only need 275 feet, can be the difference in a successful project and being left needing more wire.
- At the height of wire price fluctuation era, prices changed almost every day, sometimes by 200 percent or more, depending on the wire gauge. Prices have leveled out but are still 150 percent higher than before spring 2020.
- Panel circuit breakers are another item of concern related to costs and availability. Check your local Building Department of your municipality to understand the NEC enforcement being used to ensure you install the correct circuit break type.
- Newer codes require that arc fault (AFCI) and arc fault/ground fault (AFCI/GFCI) combination breakers be installed in panels, and that includes remodeling installations as well. The cost and availability of these breakers since spring 2020 has become an issue. Be sure to have them on hand before starting your work, because they may not be available when you finish your work.
- PVC junction boxes have also been less available and more expensive since spring 2020. Many home centers are switching brands and manufacturers, so if you start with a particular brand of a PVC junction box and they no longer have them, or they are in limited supply, you may be forced to purchase boxes from other sources, which could take extra time and cost more.
- Keep your receipts. In the digital age receipts can be an afterthought. However, retailers in the construction trades are relying on them to refund the amount paid when the items were purchased, and not the current price. And with the frequent turnover in stocked items, if a SKU number is deleted from their system, having the paper receipt gives you additional protection.

Materials and Equipment

WIRES AND CABLES

Types and Designations

Technically, the metallic material through which electric current flows is called a conductor. In practical terms, most people call it wire. Wire is designated as bare or insulated, stranded or solid, single or multiple, sheathed in cable or encased in insulated cord. In residential work, most wires made of a solid conductive material, such as copper, are encased and protected in plastic insulation. Cables usually consist of two or more insulated wires wrapped together in a second protective layer of plastic sheathing. If the cable includes a grounding wire, it can be insulated, bare, or covered copper wire. Cable is commonly sold boxed in precut lengths. Stranded wires are typically enclosed in an insulating jacket, called a cord. Flexible cord is sometimes precut and packaged but is usually sold off the roll. Whether on a roll or precut, conductors are always sold by the linear foot.

Aluminum and copper-clad aluminum wires have also been used in the past, in addition to copper, as conductive materials. For any electrical work you do, you should use only the kind of wire that is already installed in your home. To find out which kind of wire you have, check the cable type at the main service panel by reading the designation printed on the plastic sheathing. (See table "American Wire Gauges," page 256.)

For example, consider the following designation: 14/3 WITH GROUND, TYPE NM-B, 600 Volts (UL). The first number shows that the insulated wires inside the cable are 14 gauge (AWG). The second number indicates that the cable contains three wires. "With ground" signifies that a fourth bare copper or green insulated grounding wire is incorporated within the cable. This may simply be designated with the letter G following the number of wires in the cable. "Type NM-B" denotes that the wire is rated at 90 degrees Centigrade (194 degrees Fahrenheit) and is encased in a nonmetallic (plastic) sheathing. Next, the maximum voltage safely carried by the cable is specified as 600 volts. And, finally, the UL notation ensures that the cable is rated as safe for its designated use.

Wire Sizes. You will be concerned mostly with solid-copper wires of 14, 12, and 10 gauge because these are most commonly used for house wiring. Again, the term wire refers to a single conductor. In a cable containing two or more wires, they will all be the same gauge. The AWG system codes the wire diameter as a whole number. The smaller the number, the greater the diameter and current-carrying capacity of the wire. Because wire size recommendations are for copper wires, you must readjust the designation to the next larger size whenever you use aluminum or copper-clad aluminum wire. (12- and 10-gauge aluminum and copper-clad aluminum are no longer manufactured and are not available.)

Aluminum Concerns. Be extremely cautious if you use aluminum wire. Though commonly used for heavy appliance circuits, aluminum wire requires special attention in switches and receptacles. Don't use aluminum wire where copper wire is designated. If aluminum wire is used in a device designed for copper wire, the wire will expand and contract as it heats and cools, eventually working loose from the terminal screws. This will create a dangerous situation and may result in an electrical fire. If your home contains copper-clad aluminum wiring, do not add aluminum wiring to it. Instead, use copper wires. If your home has aluminum wire, check whether the switches and receptacles are marked CO/

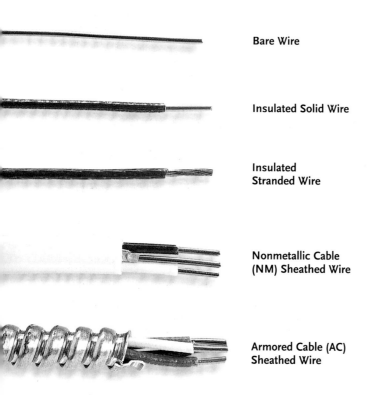

Bare Wire

Insulated Solid Wire

Insulated
Stranded Wire

Nonmetallic Cable
(NM) Sheathed Wire

Armored Cable (AC)
Sheathed Wire

Connection
Rating

Connect aluminum wire only to receptacles or switches approved for it and clearly marked with the letters CO/ALR.

Gauge	Number of Wires	Grounding Label	Type	Voltage Rating	UL Listing

ALR (rated to be connected to aluminum). If the switches and receptacles do not bear this marking, replace them with those that do. Be careful, too, when working with single-strand aluminum wire because it breaks easily. Also, never connect aluminum wire to a back-wired switch or receptacle that uses push-in terminals. Aluminum wire must always be connected to terminal screws (NEC Section 110.14). Note, too, that you can buy UL-listed crimp and twist-on connec-tors that are specifically made to connect aluminum to cop-per wire pigtails. These devices are recommended by the Consumer Product Safety Commission.

Aluminum cable is sometimes used for service-entrance cable and large appliances such as electric ranges and elec-tric furnaces. If large diameter, multistranded aluminum cable is used, the ends must be coated with a noncorrosive compound. (NEC Section 110.14)

INSULATION CATEGORIES

WIRE COMES in a variety of insulation types. Be sure that you select the appropriate type for the use and location you have in mind by checking local codes. The most common insulation categories used in residential wiring are THHN, THW, and THWN. The T stands for ordinary thermoplastic insulated cable. You will probably use more of this than any other type of cable. The letter H specifies wire that is heat resistant. A double H indicates wire that can operate at a higher temperature (up to 194 degrees Fahrenheit) than wire designated with a single letter H. The W denotes wire that can be used in dry, damp, or wet locations. The letter N (nylon) specifies that the wire also resists gasoline and/or oil.

Wire Types. THHN wire has flame-retardant, heat-resistant insulation specified for both dry and damp locations. The absence of a W, however, means that the wire is not approved for wet locations. Because nylon in-sulation is thinner than other kinds of plastic insulation, THHN wire is often used to fit more wires into a conduit. THW wire is flame retardant, and heat and moisture resis-tant. THWN wire also resists gasoline and oil. Both THW and THWN can be used in dry, damp, or wet locations. They are commonly used in place of THHN in conduit. Another type of wire, XHHW, is often used for service entrance (SE) cable in wet areas instead of THWN. The X indicates that the wire insulation is a flame-retardant, synthetic polymer.

Cable Sheathing Insulation. Indoor house circuits are usually wired using nonmetallic (NM) cable, which is wire contained in a plastic sheathing that's labeled with its specific use. This flexible cable is sometimes known by its trade name, Romex. NM cable contains insulated neu-tral and power wires and a bare grounding wire. It is used in dry locations only. Each wire is individually wrapped in plastic insulation that is color-coded according to the type of wire inside. Hot wires are typically wrapped in black and neutral wires in white. Grounding wires are either wrapped in green or bare.

The wires in NM cable for common receptacle, light, and small appliance circuits are usually 12/2G or 14/2G. Wire a 20-amp circuit with 12/2G cable. Larger appliance circuits require larger wire sizes. For example, a 30-amp clothes dryer requires 10/3G cable. (See the table, "Repre-sentative Loads and Circuits for Residential Equipment," page 290, for more information.)

If a cable is designated type UF (underground feeder and branch-circuit cable), this means that it is suitable for use in wet locations, including direct burial underground. UF cable can be used in place of wire in conduit in some areas and is permitted for interior wiring in place of Type NM cable (NEC Section 340.10). Check local code re-quirements. The distinguishing characteristic of this type of cable is that the individually insulated wires are embed-ded in solid, water-resistant plastic.

Cord Insulation. Wire designated as cord dif-fers from cable. The type of wires sheathed in cord are stranded wires. The sheathing usually consists of some type of plastic, rubber, or cloth insulation. Zip cord, for example, contains two wires, usually 18 gauge, encased in a neoprene, synthetic, or other rubberlike insulation. A thin strip of this insulation between the wires is all that holds them together. You can easily separate the wires by pulling, or zipping, them apart. Cord is used primarily for lamps, small appliances, and other wires that have plugs or receptacles attached to one or both ends of the cord. Never use them for fixed appliances.

Materials and Equipment

REPRESENTATIVE LOADS AND CIRCUITS FOR RESIDENTIAL ELECTRICAL EQUIPMENT

Appliance	Average Wattage	Volts	Gauge/ No. of Wires	Circuit Breaker or Fuse in Amps
Range	12,000	115/230	6/3	60
Built-in oven	4,500	115/230	10/3	30
Range top	6,000	115/230	10/3	30
Dishwasher	1,200	115	12/2	20
Waste-disposal unit	300	115	14 or 12/2	15 or 20
Broiler	1,500	115	12/2	20
Refrigerator	800	115	14 or 12/2	15 or 20
Freezer	350	115	14 or 12/2	15 or 20
Washing machine	1,200	115	12/2	20
Clothes dryer	5,000	115/230	10/3	30
Iron	1,650	115	14 or 12/2	15 or 20
Workbench	1,500	115	12/2	20
Portable heater	1,300	115	12/2	20
Television	300	115	14 or 12/2	15 or 20
Fixed lighting	1,200	115	14 or 12/2	15 or 20
Room air conditioner	1,200	115	14 or 12/2	15 or 20
Central air conditioner	5,000	115/230	10/3	30
Sump pump	300	115	14 or 12/2	15 or 20
Forced-air furnace	600	115	14 or 12/2	15 or 20
Attic fan	300	115	12/2	20

Wherever the information is available, use actual equipment ratings. A heavy-duty, fixed-location appliance should generally be on its own circuit. Check the manufacturer's literature to determine circuit and direct connections for any appliance before installing and connecting it to your electrical system.

Wire insulation comes in categories, each having a maximum operating temperature and ampacity rating. A—TW (Wet Locations); B—THHN (Flame and Heat Resistant, Gas/Oil Resistant); THWN (Flame Retardant, Wet Locations, Gas/Oil Resistant); C—THW (Flame Retardant, Wet Locations); D—XHHW (Service Entrance, Flame and Heat Resistant, Wet Locations)

smart tip

ESTIMATING WIRE

TO ESTIMATE THE AMOUNT OF WIRE OR CABLE YOU WILL NEED FOR A PROJECT, MEASURE THE DISTANCE BETWEEN THE NEW SWITCH, RECEPTACLE, OR FIXTURE BOX AND THE MAIN PANEL WHERE THE CABLE ORIGINATES. BECAUSE YOU WILL PROBABLY NOT BE GOING IN A STRAIGHT LINE, REMEMBER TO ALLOW FOR CURVES AND OFFSETS. TO BE SAFE, ADD 1 FOOT FOR EVERY JUNCTION YOU WILL MAKE; THEN PROVIDE A MARGIN OF ERROR BY ADDING 20 PERCENT TO THE TOTAL CALCULATED DISTANCE.

SPLICING WIRES

ACCORDING TO THE NEC, all wire splices must be enclosed in a switch, receptacle, fixture, or junction box. To make a wire splice, you must first strip insulation from the end of the wires. Although it may be used for this, a utility knife will most likely nick the wire. Instead, use an electrician's wire stripper or multipurpose tool. A wire stripper is operated either manually or automatically. (See "Stripping and Crimping Wires," page 275.) A manual wire stripper requires that you cut the insulation, without cutting the wire, and then pull the cut insulation from the end of the wire. Automatic wire strippers cut and strip the insulation in one motion.

To splice solid wire to solid wire, strip approximately ½ inch of insulation from the end of each wire. Then, using pliers, spirally twist one piece of wire around the other in a clockwise direction. Make the twist tight but not so tight it will cause the wire to break. Cap the splice with a wire connector. (You can also cap the wires without twisting first.) Some people tape around the connector as an added precaution to ensure that the wires will not come out. Splice stranded wires in the same way, but do not strip either type of wire by circling the insulation with cutting pliers and then pulling off the insulation. This will cut into the conductors and cause them to break if they are bent.

To splice a stranded wire to a solid wire, strip the same ½ inch of insulation off the solid wire, but an inch from the stranded wire. Spirally twist the stranded wire clockwise around the solid wire. Cap the splice with a wire connector.

To splice solid wire to solid wire, spirally twist one wire around the other in a clockwise direction. Cap the splice using a wire connector.

Splice a stranded wire to a stranded wire in the same way as a solid wire to a solid wire, but be careful not to cut or break the individual wire strands. Strip stranded wires to expose 1 in. of bare wire before splicing.

To splice a stranded wire to a solid wire, spirally twist the stranded wire around the solid wire, and cap the splice using an appropriate-size wire connector. Before splicing, solid wire needs to be stripped to ½ in.

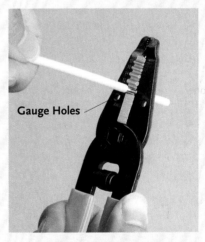

Gauge Holes

To use a manual wire stripper, insert the wire into the matching gauge hole; close the stripper to cut the insulation; and pull it toward the end of the wire.

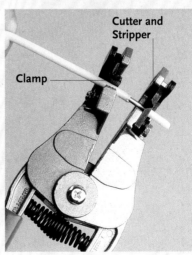

Cutter and Stripper

Clamp

Though more expensive, an automatic wire stripper combines both steps, cutting and stripping the wire insulation, in one motion.

Materials and Equipment

AMPERAGE RATINGS FOR RESIDENTIAL CABLE

AWG Size	Insulation Type	Copper		Aluminum/Copper-Clad Aluminum	
		Ordinary Use	Service Entrance	Ordinary Use	Service Entrance
4/0	THW, THWN	230	250	180	200
2/0	THW, THWN	175	200	135	150
1/0	THW, THWN	150	175	120	125
1/0	TW	125	NA	100	NA
1	THW, THWN	130	150	100	110
2	THW, THWN	115	125	90	100
2	TW	95	NA	75	NA
4	THW, THWN	85	100	65	NA
4	TW	70	NA	55	NA
6	THW, THWN	65	NA	50	NA
6	TW	55	NA	40	NA
8	THW, THWN	50	NA	40	NA
8	TW	40	NA	30	NA
10	THW, THWN	35	NA	30	NA
10	TW	30	NA	25	NA
12	THW, THWN	25	NA	20	NA
14	THW, THWN	20	NA	NA	NA

Wires sheathed in thermoplastic insulation (cable) have maximum amperage capacities (ampacities) for which they are rated. The ratings above are for typical residential wires. (NEC Table 310.16)

Wire Ampacity

When selecting wire, consider its ampacity—the amount of current in amperes that a wire can carry safely and continuously under normal conditions, without exceeding its temperature rating. For example, 10-gauge copper wire is rated to carry up to 30 amps; 14-gauge wire, 15 amps. If a wire is too small, it will present a greater-than-normal resistance to the current flowing around it, generating excess heat that could destroy the wire insulation.

UF Label   Resistance Label

Underground feeder and branch-circuit cable is marked with the letters UF. The label also indicates whether the cable is corrosion- and/or sunlight-resistant.

Underground Cable

Underground feeder and branch-circuit cable, or UF cable, can be used for interior wiring wherever NM cable is permitted. However, it is primarily approved for wet locations, such as direct burial underground. To minimize damage to the UF cable, it must be buried a minimum of 1 foot underground if it is a 120-volt circuit and is GFCI-protected. If it is not protected by a GFCI or the circuit exceeds 20 amps, bury it at least 2 feet underground. Check local code regarding direct-burial cable.

The outer sheathing on UF cable is solid thermoplastic, encasing the inner wires completely. This makes it more difficult to separate the wires from the sheathing, as compared with the wires in standard NM cable. The wires inside UF cable are solid and can be spliced in the same way as standard NM wire, but all splices must be made within a watertight box or with approved splicing devices.

ARMORED CABLE

WIRE ENCLOSED IN METAL SHEATHING is called armored cable (AC). It is sometimes called by its trade name, BX. Inside the flexible metal sheathing are insulated hot and neutral (grounded) wires and a bare bonding wire. BX is restricted to use indoors in dry locations. It is rarely used in new construction (except in high-rise buildings) because it is expensive and difficult to install. Nevertheless, it is often found in older homes. Metal-clad cable (MC) is a more common type of armored cable. The two cables look alike but are easy to tell apart if you know what to look for. MC cable includes a green grounding wire while AC cable does not. The metal covering on MC cable is not permitted to be the grounding conductor. The wires in MC cable are wrapped in a plastic tape to protect them from chafing against the armored sheathing. Be sure to insert a plastic sleeve between the wires and the armor wherever wires emerge from the armored cable.

For BX, different fittings are used to attach the cable to electrical boxes. All BX fittings work the same way—the cable goes through center of the fitting. The armor itself is connected within the fitting and is held in place by one or two clamps or a twist-on mechanism. As stated, BX is not easy to work with. To splice one BX cable into another requires cutting the armor sheathing without harming the wires inside. This can only be done using a hacksaw or a specialized tool that cuts any type of armored cable. The tool just barely cuts through the armor, which is then twisted to break cleanly, exposing the wires inside. Another drawback to BX is that it cannot turn a tight radius because of the metal sheathing. Too tight a turn will kink the armor, creating a sharp edge. Sharp edges are also created wherever armored cable is cut. This is why it is so important to always install a protective sleeve on the cut ends of the cable to protect the wires inside.

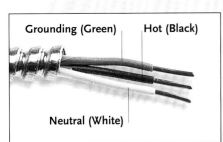

Hot (Black) Hot (Red)
Internal Bonding Strip (Ground) Neutral (White)

Armored cable (AC) is sometimes called by its trade name, BX. It consists of hot, neutral, and grounding wires in a protective metal (armor) sheathing.

Grounding (Green) Hot (Black)
Neutral (White)

Metal-clad (MC) cable is similar to AC cable, but the wires are wrapped in plastic tape instead of paper.

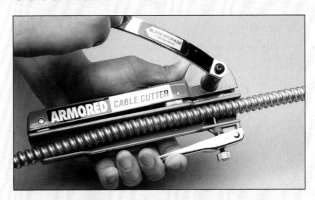

Plastic Sleeve

All types of armored cable require a plastic sleeve placed between the sharp metal edges of the cut cable and the emerging wires.

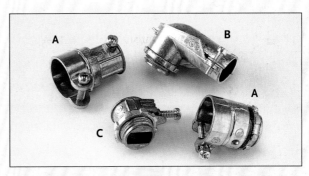

A–squeeze connectors; B–90-deg. squeeze connector; C–end connector

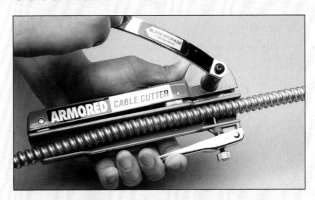

To cut armored cable easily, use a specialized cutting tool. Insert the cable in the tool, and turn the knob clockwise to tighten down on and cut the armor.

NONMETALLIC CABLE

NONMETALLIC (NM) CABLE is the most common type of cable used in residential work. Again, NM cable consists of wires encased in a thermoplastic sheathing. The wires include one or more hot wires, a neutral wire, and a grounding wire. The most common type is two wires with a ground—one hot wire in black insulation, one neutral in white, and a bare copper grounding wire. Three-wire cable is commonly used for house circuits to wire three-way switching or where an extra hot wire is needed, such as for wiring a switch-operated outlet. The third wire is typically encased in red insulation. In some cases, the grounding wire in NM cable may not be included. This is particularly true of older-style NM cable (prior to 1960).

When you work with NM cable, be sure to avoid two common errors: first, putting a kink in the wires by bending the cable too sharply and, second, damaging the cable sheathing by pulling it through too small an opening. A kink may damage the copper wire inside the cable and can cause it to overheat and create a fire hazard. This also applies to working with the individual wires—never bend them at a right angle but rather bend them gradually. As for sheathing, if it is torn by pulling it through a tight opening, around a sharp turn, or getting it caught on something, the cable may be taped as long as the insulation on the individual wire within the cable is not damaged. Otherwise it must be replaced.

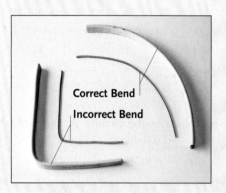

To prevent damage to wires, never bend individual wires or NM cable at a sharp angle.

Correct Bend
Incorrect Bend

A standard NM cable contains two insulated wires and one bare copper grounding wire. The hot wire is encased in black insulation and the neutral in white. In a three-conductor NM cable, the additional hot wire is encased in red insulation.

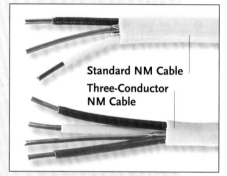

Standard NM Cable
Three-Conductor NM Cable

REMOVING NM CABLE SHEATHING

To remove the sheathing on NM cable, insert the cable into a cable ripper, and squeeze the cutting point into the flat side of the cable 8 to 10 inches from the end. Pull lengthwise down the center of the cable. Because the center wire is the bare grounding wire, if you accidentally cut too far into the cable you will not be likely to cut into the insulation on the conductor wires. Peel back the thermoplastic sheathing and the paper wrapping.

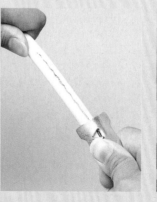

Use a cable ripper to slice open the center of the sheathing on NM cable. This will protect the insulated wires from being cut.

Pull back 8 to 10 in. of the sheathing; then cut away the paper wrapping and excess sheathing, using diagonal cutting pliers.

SERVICE PANELS

Types and How They Work

The service-entrance panel (SEP) is the main house panel. It serves two primary purposes. First, the main panel is the only location in or outside the house where all electrical power can be cut off at once. Every adult member of your household should know the location of this panel and how to cut the power in case of an emergency. Second, the main panel is the distribution point and protection center for all of the circuits. All the branch circuits, ones that go to the receptacles, switches, and appliances throughout your house, originate here.

Under the panel cover, circuit breakers and wires are two copper or aluminum strips. These are the power buses, called hot buses. Each bus is connected to a hot incoming main cable. The circuit breakers are all plugged into these two buses, which provide the breakers with power. Neutral and grounding wires from each circuit are connected to the aluminum neutral/grounding buses on each side of the hot buses. Dead center in the upper part of the panel is a very large breaker, called the main breaker. This breaker controls all of the house power. Its purpose is to monitor the current being drawn, opening the circuit when there is a short or an overload. It also provides manual control over the house power.

Panel Sizes. A typical house panel may provide 100, 150, or 200 amps. Today, 200 amps is most common, although larger all-electric-power homes may use up to 400 amps. Your house's power capacity is noted either on the panel or on the main breaker.

Panels rated for the same maximum current capacity, such as 200 amps, are subdivided by the number of breakers they can hold. For example, a 200-amp panel might contain 40 breakers plus the main breaker. This type of panel is called a 40/40 panel. The first number refers to the number of full-size breakers the panel can hold, and the second number refers to the maximum number of breakers the panel can hold regardless of breaker type. The next panel size below a 40/40 is a 30/40 panel. It can hold only 30 full-size breakers. To increase the panel to 40 breakers, half-size breakers must be used. It is preferable to use full-size breakers for safety reasons. Smaller panels may hold a maximum of 20 or 30 breakers. Avoid these panels because they will not provide breaker space for future expansion.

Circuit-Breaker Sizes. Individual breakers distribute power from the hot buses to the circuits. A standard-tab hot bus will accept only standard full-size breakers; a split-tab hot bus can accept either twin (dual) or half-size breakers. A twin breaker consists of two breakers installed within the space usually occupied by a single breaker.

Power Buses

The service-entrance, or main, panel is both the entry and distribution point for all the circuits in your home. If the panel cover, breakers, and wires were removed, you would see the two power buses into which all of the circuit breakers are plugged. The main breaker, at the top, controls power entering the hot buses. Turn off the power by moving the handle to the off position on the main disconnect. Breakers trip automatically if the circuit shorts or is overloaded.

Circuit Breaker Screw

To install an individual breaker, left, first turn off the main power; then hook the notched end onto the hot bus tab, and snap it firmly in place. A circuit's hot wire, right, is secured beneath a circuit breaker screw. Insert the bare wire end in the terminal hole, and tighten the screw over the wire.

Materials and Equipment

HOT BUSES

WHEN THE MAIN BREAKER is turned on, electricity flows through the two hot buses, or legs. These two vertical metal strips, normally aluminum or copper, extend below the main breaker to the bottom of the panel. They are electrically isolated (separated) from the panel frame. The voltage between one of the buses and the grounded bar equals 120 volts. The voltage from bus to bus equals 240 volts. This is the same voltage level that comes from the utility transformer. The main breaker acts like an on-off switch. When the breaker is on, power is carried through the circuit breaker that serves the fixture, appliance, etc. If it is a 120-volt light fixture, the current will leave the breaker and go through the black hot wire to the light. It returns through a white wire from the light, directly to the neutral bus. If an appliance requires 240 volts, such as a baseboard heater, then current flows through one side of the double-pole breaker, goes through the heating element, and returns through the other hot wire to the second pole on the breaker. No neutral is required. In either case, if the wire is carrying more current than is safe, the circuit breaker will automatically trip.

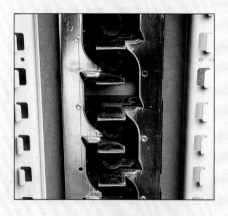

A standard hot-bus tab will only accommodate a full-size breaker.

A split tab can accommodate a twin breaker or a full-size breaker. Do not attempt to fit a twin breaker in a standard hot-bus tab.

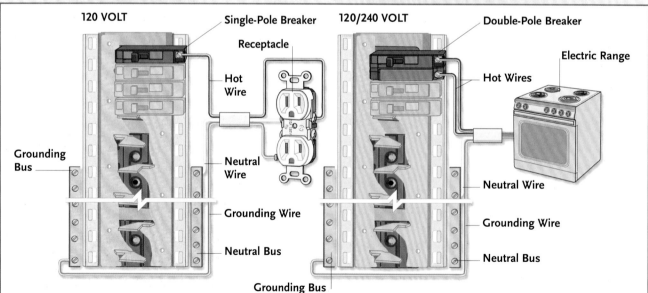

Power rated at 120 volts travels from a black wire on a single-pole circuit breaker to the device. It returns through a white wire from the device to the neutral bus. In a 12%240 volt circuit, 240-volt power flows from one pole of a double-pole circuit breaker to the appliance and back to the second pole on the breaker. Additionally, 120-volt power that runs the lights, clock, and timer travels through a hot wire and back on a neutral white wire.

NEUTRAL AND GROUNDING BUSES

AS MENTIONED EARLIER, the two aluminum bus bars running parallel with the hot buses are known as the neutral and grounding buses. All white insulated neutral wires connect to the neutral bus, while all bare or green grounding wires connect to the grounding bus. In the main panel, the NEC also requires that the metal panel frame be connected to the neutral and grounding buses. This is commonly done using a bonding (connecting) screw and strap supplied with the panel box. The strap grounds the panel frame; if a bare hot wire touches it, the breaker will trip, preventing electrocution.

On all 120-volt circuits, when power returns from the device or appliance, it reenters the main panel through a white neutral wire. The white neutral wire is connected to the grounded neutral bus, which is connected to the grounded neutral conductor in the service entrance cable. From here the current returns through the meter to the utility transformer.

The neutral bus contains two large lugs, in addition to the many smaller screw terminals. The neutral service conductor that comes from the meter is connected to the larger lug. The other lug provides a terminal for any neutral conductor that is too large to fit under one of the smaller screws on the bus.

Bonding Screw

Connecting Strap

Grounded Bus

A panel frame is usually bonded to a grounded bus by a short metal strap running between the green bonding screw on the panel and a terminal on the bus.

A large lug on the neutral bus connects the neutral cable from the utility line to the main panel.

Oversize Wire Lug

Use other large lugs to connect any neutral wire that is too big to fit into a standard screw terminal.

SERVICE PANEL INSTALLATION

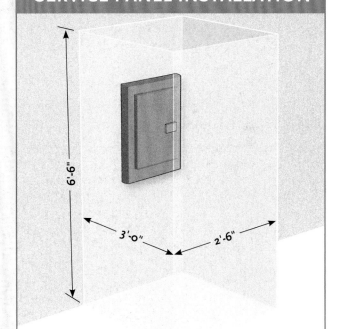

6'-6"

3'-0"

2'-6"

In new installations, a main panel is mounted back-to-back with the utility meter. This saves the expense of running cable and having to install a second cutoff panel near the meter base, as required by most local codes. Maintain clearances at front of the panel at least 3 ft. deep by 2 ft. 6 in. wide by 6 ft. 6 in. high. The panel must be readily accessible in an emergency.

CIRCUIT BREAKERS

CIRCUIT BREAKERS have replaced fuses as the preferred type of circuit protection. Technically, they are called molded-case circuit breakers, or MCCBs. Circuit breakers use a two-part system for protecting circuit wiring. When a small overload is on the circuit, a thermal strip will heat up and open, or trip, the circuit. When a massive amount of current comes through very quickly, as in a ground fault or short circuit, an electromagnet gives the thermal strip a boost. The greater the amount of trip current, the faster the breaker will trip.

The most important advantage circuit breakers have over fuses is that they can be easily reset; you don't have to buy a new one every time an appliance draws excessive current. When a breaker is tripped, it won't work unless you throw it all the way to the off position before you turn it back on again. Another characteristic of circuit breakers is that they are air-ambient-compensated—the hotter the air around them gets, the sooner they will trip. For example, if all the circuit breakers around a specific 20-amp breaker are running hot, because of an excessive flow of current, the 20-amp breaker may trip at only 18 amps.

Residential circuit breakers typically range in size from 15 to 60 amps, increasing at intervals of 5 amps. Single-pole breakers rated for 15 to 20 amps control most 120-volt general-purpose circuits. Double-pole breakers rated for 20 to 60 amps control 240-volt circuits.

Standard circuit breakers are universal and have clips

Two contacts, or pressure clips, on the underside of a circuit breaker snap over a hot-bus tab in the main panel. These contacts bring power into the breaker.

on the bottom that snap onto the hot-bus tabs in the panel box. Contact with the hot bus brings power into the breaker. Be aware, however, that some manufacturers make breakers with wire clips that mount on the side. These clips slide over the tab on the hot bus. It is a good idea to select breakers and panel boxes from the same manufacturer.

Common Breaker Types. In addition to single- and double-pole breakers, quad breakers, GFCI breakers, and surge-protection devices are also available. Single-pole breakers supply power to 120-volt loads such as receptacle and light circuits. A hot black or red wire is usually connected to the breaker. Single-pole breakers come full size or in a two-in-one configuration (twin). The latter type will only fit into a panel having a split-tab hot bus.

Double-pole breakers provide power to 240-volt appliances such as electric water heaters and dryers. If a standard NM cable is used as the conductors, both the black and the white wire are connected to the breaker. The white wire must be marked with black tape at both ends. Larger double-pole circuits have two black conductors in the circuit.

Specialty Breakers. A quad breaker falls within the half-size breaker family and can contain several configurations within one unit. It may, for example, contain two double-pole circuits, such as a double-pole 30-amp and a double-pole 20-amp circuit; it may have two single-pole circuits and one double pole; or it may provide power to some other combination of circuits. The advantage of a quad breaker is that it takes up half the space of a standard breaker. The panel, though, must be specially designed to accept quad breakers.

A GFCI circuit breaker fits into the main panel just like a standard circuit breaker. On its face is a test button but no reset. If properly installed, pressing the test button places a deliberate, preset current imbalance (6 milliamperes) on the line to verify that the breaker will trip when there is an unintended imbalance. When tripped, the breaker arm will go to a halfway off position, cutting power to the circuit.

Arc-fault circuit interrupter (AFCI) breakers are required on branch circuits that supply power to most living areas, with the exceptions of kitchens, bathrooms, and garages. These devices look like GFCI breakers. Their purpose is to detect an arcing situation, such as loose or corroded connections on a wire, and then shut down the current on the circuit before the heat generated by the arc causes a fire.

At first glance, a surge-protection device can be confusing. You will see a device that looks like a double-pole body. This type of device also has two lights that glow when power is applied to the panel. Nevertheless, a surge-protection device connects to the buses in the same as any other circuit breaker.

Limits. Circuit breakers are limited in protecting wires, and therefore life and property. Breakers other than GFCI cannot prevent electric shock, for instance. Although breakers trip at 15 amps and above, it only takes about 0.06 amp to electrocute someone. Circuit breakers cannot prevent overheating of a fixture or appliance or other device, and they can't prevent low-level faults. For a breaker to trip, a fault must occur when enough current is being demanded to exceed the trip current of the breaker. Breakers cannot trip fast enough to completely block lightning surges from entering the circuits. Circuit breakers are meant to save the wiring to the appliance—not the appliance itself.

BREAKER TYPES

A single-pole breaker is the most prevalent type in residential use. It will power anything that requires 120-volt current.

A double-pole breaker is used with a 240-volt appliance, such as a 20-amp baseboard heater or a 30-amp clothes dryer.

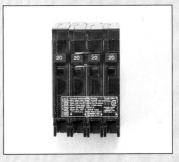

Use a quad breaker to serve two double-pole circuits in the same space as one standard double-pole breaker.

A GFCI circuit breaker will cut power to a circuit when it is tripped by an imbalance in current flow through the wires.

A surge-protection device provides protection for an entire service panel and simply installs in place of two single-pole breakers.

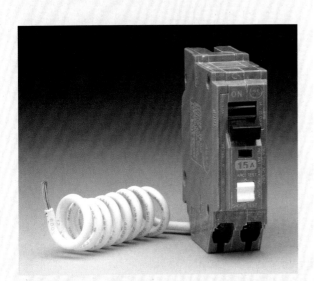

An AFCI breaker will shut down a circuit when it detects an intermittent arc of current, such as an arc caused by a loose connection.

Materials and Equipment

FUSES

THE FUSE was the most common type of circuit protection in homes prior to World War II. Fuses are still used in many older homes. The two most common types of fuses are the plug, or glass fuse, and the cartridge fuse. Plug fuses control 120-volt circuits and are commonly available in sizes ranging from 15 to 30 amps. Inside a plug fuse is a metal strip that extends from the fuse's center contact to the threaded base. The narrow portion of the strip is called the element. If the circuit is overloaded, the element will burn, disconnecting the circuit and blowing the fuse. Cartridge fuses for residential use control 240-volt circuits and typically range in size from 30 to 100 amps. The element in a cartridge fuse runs down the center of the cartridge and is surrounded by a fireproof material that resembles sand.

Most fuse panels in use today are probably quite old. It is rather common for fuse boxes like these to require troubleshooting. Loose connections in an old fuse holder may produce enough heat to instantaneously va-porize a fuse element. If a fuse or fuse holder is discolored (brown or black) or if burn or melt spots are obvious, it is recommended that you replace the entire fuse panel with a circuit-breaker panel.

Replacing a fuse with another one that has a higher amperage rating can allow excessive current on a circuit wire, damaging the wire insulation and possibly causing a fire. Type S fuses were developed to solve this problem. Because each fuse size has a different base threading design, only one size can be installed in a particular circuit.

Sometimes a fuse may blow because of a momentary surge of power coming into the electrical system. Another type of fuse, called a time-delay fuse, can withstand this kind of power surge without blowing.

Fuse Overload. When a circuit is overloaded and the fuse element melts, disconnecting, or opening, the circuit, the damage to the element can be seen easily by looking through the fuse glass.

An overload occurs whenever the amount of current drawn by one or more fixtures or appliances exceeds the fuse rating. You determine a fuse rating by the gauge of

Hot Wire
(Black)

Neutral Wire
(White)

An obsolete fuse box is commonly found in older homes. Such boxes are frequently in need of trouble-shooting or replacement.

When a black hot wire comes into contact with a white neutral wire, a short circuit results.

wire that the fuse protects. In the absence of a fuse (or other circuit protection) or when devices use too much current, the wire becomes overheated, damaging the insulation, possibly causing a fire. Some fuses can be reset rather than replaced (not recommended). Be careful that this type of fuse fits properly into your panel and does not interfere with door closure.

Short Circuits and Ground Faults. A short circuit occurs when a hot wire touches a neutral wire. This sometimes happens by accident when wires are improperly connected. It may also happen when an appliance malfunctions or a circuit is improperly wired. In any case, a short circuit will result in a massive current flow through the fuse, causing the element to destruct and open the circuit. When this happens, the view through the glass on a plug fuse will be obscured by a black/silver discoloration. If this happens to a cartridge fuse, however, it will reveal no visible sign that it has been blown. You must test the fuse using a multitester.

A ground fault occurs when a hot wire touches a grounding wire or any grounded surface. As in a short circuit, massive current flow will cause the fuse to blow. Unfortunately, you cannot tell a short circuit from a ground fault by looking at the blown fuse.

When a short circuit or ground fault occurs, a massive amount of current will surge through a glass fuse, causing the element to be vaporized.

Vaporized Element

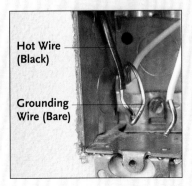

Hot Wire (Black)

Grounding Wire (Bare)

When a hot wire touches a grounding wire or grounded metal appliance frame, a ground fault will occur.

FUSE TYPES

GLASS FUSES

Element

Blown Fuse

Glass, or plug, fuses are found in older homes. Replacing a fuse with one of larger capacity is a fire hazard. On a correctly sized fuse, a metal element inside the fuse will burn and blow out (right), indicating a circuit overload or short circuit if the current exceeds capacity.

CARTRIDGE FUSES

A 60-amp cartridge fuse may be used as the main fuse in an older home. Cartridge fuses range from 30 to 100 amps. A cartridge fuse contains an element not unlike that in a glass fuse, except that it is embedded in nonflammable material (right).

TYPE S FUSES

Base Threading

The Type S fuse was designed to replace the standard glass fuse. Each Type S fuse size has a different base-threading configuration (right) to prevent a homeowner from installing a high-amp fuse in a low-amp fuse socket.

TIME-DELAY FUSES

Some glass fuses are designed to withstand a temporary surge in power without blowing. This type of fuse should be marked "time-delay" on the edge.

ELECTRICAL BOXES

Types and Capacities

Electrical boxes are used for a variety of purposes, such as holding receptacles and switches, housing wire junctions, and supporting ceiling fans and lights. Many types of boxes are made for different purposes, and they can be metal or nonmetallic (plastic or fiberglass). Today, plastic boxes are the type most commonly used. However, metal boxes are still found in many homes. Check code requirements before installing electrical boxes. Plastic boxes have the advantages of low cost and simplicity of installation.

Electrical boxes come in standard shapes for each type of use. For example, they may be shallow for furred walls, wider for ganged arrangements, or waterproof for outdoor applications. Be sure to use the right box. No matter what the purpose, though, every box must be covered and accessible. It is also important not to use a box that is too small for the size and number of wires it will house. An electrical box can hold only a limited number of wires. Determining how many wires a box can safely hold can be complicated. Requirements change as the code changes.

Although plastic boxes are labeled according to the number of wires they can house, and/or their size in cubic inches, metal boxes are not. Cubic-inch capacities for a variety of metal boxes are listed in NEC Table 314.16(A). The safest way to overcome this problem is by purchasing the deepest box that will fit into your stud wall—one that is 3¼ to 3½ inches deep. For a single-gang box, this will provide 20.3 cubic inches of wiring space. Use common sense, and don't overcrowd any box. (See "Maximum Wires in a Box," page 14.)

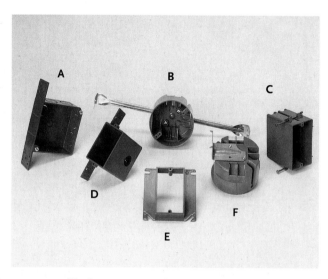

Nonmetallic boxes: A–MP bracket square box; B–adjustable ceiling box; C–receptacle and switch box; D–MP bracket switch box; E–raised device cover; F–JP bracket ceiling box

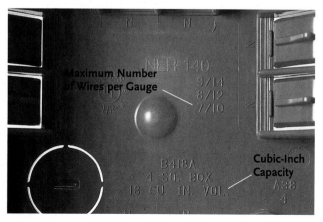

The inside of a nonmetallic electrical box, left, is labeled with the cubic-inch capacity of the box as well as the maximum permitted number of wires per gauge.

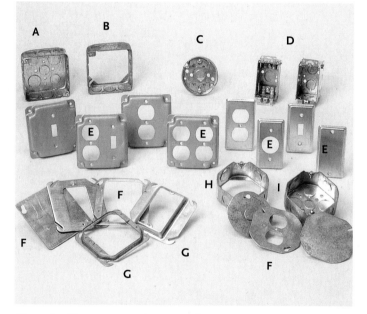

Electrical boxes come in many shapes and sizes for different purposes and are made of metal, plastic, or fiberglass. Though use of plastic boxes is widespread today, they don't meet code requirements for some jobs. Splice boxes are required for all wire junctions. **Metallic boxes:** A–square; B–box extension; C–ceiling pan box; D–receptacle and switch boxes; E–exposed box cover plates; F–concealed box flat plates; G–raised device covers; H–box extension; I–octagonal box

PLASTIC BOXES

THE MOST COMMON TYPE of plastic box is the single-gang, nail-on box. It has two integral nails that fasten it to stud framing. This type of box is commonly used in new construction and is available in several depths—the deepest having the greatest capacity.

Box Placement. When attaching nail-on boxes to studs, leave enough of the box edge protruding to bring the box flush with the finished wall. If you don't know the depth of the finished wall, use an adjustable box. Once installed, this box can be moved in and out on a slider to match the finished wall depth. The slider also allows you to change from a single box to a double without ripping apart the wall. You just unscrew and remove the single box, cut the opening to the new size, and insert the new box on the slider.

All plastic boxes must be installed carefully because they can be easily damaged. If a plastic box is hit with a hammer or if nails are driven in too far, the box will distort or break. Drive nails until they are snug, but no farther.

Ceiling Boxes. Ceiling pan boxes are typically used for ceiling fixtures. Named for its shape, a ceiling pan box may be designed to hold a fixture, such as a ceiling fan/light, weighing up to 35 pounds. If this is the case, it will be labeled. This type of box can be screwed or nailed directly into a ceiling joist. It is preferable, though, to screw the box into a wooden support such as a flat 2x6 spanning between two joists. A box having integral nails can break easily and will not support weight well. A fixture that weighs more than 50 pounds, such as a chandelier (35 for a paddle fan), cannot be suspended from a box. Instead, it must be supported independently from the box. Another way to mount an overhead fixture is by using an approved box with an adjustable bar hanger attached to it. Mounted between two overhead joists, this type of box can be positioned anywhere along the bar between the two joists.

Most plastic boxes, regardless of purpose, have internal clips that clamp onto the NM cable where it is inserted into the box. Open these clips using a flat-blade screwdriver before inserting the cable.

PLASTIC BOX TYPES

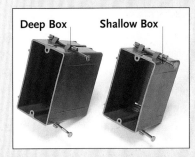

Deep Box   Shallow Box

Plastic nail-on boxes are available in many sizes, shallow or deep. Use the deepest box that can fit your space when installing receptacles, switches, and wires.

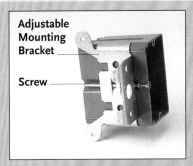

Adjustable Mounting Bracket

Screw

Adjustable boxes provide for variations in finished wall thicknesses, even after they are installed. Turning a screw on the face of the box adjusts it in or out.

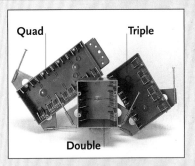

Quad   Triple

Double

Multiple-switch boxes—double, triple, and quad. A quad box should be attached to two framing studs, one on each side, to prevent wobbling.

ACCEPTABLE FOR FAN SUPPORT SCREWS PROVIDED MUST BE USED
2 PCS - #8 x 3 1/2" (P/N G429)
2 PCS - #8 x 1" (P/N G430)
PATENT NO. 5522577   LBL720

Fixture Supporting Label

Ceiling pan boxes for overhead fixtures bolt to framing. If a fixture weighs up to 50 lbs., the box must be marked "For Support"; if it weighs more, it must be supported independently.

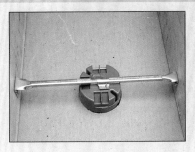

Some ceiling-fixture boxes are supported between joists with an adjustable bar hanger. You adjust the fixture location by sliding the box along the bar.

Materials and Equipment

METAL BOXES

THOUGH MORE EXPENSIVE and harder to work with than plastic boxes, metal boxes have some advantages. For one, they are available in more configurations than plastic boxes because they have been around longer. Basic boxes include the switch or receptacle box (rectangular) and the fixture or equipment outlet box (square or octagonal). One of the greatest advantages of metal boxes is that they are much stronger than plastic boxes. Because they can stand up to greater abuse, they are suitable for use in exposed locations such as unfinished basements and garages. To accommodate different finished wall thicknesses, some metal boxes have a built-in depth gauge.

Another important advantage is that some metal boxes have removable sides that allow additional boxes to be added, or ganged, to accommodate more than one device. A single-gang box, for instance, can be expanded to become a quad box.

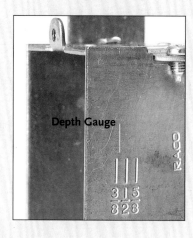

Depth Gauge

A depth gauge marked on an electrical box tells the installer where to align the box on a framing stud so that its face will be flush with the finished drywall.

ADDING SPACE TO A GANGABLE BOX

1 To add space to a gangable box, use a screwdriver to remove the retaining screw on the side of the existing box to be expanded, and take out the side panel.

2 Remove the opposite panel from a second, add-on box.

3 Remove the retaining screw from the open side of the second box, and align the screw slot over the retaining screw on the open side of the first box.

4 Tighten the retaining screw, creating one double-size box.

smart tip

BRINGING NM CABLE INTO A METAL BOX

To bring NM cable into a metal box, you must first remove one of the knockouts on the box. Some boxes have a pryout built into them that can easily be removed using a flat-blade screwdriver. Others have a circular knockout that must be punched out using a hammer and a screwdriver or knockout punch. Once the knockout hole is open, a cable clamp can be inserted into the opening. The clamp secures the cable in place and protects it from chafing against the sharp metal edges of the box opening.

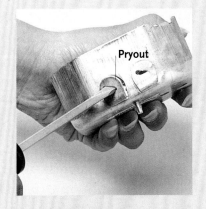

Some metal boxes have pryouts that can be removed using the flat blade of a screwdriver.

Pryout

A cable clamp screws into the pryout or knockout opening to secure the cable entering the box and protect it from chafing against the sharp edges of the opening.

Cable Clamp

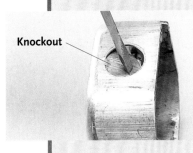

Knockout

Other boxes have knockouts that must be punched out with a hammer and screwdriver or with a special tool called a knockout punch.

WEATHERPROOF BOXES

BOXES MOUNTED OUTDOORS must be watertight. One way to achieve this is by recessing a standard box with a watertight lid in an outside house wall. Another is to mount a watertight box with a watertight lid on the surface of the exterior wall.

The problem with either method is that once the lid is opened, the box is no longer watertight; the interior is exposed. The NEC requires that when unattended equipment is left plugged into an exterior outlet, a special box or lid must be used that will keep the outlet weatherproof even while the plug is in place [Section 406.8(B)].

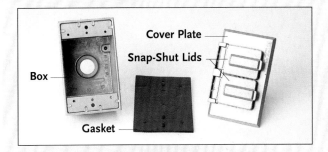

Cover Plate

Snap-Shut Lids

Box

Gasket

A watertight outdoor-receptacle box has a foam sealing gasket and a cover with snap-shut receptacle lids.

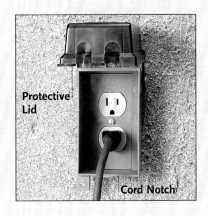

Protective Lid

Cord Notch

A weatherproof box must remain watertight even while the receptacle is in use. This type of box must have a lid that closes over the plug-in cord.

Materials and Equipment

SPECIAL BOXES

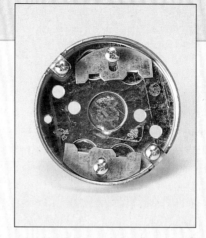

SPECIAL TYPES of electrical boxes include pancake and cut-in boxes. Pancake boxes are commonly used to mount outside entrance lights. Because of their low silhouette, they can be attached to the surface of an exterior wall yet remain hidden beneath the dome of the exterior light.

Retrofit cut-in boxes are available in metallic and non-metallic forms. Both types have flat lips, or drywall ears, on the front and some type of adjustable wing on the back. The wings expand outwardly, grabbing the back of the finished wall surface, while the metal ears on the front keep the box from falling into the opening. Metal cut-in boxes are not as popular as fiberglass or plastic because they are more expensive, must be grounded, and often have limited room for wires.

Old-work, or cut-in, boxes are for retrofits and are designed for installation in existing walls. Once inserted into a wall opening, screws are adjusted to expand side wings that grasp the back of finished drywall or plaster. Ceiling cut-in boxes should not be used to support heavy fixtures.

Pancake boxes are aptly named because of their flat, round shape. They contain minimal cubic volume and are designed to fit under the dome of an exterior light.

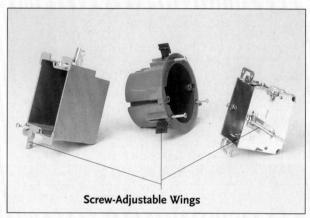

Screw-Adjustable Wings

INSTALLING A CUT-IN BOX

TO INSTALL A RECEPTACLE, switch, or ceiling cut-in box, first trace a template of the box on the surface of the wall or ceiling. Using a keyhole or saber saw, cut the opening for the box. Insert the box in the opening; then adjust and tighten the wings against the back of the drywall.

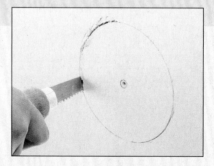

1 Trace a template of the box on the wall or ceiling surface, and cut the opening for the box.

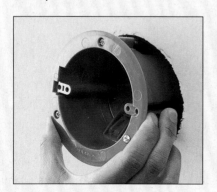

2 Insert the box in the opening, and adjust the side wings.

3 Tighten the adjusting screws to bring the wings firmly against the back of the finished wall (view from inside the wall).

BOX EXTENSIONS AND MOUNTING BRACKETS

Box Extensions

Box extensions, or extension rings, are used to add wiring capacity to a box. If a finished ceiling or wall surface lies beyond a box front or more space is needed for wiring within the box, simply add an extension ring. Use a watertight box extension for outdoor work.

Mounting Brackets

Brackets exist for mounting every type of metallic and nonmetallic box under a wide variety of installation conditions. Though some brackets are used for only one purpose, others may be used for several types of boxes. Each bracket type attaches a box differently. An A bracket, for example, attaches to the face and side of a stud, while a B bracket only attaches to the face and a D bracket only to the side of a stud. Metal framing-stud mounting brackets are also available. Other brackets are used for gangable boxes and boxes that must be backset or offset from stud work. Mounting brackets for

plastic boxes are available in fewer styles. Because of they are less durable, nonmetallic boxes are more likely to have nailing spurs than actual brackets. Discuss your wiring plans with your electrical supply retailer to be sure you are getting the right type brackets.

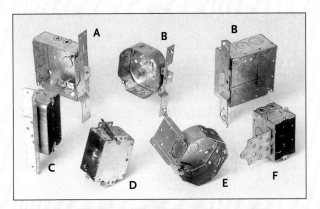

Metal mounting brackets: A–FM bracket; B–FA brackets; C–A bracket; D–S bracket; E–J bracket; F–long B bracket

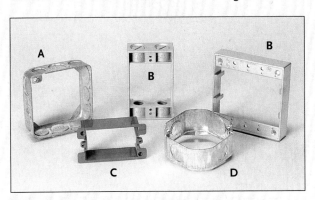

Box Extensions: A–square-box extension; B–watertight-box extensions; C–rectangular-box extension; D–octagonal box extension

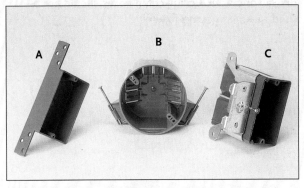

Plastic mounting brackets: A–MP bracket; B–WP bracket; C–adjustable bracket

RECEPTACLES

Duplex Receptacles

Different types of receptacles are manufactured for a variety of residential purposes. Standard duplex receptacles are the most common type available and are used to power fixtures, appliances, and residential equipment rated for 110 to 125 volts. This type of duplex receptacle has a long neutral slot, a short hot slot, and an arch-shaped ground-

ing hole. This configuration guarantees that a plug can only be inserted into the receptacle one way—so it will be properly polarized and grounded.

Tamper-Resistant Receptacles. For new construction, the NEC requires that all 125-volt, 15- and 20-amp receptacles installed in living areas must be listed as tamper resistant. These receptacles are designed so that a child cannot insert an object into one of the contact slots. Manufacturers use different methods to achieve this.

Materials and Equipment

RECEPTACLE TYPES

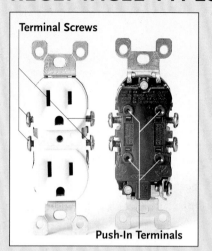

Terminal Screws

Push-In Terminals

Standard duplex receptacles have terminal screws for connecting wires. Some also have push-in terminals where 14-gauge wires can be inserted, but these connect less securely and are not recommended.

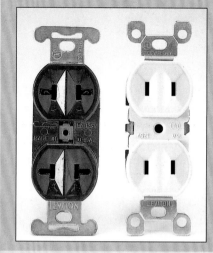

Older receptacles have only two slots. If both are the same size, as in these outlets, the receptacle is neither grounded nor polarized. If one slot is longer than the other, the receptacle is polarized but not grounded.

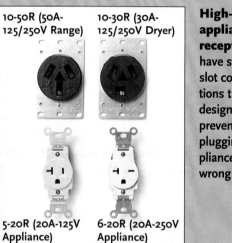

10-50R (50A-125/250V Range)   10-30R (30A-125/250V Dryer)

5-20R (20A-125V Appliance)   6-20R (20A-250V Appliance)

High-voltage appliance receptacles have specific slot configurations that are designed to prevent you from plugging an appliance into the wrong circuit.

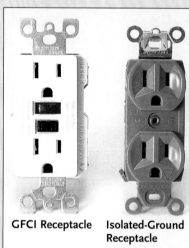

GFCI Receptacle   Isolated-Ground Receptacle

A **GFCI receptacle** protects the user against electric shock, while an isolated-ground receptacle protects sensitive equipment from power surges.

Appliance Receptacles

Other types of receptacles have slot configurations that limit their use to specific appliances or groups of appliances. For example, the hot slot on a large 20-amp appliance or tool receptacle is T-shaped, while the hot and neutral slots on an air-conditioner receptacle are horizontal instead of vertical. Appliances that draw high currents, like clothes dryers and ranges, use a single dedicated receptacle. Each type has a slot configuration designated only for the particular appliance being powered. The amperage and voltage are clearly marked on the receptacle, along with the number assigned by the National Electrical Manufacturers Association (NEMA) and the listing mark of the Underwriters Laboratories (UL). The NEMA code ensures that you are buying the correct receptacle for the appliance, and the UL-listing label indicates that the receptacle has passed rigorous testing standards.

Isolated-Ground and GFCI Receptacles

An isolated-ground receptacle is a specialized, orange-colored device. It has an insulated grounding screw and is primarily used to protect sensitive electronic equipment, such as computers, from disruptive or damaging electrical power surges. A GFCI (ground-fault circuit-interrupter) receptacle is a special duplex receptacle that protects you from a fatal electrical shock. When incoming and returning current are unequal, the GFCI cuts off the circuit in a fraction of a second, before you can feel a shock. This type of receptacle is required by code in wet locations, such as bathrooms, kitchens, basements, garages, and outdoors.

SWITCHES

Types and Designations

A switch controls the flow of power in an electrical circuit. When a switch is on, electricity flows through the circuit from its source to the point of use. The standard switch used in residential work is the toggle switch, sometimes called a snap switch. Other types include dimmer, pilot-light, timer, and electronic switches. Switches are further categorized by quality and usage. The standard, or construction grade, switch is rated for 15 amps and is the grade and type most commonly found in homes.

Toggle Switches

Toggle switches have evolved over time. Now you can perform many functions throughout a home with them. A standard, single-pole toggle switch turns a light on from only one location. But switches may also control a circuit from two (three-way switch) or three (four-way switch) locations. A single-pole switch has two terminal screws. Only this one switch can control the circuit. The hot wire connects to one terminal, and the outgoing wire to the other. A three-way switch has three terminals. One is marked com or "common"; the hot wire connects to this terminal. The other terminals are switch leads. A four-way switch has

Switches: A–toggle; B–large-button toggle; C–pilot light; D–clock timer; E–time delay; F–automatic; G–programmable; H–motion sensor

four terminals. A similar-looking switch, the double-pole switch, is used to control 240-volt appliances and is differentiated from the four-way switch by the on and off markings on the toggle.

Dimmer Switches

A dimmer switch is used to control the brightness, or intensity, of light emitted from a light fixture by increasing or decreasing the flow of electricity to the fixture. Dimmers may have standard toggle switches, rotary dials, sliders, or automatic electronic sensors that respond to the level of ambient light in a room and adjust accordingly. They can be single-pole or three-way switches.

smart tip

READING A SWITCH

Switches must be marked with labels that represent different ratings and approvals. These labels convey important information about safety and usage. The designation UND. LAB. INC. LIST, for example, means that the switch has been listed by the Underwriters Laboratories, an independent testing agency. AC ONLY indicates that the switch can only handle alternating current. CO/ALR specifies that the switch can be connected to either copper or aluminum wires. A switch marked CU can be used only with copper and not with aluminum wires. The amp and voltage ratings are given by designations like 15A–120V, which means that the switch is approved for use with circuits that carry 15 amps of current at 120 volts.

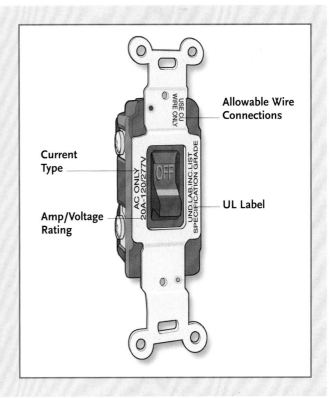

Materials and Equipment

SWITCH TYPES

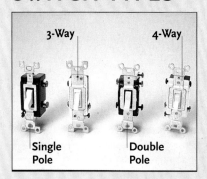

A single-pole toggle switch operates a light from one location. Other types include double-pole and three- and four-way switches.

Standard toggle switches can be side-wired at screw terminals or back-wired at push-in terminals. Older switches may be front- or end-wired.

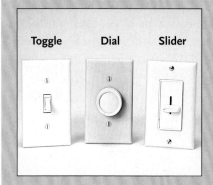

A dimmer switch controls the brightness of light emitted from a bulb. Dimmer switches may have toggle, dial, slide, or automatic controls.

A green or red light will glow on a pilot-light switch to indicate that an appliance or other type of circuit is turned on or active.

A clock-timer turns a circuit on or off at a set time of day, while a time-delay switch operates a circuit for a set length of time.

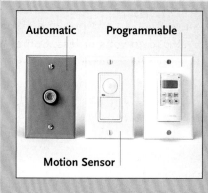

Automatic, motion-sensor, and programmable switches are types of electronic switches. Movement detected by an infrared eye will trigger a motion sensor.

Pilot-Light Switches

Pilot-light switches are usually found on appliances but are especially useful for controlling remote fixtures, like porch, attic, basement, and garage lights, because they can let you know whether or not a light is on or off. When a fixture or appliance is turned on, the pilot light is illuminated.

Timer Switches

Timer switches come in two varieties: clock and time delay. A clock-timer can be set to turn on a fixture or other device at a preset time of day. An example would be a thermostat set to turn down the heat during the day when no one is home. Another example would be a switch that turns on security lights in your home after dark or when you are

away on vacation. This type of switch can also be used to operate a lawn-sprinkler system. In contrast, a time-delay switch is designed to allow a fixture or appliance to operate for a set period of time and then shut off. An example would be a heat lamp or exhaust fan in a bathroom.

Electronic Switches

Electronic switches offer automatic control of lights and other devices. As a matter of safety, they can be overridden by using manual switch levers. An automatic switch allows a user to simply wave a hand in front of the switch to turn it on or off. An infrared beam emitted from the switch detects the movement of the user's hand and activates an electronic signal to operate the switch. A motion-sensor switch operates the same way but is designed for security lighting. When someone or something passes in front of the infrared eye, the light is activated. When the motion ceases, the light will turn itself off after a set period of time has elapsed. Outdoor perimeter or garage lighting is commonly on this type of switch. A programmable switch is a digitally controlled version of the clock-timer. It can be programmed to turn lights and other devices on and off several times a day at specified or random times. For security, this type of switch is especially advantageous when you are away from home.

LOW-VOLTAGE TRANSFORMERS

Types and Applications

Many types of household fixtures and equipment require much less power to operate than is provided by standard 120-volt house current: door chimes, low-voltage outdoor and pool lights, telephones, antennas, and thermostats are just a few examples. (See Chapter 4, "Specialty Wiring," pages 156–175.) A low-voltage transformer steps down 120-volt house current to 30 volts or less. Some fixtures may come with a built-in transformer that serves only that device. A remote transformer is externally connected and can control several devices. A special weatherproof transformer is used to power low-voltage lighting outdoors. The most common type of transformer used in residential work, however, is a simple box-mounted transformer that attaches to a junction box. Both the supply and device wires are connected to the transformer wires inside the junction box. The current is stepped down by the transformer before proceeding to the equipment.

Low-voltage transformers may be installed separately or come as an integral part of a fixture. A–remote transformer; B–lighting transformer; C–device transformer

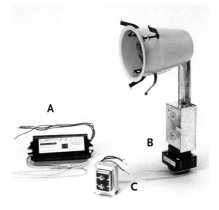

RACEWAYS

Raceway Application

To an electrician, raceway and conduit are interchangeable terms, but for our purposes a raceway houses surface wiring. This eliminates fishing cable through existing walls, allowing wire to be run along masonry surfaces. Raceways protect cable in enclosed plastic or metal casings. Raceway wiring includes receptacles, switches, and ceiling fixtures. Special connectors turn corners, providing intersections to extend branches. Raceways are grounded by an equipment-grounding conductor, a metal casing, or both. The NEC limits raceway use to dry locations not exposed to physical damage. Raceways are permitted to contain a certain number and size of wires for each intended use.

Raceway Components

Raceway components are available in metal or plastic and must be joined mechanically and electrically to protect wires. Raceway fasteners must be flush with the channel surface so that they don't cut the wires. Raceways must be flame-retardant; resistant to moisture, impact, and crushing; and installed in a dry location.

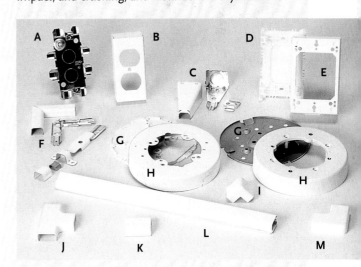

Typical raceway components: A–backing plate; B–receptacle coverplate; C–reducing converter and cover; D–tongued mounting plate; E–extension box; F–elbow connector and cover; G–fixture mounting plates; H–fixture extension boxes; I–90-deg. connector; J–T-connector cover; K–straight connector cover; L–channel; M–L-connector cover

Materials and Equipment

CONDUIT

Conduit Components

Common types of conduit are shown opposite and on page 280. Each conduit type uses specific connectors and fittings. Rigid metallic conduit is threaded on both ends, with a preattached coupling on one end. The metal is usually galvanized and may be finished in enamel or plastic for use in corrosive environments. Rigid metallic conduit must be supported every 10 feet and within 3 feet of any connected junction box. Other fittings include compression connectors, elbows, couplings, and locknuts. Although its walls are thinner, IMC is similar to rigid metal conduit and uses the same connectors and fittings. EMT is thinner than rigid metallic conduit and IMC. Unlike rigid metal, it is not threaded and can only be used with its own connectors and fittings. Both IMC and EMT follow the same code requirements as rigid metallic conduit. Helically wound flexible metallic conduit is used for areas with tighter turns and where equipment vibrations occur. Liquid-tight flexible metallic conduit is used in locations subject to liquids and vapors, including burial underground. Flexible metallic conduit must be supported every 4½ feet and within 1 foot of electrical boxes. Because it has higher resistance than rigid metal, it is independently grounded with an internal wire.

Rigid nonmetallic conduit is used for underground wiring because it is lightweight and resistant to corrosion and moisture. ENT is permitted in wet indoor areas, in concrete slabs, or in any building, but must be concealed behind fire-rated drywall. Both types are toxic when burned, so check local codes before using. Connectors and fittings for nonmetallic conduit are attached using approved cement. Bend the conduit by heating it with hot air or an infrared heater. Support nonmetallic conduit every 3 to 8 feet, depending on size, and within 3 feet of a junction box.

RACEWAY WIRING

Raceway receptacles are conventionally wired. An existing box is extended with a plate and extension frame to accommodate the raceway channel. Raceway wiring adds receptacles, switches, and fixtures without opening walls or ceilings.

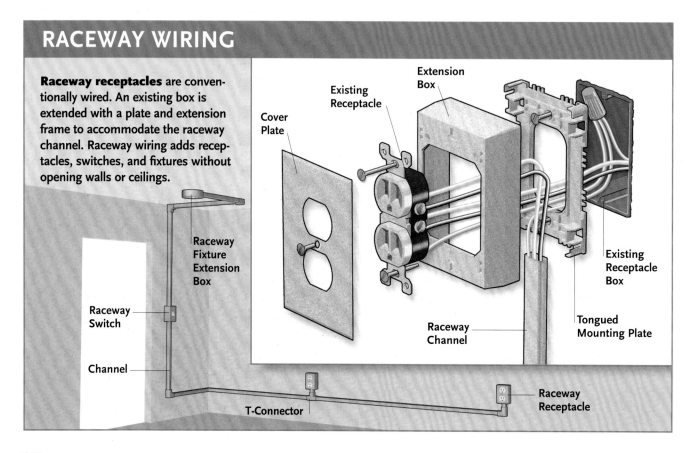

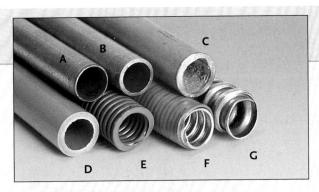

Metallic and nonmetallic conduit types:
A–electrical metallic tubing (EMT); B–intermediate metallic conduit (IMC); C–rigid metallic conduit; D–rigid nonmetallic conduit; E–electrical nonmetallic tubing (ENT); F–liquid-tight flexible metallic conduit; G–flexible metallic conduit

Rigid metallic and intermediate metallic conduit (IMC) connectors and fittings: A–setscrew couplings; B–long compression 90-deg. elbow; C–short 90-deg. coupling; D–threaded connectors; E–3-piece coupling; F–insulated bushing with ground lug; G–locknut; H–bonding locknut; I–sealing locknut

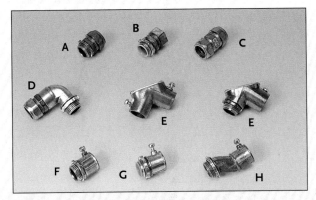

Electrical metallic tubing (emt) connectors and fittings: A–compression connector; B–insulated throat compression connector; C–compression coupling; D–90-deg. short-angle connector; E–90-deg. setscrew ell couplings; F–insulated throat setscrew connector; G–setscrew connector; H–offset setscrew connector

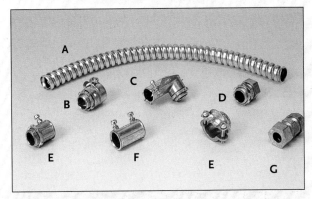

Flexible metallic conduit connectors and fittings: A–flexible metallic conduit; B–squeeze connector; C–90-deg. squeeze connector; D–compression connector; E–setscrew connectors; F–setscrew coupling; G–compression coupling

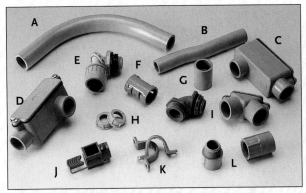

Rigid nonmetallic conduit and electrical non metallic tubing (ENT) connectors and fittings: A–sweep bend; B–offset connector; C–LB fitting; D–LBL fitting; E–multiposition fitting; F–ENT coupling; G–coupling; H–bushings; I–90-deg. connectors; J–NM cable connection; K–conduit clamps; L–threaded couplings

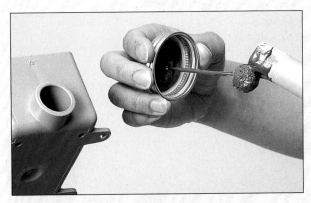

Nonmetallic conduit connectors and fittings are welded in place using a particular type of solvent called conduit cement.

Resource Guide

This list of manufacturers and associations is meant to be a general guide to additional industry and product-related sources. It is not intended as a listing of products and manufacturers represented by the photographs in this book.

Alpha Wire
Phone: 800-522-5742
www.alphawire.com
Manufactures electrical products, including wire, cable, tubing, and connectors used for electrical work.

Amana
Phone: 866-616-2664
www.amana.com
Manufactures refrigerators, dishwashers, and cooking appliances.

American Grounding Systems, Inc.
Phone: 541-336-2426
www.americangroundingsystems.com
Manufactures grounding straps and wires. The Website offers an online catalog.

Artemide
Phone: 631-694-9292
www.artemide.com
Manufactures lighting fixtures.

Baldinger Architectural Lighting
Phone: 718-204-5700
www.baldinger.com
Produces decorative, custom-made lighting fixtures.

Bosch Home Appliances
Phone: 1-800-944-2904
www.bosch-home.com
Manufactures major and small appliances.

Emerson Electric Co.
EasyHeat
Phone: 314-553-2000
www.appleton.emerson.com/en-us/easy-heat
Manufactures floor warming systems.

Energy Star
US EPA
Phone: 888-782-7937
www.energystar.gov
A joint program of the U.S. Environmental Protection Agency and the U.S. Department of Energy, Energy Star helps us all save money and protect the environment through energy-efficient products and practices.

FC Lighting, Inc.
Phone: 800-900-1730
www.fclighting.com
Sells commercial and architectural lighting fixtures in custom colors, shapes, and sizes.

Fisher and Paykel Appliances, Inc.
Phone: 888-936-7872
www.fisherpaykel.com
Manufactures kitchen appliances.

General Electric
Phone: 203-373-2211
www.ge.com
Manufactures appliances and electronics.

Ginger
Phone: 949-417-5207
www.gingerco.com
Manufactures lighting and bathroom accessories.

Haier America
Phone: 877-337-3639
www.haieramerica.com
Manufactures electronics and appliances, including wine cellars.

Home Ventilating Institute
Phone: 855-484-8368
www.hvi.org
A nonprofit association that provides services to manufacturers of home ventilating products and information to consumers.

Intermatic, Inc.
Phone: 815-675-7000
www.intermatic.com
Manufactures a wide variety of outdoor lighting products, such as low-voltage and solar lighting systems, and lighting controls.

In the Swim
Phone: 800-288-7946
www.intheswim.com
Sells aboveground pool filters, pumps, and cleaning supplies.

Jacuzzi Inc.
Phone: 844-602-6064
www.jacuzzi.com
Manufactures spas and shower systems.

Jenn-Air, a division of Maytag
Phone: 800-536-6247
www.jennair.com
Manufactures kitchen appliances.

Kichler Lighting Co.
Phone: 866-558-5706
www.kichler.com
Manufactures residential lighting fixtures for both outdoor and indoor systems and offers a wide variety of fixture styles and finishes.

Leviton
Phone: 800-824-3005
www.leviton.com
Manufactures lighting products such as controls, switches, wallplates, and structured cabling systems.

LG
Phone: 800-243-0000
www.lg.com
Manufactures major appliances.

LightBulbs.com
Phone: 800-948-1063
www.lightbulbs.com
The internet's largest and most complete light bulb store, with more than 10,000 light bulbs and accessories available to order online.

Lightology
Phone: 866-954-4489
www.lightology.com
Manufactures lighting fixtures.

Maytag Corp.
Phone: 1-800-344-1274
www.maytag.com
Manufactures major appliances.

Master Spas
Phone: 800-860-7727
www.masterspas.com
Manufactures polymer spas for both indoor and outdoor use.

National Electrical Manufacturers Association
Phone: 703-841-3200
www.nema.org
Develops technical standards for electrical equipment, helping consumers select safe, reliable products.

National Fire Protection Association
Phone: 800-344-3555
www.nfpa.org
A nonprofit organization that provides life, electrical, and fire safety information to the public. They are responsible for the National Electrical Code, as well as other important codes that ensure safety.

Nuheat
Phone: 800-778-9276
www.nuheat.com
Manufactures radiant floor heating.

NuTone, Inc.
Phone: 888-336-3948
www.nutone.com
Manufactures ventilation fans, medicine cabinets, and lighting fixtures.

Osram Sylvania
Phone: 978-570-3000
www.osram.com
Sells a wide variety of commercial and residential lighting products. The website offers consumers product information, as well as information on lighting materials, components, and electronics.

Pool & Hot Tub Alliance
Phone: 703-838-0083
www.phta.org
An international trade association promoting the safety and proper maintenance of pools and spas. NSPI also provides free information on building and maintaining pools and spas.

Remcraft Lighting Products
Phone: 305-687-9031
www.remcraft.com
Manufactures lighting fixtures.

Restoration Hardware
Phone: 800-762-1005
www.rh.com
Manufactures indoor and outdoor furniture, windows, and lighting accessories.

Schonbek Worldwide Lighting Inc.
Phone: 800-836-1892
www.schonbek.com
Manufactures crystal lighting fixtures.

Seagull Lighting Products, Inc.
Phone: 800-985-9475
www.seagulllighting.com
Manufactures lighting fixtures.

Sharkline
Phone: 631-951-9800
www.sharkline.com
Manufactures pools, decking systems, liners, and accessories. The website offers consumer information on safety and technical issues.

Sharp
Phone: 800-237-4277
www.sharpusa.com
Manufactures consumer electronics.

Square D/Schneider Electric
Phone: 877-342-5173
www.squared.com
Sells and distributes electrical control products, such as circuit protectors, for residential and commercial use.

Sub-Zero Freezer Co.
Phone: 800-222-7820
www.subzero.com
Manufactures professional-style refrigeration appliances.

Super-Temp Wire and Cable, Inc.
Phone: 802-655-4211
www.super-temp.com
A cable manufacturer that specializes in multiconductor and RF cables, and Teflon insulated single conductors.

Thermospas
Phone: 800-603-3556
www.thermospas.com
Designs, manufactures, and installs spas, hot tubs, and accessories for residential use.

Viking Range Corp.
Phone: 662-445-1200
www.vikingrange.com
Manufactures professional-style kitchen appliances.

Warmly Yours
Phone: 800-875-5285
www.warmlyyours.com
Manufactures radiant floor heating systems.

Waytek Inc.
Phone: 800-328-2724
www.waytekwire.com
Sells electrical wiring supplies, including wire, terminals, connectors, accessories, circuit protection, cable ties, and heat-shrink products.

Whirlpool Corp.
Phone: 866-698-2538
www.whirlpool.com
Manufactures home appliances and related products, including a drying cabinet and an ironing center.

Wiring Products, Ltd.
Phone: 800-549-0243
www.wiringproducts.com
A one-stop online source for electrical supplies.

Wolf Appliance Company,
a div. of Sub-Zero Freezer Co.
Phone: 800-332-9513
www.wolfappliance.com
Manufactures professional-style cooking appliances.

Glossary

A/V Audio/video.

AWG American Wire Gauge; a system of sizing electrical wire.

Accent lighting Spot lighting that focuses on decorative or architectural features.

Alternating current (AC) An electrical current that regularly reverses its direction, usually at 60 cycles per second.

Ambient lighting Indirect, background lighting.

Ampere, amp A quantity of electric current flow due to one volt of electricity across one ohm of resistance.

Ampacity Current-carrying capacity of an electrical wire in amps.

Applications cable Electrical or fiber optic voice, video, and data communications cable.

Arc fault Intermittent flow of electricity aross a gap, such as an arc created by a loose connection.

Arc-fault circuit interrupter A type of circuit breaker that shuts down an electrical circuit when it detects an arc fault.

Armored cable Cable sheathed in flexible metal.

Backfeed Electricity fed back into a utility system while a standby generator is running. A double-pole, double-throw transfer switch is required to prevent this from happening, protecting the generator, wiring, and appliances from damage when service is restored.

Ballast Device that controls current in a fluorescent tube.

Bar hanger Bracket placed between joists or rafters to support a fixture box.

Bare wire Uninsulated grounding conductor in a cable.

Base pin Contact on the end of a fluorescent tube.

Bell wire Thin wire used for making doorbell connections.

Bipin Fluorescent tube having two base pins on each end.

Bonding Connecting metal parts to make an electrically conductive path.

Bonding jumper A connection that ensures continuous conductivity between metal parts required to be electrically connected.

Box extension Device attached to an electrical box to increase its capacity.

Branch circuit Wiring from a final fuse or circuit breaker to the outlets.

Breaker See *Circuit breaker.*

Brownout Partial loss of electric power.

Bus bar Common electric conductor for multiple circuits.

CFM Cubic feet per minute; usually a measure of air-volume movement.

CO/ALR Label designating approval for use with aluminum wire.

COM Common terminal.

CU/AL Label designating approval for use with copper, aluminum, or copper-clad aluminum wires.

Cable One or more wires enclosed in protective metal or plastic sheathing.

Cable sheathing Metal or plastic casing around wires in cable.

Category 5 (CAT 5) wire Four twisted pairs of high-quality copper wire enclosed in sheathing; used for phone, fax, modem, and high-speed digital computer transmissions. Has high immunity to interference.

Choke ballast A small coil of wire that limits the amount of current flow in a fluorescent fixture.

Circuit breaker Protective device that opens a circuit if an overcurrent occurs.

Circuit capacity Maximum current a circuit can safely carry.

Coaxial cable A primary conductor wire enclosed in concentric plastic foam insulation. It is covered by braided wire that acts as a secondary conductor and a shield against interference.

Common Applications Language (CAL) Language that allows diverse household systems to be integrated under one system of control.

Communicating thermostat An interactive thermostat that can be remotely controlled.

Communications cable Voice, video, and data communications.

Community antenna television (CATV) Source for cable television signals transmitted to multiple receivers.

Conductor A wire or material that offers minimal resistance to the flow of electricity.

Conductor cable Nonmetallic sheathing encasing two or more conductors.

Conduit Metal or plastic protective tubing that encloses electrical wires.

Conduit nipple Short section of conduit used to connect an interior junction box to an outdoor receptacle box, or an LB connector.

Connecting block Central-distribution junction hardware for telephone circuit.

Consumer Electronic Bus (CEBus) Design protocol established by the Electronics Industry Association.

Continuity tester Device used when power is turned off, to detect an electrical path between two points.

Continuous load A load where the maximum current continues for 3 hours or more.

Controller A device that, in a predetermined way, controls the electric power delivered to another device to which it is directly or remotely connected.

Cord Flexible wiring used for household plug-in appliances; not intended to be used as permanent circuit wiring.

Crimping ferrule Compression sleeve used to connect bare grounding wires.

Current Flow of electrons through a conductor.

Cut-in box Electrical box designed to install easily in existing construction.

Design protocol Control standard for home automation devices.

Detector Device that senses changes in ambient conditions due to temperature, motion, smoke, gas, flames, etc.

Digital satellite system (DSS) System that distributes video signals via satellite to an antenna dish receiver.

Digital versatile disc (DVD) Formerly digital videodisc; digital movie disc format having multiple layers.

Dimmer switch Variable intensity light switch.

Direct current (DC) An electrical current that flows in one direction only.

Double-pole switch A switch having two blades and contacts to alternately open or close power to a load from two sources.

Dry niche Pool light housing that is sealed against the entrance of water.

Duplex receptacle Two 120-volt receptacles that are internally connected and housed in one receptacle box.

Electrical box Metallic or nonmetallic enclosure used for housing wire splices.

Electrical metallic tubing (EMT) Thin-walled steel tubing (conduit); not threaded.

Electrical nonmetallic tubing Polyvinyl chloride (PVC) conduit that must be concealed behind finished surfaces.

End-of-run Receptacle or switch box at the end position in a circuit.

Energy efficiency rating (EER) Measure of relative energy consumption.

Equipment grounding conductor Conductor that connects noncurrent-carrying metal parts of equipment to a grounding conductor and/or grounding electrode conductor.

Escutcheon plate Protective plastic or metal plate.

Expansion loop Slack left in any cable to allow for expansion and contraction.

Extension ring Device added to an existing electrical box to increase its wire capacity. See *Box extension*.

Federal Communications Commission Regulatory agency for broadcast communications in the United States.

Feeder cable Circuit conductors between the service equipment and the final branch-circuit overcurrent device.

Feedhorn Device at the focal point of a satellite dish that receives signals reflected from the dish.

Fish tape Flexible metal or nonmetal strip used to pull cables through walls and conduit.

Fixed-temperature detector A heat detector that uses the low melting point of solder or metals that expand when exposed to heat to detect fire.

Flame detector Infrared (IR) or ultraviolet (UV) detector that senses and responses to the IR or UV emitted by flames.

Fluorescent tube A glass tube having an internal phosphor coating that, when exposed to an electric discharge, transforms ultraviolet light into visible light.

Four-way switch Switch used with two three-way switches that allows a circuit to be turned on or off from three places.

Fuse Safety device that melts to break a circuit, protecting the conductors from burning.

GFCI (ground-fault circuit interrupter) A safety device that breaks a circuit when it senses a difference in flow between line and ground current.

GFCI circuit breaker A combination circuit breaker and GFCI installed in the service panel in place of a regular circuit breaker. It monitors current flow in both hot and neutral wires. When the breaker detects unequal current in the wires it immediately shuts off power and protects the entire circuit.

Ganging Joining two or more device boxes together.

Generator A device that converts mechanical energy to electrical energy.

Glow switch See *Starter switch*.

Ground Connection between an electrical circuit or electrical equipment and the earth.

Grounding rod See *Grounding electrode conductor*.

Grounding conductor Wire that grounds a circuit or equipment but doesn't normally carry current.

Ground terminal See *Grounding rod*.

Grounding bus bar An electrical bus to which equipment grounds are connected and which is itself grounded.

Grounding electrode conductor Grounding wire that connects the ground electrodes to the grounded wire from the public utility (white neutral wire).

Grounded neutral The grounded wire that completes a circuit and returns current to the power source.

Grounding rod A metal conductor entrenched in earth that maintains ground potential on other conductors connected to it.

Grounding screw Terminal screw to which a bare or green grounding wire is connected.

HSTV Home satellite television.

Hanger bracket Adjustable bracket from which a ceiling box/fixture is suspended between ceiling joists.

Hardwired Directly connected by electrical wires or cables.

Hertz A unit of frequency measuring one cycle per second.

Glossary

Hickey   Threaded fitting used to connect a light fixture to a ceiling box.

Home automation   System for remotely controlling the operation of electrical devices in a home.

Home networking   Complete home connectivity. Sharing of internet access, printers, and files by all computers in a home.

Hot bus   Metal bar in an electrical panel that serves as the common connection between the circuit breakers and the hot line conductors.

Hot conductor   Ungrounded live wire carrying electrical current.

House code   One of 16 address groups used in X-10 automation control.

IR   Infrared.

Impedance   Opposition to current flow in an alternating current circuit.

Infrared detector   Device that senses and responds to flickering infrared radiant energy, such as that emitted by flames.

Infrared transmission   Signal transmission along a beam of infrared (IR) light.

Instant-start starter   Applies high voltage to initiate a flow of electrons through a fluorescent lamp without preheating the electrodes.

Insulation-contact   Recessed light fixture housing approved for direct contact with insulation; also insulated ceiling.

Insulation displacement connector (IDC)   Telephone circuit junction wiring block having a gas-tight seal that prevents bimetal corrosion.

Insulator   A nonconductor of electricity.

Integral transformer   Low-voltage transformer built into a device such as a light fixture.

Interactive television (ITV)   Television that permits user interaction, such as in game playing and voting, and can give immediate feedback.

Intermediate metallic conduit (IMC)   Threaded rigid metal conduit, but with thinner walls.

Ionization detector   A sensor that ionizes the air between electrodes, causing a current to flow. Smoke particles interfering with this flow set off an alarm.

Isolated-ground receptacle   A bright orange receptacle that is wired to a separate grounding system and protects computer equipment from power surges.

Jumper wire   Short length of single conductor wire used to complete a circuit connection.

Junction   Where wire splices, cable or raceway joints occur.

Junction box   Box in which all standard wiring splices and connections must be made.

Kilowatt   1,000 watts.

Kilowatt-hour (kWh)   Amount of energy expended in one hour by one kilowatt (1,000 watts) of electricity.

LB connector or fitting   A 90-degree connector used to bring cable through an exterior wall.

Lamp   A device that generates light.

Laser disc (LD)   High-resolution disc on which programs can be recorded for playback on a television set.

Lightning rod   A grounded metal rod placed on a structure to prevent damage by conducting lightning to the ground.

Line cord   Flat, four-conductor cord used to connect a telephone or other accessory to a phone jack.

Load   A device or equipment to which power is delivered.

Local-area network (LAN)   A system that links electronic equipment, such as computers and fax machines, to form a shared network within a limited area.

LonWorks   A networking technology for automation controls.

Low-voltage   Voltage stepped down from 120 volts to 30 volts or less.

Low-voltage transformer   An electrical device with two or more coupled windings that step standard 120-volt power down to 30 volts or less.

Lumen   Flow rate of light per unit of time, defining quantity of visible light.

Luminaire   Lighting fixture.

Luminosity   Relative brightness.

Macro   A single customized programming instruction that results in a series of actions or responses.

Magnetic flux   The total number of magnetic lines of force passing through a bounded area in a magnetic field.

Main breaker   Circuit breaker through which utility power enters the main panel and connects to the hot bus.

Metal-clad (MC) cable   Copper-type THHN/THWN cable with two or more conductors and an insulated ground. The conductors are wrapped in binder tape and the assembly is then clad in aluminum or steel armor.

Meter   Device designed to measure the flow of an electric current.

Middle-of-run   Receptacle or switch box lying between the power source and another box.

Motion/sensor detector   Passive infrared (PIR) detector that senses movement across a detection field.

Nailing spur   Nailing bracket attached to an electrical box.

National Electrical Code (NEC)   Regulations governing the minimum safe installation of electrical systems and components.

Network Connection between computers, peripheral equipment, and communications devices that permits the sharing of files, programs, and equipment.

Network interface device Telephone utility device that connects house wiring to a telephone network.

Neutral bus bar Bus bar connecting the utility neutral wire to the house neutral.

Neutral conductor Gray or white grounded conductor used to complete a circuit and return current to its source.

Noninsulation-contact fixture Recessed light fixture housing not approved for direct contact with insulation; requires minimum of 3 inches clearance; also noninsulated ceiling.

Nonmetallic cable Two or more electrical wires enclosed in moisture-resistant, fire-retardant, nonmetallic (plastic) sheathing.

Non-polarized Having two positions or poles that are not exclusively positive or negative.

Ohm Unit of electrical resistance in a conductor.

Ohm's Law Current in a circuit is directly proportional to voltage and inversely proportional to resistance.

Occupancy detector A device that reacts to variables such as heat and motion to detect the presence of people.

Overcurrent Current that exceeds the rated current of equipment or the ampacity of a conductor.

Overload An excessive demand for power made upon an electrical circuit.

PIR detector See *Passive infrared detector.*

Pancake box Low-profile round electrical box that can be concealed behind or within a light fixture.

Parabolic aluminized reflector (PAR) lamp Bulb having an internal reflector of aluminum.

Passive infrared (PIR) detector Device that emits no signals but senses the body heat of anyone moving nearby.

Photocell A device having an electrical output that varies in response to invisible light; an electric eye.

Photoelectric detector Sensor that responds to changes in light levels caused, for example, by smoke particles.

Pigtail Flexible conductor that connects an electrical device or component to an electrical circuit.

Plug A fitting, with metal prongs for insertion into a fixed socket, used to connect an appliance, lamp, or motor to a power supply.

Plug configuration Number and pattern of prongs on a plug.

Point of demarcation Interface between telephone utility wiring and telephone wiring in a home.

Point-of-use protection Surge-suppression device used to filter line noise at the point where an appliance is plugged into it.

Polarized Having two contrasting positions, such as a positive and a negative pole.

Polyvinyl chloride (PVC) A thermoplastic resin used to manufacture nonmetallic conduit, boxes, and other electrical components.

Power horn Security alarm; siren.

Power line carrier control (PLC) Home-automation control system that uses the existing AC wiring in a home to transmit signals to receivers used to remotely switch lights and appliances.

Preheat starter Device that preheats the electrodes of a fluorescent lamp to arc start.

Primary winding The transformer coils wound on the input side of the transformer.

Programmable switch A switch that can turn lights on or off according to a preset schedule.

Pulse Brief, sudden change in a normally constant current.

Punch-down tool Special tool used for punching down IDC blocks.

Quad-shielded cable Coaxial cable having two layers of foil shielding, each covered by a layer of braided shielding.

RG-6 quad-shielded cable Coaxial cable with insulated center wire and four layers of shielding; supports hundreds of channels and digital data. Used for cable TV, digital satellite systems, cable modems, and high-speed interactive video servers. Highly immune to interference.

Rain-tight Able to prevent the entry of water in a driving rain.

Rapid-start starter A device that uses a low-voltage winding to preheat fluorescent lamp electrodes to start an arc.

Rated power Electrical output a generator can provide continuously.

Rate-of-temperature detector Device that detects and responds to a rapid change in air temperature such as that produced by fire.

Receptacle Contact point at an electrical outlet for the connection of a plug.

Reflector lamp An incandescent lamp with a reflector built into the bulb.

Register To transmit and record remote coding information from a controlled device to a central controller.

Residential gateway A device that allows multiple PCs to share a high-speed internet connection and peripherals, such as printers; enables homes to have their own network without extra wiring.

Remote transformer The use of remote transformers eliminates electrical interference caused by dimmers and provides simpler wire installation.

Resistance Opposition to current flow in a conductor, device, or load measured in ohms.

Glossary

Ribbon wire Zip cord consisting of low-voltage conductors each with a different color plastic sheathing.

Ringer equivalency number (REN) A number, usually 1.0 or less, that represents the amount of power needed to ring a telephone.

Run wattage Power it takes to keep an appliance running after the initial startup surge.

Secondary winding The transformer coils wound on the output side of the transformer.

Service drop Overhead utility lines that bring electric service to a home.

Service entrance panel (SEP) Point where utility power enters the house wiring.

Short circuit Undesirable contact between two hot wires or a hot and a grounded or grounding wire.

Single-pole switch Electrical switch having one movable contact that connects two terminals.

66 block Connection block for a telephone circuit. Also called M block.

Smart House A control standard for home automation applications, such as entertainment, lighting, security, and temperature control.

Smoke detector An ionization or photo electric device that sounds an alarm when is senses products of combustion; it does not sense the presence of heat, flames, or gas.

Snap switch See *Toggle switch*.

Socket Metal shell into which a light bulb or plug fuse is inserted.

Spike Sudden and pronounced increase or surge in power.

Splice Mechanical connection between wires.

Splice box Square or octagonal junction box for splicing wires; accessible, plate-covered box that can be installed in a wall or ceiling.

Spread spectrum modulation Power-line transmission that starts at one frequency and is changed to another during its cycle.

Standby generator Portable residential electric generator designed to power selected appliances or lamps temporarily during a power outage.

Starter switch A switch that works with a ballast to start a fluorescent tube only when sufficient power is available.

Start-of-run Receptacle or switch box at the beginning position in a circuit.

Step-down transformer A transformer that reduces electrical voltage to a lower voltage at the secondary output terminals.

Stranded wire Wires spun together to form a single conductor.

Structured wiring Wiring system composed of a central hub, high-performance cabling, and high-quality outlets; services can be redirected as needs change.

Surface raceway A surface system for installing wiring, switches, receptacles, and fixtures without the need for demolition work.

Surge arrester or suppressor Device that diverts heavy electrical surges to a grounding system.

Surge wattage Power it takes to start an appliance. When it first kicks on, the appliance requires an initial surge. A generator must be able to accommodate the surge wattage. If it doesn't have enough power, the generator and connected appliance motors can burn out.

Switch Electrical control for turning power to a device on or off.

Switch box Electrical box used to contain a switch or receptacle.

Switch loop Installation in which power bypasses through a switch box and then loops directly back to the fixture.

TVRO Television Receive Only.

Task lighting Point-of-use directional lighting.

Telephone cable Four- or eight-wire cable use to connect telephone outlets. Also called station wire.

Telephone jack Device having a female connecting socket into which a telephone circuit wire may be plugged.

Terminal A position in a circuit or device at which a connection is normally established or broken.

Terminal screw A screw on a device where a wire connection is made.

Thermal-protected ballast Ballast protected against overheating resulting from an overload or a failure to start.

Thermoplastic Becoming soft when heated and hard when cooled.

Thermostat A device that automatically responds to temperature changes and activates switches controlling HVAC equipment.

Three-way switch An electrical switch used to control lights from two locations when used with others switches.

Time-delay fuse A plug fuse that can, for a limited time, withstand a heavy electrical load without blowing.

Toggle switch Snap on/off switch activated by a lever.

Transfer switch Device that switches a load from its main source, such as a public utility, to a standby power source, such as a home generator.

Transformer A device that steps voltage up or down.

Transponder A control device that receives a remote signal and then sends out a signal of its own to another device.

Traveler wire   A wire that transfers electricity from one three-way switch to another.

Tubing   Thin-walled electrical conduit.

Twisted pair   Two single, insulated wires twisted together to reduce interference with other pairs of wire.

Twistlock   Receptacle or plug that can be locked in place, preventing accidental removal.

Type-S fuse   A plug fuse that can only fit into a fuse holder or adapter having the same amperage rating.

UL label   Underwriters Laboratories' mark of evaluation and listing.

Ultrasonic sensor (US)   Device that emits a high frequency sound and then listens for changes in the echo.

Ultraviolet (UV) light   Range of invisible light just beyond violet in the spectrum.

Underground feeder (UF) cable   Outdoor cable approved for direct burial.

Underwriters' knot   A knot that ensures electrical wiring connections in a fixture will withstand the strain if the cord is jerked.

Underwriters Laboratories   Organization that sets standards of manufacture, testing and evaluation of electrical products.

Unit code   One of 16 individual addresses used for X-10 automation control.

Utility line   Power supply cable provided and owned by a utility company.

Video cassette recorder   Device for recording and playing back videotapes.

Volt   Unit of electromotive force; pressure required to move one amp through a resistance of one ohm.

Voltage   Potential difference between any two points in an electric circuit.

Watertight   Designed for temporary immersion in or exposure to water; sealed with waterproof gaskets.

Watt   Unit of electrical power usage.

Weatherproof   Constructed to function without interference from weather.

Wet niche   Pool light housing in which the fixture is completely surrounded by water.

Whole-house protection   Comprehensive surge protection involving both main panel and point-of-use surge arrestors, or suppressors.

Wide-area network (WAN)   Computer or data communications network connecting devices over a greater distance than a local-area network (LAN).

Windings   The wire coils of a generator, motor, or transformer.

Wire   A flexible metal strand of various lengths and diameters, often electrically insulated, used to conduct electricity.

Wire connector   Device for twisting two or more wires together.

Wire shield   Metal guard nailed to a framing member to protector wiring behind from nail or screw penetration.

X-10 technology   System that allows remote control of lights and appliances using the existing wiring in a home.

Zero voltage   The level of voltage of any ground connected to the earth.

Zip cord   Two-wire cord designed to split when pulled down the middle.

Index

Index

Photoelectric smoke detectors, 165
Pilot-light switches, 310
Plastic boxes, 303
Pliers, 274
  diagonal-cutting, 274
  lineman's, 274
  long-nose, 274
Plug fuse, 301
Plugs
  attaching, to Category 5 cable, 245
  installing quick-connect, 63
  standard, 61–62
Plumbing, home automation and, 234
Point-of-use surge protection, 217
Pool lighting, underwater, 208–09
Power generator, 255
Power-line carrier control, 229–30
Power outdoors, extending, 186–87
Power reduction, 231
Power surge, protecting against, 211
Programmable switches, 310
Punch-down blocks, 174
Punch-down tool, 278
Push-in terminals, 37

Q

Quad breaker, 299
Quartz halogen lamps, 92

R

Raceway application, 311
Raceway components, 311
Raceway receptacles, 312
Raceway wiring, 312
Radiant floor heating, installing
  radiant floor heating, 142–43
  Schluter underlayment system, 144–47
Range finder, 281
Range hood, 132–33
  wiring ducted, 132–33
Range receptacles, 115–17
Ranges, 115–16
  amp circuit for gas, 12
Receptacles, 307–8
  analyzer for, 285
  appliance, 310
  countertop, 13
  dryer, 117–18
  duplex, 32–49, 307
    with split controlled by end-of-run switch, 40
    with split controlled by start-of-run switch, 40
  end-of-run, 34
  GFCI, 44–41
    installing, 48–49
    protection in electrical circuits history, 46–47
    high-voltage, 41–43
    history of, 32
    interpreting, 41

island, 124–25
isolated-ground, 310
middle-of-run, 35
multiple 120-volt duplex circuit, 36
outdoor, 190–91
raceway, 312
range, 115–17
sequential 120-volt duplex, 36
single-pole switch with light fixture and duplex, 3
split, controlled by end-of-run switch, 39
tamper-resistant, 307
USB 120-volt dual-purpose residential receptacles, 33
wiring split-circuit receptacle, 37
wiring switch/receptacle, 38–40
Recessed fixtures, 106
Recessed lights, 93–95
  insulating around, 93
Recessed wall heater, 151–52
  installing, 152
Resistance, 257
Resistance heaters, 148–51
Retrofitting a Dishwasher with a Flexible Cord System, 112–115
RG-6 coaxial cable, 244
Rigid conduit, 178
Router, 23

S

Safety
  disposal, 119
  generator, 227
  tools for, 284
  working, with electricity, 265–66
Safety equipment, 153–55
  carbon monoxide (CO) detectors, 155
  hardwired smoke detectors, 153–54
Safety glasses, 284
Satellite TV system, installing, 170–71
Saw
  cordless reciprocating, 283
  utility, 283
Schluter underlayment system, installing, 144–47
Screwdrivers, insulated, 276
Sensors
  alarms and, 165–66
  timers and, 184
Sequential 120-volt duplex receptacles, 36
Service-entrance panel, 259, 261–62
Service entrance round (SER) cable, 115
Service panels, 295
  circuit-breaker sizes, 295
  sizes, 295
Short circuits, 266, 301
Sidewalks, trenching under, 190
Signal transmission methods, 233
Single-pole breakers, 298–99

Single-pole dimmer switch, 60
Single-pole switches, 50–52
  to light fixture, 51
  with light fixture and duplex receptacle, 39
Single-pole toggle switch, 310
Small appliance branch circuits, 12
Smart Home Technology and Apps, 250–53
Smart House, 233
Smoke detectors, 165
  hardwired, 153–54
  photoelectric, 165
  smart smoke detection alarms, 252
Spas, 206–8
Special boxes, 306
Specialty breakers, 298–99
Specialty switches, 162
Specialty wiring, 157–59
  applications, 150–75
  low-voltage power, 157–59
Split-circuit receptacle, wiring, 37
Split receptacle controlled by end-of-run switch, 39
Sprinkler system, 236
  automated, 238–40
  smart sprinkler controller, 253
Standard plugs, 61–62
Standard round-cord plug, replacing, 62
Standard toggle switches, 310
Start-of-run switch, duplex receptacle with split receptacle controlled by, 40
Stationary emergency power generator, 222
Step-down utility transformers, 260
Straps, 276
Striking tools, 281–83
Stripper, automatic wire, 275
Structured cabling, 244, 246
  outlets for, 246–47
Structured media center, 248
Structured wiring system, 229
Surface-mount fixtures, 96–97, 106
Surface wiring, 21
Surge arrester, 217
Surge control, home automation and, 231
Surge protection, 217–19
  devices for, 298–99
  electrical, 217
  point-of-use, 217
  whole-house, 217
Suspended fixtures, 106
Swimming pools, 203–9
  aboveground, 203–5
Switches, 50–60, 309–11
  clock-type, 162
  dimmer, 59–60, 309
  electronic, 310–11
  four-way, 58–59

Index

Photo Credits

Interior photography by Brian C. Nieves/CH, except as noted.
Supplemental studio photography by Hal Charms/CH.

front cover: *bottom left* oasisamuel/Shutterstock.com; page 1: *top left, bottom left & top right* John Parsekian/CH; *bottom right* Merle Henkenius; pages 4–6: *all* John Parsekian/CH; *bottom right* John Parsekian/CH; pages 8–9: *all* John Parsekian/CH; page 17: Charles T. Byers; page 33: *all* Charles T. Byers; pages 46–47: *all* Charles T. Byers; pages 68–69: *all* Freeze Frame Studio/CH; page 71: *all* John Parsekian/CH; pages 72–73: *all* Charles T. Byers; pages 74–77: *all* Merle Henkenius; page 78: John Parsekian/CH; pages 80–81: *all* Charles T. Byers; page 87: *bottom* courtesy of GE; pages 90–91: *all* Merle Henkenius; page 94: *bottom left* Mark Samu, design: The Tile Studio; page 100: *top left & bottom left* John Parsekian/CH; page 101: *all* John Parsekian/CH; page 102: *top* Freeze Frame Studio/CH; *bottom* courtesy of Osram Sylvania; page 103: *all* Freeze Frame Studio/CH; pages 104–105: *all* Merle Henkenius; page 106: *all* courtesy of Rejuvenation; page 107: *left* Mark Samu; *right* courtesy of Kohler; page 108: Merle Henkenius; page 110: *top left* courtesy of Kohler; *right* Charles T. Byers; page 111: *top sequence* Charles T. Byers; pages 112–115: *all* Charles T. Byers; pages 120–121: *bottom sequence* Merle Henkenius; pages 122–125: *all* Merle Henkenius; page 132: *top left* courtesy of Merillat; pages 135–137: *all* Freeze Frame Studio/CH; pages 138–139: *all* Merle Henkenius; pages 140–141: *all* Charles T. Byers; pages 142–143: *all* John Parsekian/CH; pages 144–147: *all* Charles T. Byers; page 169: *top left* Miles Boyer/Shutterstock.com; *bottom left* Joni Hanebutt/Shutterstock.com; *right sequence* Charles T. Byers; page 176: John Parsekian/CH; page 180: *top right* John Parsekian/CH; page 184: *top right* courtesy of Malibu Lighting/Intermatic, Inc; *bottom right* Peter Tata; page 185: *bottom right* courtesy of California Redwood Association; pages 196–197: *all* Merle Henkenius; pages 198–199: *all* courtesy of Malibu Lighting/Intermatic, Inc; page 200: *bottom left & center* courtesy of Malibu Lighting/Intermatic, Inc; page 202: courtesy of Sharkline Pools; page 203: *top* courtesy of Jacuzzi, Inc.; *bottom* courtesy of National Pools & Spa Institute; pages 204–207: *all* John Parsekian/CH; page 210: John Parsekian/CH; page 211: Kent Wood/Peter Arnold, Inc.; page 222: *top left* John Parsekian/CH; page 226: *top left, top center & bottom center* John Parsekian/CH; page 228: John Parsekian/CH; pages 244–249: *all* John Parsekian/CH; page 250: *top left* Juan Ci/Shutterstock.com; *top right* Jaimeandkyleshootstock/Shutterstock.com; *bottom* RaspberryStudio/Shutterstock.com; page 251: *top left* RossHelen/Shutterstock.com; *top right* BrandonKleinPhoto/Shutterstock.com; *bottom* New Africa/Shutterstock.com; page 252: *top left* Audio und werbung/Shutterstock.com; *top right* Catherine.Things/Shutterstock.com; *bottom* Vantage_DS/Shutterstock.com; page 253: *top left* Happy_Nati/Shutterstock.com; *top right* mariakray/Shutterstock.com; *bottom* Piotr Wawrzyniuk/Shutterstock.com; page 254: John Parsekian/CH; page 260: *top left* courtesy of the Bureau of Reclamation; page 272: John Parsekian/CH; page 286: Merle Henkenius; page 299: *bottom left* John Parsekian/CH; back cover: *bottom left* Charles T. Byers

Acknowledgments

Special thanks to the following: DirecTV, US Electronics, Rainbird, Dave Houser for pool sequence shots, Automatic Lightning Protection, Gen/Tran, Umberto Ciliberti for backup generator shots, Makita Tools, Ryobi Tools, Triple S, Home Intelligence, X-10, NuHeat, and Leviton Integrated Networks Group. Their cooperation was key to the completion of this book.

Metric Equivalents

Length

1 inch	25.4mm
1 foot	0.3048m
1 yard	0.9144m
1 mile	1.61km

Area

1 square inch	645mm²
1 square foot	0.0929m²
1 square yard	0.8361m²
1 acre	4046.86m²
1 square mile	2.59km²

Volume

1 cubic inch	16.3870cm³
1 cubic foot	0.03m³
1 cubic yard	0.77m³

Common Lumber Equivalents

Sizes: Metric cross sections are so close to their U.S. sizes, as noted below, that for most purposes they may be considered equivalents.

Dimensional lumber	1 x 2	19 x 38mm
	1 x 4	19 x 89mm
	2 x 2	38 x 38mm
	2 x 4	38 x 89mm
	2 x 6	38 x 140mm
	2 x 8	38 x 184mm
	2 x 10	38 x 235mm
	2 x 12	38 x 286mm
Sheet sizes	4 x 8 ft.	1200 x 2400mm
	4 x 10 ft.	1200 x 3000mm
Sheet thicknesses	¼ in.	6mm
	⅜ in.	9mm
	½ in.	12mm
	¾ in.	19mm
Stud/joist spacing	16 in. o.c.	400mm o.c.
	24 in. o.c.	600mm o.c.

Capacity

1 fluid ounce	29.57mL
1 pint	473.18mL
1 quart	0.95L
1 gallon	3.79L

Weight

1 ounce	28.35g
1 pound	0.45kg

Temperature

Fahrenheit = Celsius x 1.8 + 32
Celsius = Fahrenheit - 32 x ⁵⁄₉

Nail Size and Length

Penny Size	Nail Length
2d	1"
3d	1¼"
4d	1½ "
5d	1¾"
6d	2"
7d	2¼"
8d	2½"
9d	2¾"
10d	3"
12d	3¼"
16d	3½"

More Great Books from Fox Chapel Publishing

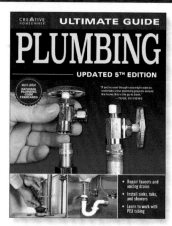

Ultimate Guide: Plumbing, Updated 5th Edition
Paperback • 312 pages • 8.5 x 10.8
978-1-58011-861-3 • Code #8613U
$24.99 US / $29.99 CAD

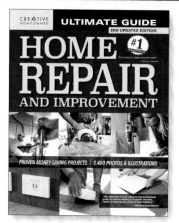

Ultimate Guide to Home Repair and Improvement, 3rd Updated Edition
Hardback • 608 pages • 8.6 x 10.8
978-1-58011-868-2 • Code #8682
$29.99 US / $37.99 CAD

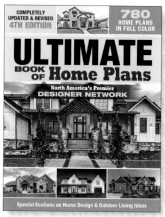

Ultimate Book of Home Plans, Completely Updated & Revised 4th Edition
Paperback • 528 pages • 8.5 x 10.8
978-1-58011-569-8 • Code #5698
$21.99 US / $26.99 CAD

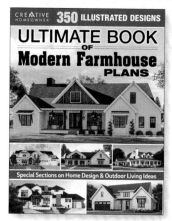

Ultimate Book of Modern Farmhouse Plans
Paperback • 288 pages • 8.5 x 10.8
978-1-58011-870-5 • Code #8750
$22.99 US / $28.99 CAD

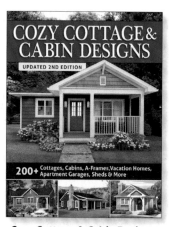

Cozy Cottage & Cabin Designs, Updated 2nd Edition
Paperback • 240 pages • 7 x 9
978-1-58011-568-1 • Code #5681C
$18.99 US / $23.99 CAD

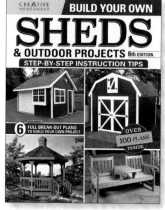

Build Your Own Sheds & Outdoor Projects Manual, Sixth Edition
Paperback • 168 pages • 8.5 x 11
978-1-58011-570-4 • Code #5704
$16.99 US / $20.99 CAD

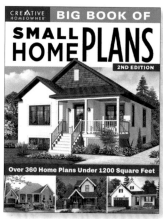

Big Book of Small Home Plans, 2nd Edition
Paperback • 288 pages • 8.5 x 11
978-1-58011-869-9 • Code #8699
$14.99 US / $18.99 CAD

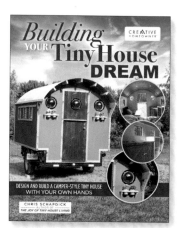

Building Your Tiny House Dream
Paperback • 176 pages • 8 x 10
978-1-58011-847-7 • Code #8477
$19.99 US / $24.99 CAD

How to Garden Indoors & Grow Your Own Food Year Round
Hardback • 192 pages • 8 x 10
978-1-58011-574-2 • Code #5742
$34.99 US / $44.99 CAD

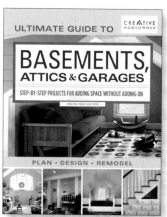

Ultimate Guide to Basements, Attics & Garages, 3rd Revised Edition
Paperback • 216 pages • 8 x 10
978-1-58011-842-2 • Code #8422
$19.99 US / $24.99 CAD

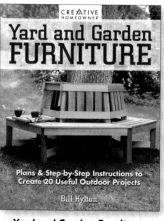

Yard and Garden Furniture, 2nd Edition
Paperback • 192 pages • 8 x 10
978-1-58011-850-7 • Code #8507
$19.99 US / $24.99 CAD

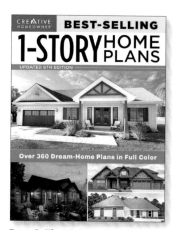

Best-Selling 1-Story Home Plans, 5th Edition
Paperback • 288 pages • 8.5 x 10.8
978-1-58011-567-4 • Code #5674
$16.99 US / $20.99 CAD

Shop Online at www.FoxChapelPublishing.com